CAPTIVES AND VOYAGERS

Antislavery, Abolition, and the Atlantic World

R. J. M. BLACKETT AND JAMES BREWER STEWART, *Series Editors*

CAPTIVES  VOYAGERS

BLACK MIGRANTS ACROSS
THE EIGHTEENTH-CENTURY
BRITISH ATLANTIC WORLD

Alexander X. Byrd

LOUISIANA STATE UNIVERSITY PRESS ❋ BATON ROUGE

Published by Louisiana State University Press

Manufactured in the United States of America
First Printing

DESIGNER: *Amanda McDonald Scallan*
TYPEFACE: *Minion*
TYPESETTER: *J. Jarrett Engineering*
PRINTER AND BINDER: *Thomson-Shore, Inc.*

Library of Congress Cataloging-in-Publication Data

Byrd, Alexander X., 1968–
    Captives and voyagers : black migrants across the eighteenth-century British Atlantic World /
Alexander X. Byrd.
        p. cm. — (Antislavery, abolition, and the Atlantic world)
    Includes bibliographical references and index.
    ISBN 978-0-8071-3359-0 (cloth : alk. paper) 1. Slavery—Great Britain—History—18th century. 2.
Blacks—Great Britain—History—18th century. 3. Slave trade—Nigeria—History—18th century. 4.
Sierra Leone—History. I. Title.
    HT1161.B97 2008
    306.3'62094109033—dc22

                                                                                    2008018831

For Jeanette

CONTENTS

ACKNOWLEDGMENTS

I have accumulated a great many debts in researching and writing this book about transatlantic black migration across the late eighteenth-century British empire. They are debts I can never discharge, but it is a great pleasure to have the opportunity to acknowledge a few of them here.

I first seriously grappled with the questions and concerns at the heart of this book as a history graduate student at Duke University. In Durham, Janet Ewald, the late John Cell, Bill Chafe, Raymond Gavins, Barry Gaspar, Lawrence Goodwyn, Sydney Nathans, Richard Powell, Julius Scott, and Peter Wood, among others, pushed me to read more closely, to write more clearly, and to think more imaginatively. When it came time to take exams and to write the dissertation, Jan chaired a committee consisting of Jack, Ray, Julius, and Peter. These five were demanding and generous in ways that will continue to benefit me, I am certain, for as long as I write and teach history.

I am especially grateful to graduate students whose tenures at Duke coincided with mine. I had the great fortune of arriving in Durham at a time when a lively group of slavery scholars, Afro Americanists, and students of early America were also there. So I benefited enormously from the company of Herman Bennett, Rod Clare, Matthew Countryman, Kathryn Dungy, Karen Ferguson, Charles McKinney, James A. McMillin, Jennifer Morgan, Celia Naylor, Ifeoma Nwankwo, Paul Ortiz, Kara Miles Turner, and others. Luckily, I also first met Vincent Brown, Stephanie Smallwood, and Claudio Saunt at Duke. They have remained great friends and interlocutors ever since. I don't have words for what Annie Valk and Leslie Brown have meant to me, my family, and this project over the years. I am simply thankful.

I finished both the dissertation and the ensuing book as a member of the department of history at Rice University. John Boles, Carl Caldwell, Edward Cox, Rebecca Goetz, Ira Gruber, Atieno Odhiambo, Paula Sanders, Allison Sneider, and Kerry Ward read parts of the manuscript (and some among those listed read all of it). I appreciate their feedback very much.

As department chairs, Gales Stokes, John Zammito, Carl Caldwell, and Martin Wiener were each remarkably generous and supportive. Caroline Levander, Michael Emerson, Anthony Pinn, Maarten Van Delden, and other participants in Rice's Americas Colloquium have encouraged my work a great deal. Beatriz González-Stephan and Juan Carlos Rodriguez provided a welcome opportunity to present some of the book's findings as they concern the idea of el gran Caribe. Paula Platt, Rachel Zepeda, and Anita Smith deserve special recognition.

Beyond Rice, I am grateful to scholars who have shared their work, engaged mine, and encouraged me along the way, among them, Nancy Hewitt, Mark Smith, Vincent Carretta, G. Ugo Nwokeji, Carolyn Brown, Ray Kea, Philip Morgan, Paul Lovejoy, Nell Painter, David Gutierrez, James Stewart, Hasia Diner, and Gautam Ghosh. Over many years, Richard Blackett and Colin Palmer have been especially helpful in this regard.

As a dissertation in progress and later as a book manuscript, this project has benefited from fellowship assistance that allowed me to concentrate on research and writing for extended periods of time. It gives me great pleasure to acknowledge the generous support the book and its author have received from The Graduate School at Duke University, the Center for Documentary Studies, the Ford Foundation, The Social Science Research Council's International Migration Program, the American Council of Learned Societies (through the Andrew W. Mellon Fellowship for Junior Faculty), the Shelby Cullom Davis Center for Historical Studies at Princeton University, and the Woodrow Wilson National Fellowship Foundation (through a Career Enhancement Grant). I am particularly grateful to John and Paula Mosle for their support of assistant professors in Rice's School of Humanities.

I am indebted to the librarians and archivists at all of the repositories listed in the bibliography, and am especially grateful to the staff at the National Archives, Kew; the British Library; the Bodleian Library, Oxford; the Manuscripts Department of Cambridge University Library; the National Archives of Nigeria, Enugu; the National Library of Wales, Aberystwyth; Duke University's Rare Book, Manuscript, and Special Collections Library; and Fondren Library at Rice University. Lord Clarendon was especially gracious in allowing me to make use of material on deposit at the Bodleian Library. I am grateful to Sir Edward Dashwood for permission to make use of documents at the National Library of Wales. The staff at LSU Press, especially Rand Dotson have been tremendous. Working with Derik Shelor, who copyedited the manuscript, was a joy.

I explored some of the issues raised in *Captives and Voyagers* in two previously published essays: "Violence, Migration, and Becoming Igbo in

Gustavus Vassa's *Interesting Narrative*," published in *Constructing Borders/ Crossing Boundaries: Race, Ethnicity, and Immigration,* and "Eboe, Country, Nation and Gustavus Vassa's *Interesting Narrative*," which appeared in the *William and Mary Quarterly.* I am grateful for permission to draw on material from those essays here.

The support of family, friends, and community have been critical to the book's completion. I am terribly grateful to C. T. Woods-Powell, the O'Gradys, the Scatliffs, the Molinas, the Nelsons, the Arches, the Poduskas, the Blythes, the Simmonses, the Buckners, the Princes, the Prices, the Fraziers, the Bowmans, Nancy Byrd, and the wonderfully loving folks on and below Ditney Hill. I have benefited enormously from the stimulation and inspiration provided by the men and women comprising Lincoln Memorial Baptist Church in Durham, North Carolina; Jerusalem Missionary Baptist Church in Houston, Texas; and Grant Chapel AME Church in Trenton, New Jersey. The barisiti at Salentos, especially in the last months of the book's coming together, fueled large chunks of the project.

My mother never asked too many questions about this book, though she inquired about many other things (which was very useful when it came to helping me keep things in perspective). Being born her son was my greatest fortune. Once I arrived in graduate school, my stepmother and late father took to sending me clothbound books for birthdays and Christmases. I am grateful for the ensuing library and their unflagging confidence. I doubt that my children know anything about this book (which I write with some pleasure). Still, they encouraged me beyond words. My wife, these many years, has been exactly what I needed (and all that I ever wanted).

Before getting under way, I want to acknowledge a point about the book's nomenclature in referring to some of its black subjects. In the pages that follow, I tend to avoid the phrase African American. I have nothing against the term in general, and I happily use it in other writings and in everyday speech to refer to blacks in the United States in the modern period. But this particular political, geographic, and temporal connotation is precisely why I mostly avoid the term in *Captives and Voyagers.*

CAPTIVES AND VOYAGERS

BLACK MIGRATIONS

On an overcast afternoon in the wet season of 1787, three trading ships working in the Sierra Leone River were interrupted in their business by the approach of a lone British war sloop and a leash of creaking transports, the sloop firing cannon to announce its arrival. The traders already in the estuary—some, no doubt, Guineamen awaiting their human cargos—had just been joined by a floating complement of free settlers. Here, where the French, the English, the Portuguese, and the Danes had long depended on the river for a steady flow of African slaves, a small reversal was under way. The HMS *Nautilus* had just escorted the *Belisarius*, the *Atlantic*, the *Vernon*, and some four hundred colonists, the majority of them impoverished black Londoners, to take possession of a sliver of land along the peninsula at Sierra Leone. After almost a year of being readied for sea and a month en route, the just arrived "black poor," as they were called in the British capital, were suddenly the founders of what would later be styled "free English territory in Africa."[1]

The same summer that the *Belisarius*, the *Atlantic*, and the *Vernon* approached Sierra Leone, but an ocean away, ships bearing black cargo were few and far between on the more established British colony of Jamaica. It was foolish to risk a slaving venture during the hurricane months (indeed, as foolish as it was to plant a colony in Sierra Leone during the wet season). But when the trade picked up, in the time between the end of summer and the end of the year, at least seven Guineamen slouched into Jamaican harbors. Four of these ships—the *Emilia*, the *King George*, the *King Pepple*, and the *Preston*—had arrived from the Bight of Biafra, a mainstay of British slaving south and east of the fledgling Province of Freedom. The nearly twenty-five hundred Africans on board had embarked mostly at Bonny and New Calabar in what is now southeastern Nigeria.[2] Thus they had been forced from some of the busiest slaving ports in eighteenth-century western Africa to what was then the largest slave entrepôt in the North Atlantic. Unlike the émigrés from London who were at the time still struggling to carve out lives as free men and free women in western Africa, these thousands arriving in Jamaica from the Bight of Biafra had a very different kind of encounter ahead. The congeries aboard these ships were doomed to spend the season learning to make lives as American slaves. Either that or flee. Or die.

The conventional image of transatlantic migration across the British empire is rarely cast so darkly, yet much of the British colonial world was made through just these kinds of black migration. In the years spanning 1630 to 1780, more than two and a half times as many Africans arrived in Great Britain's Atlantic possessions as did Europeans, and in the critical near century from 1700 to 1780, more than four times as many Africans as Europeans departed their homelands for British colonies.[3] As far as the transatlantic movement of people was concerned, the late eighteenth-century British empire was overwhelmingly black. This is a book about the migrants who made it so. It examines the nature of their movements, explores the social consequences (personal and corporate) of their dislocations, and, more than anything else, scrutinizes their lives as people in motion across a European New World empire.

The book focuses on the two largest streams of free and forced trans-oceanic black dislocation across Great Britain's western empire: the slave trade from the Bight of Biafra to Jamaica, and free black migration to Sierra Leone. When pondering the human articulation of Great Britain's eighteenth-century Atlantic empire, admittedly, these two migrations hardly leap to mind. New England's Great Migration and the demographic catastrophe that was early Virginia, for instance, are no doubt much more commonly thought of when the subject is the movement of people to, from, and within Great Britain's Atlantic empire. The pairing at the heart of the book is not iconic, but it should be. A primary burden of the pages that follow is to naturalize the coupling, to underline how important the experiences of black migrants are for grasping the shape and texture of the British Atlantic world (a world set off from other parts of the eighteenth-century British colonial world by the sheer vastness and sheer blackness of migration across and between it).

That the slave trade to Jamaica and free black migration to Sierra Leone are not now commonly braced, though, is certainly understandable. A great deal separated the two movements. The difference in magnitude between them was enormous. In contrast to the intermittent trickle that was transatlantic movement to Sierra Leone, the slave trade from the Bight of Biafra was a torrent involving hundreds of ships and tens of thousands of people. In the five years coinciding with the initial colonization of Sierra Leone (1787–1792), when just two convoys of fewer than twenty ships transported a little under 2,000 free blacks to the west African Province of Freedom, surviving ship records document that nearly 250 Guineamen loaded more than 78,000 African slaves along the Bight of Biafra (a difference almost too great for words).[4]

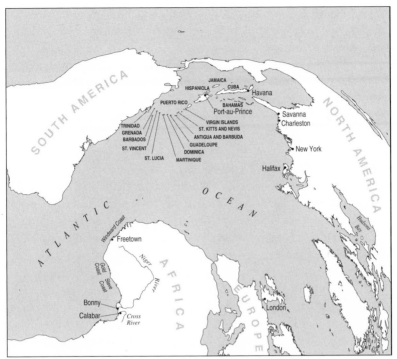

Figure 1. The North Atlantic in the late eighteenth century
Source: Map drawn by the Cartographic Laboratory, Department of Geography, University of Wisconsin

There was also the matter of status: migrants to Sierra Leone were set-tlers, not slaves. They were colonists in the common sense of the word—men and women who embarked for western Africa of their own volition, even if not under conditions or circumstances of their own making. Those carried from western Africa, of course, did not embark freely. So at two elemental levels the differences were stark. The slave trade from the Bight of Biafra was the macabre business of ferrying hundreds of thousands of dead and dying dark bodies for the chance of profit. The migration of free blacks to Sierra Leone was an attempt by a few thousand settlers to improve their lot, an effort, as the settlers themselves once described their intentions, to see their "Children free and happy."[5]

Put this way, there could hardly be more separating these two move-ments. But this is not the only way to put things, nor perhaps the best. There were real differences, in numbers and in conditions, between the migrations comprising the colonization of Sierra Leone and the continued re-peopling of British Jamaica. But the movements were also intimately related. First, free black migration *to* western Africa was, quite simply, a consequence of the slave trade *from* western Africa. The connection is most apparent from the vantage of politics, high and low, where British philanthropists and moralists who believed at the height of the British slave trade that their nation's implication in African slavery was both wrong in a moral sense and unnecessary in a practical one encouraged the creation of a free British foothold in western Africa. For those activists, organizing a black settlement at Sierra Leone was, among other things, an attempt to strike at the Atlantic slave trade by demonstrating that free labor might produce much—even if not all—of what was asked of slave labor in the Americas.[6]

The movements were connected in other ways, too. In British North America, free blacks looking for a better place to try their liberty followed news from Sierra Leone as closely as they could, and in Jamaica planters and merchants whose livelihoods depended on the slave trade paid more than passing attention to the purpose and prospect of free black migration to Africa. And if there is little evidence that the island's slaves followed the course of free black migration to Sierra Leone, it is certain that they knew a great deal indeed about the forces of British antislavery that gave impetus to that migration. In these ways, the apparently contradictory journeys of forced migration to Jamaica and free emigration to western Africa connected and were connected by political ideas and desires (and lamentations, too) across the British Atlantic world.[7] Furthermore, such connections between migrations to and from western Africa were themselves embodied, sometimes perfectly, in the lives of contemporaries. Among the migrants who made for Sierra Leone were settlers who had been born in Africa, who were previously slaves in the Americas, and who had themselves survived earlier transatlantic voyages as prisoners aboard European Guineaships.[8] The story of the slave trade from the Bight of Biafra to Jamaica and the story of the journeys made by free blacks toward the colonization of Sierra Leone need to be told together because in important ways—in time and in the minds of their protagonists—this was how they unfolded.[9]

Additionally, the two transatlantic journeys offer a particularly powerful and illuminating way to address some of the most pressing questions about migration, migrant society, and the late eighteenth-century British colonial world. First, the pairing's focus on black migrants addresses a significant fact about British Atlantic migration that the historical literature still has yet to recognize fully: the vast majority of Great Britain's Atlantic migrants were of African descent. The focus on black migrants invites reflection on the relationship between black migration and other more studied, if smaller, transatlantic movements across Great Britain's western colonial world.

Second, the starkest difference between the two migrations undergirds the most powerful rationale for the movements' being examined concurrently: At the height of the eighteenth-century British slave trade, Africans and Afro-Americans in the British colonial world imagined and shaped an antithetical transatlantic movement. The differences between black migration to Jamaica and Sierra Leone speak to the nature of and the possibilities within the revolutionary eighteenth century's most important set of opposing ideas. Examined together, transatlantic black migration to Jamaica and to Sierra Leone illumines when and how condition of servitude mattered in the lives of a set of people then crisscrossing Great Britain's Atlantic. Elizabeth Freeman, once a British subject but later one of the first slaves in the new United States to sue for her freedom, often expressed the difference with some poignancy. "Any time, any time while I was a slave," she said, "if one minute's freedom had been offered to me, and I had been told I must die at the end of that minute, I would have taken it."[10] This is a powerfully moving sentiment, but it merits interrogation. For black migrants, for people in motion across the British empire, just what was the difference between slavery and liberty? This is one of the book's essential questions.

The book's focus on both enslaved and free migrants also allows close attention to a question that dominates historical writing on migration across the British Atlantic world: For emigrants themselves, what were the social and cultural consequences of their dislocations? To date, the historiography on migrations has given us clear and relatively concise ways to judge and to speak about the social and cultural consequences of Atlantic migration. For enslaved African migrants to the Americas, for instance, John Thornton has stressed the social and cultural continuities that characterized immigrant life on the other side of the Atlantic. Writes Thronton: "Although many scholars discuss the possibility of the survival of African culture into the present day, an important issue to be sure, the fact is that in the eighteenth century African culture was not surviving: It was arriving. Whatever the brutalities of the Middle Passage or slave life, it was not going to cause the African-born to forget their mother language or change their ideas about beauty in design or music; nor would it cause them to abandon the ideological underpinnings of religion or ethics—not on arrival in America, not ever in their lives."[11]

For eighteenth-century European migrants to British North America, Bernard Bailyn is largely of a different persuasion. Bailyn has underlined the ways that American contexts challenged, battered, and transformed European intuitions, ideas, identities, and possibilities. He thinks it important not to "minimize the primitiveness and violence, the bizarre, quite literally outlandish quality of life" that characterized European society in British

North America. "Partly," writes Bailyn, "this wildness, extravagance, and disorder were simply the products of the inescapable difficulties of maintaining a high European civilization in an undeveloped environment."[12]

At the center of this book, too, then, is the kind of question that animates nearly every social history of eighteenth-century migration across the Atlantic world. For the captives and voyagers who peopled Great Britain's most prolific sugar island and established its first African settler colony, what demands did their respective transatlantic journeys make on their society and how did their society affect and shape their journeys? It is a kind of question whose answers stand to benefit from it being posed in less familiar ways. Consequently, this book is propelled by the premise that it is possible to gain new purchase on the history of eighteenth-century transatlantic migration by examining free and forced migration together, and by paying careful attention to the social consequences of the actual processes of emigration.

As an interpretive and analytical innovation, studying free and forced migration together is one thing (it is, after all, not often done). Studying the social consequences of transatlantic migration by paying close attention to transatlantic migration, however, has a rather tautological ring. The tautology, though, speaks to a peculiar historiographical condition. Historians of Great Britain's Atlantic empire take up the matter of immigration (the circumstances surrounding migrants' arrival and settling of new land) more often than they do emigration (the circumstances surrounding migrants' departure from their former home). Consequently, they often neglect the shape and repercussions of migration itself, choosing instead to infer the effects of dislocation from its various aftermaths. In this sense, some of the best early American migration history is more the history of European settlement in British America than it is the history of transatlantic migration proper.[13] Further, in eighteenth-century African American historiography, migration has come to be seen, in the main, as transport—perhaps harrowing but not necessarily affecting. Thus, much of the recent scholarship on Afro America underlines the reconstruction and sometimes the outright transplantation of black migrants' former society and institutions in the Americas. Igbo power ways and food ways arrived in the Chesapeake and Kikongo language washed over St. Domingue, in the same way that East Anglian religiosity apparently covered New England.

Such matters of migration and social and cultural resiliency are issues that scholars of Afro-America have paid particular attention to over the past forty years, especially in debating questions relating to the impact of African culture and society in the New World.[14] This study joins that conversation through a history of the societal "uprootings and regroundings" that characterized two great black migrations of the eighteenth-century.[15] A key argument of the book is that the stages that characterized all kinds of transatlantic migration, free and forced, could and did have a significant impact on the ways migrants perceived, organized, and understood themselves, and in how they were perceived organized and understood by others. Migration, to put it another way, was not so much the transplantation of a particularly society from here to there. It was rather, much more often, a vehicle whereby societies were transformed between here and there.

One of the benefits of following the movements of free and forced black migrants in the ways described above is that it brings into sharp focus—and from the perspective of black migrants—the relationship between the African diaspora and the British empire. Such a focus underscores the ways in which the social and political exigencies of empire shaped black migrant experience and vice versa. So the book's particular focus on free and forced transatlantic black migration not only illuminates how the choices, struggles, and aspirations of migrants' themselves affected their experiences and in turn helped to define the substance of their diaspora, but the volume is also an examination of how black migrants came to understand and insinuate themselves into the British empire.

For all that separated Sierra Leone and Jamaica, when black migrants arrived in either, they also arrived in the British empire. Black migrants affected and were themselves affected in important ways by British imperial power and politics—in guises formal and informal. The relationship between ethnicity and migration is a subject to which historians have paid particular attention of late; the relationship between black migration and empire—for free and enslaved migrants alike—is equally important. So at the same time, for instance, that we inquire into the *Africanness* of captives vis-à-vis their departures from their homelands, we need also to investigate their *Britishness* vis-à-vis their arrival at what was in the late eighteenth century the heart of the British American colonial world.

What were the social and cultural consequences of transatlantic migration for emigrants themselves, whether enslaved or free? In the late eighteenth century, what was *black* about the British Atlantic world and what was British about the experiences of blacks within that world? Those are the central animating questions of *Captives and Voyagers*. Answering them gives view to the historical articulation of a transatlantic, black, British, colonial space, and its origins in the transformative movements—in the departures, the voyages, and the landings—of tens of thousands of black men and women, enslaved and free.

Part I of this book focuses on black captives, Part II on free migrants. Part I contains four chapters. The first two examine the emigrant experience from the region of western Africa from which most black migrants to Great Britain's Atlantic empire hailed, the Biafran interior of present-day southeastern Nigeria. The next two chapters explore black settler society in the region of the British colonial world to which most enslaved migrants in the British Atlantic world were bound, the island of Jamaica. Taken together, the chapters comprise an argument concerning the articulation of black society within and between the Biafran interior and Jamaica. Chapter 1 argues that the movement of enslaved men, women, and children within the interior of Africa was critical to the development of black society as it would come to be articulated in the Americas in ethnic national terms. The black ethnic publics of the Americas were as much a product of enslaved peoples' displacement *out* of their homelands as they were artifacts of their African origins. The second chapter argues that the slave ship experience extended and in important ways solidified this process of ethnic identification.

Chapters 3 and 4 turn from emigration to immigration, from migration through and out of Africa to enslaved migrants' arrival in and adjustment to life in British America, from a regional African focus (with attendant attention to questions of ethnic identification and migration) to a regional imperial focus (with attendant attention to the relationship between migration, ecology, white power, and imperial politics). The shift of attention from embarkations to disembarkations necessitates a broader view of the book's migrant subjects, and so while the first two chapters focus on Biafrans and their particular migrant experiences out of Africa, the following two take a more expansive view of African arrivals in the British Americas, reflecting the experiences of migrants themselves and the ways that departures from an African slaving port differed from arrivals in a British Atlantic slave society. In Jamaica, because much of black life centered on work, the continuing articulation of migrant society, from wherever the migrants hailed in Africa, was significantly affected by the people who also defined so much of slaves' labor: white slaveowners and their functionaries. Chapter 3 argues that the nature of white power and white decision making significantly affected how captives adjusted to their new lives in British America. This fact cannot and should not be ignored. Further, the generation of captives who arrived in Jamaica in the late eighteenth century—again, from wherever they hailed in Africa—navigated a particular ecological and ideological environment that threw up incredible limits concerning the worlds they would build and join, but which at the same time offered remarkable opportunities. Chapter 4 explores black social relations across a landscape characterized by nearly constant environmental disasters and the ubiquitous social upheaval that characterized the revolutionary late eighteenth century at the center of British America.

The chapters in Part II of the book examine free black migration across the eighteenth-century British Atlantic world. Chapters 5 and 6—focusing on black migration from London to Sierra Leone in the 1786—and chapters 7, 8, and 9—focusing on black migration from the British Maritimes to Sierra Leone some five years later—argue that, not unlike captives exported from Biafran ports, the society of free migrants bound for Sierra Leone were significantly affected by social and physical movements preceding their actual migrations to western Africa.

The final chapter examines the London migrants' arrival in Sierra Leone. The same material and political factors that were important to the ways enslaved migrants seasoned, or acclimated, in Jamaica were critical in Sierra Leone. In examining the world black migrants built in western Africa, the chapter pays particular attention to the social consequences of migrants' adjustment to difficult environmental circumstances, to the relationships immigrants built with people already present in Sierra Leone, especially people representing other outcroppings of the British empire, and to how migrants responded and contributed to the volatile, revolutionary sentiments that ricocheted across the Province of Freedom just as they did Jamaica. The migration from London to Sierra Leone was considered at the time a failure, and it is still often portrayed as such today. The final chapter argues that for understanding the whole course of early migration to Sierra Leone, the initial settlement cannot be dismissed so lightly. The way this first wave of black migrants seasoned in Sierra Leone largely determined what was possible for subsequent migrants to the colony.

Considered together, the sheer weight of forced migration to Jamaica in the late eighteenth century and the special circumstances of free black migrants to Sierra Leone—the fact that as former slaves many suffered from the presumptions of slavery—draw stark attention to a point raised by David Eltis in his work on comparative migration: the fact that coercion, and not choice, fundamentally shaped and defined the bulk of *all* transatlantic movement in the eighteenth century.[16] Of course, violence and coercion are not matters that have been ignored in the literature on the slave trade, nor are they completely absent from work on contemporaneous free transatlantic migration. Rather, the issue is that violence and coercion are more acknowledged as part of the experience of transatlantic migration than they are analyzed for the profound ways they shaped the process of emigration and the subsequent formation of immigrant communities.[17]

At its core, this book is a study of human movement under horrendously oppressive circumstances. It is a twin story of desperation—of people desperately choosing or desperately being forced to move, to go. Shadowing black migrants across the eighteenth-century British Atlantic empire under such circumstances and studying the lives they made in motion, more than anything else, shows just how central violence and disaster, and emigrants' responses to duress and catastrophe, were to the formation and articulation of black migrant society. This is true of the free settlers at the margins of the British empire where the book ends, but it is especially so at the emigrant center of the eighteenth-century British Atlantic world, the Biafran littoral and interior, where this story of free and forced migration begins.

PART I

CAPTIVES

By the 1740s, merchants and slave traders along the Biafran littoral and their connections in the interior succeeded in consolidating long-existing trade networks while aggressively forging new ones. In the resulting commercial transformation, the trading men and women of Bonny and Elem Kalabari (also known as New Calabar) in the eastern Niger Delta and Old Calabar in the Cross River began funneling more captives toward the Americas than at any other time in the region's history. By the second half of the eighteenth century, traffic from these three Biafran towns accounted for a greater share of Great Britain's *total* transatlantic traffic in slaves than any other three ports in western Africa.[1]

Each of these seaports was remarkable in its own right. Bonny may have been established as a trading town as early as 1500. In *Esmeraldo de Situ Orbis,* a sixteenth-century summary of Portuguese maritime knowledge, Duarte Pereira described a bustling town of some two thousand inhabitants at the mouth of the Rio Real that may have been one of Bonny's early incarnations. Enormous trading canoes, some large enough to ferry eighty men, piloted the waterways surrounding the settlement, facilitating a brisk up-river trade in salt, yams, cows, goats, and sheep. In addition to this trade in foodstuffs and livestock, a vigorous market in slaves was carried on as well.[2]

The Bonny of the late 1700s, though its economy and society had no doubt changed dramatically since first visited by Portuguese caravels, could still be described commercially in much the same language as used by Pereira. At the end of the eighteenth century, the town consisted of a "considerable number" of small houses framed with supporting poles and covered with mats—the whole plastered together with the red earth of the eastern delta. Most were built close to the river, so water frequently washed their foundations, turning the surrounding ground into a swampy morass.

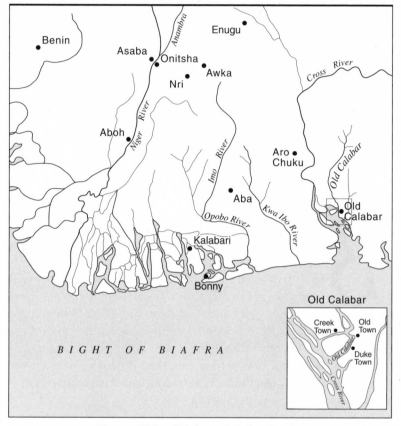

Figure 2. Bight of Biafra and Biafran interior
Source: Map drawn by the Cartographic Laboratory, Department of
Geography, University of Wisconsin

As many as fifteen Guineamen might anchor off Bonny at a time—some ships beginning, others ending, and a number in the middle of the tedious business of taking in slaves. Telltale signs of the town's integration into the Atlantic and upriver trades were evident throughout the community: Bonny's cityscape was shot through here and there with the trading complexes, warehouses, and canoe landings of trade-rich aristocrats, merchants, and their retinues. Evidence of the town's peculiar commercial orientation even carried through the very air of the place: now and again the murmuring of merchants, traders, and slaves, the calls of livestock and wildlife, and the sounds of the river itself were drowned out by the cannon of slave ships announcing their coming or going, or by the fanfare of canoe traders who burst into song and music, and hoisted their colors before paddling to upstream markets to trade for slaves. And over the whole place hung a pall of death: The stench of rotting bodies emanated from the burial grounds of European seamen who had expired while waiting for slaves and were interred in shallow graves opposite the town proper.[3]

Behind Bonny, accessible from the Rio Real estuary, lay the trading town of Elem Kalabari—referred to by Europeans as New Calabar. In the seventeenth century, the settlement was described by British slave trader James Barbot as being very similar to Bonny, its larger neighbor farther toward the coast. "The town," wrote Barbot, "is seated in a marshy island often overflow'd by the river, the water running even between the houses, where there are about three hundred in a disorderly heap." In 1699, Barbot's trading voyage to the eastern delta consisted, in the main, of sailing back and forth between Bonny and New Calabar gathering nearly six hundred slaves for the three hundred-ton frigate *Albion*.[4]

Decades later, at the height of the Atlantic slave trade, the place of trade slaves in the town's economy had expanded significantly, but the general processes remained the same as when Barbot had sailed there three generations earlier. British traders to the eastern delta still ran between Bonny and New Calabar drawing slaves from canoe traders who had in turn transported them in parcels from upriver markets. Only, by the late eighteenth century New Calabar was almost wholly oriented toward the sea. The Atlantic and its trade mattered there to more people and for more reasons than it ever had before.[5]

The third major eighteenth-century slaving port in the Bight of Biafra was not in the Niger Delta proper, but farther east in the estuary of the Cross River. Old Calabar lay about thirty miles up the river and was really three settlements founded one after the other during the early seventeenth century: Creek Town, Old Town, and Duke Town. Anachronistically, Old Calabar was much younger than New Calabar (and Bonny as well for that matter), and in all likelihood did not develop into a regional Atlantic entrepôt until the mid-1700s. Still, as early as 1668 there was enough general knowledge among Europeans about the towns that the English sailor John Watts, in a fictionalized account of his ordeal in the Cross River, assumed that his audience had already heard a great deal about the geography and folkways of the area. In discussing the people, landscape, trade, and manners of Old Calabar and environs, Watts admitted that the information he would offer on those heads was "no more than others have spoken formerly, who have been in the same Country."[6]

In the late eighteenth century, however, it is clear from the descriptions offered by British slave traders that Old Calabar was different from its counterparts farther west. British mariners painted New Calabar and Bonny as
water-logged trading towns given over almost entirely to the Atlantic trade
in slaves.[7] The approach to Old Calabar, in contrast, betrayed a diversified economy. "The Banks of the rivers, till you come near the Towns, are
covered with Mangrove Woods," reported one British captain, but nearer
to the settlements themselves, "the Land is cultivated, and produces Rice
and Guinea Corn; and there appeared to be a great Quantity of Cattle." In a
travelogue of the west African coast, the Briton John Adams added that Old
Calabar exported a significant quantity of palm oil and barwood in addition to participating in the lucrative trade in human beings. To distinguish
the town further from its neighbors, Adams added, "Many of the natives
write English, an art first acquired by some of the traders' sons, who had
visited England, and which they have had the sagacity to retain up to the
present period."[8]

The journal of one such African trader, recounting the death of a town
oligarch named Edem Ekpo, provides a telling glimpse of Old Calabar and
of some of its most unfortunate inhabitants, its slaves.[9] Old Calabar teemed
with slaves. At any moment, hundreds were confined aboard European
Guineamen in the Cross River or at the houses of traders in preparation
for sale to waiting ships. Many others were integrated into the fabric of Old
Calabar society as domestic and agricultural laborers. Of these, some were
little more than chattel, others carried on with great privilege, and a few
were among the most powerful men on the river. But at moments such as
the death of a great man, the subjugation at the base of every slave's experience came to the fore—as it were slaves, almost exclusively, who perished
during the funeral celebrations that followed.

At Edem Ekpo's interment, the principal men of Old Calabar murdered nine slaves in the dead man's honor. Weeks later, the residents of a
settlement at the northern edge of the town "cutt one women slave head."
Six days later "3 head cutt of[f] again." The next day a Taeon town man
brought the head of a stranger in honor of Duke's death. But the apogee of
mourning came during a torrential rain in the early hours of November
6, four months after Ekpo's demise, when a crowd of slaves was led into
the great hall of the Ekpe Society—the fraternity of ruling men—to be
decapitated by the gentlemen of the town: "5 clock morning we begin cutt
slave head of[f] 50 head of[f] by the one Day. . . ."[10]

For enslaved Africans at Old Calabar, this kind of violence was ordinary, and the violence to slaves that punctuated the funeral celebrations of

Edem Ekpo was of a kind that characterized all of the Atlantic slave trade.[11] Whether in the Bight of Biafra at the emigrant center of the British empire or on Jamaica at the empire's complimentary black immigrant core, captives forced to navigate such conditions emerged changed people.

ONE

THE SLAVE TRADE FROM THE BIAFRAN INTERIOR

Violence, Serial Displacement, and the
Rudiments of Igbo Society

Who were they and where did they come from, the thousands of slaves who perished, passed through, or were integrated into the social fabric of Old Calabar, Bonny, and Elem Kalabari? Coming to terms with these two fundamental questions focuses attention on the matter of how enslaved migrants from the emigrant heart of the British empire were affected by their journeys. Contemporaries tended to speak of these unfortunates in ethnic national terms. Eighty percent of the slaves sold at Bonny, and a robust majority of those loaded at Elem Kalabari and Old Calabar, calculated slave trader John Adams, "are natives of one nation, called Heebo." American planters engaged in the Africa trade and slaves knowledgeable about the trade in and around Biafra adapted a similar descriptive nomenclature. Gustavus Vassa, the eighteenth-century slave turned British abolitionist, described himself and the area in which he apparently lived as a boy as "Eboe," and in a telling turn of phrase concerning the British slave trade, Jamaican planter Simon Taylor designated Guineamen that arrived at Kingston from Biafran ports as "Eboe Men."[1]

Understandably, this has become the language of slave trade historians, too, and recent African diaspora scholarship has explored in detail the significance of various African *nations* in the Americas. Work on Igbo slaves in the New World describes what Igbo came to mean and represent in the Americas, and how Igbo slaves shaped and contributed to their new societies.[2] But a foundational issue remains: Though Igbo slaves abounded on American plantations in the eighteenth century, there is very little evidence that there were people who understood themselves as such in the Biafran interior of the same time. Most students of Igbo migrants in the African diaspora acknowledge this point. Accounting for the apparent anomaly, however, and grappling with the issues it raises concerning the nature of Igbo society and the history of African nations in the diaspora remains largely undone. To date, African nations in the diaspora, Igbo among them, are generally understood as "the locus for the maintenance of those elements of African culture that continued on American soil."[3] This is undoubtedly true, but this is not all the nation was. Indeed, as far as the Igbo nation in the diaspora is concerned, this is more a description of one aspect of the nation's *potential* as a social formation than it is an account of its origins. The origin of the Igbo nation in the diaspora was not simply a cultural imperative. At its base, it was also a social imperative born of migration—in particular the violent, alienating dislocation that characterized slave trading in the Biafran interior. In ways too important to ignore, the Igbo of the Americas were made so through their migrations.

The majority of slaves cast away from the Niger Delta, and a preponderance of those shipped from the Cross River estuary, originally hailed from a vast hinterland behind the Bight of Biafra, located in the southeast quadrant of present-day Nigeria. In the eighteenth century, society and culture across this region was as diverse as the landscape itself.[4] Historically, the area was dotted with hundreds of independent polities, best referred to as village groups. In the main, these village groups were arrays of smaller settlements where ties of kith, kin, and proximity informed political and economic cooperation, as well as a certain corporate feeling and identification. Village groups themselves divided into smaller settlements, which were in turn sets of individual, patrifocal compounds physically connected one to another by series of paths. Spatially and politically, the internal organization of individual village groups varied throughout the region. Some were rather compact units led by congresses of leading men distinguished by their age and experience. Others were far-flung affairs governed collectively by the prominent men of certain titled societies. Yet others resembled small kingdoms, with political power concentrated into the hands of a single ruler.[5]

The inhabitants of the region spoke a group of related dialects. Yet language in the Biafran interior, as with forms of political power, was significantly localized. Linguistic patterns varied—sometimes slightly, sometimes quite significantly—from village group to village group. The dialect spoken at Onitsha in the late eighteenth century, for example, probably prevailed scarcely twelve miles to the south and a scant five miles east. Traveling west, it survived only in the talk of traders. Frontiers of dialect and language could be even more extreme farther east, particularly along the Cross River. Nevertheless, with mutual adjustments in grammar, tone, and locution, men and women from different locales could often make themselves understood to one another. But the feat was not transparent. It often could not be effected without conscious effort or recourse to some

experience in such matters; neither could it be accomplished without revealing degrees of social and cultural differentiation between the speakers.
And sometimes, for all intents and purposes, cross-dialect communication
was simply impossible.[6]

An abiding localism centered on the village group characterized society and culture in the eighteenth-century Biafran interior: No manifest
institutional authority exercised control over any significant part of the
region; a plethora of locally focused aesthetic ideas flourished the area over;
and a mosaic of dialects colored various corners of the whole expanse. The
village group—its land, its politics, its rituals, and its dialect—was often
the largest corporate unit.[7]

This is not to say that there did not exist general principles that informed
life and labor the region over. Yam cultivation, for instance, predominated
throughout the region, and the dialects of the Biafran interior were just
that, dialects of a larger tongue. And some political and philosophical ideas
possessed a wide currency. An imperialism of ideas centered on titles of
personal achievement and rituals associated with the fertility of the land,
for instance, radiated from the Nri village group in the Anambra River
basin out toward many other settlements in the region. Neither was the
localism of the Biafran interior akin to stagnation or isolationism. Village
groups were connected by extensive ties of trade, marriage, conflict, and
consultation, and every village group was itself something of a growing, living, social organism—colonizing new ground, acculturating new members,
breaking off from previous concerns, and sometimes dying out altogether.[8]

Nonetheless, the expansion and transformation of various village
group-based polities informed rather than mitigated against the essential
localism of the area as a whole. Village groups, for instance, did not so
much expand as segment, and hegemony was a more common outcome of
conflict than was actual conquest.[9] Political and cultural expansion in the
Biafran interior invariably resulted in new or transformed localisms rather
than real imperialisms. Similarly, the cultural and political principles pre-
eminent across the region did not so much inform broad generalization as
enforce the importance of particularism, for the cultural and political notions that were perhaps most widespread and deeply rooted throughout the
Biafran interior were ones that undermine normal generalization: namely,
individualism and personal achievement.[10]

Accordingly, it should come as little surprise that the peoples of the
Biafran interior have tended to divide the world "dichotomously" into
categories of "we" and "they"—with "we" referring either to relations
or their village group and its components, and "they" serving to denote

everybody else.[11] Thus to its inhabitants, the Biafran hinterland was a patchwork of polities, ethnicities, cultures, ecologies, and professions; and people across the whole expanse tended to refer to themselves and to others accordingly. Along the lower Niger, for example, the inhabitants conceived of themselves politically by their village groups, Onitsha people and Aboh people, for example. These groups also referred to peoples in their purview who likewise lived along the Niger as *Olu*, riverine people. Elsewhere in the Biafran interior, there were *Enugu* and *Aniocha*—people from the hills and people who live on the eroded soils, respectively—and *Ndiuzu* and *Umudioka*—blacksmiths and carvers. And there were communities that situated themselves in relation to their ancestors, as with the village groups Ngwa-Ukwu and Onicha-Ukwu.[12]

It is doubtful, however, that there were peoples who would have referred to themselves as Igbo.[13] The first Europeans to make their way into the Biafran interior and early students of west African languages came to this realization rather quickly. The Reverend Sigismund Koelle, who compiled a comparative vocabulary of African languages, paid particular attention to this anomaly in his *Polyglotta Africana*. Koelle interviewed slaves shipped from Biafran ports who were emancipated at sea and thus never arrived in the Americas; and in attending to what he referred to as the Igbo dialects of the Niger Delta languages, he began with a rather startling observation. Though it was customary that Africans "who have come from the Bight are called Ibos," the reverend ascertained through conversation with said Igbos "that they never had heard" the term until their emancipation and resettlement. Instead, the philologist's informants claimed a number of different affiliations: Isoama, Mbofia, Isiele, and Aro among them.[14]

Even seventy years ago, colonial officers and anthropologists working in southeastern Nigeria encountered a similar situation when they went looking for the Igbo. In the early 1930s, a colonial anthropologist sent to assess the social and political structure of an Igbo sub-tribe reported back that his subjects "declare that they are not Igbo and refer to all the other Igbo speaking peoples as Igbo." Further, among many twentieth-century village groups, "Eaters of Ibo" prevailed as a name taken by age-grade societies throughout the region. The title connoted that the young men, far from considering themselves Igbo, styled themselves as conquerors of Igbo.[15]

What was meant by these uses of Igbo? In many parts of the Biafran interior, the term Igbo was an insult and expression of contempt. No village group used it to describe their "we," rather it was almost always employed to denote a "they." Along the Niger, various riverine communities used Igbo to describe and vilify peoples living behind the river's course as well

as those residing in the adjacent uplands: "Those who did not wash." West
of the Niger, the expression was an epithet used to denigrate the peoples
dwelling just on the other side of the waterway. Among the inhabitants of
Onitsha and Nri, the term was used in elevating themselves from surrounding polities that lacked well-developed notions of kingship, as in the con-
descending proverb "Igbo have no kings." In other parts of the interior, as
suggested by Koelle, the word "Igbo" may have gone completely unheard.[16]

Thus in the introduction to his eighteenth-century memoir, *The Interesting Narrative of the Life of Olaudah Equiano, or Gustavus Vassa, the African,*
Gustavus Vassa perhaps relayed even more than he intended about the cultural and social consequences of the slave trade when he claimed Eboe as a
birthplace.[17] Among the lettered classes in eighteenth-century Great Britain,
Vassa was probably the best known African in the empire. He penned correspondence to the London press, petitioned the government against the slave
trade, and was the one-time commissary to the nation's first colonial experiment in western Africa (the British settlement at Sierra Leone). In his life-
time, Vassa's memoir went through nine British editions and was reviewed
in such journals as *Gentleman's Magazine* and *The Analytical Review.*[18]

According to his *Interesting Narrative,* Vassa was born in the Biafran
interior around 1745. At the age of eleven he was kidnapped from his family's compound, spirited in stages to the Niger Delta, and sold into the
Atlantic trade.[19] But unlike countless others suffering a similar fate, Vassa
did not live and die in chattel slavery on an American plantation. Through
luck, pluck, hard labor, and the "mercies of Providence," he managed subsequently to purchase his freedom after some ten years in bondage. In 1789,
he published the story of his life.

Despite the claims in his memoir, we cannot be certain that Vassa indeed
hailed from the Biafran interior. At other moments in his life, he claimed
South Carolina as his birthplace.[20] We can be more certain, however, that
the story Vassa told about the slave trade in his *Interesting Narrative* was
firmly rooted in sources from the Biafran interior.[21] As such, when carefully
considered and contextualized, Vassa's account throws considerable light
on the subject of the origins of the Igbo nation in the eighteenth-century
diaspora and the slave trade within and from the Biafran interior.

In the popular imagination, the middle passage stands out as the defining
moment of the Atlantic slave trade. Yet in time, the overseas voyage from the
African littoral to the Americas represented perhaps the shortest leg of captives' whole disparaging odyssey. On average, for instance, English Guineamen calling at the Bight of Biafra sailed nearly seventy days to reach Jamaica.
These same ships anchored at Biafran ports an average of 103 days collecting

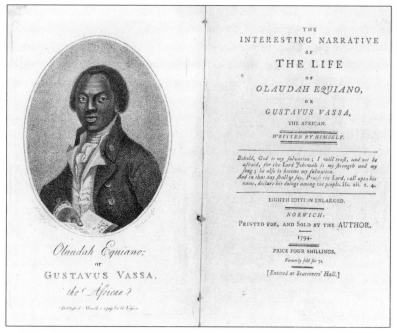

Figure 3. Frontispiece and title page from *The Interesting Narrative of the Life of Olaudah Equiano, or Gustavus Vassa, the African,* 8th ed. (Norwich, 1794) *Source:* Library of Congress.

their human cargo. But even before reaching the ships, slaves from the interior could be many months moving from their former homes to the coast.[22]

The consequences of this trek through the interior should be neither overlooked nor underestimated. The trails captives followed in the interior were characterized by grinding, disjointed movement and profound alienation, the total effect of which was to separate enslaved Africans from the physical and social moorings of their homelands. The trade forced captives into new connections, attenuating former locally based ties. In the end, the serial displacement and violence inherent to slave trading in the interior prepared the way for people who previously would not have known themselves as Igbo to begin to see themselves as such.

The story Vassa told of his enslavement in the Biafran interior brings this process into clear view: One day, while the adults of his village were in their fields or otherwise engaged, the young Equiano and his sister were set upon in their father's compound by two men and a woman who, as Vassa put it, "got over our walls, and in a moment seized us both."[23] Moving with expert stealth, the kidnappers bound and gagged the two children and dragged them out of the compound before either one was able to call for help or to offer any real resistance. The trio carried the children through the surrounding woods until nightfall, when they took refuge in a small house to eat, which the children refused, and to sleep, which the young captives welcomed.[24]

The next morning the thieves continued with their contraband. "For a long time," wrote Vassa, "we had kept the woods, but at last we came into a road which I believed I knew." The familiar road sparked hope in Equiano that they might yet be saved, and seeing a group of people on the byway, but at a distance, he cried for help. In response, his captors tied his limbs tighter, reapplied a gag, and placed him in a sack in which they carried him until nightfall. Once more they stopped for rest and sustenance, but the children again refused to eat.[25]

The following morning the kidnappers stirred the two children from their slumber only to separate them. According to Vassa, though the siblings begged to be kept together, and though they held on to each other for dear life, the traders and the demands of the trade prevailed. "[S]he was torn from me, and immediately carried away, while I was left in a state of distraction not to be described." Equiano's travels continued for many days afterward, during which he "cried and grieved continually." For a time, he ate only what he was forced, and on this leg of his journey he changed masters frequently. His initial kidnappers passed him on along the pathways of the interior; presumably, his sister suffered a similar fate.[26]

After some time in the trade, Equiano was at last purchased by a smith, who employed the young slave in working the bellows of his forge and in assisting a slave woman with the cooking. He understood the dialect of the people, and though treated as an outsider—he was forbidden to eat with the free-born children and at times feared grave treatment at the hands of his master—he was at the very least finally set still. The stop, however, did not last. Before long he was sold away again.[27]

This time, the trader or traders who purchased Equiano marched him toward the sea. They carried him on their shoulders when he tired and could walk no farther, and apparently he traveled in the company of others damned to similar fates. They marched and marched and marched, stopping only in the evenings to sleep. During this circuit of his journey, Equiano's path and that of his sister crossed once again. One evening when the traders who held him stopped for the night, those who had charge of his sister happened into the same way station. Their reunion lasted one night. In the morning, they were again pushed separate ways.[28]

Following a great deal of travel through the interior, and after having changed hands at least three more times, Equiano was sold into a wealthy household somewhere in the Biafran wetlands, a town Vassa called Tinmah. He hoped it was his fortune to be adopted into this family, for they treated him more like a son than a slave. But after some two months, he was snatched from his bed in the early morning and sold away yet again. "The change I now experienced," Vassa remembered of the moment, "was as painful as it was sudden and unexpected." The overland journey that followed landed Equiano at "the banks of a large river, which was covered with canoes in which the people appeared to live with all their household utensils and provisions of all kinds." Here, he was placed into one of the dugouts and "continued to travel, sometimes by land, sometimes by water, through different countries, and various nations, till, at the end of six or seven months" he arrived at the coast.[29]

According to Vassa's account, then, the slave trade from the Biafran interior funneled captives from the uplands to the coast in spasms. The serial nature of the trade meant that captives were not only separated from their homes as time wore on, but they could not even count on remaining for long with fellow captives taken in the vicinity. For slaves, the consequence of such movement was the continuous introduction to new people and places. Moreover, though Vassa wrote little of the matter himself, the journey of enslaved Africans through the interior was characterized by levels of violence and denigration that compounded the inherent alienating effect of the movement itself. According to oral histories of the slave trade collected by Boniface Obichere, slaves were pushed hard through the elements and down the interior's roads and pathways, suffering all the while from hunger, disease, and maltreatment at the hands of their captors. When drivers encamped a slave coffle near a village or market for recuperation, the string of captives were usually held apart from the local population in adjacent areas designated for the use of slave traders and their prisoners. Slaves who perished on the way to market or at market were not buried. Rather, they were thrown to rot into the "bad bush," grounds used by local people to dispose of those who died tainted by some abomination. Slaves in transit, argues Obichere, suffered such harsh usage, in part, precisely because they were so far from home and thus so far from any potential protectors or relations. The slave coffles, quite simply, were full of the foreign born and strange accents. Slaves in transit were utter outsiders, pariahs, and they suffered as such.[30]

In the *Interesting Narrative*, the effects of continual dislocation and the power slaveowners held over captives is absolutely clear. Combined, the two phenomena dislodged captives from their former sense of society and place and encouraged them to work out and accept new connections. Relating his experience with the smith who was his first master, Vassa detailed this shift rather dramatically. After about a month in the smith's compound, Equiano was allowed some leeway from his betters. When trusted away from his master's place, he connived constantly about how and whether he could make it back to his father's. The information he gathered convinced him that if the right circumstances presented themselves, it was not out of the question to try for home.

An opportunity soon arose. After having accidentally killed one of his master's fowls, Equiano ran to the thickets surrounding his owner's compound so as to escape punishment. While in hiding, he heard those seeking him suppose out loud that he was trying to make his way back from where he came. They reasoned that "the distance was so great, and the way so intricate" that the little slave would never reach his goal. He would die in the forest first. The conversation completely unnerved Equiano:

> I had before entertained hopes of getting home, and I had determined when it should be dark to make the attempt; but I was now convinced it was fruitless, and I began to consider that, if possibly I could escape all other animals, I could not those of the human kind; and that, not knowing the way, I must perish in the woods.

Contrite, accepting what appeared to be his fate, and reeled in, perhaps, by the discouraging ruminations of his would be captors, the slave returned to his master.[31]

Separated from his homeland by several months and many miles, Equiano resigned himself to the possibility that he might never again see his family. Thereafter, he attempted to insinuate himself into the ways and means of those among whom he was exiled. He mastered the dialects of his captors and whenever sold into another household tried in vain to make himself a transparent member of his new society. The sharp, serial displacement occasioned by the trade and the temporal separation it effected between Equiano and his home demanded as much.[32]

In general, research on slavery in Africa reveals that the exigencies and transformations apparent in Vassa's *Interesting Narrative* were not at all uncommon to the condition. Reviewing more than fifteen local studies of slavery in Africa, Suzanne Miers and Igor Kopytoff have argued that enslavement and the internal African slave trade tended to inflict upon captives "a traumatic and sometimes violent withdrawal from kin, neighbors, and community, and often from familiar customs and language." So, when first settled into new societies, captives were in a "state of marginality," their old senses of place, self, and identification enfeebled and new ones yet to be fully determined. In time, however, captives often incorporated themselves into their new surroundings. Sometimes this incorporation led to a captive achieving status as a full member of their new society. More often it did not. But incorporation almost always entailed—and Vassa's *Interesting Narrative* is but an eighteenth-century illustration—the slow recession of former social ties and the domestication of new ones.[33]

There is little evidence concerning what was on the minds of other eighteenth-century slaves pushed through the Biafran interior, but we do know that the displacement that formed Equiano's experienced was not at all uncommon. Alexander Falconbridge—an abolitionist, formerly a surgeon in the Guinea trade, and familiar with affairs along the Niger Delta—believed that none of the slaves he saw boarded at Bonny were natives of the coast. He had quizzed several aboard the ships he served concerning their origins and was convinced from their replies that those loaded at Bonny came to port from a great distance and had passed "through several Hands" before arriving.[34] James Penny, himself the captain of a slave ship and no friend to abolitionists, conceded the same point in his testimony to Parliament. According to notes entered in the "Report of the Lords of the Committee of Council appointed for the Consideration of all Matters relating to Trade and Foreign Plantations," Penny attempted an icy precision in addressing the matter. "Mr. Penny believes," reads a summary of his testimony, "that some of the slaves are brought from Countries still more distant in the interior Parts of Africa. They sometimes find from the Slaves that they have travelled Two Moons (or Months) before they arrived at the Sea Coast. They may travel at the Rate of from Twenty to Twenty-five Miles a Day." Thus Penny conceded that he had regularly taken aboard his ship men and women who from appearances gave no reason to doubt that they had just been forcibly marched some 1,200 miles from the interior to the coast.[35]

Penny's opinion is perhaps an exaggeration, but the assertion is useful because it directly confirms Falconbridge's claim concerning the great distances traveled by slaves loaded in the Niger Delta. Also, through its unintended allusion to the condition of slaves boarded at Bonny, Penny's testimony indirectly supports the contention that others loaded at Biafran ports had survived circumstances similar to those described in Vassa's *Interesting Narrative*. That is, during their journey toward the Atlantic they were *used* as slaves as well as *traded* as slaves. It is a point made more directly by a perceptive ship captain who, after waiting for slaves in the Bonny River for some two weeks with little to show for it, wondered whether the trade would soon pick up. In the interior, he reasoned, the harvest would soon be over. In all likelihood, farmers in the hinterlands would then release some of their slaves into the hands of traders, who in turn would funnel them toward the ships.[36]

After having passed through many hands in the hinterlands, slaves bound for the Atlantic were sold to the coast from markets on the outermost edges of the interior.[37] The arrival of enslaved Africans at these upland markets, or fairs as they were called, marked their entry into the Atlantic world, and it is from the Atlantic that a clearer view emerges of the origins of the Igbo identity ascribed to and eventually internalized by such slaves. In contra-distinction to circumstances in the interior, residents of the trading towns of the Biafran littoral held and articulated fairly well-developed notions of being Igbo. In a fundamental way, consequently, the origins of Igbo society in the Americas owe a great deal to the nature of captives' sojourn along the Biafran coast—namely to captives' continuing alienation within the urban contexts of such Atlantic towns as Bonny, Elem Kalabari, and Old Calabar.

When European slavers anchored off Bonny, New Calabar, or Old Calabar, the principal traders of those towns dispatched people upriver to purchase slaves in bulk from the various trade fairs held on the near mar-gins of the interior. As recalled by Alexander Falconbridge, preparations for such missions were "very considerable." Wrote Falconbridge: "From twenty to thirty canoes, capable of containing thirty or forty negroes each, are as-sembled for this purpose; and such goods put on board them as they expect will be wanted for the purchase of the number of slaves intended to buy. When their loading is completed, they commence their voyage, with colors flying and musick playing, and in about ten or eleven days, they generally return to Bonny with full cargoes."[38]

The coastal traders loaded their canoes with goods acquired "on trust" from slave ship captains, and they were sometimes obliged to visit sev-eral markets before returning with a full complement. When supply was greatest, trading firms on the coast were capable of delivering enormous numbers of slaves. On a single day in April 1791, traders at Bonny busied themselves with the appetites of some thirteen ships then anchored in the river. All told, these vessels contained between them more than four thou-sand slaves and were waiting for more.[39]

Laboring under such demands of volume, traders found it in their interest to expedite their missions upcountry. Under such conditions as prevailed at Bonny in April 1791, the more rounds a firm completed into the interior the greater its potential profits. In addition, canoe traders were under pressure to collect slaves from the interior before news concerning the number and/or status of ships at the coast reached the inland slave marts, for suppliers behind the coast set prices according to their perception of demand at the Atlantic.[40]

For slaves on sale at the fairs, these acute demands of the Atlantic African market translated into further degrees of disparagement and alienation. Going upriver and back, traders gave only the slightest attention to the care of their cargo. A canoe trader was liable for the health of his slaves during the journey to the coast, but his responsibility expired eight to twelve hours after making a sale to a ship. Thus, when at market, traders undoubtedly felt more pressure toward affecting a reasonable return time, acquiring a sufficient volume, and maintaining control over their cargo than anything else. To these ends, persons bought at the fairs were fastened tightly—many simply by the arms, the stronger by the legs as well—thrown into the bottom of a canoe, and spirited toward the sea.

Up to thirty individuals could be piled into the average pirogue. Alexander Falconbridge, who had observed this aspect of the trade firsthand, recalled that slaves were sometimes secured lying down so that they made the journey "in great Pain" from the strictness of their bonds. In addition, they were "often almost covered with Water" from the seepage of the canoes and the "violent rains" common on the approach to the coast. Compounding these injuries, during their riverine journey slaves were afforded only a scanty allowance of food. Falconbridge described the portions as "barely sufficient to support nature," a rationing no doubt understood by the traders as a way to cut costs while simultaneously decreasing time in transit.[41]

Bone-soaked, half-starved, and packed as tightly as feasible into the canoes of their present captors, slaves from the interior made for the Atlantic trading towns of the Biafran coast. Their entries bespoke a continuing degradation. At Bonny, it was the practice that scores of slaving canoes arrived in union and according to a schedule, usually on a Thursday or Friday by the English calendar. Having appeared together, the fleet would disperse to land its cargoes at the town's various trading concerns. Canoe slaves were disembarked and led into the way stations of the principal traders. Even a newcomer in town could quickly grasp the nature of this late-week ritual, for those disembarked from the boats were pinioned with "Twigs, Canes, Grass Rope, or other Ligaments of the Country." At the traders' houses, slaves were "Made up for Sale," a process that included being rubbed down with oil and given a full meal.[42]

Having heard of a canoe fleet's arrival, captains anchored astride the town, waited a time, and then made their way to the trade houses, where they examined the slaves presented to them and quizzed the traders and the slaves themselves concerning the present cargo. According to Falconbridge, the first matter to be ascertained was the approximate age of the slave. Thereafter, people from the ship would "minutely inspect" the person of the slaves for bodily defects and "inquire into the state of their health." The former Guineaship surgeon outlined the course and purpose of this scrutiny as follows: "if they are afflicted with any infirmity, or are deformed, or have bad eyes or teeth; if they are lame, or weak in the joints, or distorted in the back, or of a slender make, or are narrow in the chest; in short, if they have been, or are afflicted in any manner, so as to render them incapable of much labour; if any of the foregoing defects are discovered in them, they are rejected."[43]

Likely candidates were bargained for, and almost as quickly as the slaves had arrived they were dispatched to waiting ships—either via traders who had brought them down in the first place or by boats belonging to ships then in the river. Whatever the case, these exchanges between captains and canoe traders were most often made at twilight.[44] So the day after a fleet arrived in town, if sales were brisk, it was as if the unfortunates aboard yesterday's canoes had all but disappeared.

By the time they made Bonny, New Calabar, or Old Calabar, slaves from the Biafran interior were deeply alienated. Almost every detail about their sojourn to the sea had served to separate them from the social details of their former homes. They arrived at the Atlantic strangers, and in the eighteenth century the residents of Bonny, Elem Kalabari, and Old Calabar had a specific name for such people. The foreigners brought down the river to be sold into waiting ships, whatever and whomever they used to be, were called Igbo.[45]

There is evidence from Bonny and Elem Kalabari that this nomenclature persisted throughout the eighteenth century. On a late seventeenth-century map giving the approach and soundings of the New Calabar River, for instance, the terra incognita beyond Elem Kalabari bears the label "The Hackbous Country is some Leagues above N. Calabar Town." James Barbot, who sailed to Elem Kalabari and Bonny in 1699 as supercargo aboard the slave ship *Albion*, referred several times in his journal to the people who lived beyond the littoral as Hackbous. In their deployment of the word, both the map of the New Calabar River and Barbot's journal undoubtedly followed the custom of the Bonny and Kalabari peoples from whose perspective European traders faced the interior.[46]

On one level then, people at the coast wielded Igbo in a fashion similar to how it was probably used in the interior, as a way to refer to strangers and foreigners.[47] But there were key differences, too. In the polyglot,

Atlantic trading towns of Elem Kalabari, Bonny, and Old Calabar, there are indications that Igbo referred only to certain kinds of strangers—not simply those from beyond the towns in general, but those from beyond the littoral. At the coast, Igbo were not strangers from the pale, aliens abutting the territory and dependencies of the towns. Rather, they were the strangers beyond those strangers. Guinea sailors speaking in the manner of the African merchants with whom they traded for slaves at the coast understood the distinction quite well: "The Slaves that are sold to the Europeans are generally procurred by people that live in the Up Country, as it is called by the people of Bonny—supposed to be the country between the Sea Coast and the Ebo Country."[48]

At the coast, Igbo took on a colonizing expansiveness lacking in its use in the interior, and in the towns themselves there is evidence that people infused Igbo with meaning beyond the broad regional stereotypes apparent above. There were, for instance, settlements in the delta that traced their founding and lineage to Igbo progenitors from the interior, in ways distinguishing themselves from their neighbors.[49] And with the ratcheting up of the slave trade in the eighteenth century and the influx to the delta of slaves, traders, laborers, and opportunists from the interior that this commercial explosion entailed, differences real and putative between newcomers from the hinterland and their progeny, on one hand, and indigenes and more established residents, on the other, took on an even more palpable meaning.

Work on the origins and social history of the trading towns of the Biafran littoral shores up the point. G. I. Jones, Robin Horton, and K. O. Dike have shown that key components of Elem Kalabari, Bonny, and Old Calabar society were dedicated to the acculturation of Igbo immigrants from the far interior.[50] At Elem Kalabari, the *koronogbo,* a subset of the Ekine fraternity of leading men, made it its business to roam the town on appointed nights accosting everyone they met. According to Horton: "If those challenged gave their names with a good Kalabari accent, they were allowed to go their way." If, however, "they gave their names with an accent betraying Ibo or Ibibio origin"—betraying that is, origins in the interior or the eastern delta—they were assaulted as an object lesson for the poorly acculturated.[51] At Old Calabar, the Ekpe Society played an analogous role, serving as a vehicle by which Igbo slaves and strangers from the interior could domesticate themselves into local society by mastering the language, customs, and associations of the town to which they now belonged.[52] At Bonny, the prevalence and tenacity of spoken Igbo, in the eighteenth century down to the present, suggests that acculturating institutions in operation there were in some matters no match for the volume of immigration from the hinterland.[53]

Work on ethnicity formation and African cities suggests that the particular difference Igbo signified at Bonny, Elem Kalabari, and Old Calabar, in contradistinction to its more indiscriminate use in the interior, was illustrative of the kinds of social formation common in cities, where urban material conditions and politics encouraged people to identify with one another, to define others, and to associate according to characteristics made pertinent by the peculiar conditions of urban life. In cities, social and cultural distinctions that may have been operative outside the urban crucible are not always maintained within it. For migrants in nineteenth- and twentieth-century African cities, for instance, frayed connections to their former homes and the insecurity and scramble of urban life combined with other exigencies to encourage immigrants to associate on the basis of broad familiarities of language, culture, and "assumed kinship" to ameliorate their prospects in ways that gave rise and continue to give rise to new ethnicities.[54] So too it must have been in the Atlantic trading towns of Bonny, Elem Kalabari, and Old Calabar—filled as they were with not just indigenes but with merchants, traders, and slaves from outlying areas near and far. Hunters, traders, refugees, smiths, and especially slaves, who in the interior understood themselves as Aro, Ngwa, Aboh, et cetera, were referred to at Bonny, Elem Kalabari, and Old Calabar—though not always indiscriminately—as Igbo.

More to the point, there is evidence that Bonny residents who originated in the interior came to internalize and act on the amalgamating ideology whereby matters of language, physiognomy, and practice that meant little in the social and ethnic geography of the interior could mean a great deal in the geography of the coast. At Bonny, for example, European slave traders, town indigenes, and residents originating in the hinterland all understood what it meant to send an ailing Ebo slave from ship to shore to recuperate "in [the] charge of one of her own countrywomen"—a declaration of kinship that would have made little sense in the interior.[55]

The existence of such affiliations in the Atlantic trading towns of the Biafran littoral is important to point out and to explain, because the same urbanism that gave rise to notions of Igboness at Bonny, Elem Kalabari, and Old Calabar prevailed in even greater measure aboard the European Guineaships into which captives from the interior passed following their sojourn at the coast. The slave ship was itself a kind of city, a crucible where the name foisted upon slaves during their treks through the hinterland and at the littoral developed further into captives' new society.

TWO

THE SLAVE SHIP AND THE BEGINNINGS OF IGBO SOCIETY IN THE AFRICAN DIASPORA

What did it mean to be an Igbo man or woman in the eighteenth-century Atlantic world? Was it a shared language? A spate of common beliefs and practices? A way of viewing the world? Scholars who have addressed Igbo society and culture in the African diaspora have tended to answer such questions affirmatively. Viewing Igbo society in these ways recognizes what Igbo ultimately came to mean by calling attention to some of the cultural foundations on which captives from the Biafran interior built that meaning. Being Igbo, becoming Igbo, was a process and not a given, but it did not proceed from nothing. It was facilitated by affinities of language, cosmology, politics, and philosophy.[1]

But an approach to Igbo origins that depends on the explanatory power of apparently coherent foundational elements such as language and religion has real analytical limits, too. The approach neglects the fact that a central impetus (perhaps the central impetus) behind the formation of diasporan Igbo society and culture was not some natural coherence among Igbo people *in the making,* but the centripetal exigencies of violence and suffering that defined the ordeals of enslaved African men and women from the Biafran interior. Thus, to describe Igbo culture and society by what it *was,* to underline its constitutive substance to the neglect of the rudiments of Igbo society and culture predicated not on what *was* but on loss and absence, is to leave critical aspects of being Igbo under interrogated and insufficiently described.

The eventual boundaries of diasporan Igbo society and culture were no doubt affected by affinities of language, politics, and cosmology, but the process originated in a context of material, social, and cultural privation that was itself fundamentally constitutive. Following the men, women, and children herded onto slave ships at Bonny, Elem Kalabari, Old Calabar and environs in the eighteenth century, and casting an eye toward the human connections they cobbled together within this state of affairs, offers a view of diasporan Igbo society in the making that draws this point quite plainly.

The twin cruces of diasporan Igbo origins were terror and desperation. Thus, to come to full terms with the meaning and substance of Igbo society and culture in the eighteenth-century diaspora, it is necessary to pay close attention to the circumstances and routines that characterized the dystopian world in which many Africans from the Biafran interior began to generate for themselves what it meant to be Igbo: the slave ship.

In general, enslaved Africans aboard ships at Bonny, New Calabar, and Old Calabar followed days distinguished by meals, moments of exercise, and a series of comings and goings from between decks (the term for the raised cargo deck or decks beneath the main deck) to above. Each morning— according to the weather and the inclination of the ship's master—the whole body of slaves was brought above. In ships where children and women were kept between decks during the evening, they were helped above during the day and set in place without restraints, as women and children were, in general, never fettered.

Male captives, who were almost always restrained while at the coast, faced a slightly different morning routine. When men slaves were first brought on board, the country ligaments—"small cords twisted, from the bark of trees and grass"—by which canoe traders bound captives as they carried them to the ships were cut. Guineaship armorers replaced these cords with irons, manacling pairs of men by their hands and sometimes by their hands and feet (the left wrist or ankle of one to the right wrist or ankle of the other). As male captives were brought from below each morning, a sailor examined each pair's shackles as they gained the deck to ensure they were still secure. Other crew caught each emerging couple, arranged them along the deck, and reeved a long chain through the leg shackles of each pair, effectively tying the entire group to the ship itself.[2]

With the women and children at their places and the men tied to each other and to the deck, sailors offered wash water while the surgeon and his mate offered cordials—a mixture of vinegar and fruit juice meant to prevent scurvy—to the entire group and drams and other medicines to the sickest among them.[3] Afterward, the men, women, and children on deck were divided into messes consisting of groups of ten or so people on their haunches surrounding a single tub of about three gallons. This division was accomplished at the sailors' prodding, whereupon "a warm Mess is provided for them, alternately of their own Country Food, and of the Pulse carried from Europe for that Purpose, to which Stock Fish, Palm Oil, Pepper, &c. are added."[4] Along the Bight of Biafra, the country meal consisted of regional staples purchased at the coast, mainly yams and eddoes, with the sick sometimes allowed small portions of bread in addition.[5]

Following breakfast, the slaves were once again provided wash water, and the ship's crew directed the cleaning of the upper deck, which after meals invariably became stained with a patina of the stews and porridges just fed to the slaves.[6] Afterward, at the crews' urging, enslaved Africans were bid to sing and jump about. "This Exercise which is called Dancing," recalled a sailor who had been in the Guinea trade as a boy, "consists in jumping up and rattling their Chains. It is done to the Beat of a Drum."[7] After exercise, it was the custom to ply the captives with tobacco, which some smoked in pipes and others held in their mouths as snuff.[8] Additionally, the crew distributed beads and other baubles among the women and girls, who fashioned out of them various kinds of "fanciful Ornaments for their Persons."[9]

Come late afternoon, captives "were again messed, as in the Morning," and in the evening the slaves were directed below. In some ships, the entire cargo was sent between decks to separate apartments—divided at the least between men and women and sometimes with separate spaces designated for men, for boys, for women and girls, and for the sick.[10] In other ships, with evening, the entire space between decks was given over to the men, while women, children, and the sick were suffered to spend the night on deck.[11]

This general routine of rising, coming on deck, washing, eating, exercising, and going below framed the lives of enslaved Africans aboard European slavers. But to begin to grasp the actual context of shipboard survival, it is vital also to come to terms with the general material conditions under which this routine played out. Evidence concerning these conditions is stark in support of one overriding point: every moment by which a captive might mark the passage of time aboard a slaver—the entire routine of life on a Guineaship—was punctuated by violence and privation.

Slaves from the interior filed into Guineamen that upon their own arrival in harbor had transformed themselves from sailing ships into floating stockades. At anchor, a slaver's sailors struck and stowed its sails, replacing the apparatus that was normally about the deck with a network of awnings, lattice works, nets, and gangways forming a series of chambers across the surface of the ship. About the vessel itself, the crew might raise a scaffolding that circled several levels from bow to stern. Henry Smeathman, an amateur botanist familiar with river trading in western Africa, held that a slaver at anchor was an "extraordinary spectacle," perhaps "better supposed than described." "The first thing" that caught the eye, wrote Smeathman, "was the odd appearance of the ship, which was barricadoed round and raised in an extraordinary manner. On her quarter deck was built a round house & over it a temporary one, cover'd with a canvass-awning, where the Captn.

& officers live & have view over all the Ship; the main deck was strongly barricadoed at the main mast & so kept distinct from the quarter deck; there were scaffoldings made on each side of the ship for the convenience of washing & cleansing the ship & for the unfortunate passengers on certain occasions to retire to."[12]

Guineamen at anchor cast various profiles depending on their size, shape, and tonnage. There were barks, sloops, snows, schooners, brigs, and ships, but when attired as was the custom when waiting in the Biafran rivers, all offered similar accommodation. Invariably, the ships were damp, dank, and close. The houses built on board, ostensibly for shelter, in truth served to insulate a ship's hold so during the day the space between decks sweltered. When fires burned for cooking, or at night for warmth, a slaver's house trapped vapors rising from the green mangrove generally used as fuel along the coast. So Guineamen in the river continually produced an acrid smoke and were almost constantly enveloped by a thin haze that worked a chronic red into the eyes of the ship's inhabitants. Under the best of circumstances, Guineamen were miasmal, vermin-infested keeps; when loading, the ships sank into even greater complexes of filth and discomfort.[13]

For captives, passing the evening below deck was perhaps the most demanding part of their daily routine. To begin with, as a slaver began to fill, there was the problem of space. Purpose-built and retro-fitted Guineaships were, in the main, multi-decked ships consisting of two or more levels below their main deck. The space between the floor and ceiling of each deck often measured between four and six feet in height. To accommodate more slaves, however, most eighteenth-century Guineaships also had platforms extending from the walls of the ship toward the center of each deck, so that effectively, except for those relatively few Africans lying in the center of the deck or just below a grating to a superior deck, each captive had less than three feet of vertical space in which to raise her head. Only the smallest of children could sit up.[14]

As little room as there was between a slave's berth and the effective ceiling formed by the platform or deck above, captives had even less space across the span of their backs. The economic necessity of filling the ship with as many slaves as feasible—called the ship's complement—meant that people were laid shoulder to shoulder and sometimes front to back on their sides.[15] As a slaver began to fill, captives between decks found themselves confined in what a former Guinea surgeon described as "not so much room as a man in his coffin."[16]

Such closeness created a debilitating atmosphere. A British naval officer who testified to Parliament that he did not think Africans received any real "inhuman Treatment" at the hands of slavers admitted the exception was the fact that slaves "were so crouded" between decks "that the Stench of the Hatchway was intolerable," even in ships far from their full complements. The confined perspiration and excrement of hundreds of bodies combined for an injurious effect even to eighteenth-century noses.[17]

Under normal circumstances, then, in good weather—when a ship's air ports were open and its gratings uncovered—the temperature and fetor between decks insured that captives constantly contended with waves of heat exhaustion and nausea.[18] When a ship's air ports had to be shut and its gratings covered due to storms or swells, the normally putrid conditions between decks deteriorated even further. "They make an hideous Yelling on these Occasions," reported one Guinea sailor.[19] A witness to similar circumstances aboard another ship concurred, testifying that conditions between decks were "peculiarly distressing" in poor weather. Under such circumstances, it got so hot below that the Africans "nearly suffocated," with some becoming clearly "insensible" and remaining so for days and weeks afterward.[20]

The cost of each evening's stowing became evident as captives were brought on deck each morning. Their naked and nearly naked bodies drenched in sweat and stained with urine, feces, and mucus, many slaves were quite disorientated by their hours below and climbed above half conscious, half fainting. Every few mornings there were those who did not emerge at all, requiring sailors to search the berths, cutting the dead from the shackles of the living. Some of these, quite simply, had suffocated.[21] Others had expired from causes that eighteenth-century minds and medicine could not readily comprehend, but explained in ways that made clear how intolerable conditions were below. "I have seen them go down apparently perfectly well at night, and found dead in the morning," testified one former surgeon. Asked whether he thought the atmosphere below had ever caused such casualties, the officer replied: "Yes, I believe it has, having seen them frequently brought upon deck, some fainting; and I have also seen some die within a few minutes after they have been brought upon deck, which proceeded from the corrupted state of the air and heat jointly."[22]

When above deck during the daytime, captives were free from the worst depravations of life below. All the same, their daytime routine presented horrors of its own. Meals, for instance, were fraught with threat and violence. As was the case in the interior—where fear, depression, and disease sometimes made recent captives incapable of taking the food offered by their captors—it was common for slaves aboard Guineaships to refuse sustenance. When refusal stemmed from inclination, Africans balking at the porridge of European provisions offered them as one of their meals, mealtime became an arena of intimidation, with ship masters and Guinea crew making it known to slaves that refusing horsebeans, peas, and other foreign foods meant being denied their country provisions later. When captives rejected food with greater intransigence, perhaps owing to illness, they were subject to whippings and other punishments, even to the point that correction approached the death or dismemberment of the captive in question.[23] Some slaves were beaten so badly for refusing meals that the effects of their punishment, not the consequences of their fast, appeared in hindsight the true cause of their demise.[24]

Diligent ship masters ordered that meals be followed with a period of physical activity, thinking "that the Slaves should take Exercise for the Benefit of their Health."[25] Slave trade apologists pointed to such activity as both evidence of slaves' general cheerfulness and of slave traders own humanity, suggesting that self-interested slavers encouraged captives in various amusements in order to insure the good health and disposition of the cargo.[26] Those less friendly to the trade pointed out that in practice exercising slaves was, for the captives themselves, not quite the benign enterprise described by others. "They are made after each meal to jump up and down upon the beating of a drum," countered a Guinea sailor surprised at how others characterized the shipboard routine. This, he continued, "is what I have heard called dancing, but not what I consider dancing, as it is not to music of their own."[27] Further, this dancing could quickly become more a diversion for the crew than anything else, as the unfettered, mostly women and children, were driven one into the other at random, while those in manacles and secured to the deck were made to "jump up and rattle their Chains." Sailors sometimes compelled captives to chant in pidgin English during the chaos, as on one ship where the women were made to proclaim while exercising how good it was to live and eat "among White Men."[28] Injury was quite often added to insult for those who would not or could not dance. "If any of them appear sluggish and unwilling," goes a representative comment on how sailors kept captives active, "the Mates and Boatswain, who carry a Cat of Nine Tails with them for that Purpose, never fail to exercise it upon them."[29] The intimidation and violence characterizing the start of the day aboard a Guineaship and coinciding with the first feeding continued unabated into the mid-day exercise.

Into the afternoon, captives' routines repeated themselves—there was another feeding followed by another period of exercise—before slaves were crowded back into their nighttime habits. If the master neglected to order that the berths be cleaned while the Africans were above, then captives returned to the same filth they had left hours earlier. If the officers had indeed issued such an order, then Africans filed back onto berths that had either been scraped and swept, or washed and scrubbed by a contingent of the ship's sailors. If scraped, the filth between decks had been simply spread thinner; if washed, the berth's morning squalor had been diluted with water, vinegar, and lime juice.[30] In any case, captives were handed off from above to groups of sailors between decks who were "employed in stowing or packing them together; such as in adjusting their Arms and Legs, and prescribing a fixed Space for each."[31] In ships where women, children, and the sick spent evenings above deck, their own night was less suffocating, though sleeping among the ship's crew was oppressive in other ways.

It should be pointed out that a Guineaship's routine and the immediate material conditions in which it played out exacerbated a characteristic of captivity that, though it no doubt began in the interior, came to a head within the close confines of the slave ship: ubiquitous morbidity and mortality. Along with the routine violence and privation already outlined, extraordinary instances of death and sickness rounded out the context of life aboard a Guineaship, especially along the Bight of Biafra.

On this point, research on the incidence of death and disease among African slaves is dense, contradictory, and at moments highly technical. But several important matters emerge from the literature with some clarity. It is clear, first of all, that Guineaships, for both crew and captives, were the deadliest form of transoceanic transport and commerce in the eighteenth century.[32] Second, for the latter half of the eighteenth century, slave deaths on Guineaships—in transit and on the coast—varied remarkably from ship to ship but averaged on the whole between 10 and 15 percent.[33] Third, there is an emerging consensus that a hefty plurality of slave deaths—almost a majority—resulted from progressively debilitating gastrointestinal diseases and that the general incidence of death aboard slave ships tended to rise as the journey unfolded (quite simply, Guineaships became more deadly the fuller they got and then the longer they stayed at sea). Lastly, and this is perhaps most important for the subject at hand, whatever the changing general incidence of mortality and morbidity up and down the west African coast, ships slaving at ports in the Bight of Biafra were perennially more dangerous to the health and lives of African captives than those calling at ports along any other west African region.[34] The Bight of Biafra was the sickliest, deadliest stretch of western Africa, averaging in the first half of the eighteenth century levels of mortality twice as high as the rest of Atlantic Africa. In the period 1702–1750, for instance, when Guineaships calling on the rest of western Africa averaged losses per voyage of around 15 percent, ships calling at Biafran ports routinely lost more than 40 percent of the slaves put on board.[35]

The threat of death and the incidence of death on a Guineaship—and the illnesses that precipitated and preceded both—heightened the violence and privation ordinarily attending any one part of a slaver's daily routine. Thus the ordinarily suffocating, filthy conditions between decks deteriorated by another degree of magnitude whenever the ship's slaves succumbed in significant numbers to illness—especially when the ailment in question was that most common of Guineaship afflictions, dysentery.

A catchall for several kinds of gastrointestinal infections that are spread by fecal-oral contact, dysentery inflicted fever, nausea, debilitating cramps, and diarrhea. Its cure, one candid Guinea surgeon admitted, was beyond the comprehension of eighteenth-century medicine.[36] Even describing its effects taxed the language of those who witnessed it. "I cannot conceive any situation so dreadful and disgusting," wrote a sailor about an outbreak on a slaver on which he worked, "the deck was covered with blood and mucus, and approached nearer to the resemblance of a slaughter-house than any thing I can compare it to."[37] The best description a witness to another incident could offer was simply, "the Scene is shocking."[38]

The prevalence of morbidity and the fear of mortality that dysentery generated among a ship's officers could add another level of cruelty to outbreaks of sickness when Guinea crews attempted to quash the spread of infection. At Elem Kalabari in the 1760s a young girl aboard the slave ship *Britannia* came down with the smallpox. The *Britannia*'s complement was five hundred, but at the time the malady was discovered the ship had only about three hundred slaves on board. Figuring that New Calabar's traders would quarantine the ship should they find out about the girl's condition, the master ordered the infected child taken into the hold and hidden in an empty water puncheon. Despite this crude measure of prevention, the disease took hold among captives between decks, and the *Britannia* was obliged to sprint from New Calabar short of her full load. The "Situation of the Slaves became such, as no Pen nor Language is able to describe. The Sick Births were incapable of containing all that were ill. Those only could be admitted into them, who were so bad as not to be capable of moving. There they lay in One Mass of Scab and Corruption, frequently sticking to each other and the Decks, till they were separated to be thrown into the Sea. Six, Eight, and Ten were thrown overboard in a Morning from different Parts of the Ship."[39]

Of course, Guineaships did not sink immediately into the conditions and habits described above, and in any case all of the hundreds of African captives aboard any one slaver did not experience the ship in completely uniform ways. So although it was customary, for instance, for Guinea crewmen to lash men and boys who would not take their exercise, such encouragement was not generally meted out in equal measures to women and girls who likewise refused.[40] Though slaves customarily messed twice a day—once with country provisions and then with rations from Europe—circumstances sometimes demanded that meals be missed altogether or carried on short rations.[41] Though captives suffered in general from the suffocating heat prone to build up between decks, it was not unheard of for naked slaves to suffer equally, depending on the time of day and the season of the year, from cold and exposure.[42]

It must also be kept in mind that many of the conditions and routines described above became general only generally, owing to the incremental nature of slave trading. Canoe traders at Elem Kalabari, Bonny, and Old Calabar might bring hundreds of captives down to the coast at a time, but the captives' experiences aboard any particular Guineaship began in smaller parcels, as traders divided their quarry between several ships. So captives from the interior boarded ships at the rate of five to ten per day in general, and at higher rates when the market was flush just after traders returned from the fairs in the interior, and on particular ships as the ship moved up in priority. The situation of the ship *Rodney,* which slaved along the Biafran coast in the spring of 1791, is illustrative. The *Rodney* arrived at Bonny on April 7. In the two weeks following the ship's arrival, about twenty slaves were aboard. By May 2, thirteen days after her arrival, the same twenty-odd captives were still the *Rodney*'s only prisoners (when the *Rodney* made the river in April there were thirteen ships ahead of her). Later in the month, things began to pick up. By May 16 the ship held more than 120 slaves. Nine days later some forty more captives were aboard, and by July 1, as the *Rodney* turned out of the Bonny River, the ship carried with her some 370 enslaved Africans.[43]

Without question the *Rodney* encountered by the first slaves to board the ship during its first weeks at Bonny was not the same *Rodney* experienced by Africans forced on weeks later, when the ship was much closer to its complement. Different parcels of captives experienced the ship according to the "generation" in which they were brought aboard; and each generation's encounter with the ship evolved toward the general conditions and routines described above only as more slaves were brought on board. Such differences could have profound consequences for order and society shipboard—none more dramatic, for instance, than the custom of leaving unfettered "the first eight or ten" Africans to join a slaver, while manacling thereafter every other man hoisted aboard.[44]

How did slaves negotiate the changing demands of life aboard European slavers? What kind of society was possible, and necessary, within such a world? Those who observed slaves being brought shipside agreed that, whatever the captives' various physical states, they were saddened, dispirited, and confused when first brought on board. When asked to quantify these observations—exactly what proportion of slaves gaining the ship appeared to suffer some kind of melancholy?—Guineaship crews who had witnessed the parcels of slaves hoisted daily on board slave ships resorted to such absolutes as "All" and "Always."[45] In general, "A gloomy pensiveness seemed to overcast their countenance."[46]

The routine and conditions shipboard did little to ameliorate this despondency. If anything, the privation, violence, and sickness characteristic of slave ship imprisonment pushed many into further degrees of anguish, fear, and depression. As captives were initiated into the exigencies of slave ship life, it was not uncommon, for instance, for slaves to be overcome with an overwhelming desire for death. Ravaged by dysentery, and beyond despair at her captivity, a woman aboard the Bonny slaver *Alexander* was asked by the ship's surgeon whether there was anything she wanted, anything that might make her more comfortable. She replied through an interpreter with a sentiment the *Alexander*'s surgeon had heard often during his career: she "wanted nothing but to die."[47]

Some slaves acted positively on this kind of despair. Stirred to depths of emotion stemming partly from depression and partly from insurrectionary rage, slaves sometimes attacked the lattice works, nets, and awnings comprising a slave ship's house in desperate efforts to destroy themselves or escape into the rivers astride Bonny, Elem Kalabari, and Old Calabar. Sometimes these attempts were solitary affairs of desperation, as when a man out of a parcel of about ten slaves brought aboard the *Alexander* forced his way through the ship's starboard netting and into the Bonny River, where he was "either drowned or devoured by the sharks." Sometimes they were spectacular feats of cooperation, as when a gang of nearly twenty slaves destroyed themselves leaping en masse from the ship *Enterprize* into the Bonny.[48] Sometimes suicide was a pitiable mixture of individual despair and initiative, coupled with communal acquiescence, as when a woman aboard a Bonny slaver conspired while on deck to obtain and carry below a measure of ship's yarn. While between decks, "she made a noose . . . put her neck in it" and rolled off the platform on which she was berthed, snapping her neck. Apparently, she carried out preparations for her destruction within full view of fellow captives in the women's room and took her life just as the ship's crew was about to bring the Africans on deck for another day. The crewmen who found her reported that she was dead but still warm.[49]

That the fear and despair engendered by the slave ship itself, and not necessarily enslavement in general, was enough to push captives toward suicide is clear from the death of a woman pulled aboard the Bonny ship *Emilia* in the late 1780s. Her first three or four days on the vessel, the woman refused all food and moaned and cried continually. As was sometimes the practice with sick slaves, the ship's master sent the woman to town to recover, hoping that she might take food if not confined shipboard.[50] Lodged at Bonny with associates of the ship, the woman apparently recuperated at a nice pace. But in her health, when she discovered that she would soon be taken from town and returned again to the ship, she hanged herself rather than return.[51]

In the scheme of slave ship mortality, documented suicides were relatively rare; it was more common for Africans to simply suffer their depression. Of these, some were completely consumed by their despair, even to the point of complete breakdown. Aboard the *Elizabeth*, which slaved at Bonny during the rainy season of 1788, there was a man who came on board looking only as troubled as all the others. He soon distinguished himself, however, from the ordinary discouragement that seemed to characterize all captives. After a while on board, the man "became to look pensive and melancholy" and "a certain degree of wildness appeared in his countenance." At mealtimes he would sometimes "eat his food voraciously" like a lunatic, sometimes "as if insensible what it was; at other times he refused it entirely." As the days passed, he began also to shout out in ways and at times that rankled both the crew and his fellow prisoners—clamoring again and again, "Armourer," "Armourer," eerily imitating the call the ship's crew cried when they needed either to take slaves out of or put them into chains.[52] Aboard the *Ruby*—which slaved in the Bight of Biafra but outside the arc between the eastern Niger Delta and the Cross River—there was a woman who troubled the ship's company with so many outbursts the crew took it as a sign she had lost her mind: at "Times she cried excessively, at other Times she laughed in the same Excess; at other Times she made a most dreadful Noise."[53]

But most captives did not go mad. Rather, they managed their despair in waves, alternately succumbing to and fighting through their misery. There was such a woman aboard the *Emilia* in one of its missions from Bonny. At times she was so unpredictable that when above deck the crew thought it prudent to fetter her just as they did the men; at other times she appeared perfectly resigned to her condition. Throughout the *Emilia*'s stay at Bonny and over the course of the ship's voyage to Jamaica, the woman swung regularly between these two extremes: At one moment calm and relatively peaceful, then flailing and inconsolable.[54]

In a similar vein, the account of Equiano's captivity in Gustavus Vassa's

Interesting Narrative is remarkable for the alternating cycles of terror and resignation through which he passed while shipboard. At one moment Equiano was so sick as to wish intently for death. The next, after being comforted by fellow slaves, he admitted himself a "little revived." Next he was completely terrorized by the barbaric punishment meted out to some of his fellows; then his fear was replaced in some measure with utter astonishment at the pulleys, ropes, masts, and other workings of the ship. When once again conditions below—"the galling of the chains . . . the filth of the necessary tubs. . . . The shrieks of the women, and the groans of the dying"—filled him with an awful nausea and foreboding, Equiano again wished simply to pass away. But this dejection too was spotted with moments of wonder and surprise—at among other things, flying fish, the ship's quadrant, and spectacular cloud formations over the ocean sky—all of which intermittently interrupted the ship's more constant terrors, like the routine of pitching dead slaves overboard.[55]

Sometimes captives stifled their despair collectively. It was not uncommon that mingled among the smokes and stenches that tumbled off Guinea-ships there were dirges too. Alone and in groups, captives were known to chant plaintively day and night. Ship's crewmen who bothered to inquire into these songs through interpreters understood that the slaves were "lamenting the loss of their country and friends" and that the "Songs usually contain the History of their Sufferings, and the Wretchedness of their Situation."[56] Slaves who continued such lamentations against the wishes of a knowing and disapproving ship master paid dearly.[57]

Just as captives were affected by and acted on their despair in differing degrees—from suicide, to madness, to domestication—it appears that slaves, depending on their backgrounds and experiences shipboard, had different degrees of despair with which to deal. Women and the young adjusted to the routine and conditions aboard Guineaships more readily than did men, or so it appeared to ships' crews. So, although the Parliamentary record perhaps contains more graphic incidences of female suffering and suicide, when asked to speak in general about the despair Africans' exhibited shipboard, witnesses pointed out continually that the disposition of women and the young appeared to improve as the ship became more and more familiar to them, while men's conditions changed little from their first boarding the ship. A sailor with experience at Old Calabar claimed as follows concerning the depression into which slaves sank upon gaining the ship: "this Despondency, with the Men, continues in general—It wears out sooner with the Women." The sailor explained the difference by calling attention to the fact that the women were hardly ever fettered and were in general more liberally fed.[58] Guinea crews from throughout western Africa made similar observations, noting, "That the Females and Boys soon recover their Spirits—the Men seldom; they remain gloomy a great while."[59]

It was generally held that captives harvested from the littoral—that is, from among the communities of slave-trading middlemen with whom ship masters did business—reacted differently to captivity than did their counterparts who were brought from deep in the interior.[60] Slaves who understood their captivity as juridical, and as an alternative to execution, appeared to move more quickly from despair to resignation.[61] And there were aboard every ship a class of people who throughout their ordeals managed, on balance, to keep their wits about them, by disassociating themselves from both the horrors they witnessed and the horrors they suffered. Africans who did not appear to take "their situation so much to heart" nor "reflect much" on their current circumstances appeared, at least to their captors, to achieve a balance of mind as the days and weeks of their captivity wore on.[62]

The conditions that forced enslaved Africans to contend constantly with panic and despair—separation from their kith and kin, and the violence, privation, and scarcity characteristic of existence shipboard—also had the effect of debasing relations among slaves, especially where captives' desperation intersected with their reflexes of self-preservation. In this case, desperation fomented among captives a pervasive physical struggle for, among other things, space, nourishment, and basic security. Among captives then, as it was between slaves and crew, Guineaship violence was general. This was especially true as a ship progressed toward its complement and among enslaved men who were constantly shackled one to another. A veteran of several slave voyages understood that "It is frequently the case . . . in all Slave Ships" for the men to quarrel among each other, and a defender of the slave trade was forced to temporize when asked whether "a numerous Body of Slaves are not more annoyed by each other than a lesser Number?" "It depends," he equivocated, "on the Size of the Ship in Proportion to the Number of Negroes on Board."[63]

Every moment in a Guineaship's normal routine had the potential to generate violent outbreaks among the slaves. Mealtimes were frequently the scene of confrontation, as captives fought, no doubt, over portions, position at the tub, or over matters begun in close quarters elsewhere and simply resolved at mess time when prisoners had more physical room for maneuver. There is evidence that these conflicts were rooted in matters of simple self-preservation, but were also part of the more complex, though not unrelated, work of creating a social hierarchy among people who were otherwise strangers. Mealtime quarrels often consisted of insult and intimidation, such as slaves hurling European provisions into the face of their rivals. But if these kinds of battles increased in frequency and intensity as a ship's rations decreased, then the weakest and smallest of slaves could find themselves "obliged to be content with a very scanty portion" of the food intended for them.[64]

The routine between meals—when Guinea crew exercised slaves or simply allowed them time in the fresher air above deck—also provided an arena for conflict. Above deck, as detailed earlier, it was customary that men slaves were not only chained to a partner but that the whole male complement was then chained together and then to the ship itself.[65] Boys, in general, were allowed on deck unfettered and took advantage of such circumstances. Whether the boys were retaliating for the kind of harassment the strong meted out to the weak at mealtimes, and that undoubtedly went on below as well, is not known. In any case, it was "not unusual for the Boy Slaves, who are brought on board, to insult the Men who, being in Irons, cannot easily pursue and punish them for it."[66] The small indulgences allowed slaves between meals—beads, tobacco, and games of chance—also became matters of contention as the most desperate scrambled to establish any kind of material advantage over their fellow prisoners.[67]

The struggles that occurred below deck after captives were down for the evening were more severe than those that transpired above. First and foremost, especially in a ship nearing its complement, captives fought furiously for what between decks was the most precious commodity: space. So crew who every night went below to stow slaves were constantly fighting against the natural progression in which the strong continually carved out more space for themselves than ship masters, with their notions of economy, thought proper.[68] Said one Guinea sailor of the jostling below deck, particularly among the men, "They frequently disagree in the night about their sleeping places."[69] Such disputes were more frequent among persons who, because of differences in language or dialect, could not readily understand one another.[70]

Between-deck disturbances grew particularly violent when pairs of shackled captives had to move from their berths to the necessary tubs, which the Guinea crew placed below for the slaves to relieve themselves. On such occasions, again especially as a ship reached its complement, captives tended to step on and fall over their fellow prisoners, producing all manner of disputes and quarrels along the way. When so detained, some pairs gave up altogether on trying to reach the tubs and simply relieved "themselves as they lie," which only sparked further "broils and disturbances" among those nearby. Women, who were generally unfettered when between decks and kept in a room separate from the men, were not subject to the same kind of material instigation as were the men. Nonetheless, there is some indication that their barracks, too, were arenas of dispute and intimidation. Guinea masters, with their eye on their superiors' bottom line, professed they had to be ever vigilant in every part of the ship that "that the strong do not oppress the weak."[71]

It should be understood that although violence and contention were prime characteristics of Guineaship society, the same desperation that infused shipboard relationships with so much brutality also occasioned among captives a remarkable amount of social courage, sacrifice, even altruism. The behavior of relatives bound to the same ship suggests that desperate conditions could strengthen former bonds among captives. Aboard the *Elizabeth*, which called at Bonny in 1788, there was a titled man from the Biafran interior who took deathly ill upon boarding the ship. With the attention and indulgence of the crew he convalesced a little, until an enslaved woman was brought to the ship who professed to be the sick man's sister. She took over the man's care with a commitment and show of affection that itself affected sailors heretofore ignorant and suspicious of the fact that Africans were "equally susceptible of affections and tenderness as most other people." "The first thing" the woman did "of a morning, was to come up and enquire how he did." The man eventually succumbed to his sickness, which cast his sister into spiraling depression.[72] Family who found each other aboard the same slave ship greeted and responded to one another with raptures of joy and concern similar to the pair on the *Elizabeth*. According to one former sailor, "Such Scenes are frequently to be found in the Slave Vessels."[73]

It is clear from other eyewitness testimony that attempts at reestablishing shipboard some semblance of civil society were not restricted to captives who knew each other formerly. In ways large and small, strangers too responded to the circumstances of their ships in ways making it clear that they couched the struggle to preserve their lives within a struggle to preserve some portion of their dignity. So although conditions between decks could and did contribute to the creation of a perilous atmosphere— where, as we have seen, moving from one's berth to the necessary tubs might end in violent assault at the hands of one's fellow prisoners—captives also displayed remarkable instances of cooperation in the face of conditions that, on their face, mediated against such a spirit. On some slavers, as the ship reached its complement and captives were stowed closer and closer to one another, it was common to find slaves adjusting themselves in order to minimize conflict, lying "in such a manner that one does not breath[e] into the other's face."[74] Captives loaded at Bonny were sometimes known to achieve an amazing shipboard rapport. "Their mutual affection is unbounded . . . ," wrote one Guinea master, "I have seen them, when their allowance happened to be short, divide the last morsel of meat amongst each other thread by thread."[75]

Insurrection and the cabals that kept Guinea crewmen ever aware of its possibility provide some of the most dramatic examples of the kind of sacrifice and cooperation that could stem from captives' desperation.[76] Aboard the *Ruby*—which slaved in the Bight of Biafra but east of Old Calabar—the ship's men slaves swung between extremes; desperation resulting in internecine struggle and violence coexisted alongside group sacrifice and cooperation. On the *Ruby* the chief mate got quickly in the habit of beating "the Men Slaves with the greatest Severity for the slightest Faults" (for Guinea crew, depending on their intentions, it was possible to lash a slave without drawing blood; the *Ruby*'s mate, however, "scarcely ever failed to beat them in such a Manner as to make them bleed"). His brutality won him a particular enmity among the ship's slaves.

When the men argued or milled about too much, the mate generally descended between decks, cat in hand, to quell them. Late one evening, while the ship still lay on the African coast, a disturbance below deck caught the mate's attention, and he grabbed a lantern and went below. Whether the disturbance this night was of the kind common in the men's room, as the captives struggled for space, or whether the broil was a ruse is not known. What is known is that a group of men summarily wrested the lantern from the sailor and began to beat him with their fists and with the blunt ends of their shackles. Somehow, however, the sailor managed to make his way back to the gratings, where his colleagues above pulled him to safety and secured the opening.

The assault on the chief mate developed, or perhaps simply revealed its true nature, rather quickly after the mate made it to the main deck. The Africans below tried in vain to force themselves through the bolted hatchway after him. When that failed they turned to wrecking the bulkhead separating their room from the sick berths. From the sick room they began beating through a scuttle connecting that room to the ship's main deck. At this, the general alarm was raised, and the ship's master ordered sailors with "Muskets and Blunderbusses" into the boats on the side of the slaver. From there, pushing gun muzzles through the ship's airports, the sailors mounted a withering cross fire into the slaves' room. At the same time, crew stationed at the ship's gratings fired from above into the same rooms. It was not long before "the Insurgents yielded, and Quietness was restored."

But even then the crew did not dare to head below to take account of the situation.

The sailors wisely waited until morning to open the hatchways separating them from the ship's slaves, at which time they brought the rebels up two at a time. When the first pair reached the deck, their arms were secured tightly behind their backs before the next duo were helped up, and so on. After a while, there was a man who climbed above without the man to whom he had been shackled the night before. After this, it became clear that two other slaves were missing as well.

Sometime between the barrage that quelled the general insurrection and the next morning, when the *Ruby*'s sailors began bringing the men up two at a time, three of the ship's captives resolved not to put themselves back into the power of the crew. The captives in question knew that a cask which the crew kept in the men's room contained a number of cheap trade knives (it was there due to space constraints in other parts of the ship). From this cask, the men armed themselves, and at least two of them went beyond their original resolution to refuse the orders of the *Ruby*'s crew. Two of the three renegades entered into an oath "made by sucking a few Drops of one another's Blood." They promised that they would die before surrendering. Then they broke open a scuttle connecting the men's room to the hold, and they retreated there to wait.

There was a black trader aboard the *Ruby* when the ship's other Africans were carefully brought above the morning after the revolt. He and several armed sailors went between decks to persuade the remaining rebels to return to ranks. One of the three insurgents, perhaps the one who had not taken the oath, complied in relatively short order, came out from hiding, and walked meekly toward his pursuers. A second insurrectionist soon emerged gripping a knife in each hand, a provocation that cost him his life. After this, the last remaining African retreated deeper into the hold, with a number of the ship's crew in pursuit. When the opportunity presented itself, the sailors stabbed the man with their cutlasses, and whenever he paused to take up a position among the casks and puncheons littering the hold, they flung a mixture of boiling water and fat toward his hideaway.

After eight hours of eluding his tormentors, the captive who had promised the night before to die rather than surrender was exhausted and thus heeded the words of the black trader who had been trying throughout the ordeal to convince the rebel that he should not sacrifice himself like this. Overcome with fatigue and despair—with numerous wounds and his skin flayed, both from his pursuers' cutlasses and the scalding liquid that had been poured on him—the African climbed to the lower deck to surrender himself to the waiting sailors. Upon seeing the men assembled to receive him, however, the man suddenly doubted the intention that had brought him out of hiding. He sprinted again for the hold, but before he made the bowels of the ship a sailor wrestled the African to the ground and struck him with the butt of a pistol, fracturing his skull.

On the main deck, the ship's master perceived that the bloody creature just pulled from the hold was all but lost. Believing that even if given the best of care, the man was bound to die, the master ordered the man put in an iron collar and tied to the foremast as an example to the remaining captives. Denied food, water, and medical assistance, the man slumped down dead in three days and was thrown overboard with the ship's complement assembled as witnesses. This was, it turns out, their second object lesson. The morning after the insurrection, while this lone rebel still held out in the ship's hold, the captives gathered on deck had been made to kiss the decapitated head of his dead accomplice. When some among the slaves refused, they had the bloody neck of the severed head rubbed into their faces.[77]

Clearly, an urbanism akin to what prevailed in the slave ports of the Biafran littoral obtained as well aboard European Guineamen. The attenuation of former kinship ties through migration, the resettlement in densely populated areas characterized by both extreme material competition and extraordinary diversities of language and practice, and the necessity upon resettlement of having to come to terms with powerful, pre-existing ideologies of social categorization were hallmarks of Guineaship society as much as they were markers of African urban life. Considered together, these similarities suggest a theory of Igbo social formation in the eighteenth-century Atlantic world.

I have written at length about the serial displacement characterizing the march of slaves from the Biafran interior to the coast, the attendant erosion of former social ties such a journey entailed, and the desperate society captives encountered once finally aboard the slave ships. In the end, it appears that the kinds of Igbo identification that prevailed in the Atlantic trading towns and the articulation of Igbo society aboard European slavers was one of the ways that Africans from the Biafran interior responded to the sorry state in which they found themselves.

The impetus for this reaction was partly external, forced on slaves by their captors' power to label and organize their human cargo as they saw fit, and partly internal—an intuitive, functional response on the part of slaves to the heavy press of present circumstances.[78] At Bonny and the two Calabars, for example, it was not unheard of for ships to procure small parcels of slaves at westward layover prior to their arrival in the Bight of Biafra.[79]

Such was the practice on the ship which Hugh Crow served during his second voyage to Africa. Further, from Crow's memoir it is clear that the ship's crew thought much more highly of the slaves loaded along the Windward Coast than the larger cargo they took on in the Bight. Consequently, when the ship ran into a squall upon leaving New Calabar, the captain and crew were forced, it appears, to rely on the differences they had sown and the differences that were apparent among the ship's various parcels of slaves. "The storm and the darkness of the night," remembered Crow, "made our situation truly awful. . . . The ship, at length, began to lie over, almost on her beam ends, and dreading that the blacks might be suffocated, though at the risk of our lives, we permitted them all to come on deck." Combined, the slaves then on deck outnumbered the ship's crew by more than ten to one. "Our only dependence," recalled Crow, "was on the good disposition of the sixty whom we had shipped on the windward coast and who were of a race superior to those of New Calabar."[80]

Apparently—in the plantation tradition of gangs and drivers, and the prison custom of general population and trustees—the ship on which Crow served relied on the Windward Coast slaves to help keep order over those who had been loaded at New Calabar. That this was the case, and that the Windward Coast slaves may have been lightly armed as well, is further suggested by what Crow committed to his memoir just after relating the story of the storm: "When the storm had ceased, we saw several large canoes hovering about us, full of men, who designed, as we suspected, to cut us off. Observing, however, that we had so many windward coast men on board, they did not dare to attack us, but remained at a short distance, singing their war songs."[81]

Further evidence of the latent ethnicities that could and did emerge at the Atlantic is evident in another incident from Crow's memoir. On the vessel in question, a group of slaves from the Biafran interior drew a chalk line on the deck of the ship to serve as a boundary between their part of the ship and a section occupied by another group of slaves, known as "Appas," then also gathered on deck. After drawing the boundary, one of the "Eboe" slaves "got a piece of boiled yam, and passing to the Appa side of the line, turned his back on the Appas, holding the yam behind him, and retreated slowly towards the Eboe side." When a hungry captive from the other side of the deck crossed the chalk line in pursuit of the yam, "the Eboes, uttering a loud yell of triumph, grappled the poor fellow as their prisoner of war. . . ." According to Crow, the Igbos were "good-naturedly exemplifying the respective situation of the two countries."[82] Perhaps it was good natured, but it is hard to imagine any wrangling over food on a slaver being simply that. It is easier to conceive of the incident (along with many like it that went unreported) more darkly as an example of the role ethnicity came to play as captives labored to manage the constant, desperate struggle that was life aboard a Guineaship.

The larger point is that slave ships, like cities, contained peoples who exhibited a broad range of visible, audible, and tactile differences. For captives made in the Biafran interior, the linguistic, cultural, and historical distinctions separating a slave made near Aboh on the Niger from someone captured at Nsuka near the Igala borderlands must have paled upon entering a space where both found themselves in close quarters not only with white sailors but with enslaved Africans from lands more distant. Add to this the fact that Guinea sailors exploited inter-regional differences among their human cargo in order to better manage the ship, and it is obvious how conditions shipboard would have encouraged the development of intraregional identification and society of a kind evinced above.

There must also have been an experiential component shaping the kinds of Igbo society that developed in the coastal towns and slave ships of the Biafran littoral. As such, we should not think of Igbo, as it came to be understood in the Atlantic, as simply being born of the social compromises and cultural affinities forced and revealed by the exigencies of slave ship existence. Rather, the peculiarities of Guineaship society at the Bight of Biafra should not be overlooked as prime contributing factors in their own right. The ways in which the slave trade from the Bight of Biafra differed from the trade conducted elsewhere could profoundly influence how slaves from Bonny, Elem Kalabari, and Old Calabar experienced their captivity, and thus the substance they imparted to what it meant to be Igbo.

A critical factor distinguishing the Biafran trade from the commerce as it was conducted elsewhere has been pointed out already, the startling magnitude of death rates obtaining on ships that slaved at Bonny, Elem Kalabari, and Old Calabar.[83] Contemporaries were as aware of this distinction as are modern historians, and it influenced how principals managed ships sailing to Biafra and how merchants treated cargoes hailing from that part of the world. For instance, when the brig *Daniel* called at Grenada from Old Calabar with 189 slaves, merchant James Bailie warmed only slowly to the prospect of handling the sale. Bailie later admonished James Rogers, the ship's owner, about sending him a cargo of Calabars: "we believe you know that Negroes from this Country are not in Esteem with the windward Islands."[84] Others with whom Rogers dealt could be more direct. A Grenada merchant once told one of Rogers's captains that "He did not wish to have any thing to do with an old Callabar Cargo."[85] Over the years, this became a familiar refrain. Business partners wrote politely, "I must beg of you not to send me more consignments in this manner." Others relayed franker assessments of one or another of Rogers's Biafran ships: "we wished to have nothing to do with the Cargo." Rogers's ship masters went on and on about the difficulties of trying to unload ships hailing from Biafran ports: "they wou'd not look at the cargo"; "the other Guinea Factors Mr. Grant, Mr. Wedderburn, & others would not take her up"; "Messrs. James Baillie & Co would not have any thing to do with the Cargo."[86]

The threat and actuality of high mortality that attached itself to vessels hailing from the Bight of Biafra ensured that ships arriving from Bonny, Elem Kalabari, and Old Calabar encountered difficulties such as the ones described above more often than vessels arriving from other regions of western Africa. The effect on ship masters, owners, and slave merchants is obvious from the content and tone of the letters in which they complained about their predicament. But more to the point, the death rates that obtained aboard Biafran slavers and the reaction of merchants to these ships must have also ensured that the Africans on board such Guineamen experienced both their imprisonment and passage to the Americas in ways that distinguished them from slaves arriving from other regions of western Africa.

Consider the predicament of Africans forced to the Caribbean from Old Calabar aboard James Rogers's *Daniel*. From the spring of 1789 through the fall of 1791 this small vessel—sometimes described as a schooner, sometimes as a brig—operated directly between western Africa and the Caribbean. Apparently, the *Daniel* sometimes made its cargo by collecting slaves from other Rogers vessels then working the coast. Sometimes, however, it may have traded directly. In any case, during the three years in question more than four hundred Africans made their passage to the Americas aboard this small ship. How the *Daniel*'s slaves were received upon their arrival in the Caribbean illustrates something of the distinctive experience of captives boarded along the Biafran coast.

One hundred and eighteen Africans survived the *Daniel*'s first recorded voyaged between Old Calabar and the Caribbean during the period in question. We do not know how many perished during the middle passage, how long the ship loaded in the Cross River, nor the mortality or morbidity related to filling the ship. We can be fairly certain, however, that the schooner arrived at Barbados on or about February 18, 1789, and that the master's first attempt to discharge his cargo failed. On paper, the slaves appeared particularly well suited for Barbados, as the captives were almost evenly divided between males and females. Yet the merchant who boarded the *Daniel* to assess the slaves, a factor Rogers had used before, declined to take the cargo. He later wrote Rogers that he had refused the ship because "too large a part of the men and Women were Old people, which at this Market are very Unsaleable [*sic*] & sell low."[87]

Rebuffed at his first stop, the *Daniel*'s master directed the ship to Dominica to another merchant known to Rogers. But he also refused the ship. The *Daniel*'s master was under orders to garner an average of £35 sterling, per slave, on his cargo. The Dominican merchant thought that too high a price for a ship from Old Calabar. Politely, he wrote Rogers, "We should have been happy to have undertaken the Sale of his Cargo had the demand for Slaves from that Country [Old Calabar] been such as to have afforded us a prospect of approaching your Limits." Consequently, the ship proceeded to Jamaica.[88] Once there, in an act betraying perhaps a growing uneasiness, the *Daniel*'s master called on a merchant unknown to Rogers and offered him the cargo unconditionally—without, that is, the £35 sterling per slave average presented at Barbados and Dominica.[89]

Over the next two years, the *Daniel*'s voyages proceeded in much the same fashion, with the ship's master shopping his Old Calabar captives from island to island until finally finding a factor who would accept them, always with great reluctance, for sale. In 1790 the ship, once arrived in the Caribbean, was refused at Barbados and St. Vincent before being taken up at Grenada. At Barbados, business difficulties meant Rogers's former associates would not receive the ship "on any terms" whatsoever. At St. Vincent, "as times were so uncertain," Rogers's sometime associates reported that "they could not think of taking me up particularly as being from Old Calabar." At Grenada, the merchants who accepted the *Daniel* balked at the limits Rogers wanted and in the end needed only promise that "they wd do as much as any other house" on the island in order to be given the cargo.

During the *Daniel*'s 1791 return voyage between Old Calabar and the Caribbean, twenty of the 145 put aboard in the Cross River perished at sea. The master, apparently, did not even attempt to move the cargo when he called at Barbados in late September but sailed, rather, to Grenada. There, the first merchant house on which he called took a pass, preferring to take on a cargo just arrived from the River Congo instead.[90] A second house accepted the ship but saw it as "so disagreeable a task" that they undertook it only as a courtesy. The slaves aboard the *Daniel,* the factor later chastised Rogers, "were such a parcell that we never desire to see their like again & we should have availed ourselves immediately of quitting this Cargo had we known that they had been first refused by another House who knew their Situation too well to be plagued with such a Charge."[91]

Ships from the Bight of Biafra formed the largest part of the British slave trade, but owing to the mortality that obtained on average aboard Biafran slavers, ships from Bonny, Elem Kalabari, and Old Calabar could labor under some local competitive disadvantage once they actually reached the Caribbean. If they thought a better cargo was in the offing, American factors were inclined to accept cargoes from other parts of western Africa before taking up ships from the Bight of Biafra. The result, as illustrated in three voyages of the *Daniel,* was that vessels arriving from that region's three main slave ports, given their tendency toward sickly cargoes, were likely more prone to be shunted around from island to island and from factor to factor before finally being able to put off their captives in preparation for sale. The proofs of this tendency were at times unmistakable: In the fall of 1791, four Guineamen that had gathered their complements at Bonny lay at Montego Bay, Jamaica, trying to offload their slaves. Two of the four ships then in the bay had no prospects whatsoever.[92] The very language Caribbean merchants used when discussing cargoes from the Bight of Biafra revealed the skepticism with which they approached the ubiquitous arrivals from the Niger Delta-Cross River region. Send us a "good Bonny" ship or "one of the best of your Ebo Cargoes" they would write Rogers. In contrast, requests for Gold or Windward Coast cargoes went unadorned.[93] Apparently, one did not request ships from Biafra without first specifying that you did not want a common sort of cargo.

For African captives boarded along the Biafran littoral, the result of this stigma was, quite simply, the extension of their captivity. Whether this added time contributed to the later mortality of such slaves is unknown, but planters, merchants, and ship masters certainly thought so. A house at Grenada once accepted one of Rogers's Old Calabar cargoes because the factor, having seen the ship, suspected it would be catastrophic for the slaves and disastrous to Rogers's bottom line to refuse them. The "cruelty of sending the Slaves off in the state they were in to Jamaica the only market they could get to also weighed with us" the firm reported.[94] For their part, planters were confident that a not insignificant portion of the slave mortality that abolitionists attributed to conditions prevailing at their plantations actually belonged to the ships, as a goodly number of Africans died in Caribbean harbors after being registered at the customs house but before being offered for sale. At Jamaica, the House of Assembly estimated such losses as a 5 percent share of the island's total level of black mortality.[95] Whatever the death rate aboard Guineaships anchored in Caribbean harbors, descriptions that have survived of the conditions of captives who languished aboard such ships makes it clear that slaves shunted from island to island or from factor to factor could not help but come out the worse for the wear. Among the *Fame's* cargo, there were captives who were "Bline, one

Eye. Some Loosing fingers Some Toas," all as the ship's master scrambled to find a factor who would take the slaves off his hands.[96] It seems safe to say that, in general, slaves shipped from Bonny, Elem Kalabari, and Old Calabar were received in the Americas in ways that tended to extend and intensify the disaster that was life aboard a slave ship.

Given the language slaveholders often used to describe the condition and disposition of Africans disembarked from Biafran ports, this is an important point. Planters insisted that a prime characteristic of slaves arriving from Bonny, Elem Kalabari, and Old Calabar was their tendency toward despondency and suicide. This assertion has since become a staple in historical studies inquiring into the nature of Igbo society and the contributions of Igbo slaves to the larger Afro-American society.[97] Here, however, having already outlined some of the contingencies relating to the development of diasporan Igbo society among captives embarked along the Biafran littoral, it is profitable to do the same with notions and practices supposedly definitive of being Igbo. In the case of Igbo fatalism, acknowledging the kind of society that prevailed aboard Biafran slavers, and admitting the likely comparative experience of Biafran slaves vis-à-vis captives arriving from other regions of western Africa, suggests that what has heretofore been presented as a prime tenet of Igbo identity may be explained more clearly, or at least with less mysticism, as a consequence of the migration experience general to captives shipped to the Americas from the Biafran littoral.[98]

Since Stanley Elkins argued that the shock of enslavement denuded African captives of their native resourcefulness—turning them into "a society of helpless dependents"—terror and violence, though they were central to the institution of slavery, have not figured prominently in its historiography.[99] Instead, partly in reaction to Elkins's ill-fated argument, modern studies of the Atlantic slave trade have tended to draw down the horrors of enslavement. The most prolific students of the slave trade—cliometricians and business historians in the main—have been content to demonstrate by omission that the "evils of the slave trade," in the classic expression of the argument, "can be taken for granted as a point long since proven beyond dispute."[100] Likewise, historians of American slavery proper have been equally loathe to linger over the details and consequences of enslavement. Rather, slavery scholars, contra Elkins, have set out en masse after evidence that enslaved Africans salvaged and reiterated important aspects of their former society and culture in the Americas. To such ends, a number of studies have made delving investigations into both broad and specific African influences on slave religion, material culture, community, and folklore.[101] Some of the most recent work in the field goes beyond arguing that captives salvaged key aspects of their former society and culture in the Americas.

Ira Berlin and John Thornton have argued forcefully, and at moments quite eloquently, that the slave trade was more conduit than crucible.[102]

In a sense, this line of inquiry has served to bring the story of Africa immigrants to this hemisphere in line with the most nationalistic tales told of their European counterparts.[103] Where it was once understood that the details and context of transatlantic African immigration rendered it almost impossible for black settlers to import coherent and meaningful cultural forms, it is now routinely argued that Africans, like European migrants, transplanted folkways and traditions that helped determine the contours and course of American history: If it is true that transplanted East Anglian religiosity and orderliness stamped the Puritan northeast and that south English hierarchies checkered the American South, then it must also be admitted that Kongo cosmologies and Fante dialects had similar effects on the evolution of American religion and speech.[104]

It is hoped that the story told in this chapter raises a potential point of synthesis between Elkins and his critics, while cautioning against the development of a history of forced migration patterned too closely after a nationalistic European counterpart. On the first point, the case of enslaved migrants from the Biafran interior suggests that the cultural forms and ethnic identities previous scholars have considered proof of the connections uniting American slaves to their African homelands may in some cases be better understood as consequences of the violence and terror of their exile. In this sense the connections between Africa and the Americans denoted by Igbo are not first and foremost evidence of forms that somehow survived the slave trade; rather, they must be understood as connections that owe their existence to the disjunction the slave trade effected. The term Igbo documents, on both sides of the Atlantic, the history of African social and cultural change. As a notion of self-conscious ethnic, social, and cultural consequence, Igbo existed along the eighteenth-century Biafran littoral *and* in the Americas as a result of migration and its exigencies. Its existence proves that the forces with which Elkins was concerned were real and had real consequence, as it proves the same for the ways in which captives addressed those forces. Of African nations such at Eboe, it must also be said that they were not just social formations through which African cultural and social continuities came to be articulated in the Americas. The nation must also be understood and analyzed as an expression of loss, despair, and disjunction. The slave ship was a forcing house of social change. As we will see next, plantation Jamaica was too, and could be just as severe.

THREE

WHITE POWER AND THE CONTEXT OF SLAVE SEASONING IN EIGHTEENTH-CENTURY JAMAICA

In the late eighteenth century, British slave ships loaded more captives from along the Bight of Biafra (mostly at New Calabar, Bonny, and Old Calabar, really) than from slave ports in any other region of western Africa. Across the Atlantic, the island of Jamaica was the Bight of Biafra's American analogue. In the late eighteenth century, British ships carried more women, men, and children to Jamaica than to any other destination in the hemisphere. The island was the most productive and valuable of the United Kingdom's American possessions, and after the evacuation of New York at the end of the American war, it became the seat of British power in the region as well.[1]

But the island's imperial credentials aside, Jamaica in the late eighteenth century—its native population long since decimated, its white population transient and outnumbered ten to one by Africans and their descendents—was in many ways more African than it was British. Consequently, the inclination to interpret the lives of Jamaican slaves absent their masters, their masters' functionaries, and other whites is strong. Jamaica, in almost every way that mattered, was black. Enslaved Africans who arrived at the island from ports in the Bight of Biafra would have seen this quite clearly.

Still, how newly arrived Africans experienced Jamaica was shaped in inescapably important ways by the island's white minority, and even by whites far from the island. Thus at the center of Great Britain's American empire, enslaved Africans confronted a society in which whites were remarkably absent, but in which white power was suffused throughout. And so, just as the routines common aboard Guineamen affected what was possible for black society on British slave ships, it is impossible to understand the society that black migrants encountered and built on Jamaica without coming to terms at the same time with the context of white power in which they would first season and later carve out new lives.[2]

So now the focus changes *from emigration* from the Bight of Biafra and particular attention to the ways that the study of ethnic identification il-

Figure 4. Jamaica in the late eighteenth century
Source: Map drawn by the Cartographic Laboratory, Department of Geography,
University of Wisconsin

luminates the type of black society that slaves fashioned while in motion to the Atlantic littoral and across the ocean, *to immigration* and the ways enslaved Africans—now not just Biafrans—experienced their arrival at the migrant center of British America. What was possible for enslaved migrants landed on Jamaica? Answering the question requires an examination, first, of what arriving in Jamaica entailed for African migrants so far as the society that had colored their lives shipboard was concerned. Then, though the ultimate aim is to grasp the nature of nascent black migrant society on Jamaica, it is absolutely vital to explore the nature of the power that drew enslaved Africans to Jamaica in the first place. Why Jamaican planters bought slaves and how they bought them mattered for black society. How white planters thought new slaves should be worked and planters' resulting praxis mattered. And in the late eighteenth century—as the demand for slaves skyrocketed on Jamaica and British abolitionism simultaneously put enormous humanitarian pressures on the island's planters—the way that white power on the island began to be expressed in a particularly insidious form of paternalism certainly mattered.

Once in Caribbean waters, it was not uncommon for Guineaships bound ultimately for Jamaica to call first at one of the Lesser Antilles. Such layovers were a must for ships on short provisions and a convenience otherwise. If there was a ready market for slaves at Barbados or Dominica, for instance, there was no need to continue any farther. But if these first stops proved disappointing in potential sales, ship masters could still use the time to their advantage—unloading perhaps a portion of their cargo, inquiring into the strength of markets elsewhere, and posting letters to their partners in Liverpool, Bristol, London, and beyond before beating again northwestward.

For captives who had languished through just such a course, Jamaica presented a profile different in kind from those that marked their first arrival in the Americas. Isles that rose and gave way again quickly characterized the eastern Caribbean. Jamaica, in contrast, presented a coastline that could stretch on for more than 100 miles on a side. In the eastern sea there were impressive, singular peaks here and there. Jamaica offered whole ranges. And for the sheer convergence of African slavers, there was in the late eighteenth century simply no busier collection of ports than Kingston, Montego Bay, and their several sisters of Black River, Martha Brae, Port Antonio, Annotto Bay, and Lucea.[3] Jamaica was a slave hypermarket, the late eighteenth-century analogue to the Biafran interior: the premier slave *importer* in the North Atlantic.[4]

At first, the arrival of a slave ship at its principal destination meant very little for its captives.[5] Their routines and material conditions shifted only slightly as the ship's master disembarked to follow contacts and acquaintances that would lead eventually to the slaves' dispersal. The society and routine that characterized life aboard a Guineaship took on an added dimension only once a ship's master agreed with a merchant for the sale of his cargo and the merchant set about informing potential buyers of the coming sale. Following these signal events, the ship's crew dedicated themselves to making their prisoners once again presentable as merchandise, a somewhat different task than their previous priority of simply maintaining them as orderly, pliable cargo.

As the sale approached, captives again received much the same treatment as when they were originally sold to the ships months before. Their most obvious imperfections—sores, blemishes, and signs of infection—were tended to in order that they might fetch the highest possible prices. To these same ends, slaves suddenly found themselves sorted and shunted about—the diseased, deformed, and dying here, the weak and small there, those who best endured their recent passage at another spot. The most emaciated and debilitated among them often found themselves separated from the others and disposed of at a discount either before or after the general sale commenced.[6]

Those not disposed of as refuse slaves were, in general, either picked over at semi-private showings or exposed to the public at what was called a scramble. At the former, selected planters with whom slave merchants wished to maintain or to establish a good relationship, or the agents of such planters, were invited to examine the ship's slaves before the general sale and were permitted to purchase parcels of their choice. At these private offerings, a few potential purchasers mingled for a while among the white faces with whom captives had become familiar. These new people starred, poked, prodded, and then dragged their choices toward Jamaica's plantations, pens, shops, and town homes.[7]

The drawing of slaves in private sales could not but affect the society Africans had established thus far shipboard. Obviously, those forced away felt the change most keenly, as the ship and the routines and regime it enforced were now gone, replaced in the main with uncertainty. But even the lives of those still confined aboard ship shifted. For some, the slave to whom they were shackled when first brought on board disappeared. For others, gone was the captive who intimidated them below deck for more room and above deck for more rations. Altogether, after a private sale Africans who were friend, family, foe, or even anonymous were gone in numbers too great to go unnoticed to those still imprisoned shipboard.

Public sales tore even more vigorously at whatever modus vivendi captives had managed heretofore aboard ship. Where private sales and the ways slaves gained Guineamen along the African coast forced prisoners to cope with terrific amounts of terror and uncertainty, scrambles generated a dread magnified by the sheer chaos in which they unfolded. For sales held aboard Guineamen, it was not uncommon for slaves to be barricaded on one or another of the ship's decks. Then, at a certain signal potential buyers rushed into the holding area to secure their choices by hand, by tie, or by placing tallies on captives as marks of impending purchase. Describing scrambles at Kingston and Port Maria, Alexander Falconbridge noted that their chief characteristic was the pandemonium they inspired in potential buyers—who entered such sales with the "ferocity of brutes" and "who not unfrequently upon these occasions, fall out and quarrel with each other" over the right to secure one slave or another. A seasoned Jamaican slaveholder admitted that such scenes were "disgraceful." They could look every bit as if the Africans on board "were seized on by a herd of cannibals, and speedily to be devoured."[8]

Captives with strength—either cognizant of the opportunity afforded by the confusion or terrified by the same—sometimes fled overboard at such moments. Most prisoners, however, spent the scramble maneuvering as close as possible to friends, family, and allies. As planters and their agents rounded up purchases, the slaves they seized called out, pointed, and held fast to those whom they wanted "sent with them, wherever they were going." There were ship masters who counseled buyers concerning these attachments among slaves—relationships forged over the voyage or that preceded it—and encouraged purchasers not to part certain Africans. But such advice was only that. In the end, the sale of the ship fractured the society captives forged since their imprisonment along the African littoral, leaving as an open question whether what followed would in any way resemble what was past.[9]

Such sentiments were surely on the mind of a young woman who survived the middle passage to Jamaica in 1790 only to be torn away from the sibling with whom she had endured the ordeal. The two were sold together to a Jamaican cattle ranch from the ship in which they arrived. But when the attorney in charge of the property inspected them more closely, he sent one of them back to Kingston, protesting that he had not indeed selected this girl. Clearly, he intimated, she was a refuse slave slipped into the parcel he purchased as part of some kind of ruse. He suspected another girl had also been introduced surreptitiously and returned her as well. The factor with whom the planter worked wrote back shortly thereafter that of the two girls returned to him, "The one with the swelled arm I saw taken out of the Cabbin myself." Of the other he expressed no such personal certainty. He simply informed his associate of the effect of returning her to Kingston: "The Girl with one Eye I find has a Sister at you Penn," he wrote, "she is crying most dreadfully."[10]

The selling of the slave ship's cargo and the swift transition that followed, no doubt, had a similar effect on all who counted as a surety any circumstance thus far established on their journey to the Americas. As difficult as life was aboard European Guineaships, there did emerge for the Africans on board—after days, and weeks, and months of imprisonment—a kind of terrible normalcy. The sale of the ship's cargo disrupted this routine, introducing again a measure of uncertainty and chaos into relations among African captives and between slaves and their ostensive superiors.

What came of the crisis and transition that characterized arriving in Jamaica? "Seasoning" was the word slaveowners in the British Caribbean used to refer to the process by which recently arrived Africans inoculated themselves to the demands of their new environs. For African captives who in the late eighteenth century landed on Great Britain's most valuable American colony and who were bound for the sugar plantations that made it so, the seasoning process was a gauntlet of disease, heartbreak, famine, exhaustion, and labor (sometimes backbreaking, sometimes strange, but above all forced). During this seasoning period, all of Jamaica, despite its expansiveness, might as well have been another slave ship. The world to which African migrants had to acquaint themselves was at first quite small, and it was as demanding as the one they had just left. The consequences for black society, as experienced by African newcomers in the late eighteenth century, could be pronounced.

The average Jamaican sugar plantation contained some two hundred resident blacks, and properties that sprawled over more than a thousand acres of countryside were commonplace.[11] Yet new arrivals probably perceived little of this enormity. Even on the dozens of Jamaican estates that covered more than five thousand acres apiece, it was a relatively compact spate of improvements that made plantations obvious as such: their sugar works, slave quarters, great house, and the cultivated fields.[12]

The slave quarters or village consisted of small houses of various construction, shot through with sundry fruit trees, and all organized to form numerous compact yards and gardens belonging either to singular houses or to groups of them. The sugar works, never far from the quarters, consisted of buildings for crushing, boiling, curing, and distilling sugar cane and its byproducts. Along with these buildings intended for the manufacture of sugar, there was a small number of shops and sheds dedicated to skilled work tangential yet vital to the making of a crop—carpentry and masonry, for instance. A house for the planter or his agent, and habitations for other whites who worked on the property—overseers, bookkeepers, or perhaps a resident doctor—rounded out the ideal complex of plantation architecture.[13]

Beyond such buildings, the outlying land, by its shape and form, testified to a plantation. There were, of course, cane fields. Sometimes they were laid out in neat geometric shapes. In other instances they followed the natural contours of the land. But they were always distinct. Beyond the cane there was often some kind of pasturage or grassland, less apparent than sugar in its cultivation but obviously cultivated all the same. And beyond these fields were provision grounds on which slaves farmed various small crops for their sustenance (though these were sometimes so well sown into woodlands or ruinate as to be invisible to the uninitiated).

Of all of this, the core elements of the plantation—the area that slaves traversed regularly whether working or not—consisted of but a scant proportion of most estates' total acreage. Relying on a sample of more than one hundred eighteenth- and nineteenth-century maps, B. W. Higman makes this point in his work on the spatial economy of Jamaican sugar properties. According to Higman, the locus of an average sugar plantation—comprising shelter for its inhabitants and other constructions central to the processing of the crop—encompassed only about twenty acres. Drawing successive straight lines from each point in this complex to another and averaging the results, Higman found that "typically works, village and great house were located at the points of a triangle very nearly equilateral and enclosed by a circle with a radius of only 250 yards."[14] In this respect, even the most spectacular Jamaican sugar estate was a fairly small universe. African captives pushed from the suffocating confines of European Guineaships onto the Caribbean's third largest island and the hemisphere's most extensive slave society ultimately found themselves settled onto mere patches of land (patches not only because sugar properties actually centered on relatively small spaces, but because new arrivals' ignorance of their surroundings would have drawn down such plats even further).

For the newcomer, the social exigencies of the Jamaican sugar plantation differed hardly at all from those that prevailed aboard the Guineaships that landed them on Jamaica in the first place. As was the case aboard slave ships, African captives faced serious limitations on their movement and had to negotiate their place among already existing bodies of other captives. Slaves also had to continue to confront the same material challenges concerning food and water and mortality and morbidity that prevailed on the slave ship. And as on the slave ship, all of these imperatives were shaped by the nature of the routines forced on captives by the small number of whites who wielded power, sometimes extraordinary power, on the just arrived captives. In ways too important to dismiss, the transition captives faced in their move from Guineaship to Jamaica—their seasoning—was shaped by the ideals and habits of the men, and some women, whose appetites had brought them to Jamaica in the first place.

Whites comprised only about 10 percent of the population of Jamaica in the late eighteenth century, and on sugar plantations their numbers were even more scarce.[15] Yet the ideal estates these men variously envisioned and the actual plantation regimes they attempted to enforce are central to understanding the weight of seasoning on enslaved Africans newly arrived in Jamaica. Even before a particular cargo of captives was made on the west African coast, the rationales behind why plantation owners and their attorneys sought additional slaves, and the process and preparations they made to acquire them, combined to determine a great deal concerning the subsequent meaning and consequence of seasoning for the still en route Africans.

In the minds of Jamaican planters, of course, almost every rationale for the purchase of additional slaves had to do with the work of the plantation. Even so, on a sugar property the kinds of work for which slaveowners desired additional labor could differ significantly, and different labor needs could result in distinct receptions for newly arrived Africans. There were planters who desired additional hands for the arduous work of opening up land for sugar. Thus a Jamaican attorney advised an absentee owner as follows about additional acreage soon to be added to his property: "to take in that part of Your Estate to Join and Occupy with the rest you Should at least Want 150 good Negroes more." The new land, remarked the attorney, lay distant from the present works, and would require many more slaves to plant, tend, and process the sugar.[16] Another attorney similarly advised his client to rein in aspirations for adding to the amount of land in cane until additional hands could be had. "Yet I do not think it would be proper to put in but 15 acres more at Boxford Lodge, before we purchase some New negroes."[17] On cattle pens, a successful breeding season could create a demand for more African laborers, lest a planter risk following good fortune with disaster. So Simon Taylor advised Chaloner Arcedeckne as follows concerning purchases he made and planned for the latter's sugar property and pen: "I bought 15 Negroes for Golden Grove the latter end of October, and there is a necessity to buy some for the Penn at Batchelors hall otherwise our labour is lost in the Rearing so many Calves as I have done for you, as they and the old ones must starve for want of Pasture."[18]

Even without expansion, the natural decrease common even to long-settled properties ensured that planters needed to frequent the island's slave marts simply to maintain a property at strength, or to bring it up to some long sought but never yet reached optimal level. Along these lines, Simon Taylor counseled a client against adding acreage to his property until he had enough laborers to exploit more fully what was presently under cultivation: "The times are not favorable for buying lands in the West Indies just now, & I think you do right in not thinking of any further purchases." A planter of his friend's means, thought Taylor, had more to gain from simply improving the estate he had, which in the Fall of 1783 required "a very great number more working Negroes to do it Justice."[19] This was a common refrain. In 1784, Nathaniel Phillips thought his Phillipsfield plantation needed thirty more workers "to keep up the crops" commensurate to his expectations.[20]

Jamaican planters sometimes looked to the slave markets for reasons not directly related to the work and produce of their respective properties. In the late eighteenth century, Great Britain's maturing abolitionist movement sometimes convinced sugar planters to test the island's slave marts. So even Simon Taylor—who often lashed out at British abolitionists as dogs, traitors, and madmen—agreed nonetheless that the agitators had affected the way many slaveowners approached the management of their estates, including their buying of slaves. "One real good Effect this negroe business has had," he admitted, "is that I assure you a great deal of more attention is shown to Negroes than was before."[21] In Taylor's case, he became enamored with a plan to raise the birthrate on a plantation under his direction by purchasing female captives taken along the Biafran littoral. Eboe, averred Taylor, was "the Country to buy women off to breed," and as soon as a good ship came in he intended to purchase "10 Young Women with Cock up Bubbies." These ten would "do no other work but clean Cocos, Yams, &c. which is the lightest work I know, and they shall not interfere with the Estates work, and shall have every chance of breeding that is possible."[22]

Taylor's scheme focused on affecting birthrates. Other slaveowners feeling similar pressure turned to the slave markets in attempts to lower their property's death rates. On plantations short of hands, reflected one attorney, "Negroes are often Workt beyond their power." The solution, he thought, was to acquire "a Sufficient Strength of Negroes that three Might do the Work which two are no[w] Obliged to do." Explaining himself further, the planter admitted to owing at least part of his thinking on this matter to the abolitionists: "there would be policy, Interest & Above All the feelings of Humanity in this. which the Folks in England say we so much want. had this been the Generall plan, there never would be the Noise which is Now making in England about Slavery & the Slave trade."[23]

Understanding *why* slaveowners and their agents procured additional captives for their properties leads only partway to an analysis of the consequence of planter decision-making to the subsequent society of newly arrived Africans. It is equally important to consider the ideals comprising *how* property masters thought fresh labor should be procured. The relationship between the rationales plantation principals gave for seeking new slaves and their thinking on the process that should be followed to effect a purchase ultimately makes plain the critical role masters and their charges played in shaping the particular Jamaica at which just-landed Africans arrived.

At a most basic level, price and quality influenced how slaveowners approached the market, and thus under what conditions they forced additional Africans onto their properties. As best they could, managers avoided purchasing slaves from what they thought of as bad ships, but it was also true that a bad ship was better known in retrospect.[24] The price of a particular cargo had a more definitive effect. The terms at which slaves were available might persuade planters desperately in need of labor to hold off. So, though Nathaniel Phillips gave his manager clear instructions to put more hands onto his plantation, it was an order his agent was reluctant to carry out immediately due to the conditions then prevailing at the market. "The price of New negroes is so very high," wrote Phillip's deputy, that he had decided "not to purchase the 20 you have ordered, for these 3 or 4 months to come." At that time, he had been assured, slaves would "be very moderate."[25]

Different terms might convince slaveowners previously seeking, and thus prepared to receive, ten captives to consider corralling twice that number. In the summer of 1792, for instance, an apparently tightening market convinced Simon Taylor that it might be best to risk an immediate and unplanned purchase of additional slaves for fear of not being able to procure any later.[26] Another set of conditions could move those who were not necessarily seeking additional laborers to consider a purchase anyway, as John Graham informed his absentee employer in the midst of a steady rise in the price of slaves. Although Graham had already met instructions to put twenty additional captives on the property in his trust, "the advanced and advancing price of Negroes" convinced him that it might be in his client's "Interest that a further purchase of ten Negroes (eboe Girls) should be made before the price gets higher." He had no definite instructions on the matter, but decided to keep an eye on prices and to "hazard the purchase without your directions *as we may judge best for your Interest.*"[27]

Deliberations and decisions over the terms at which additional labor could be had affected the timing of purchases and the number of new Africans planters and their agents might attempt to settle on their properties. In turn, the number of new people brought to a plantation at one time and the season during which they settled affected captives' eventual reception. In theory, it was wise to avoid the slave ships during the hurricane season of July through October. Planters who purchased Africans during the storm season exposed them (and their investment) to possible catastrophe. Simon Taylor admitted to being "afraid to buy any New Negroes until the Hurricane months are over."[28] Once, after buying seven new slaves near a dangerous time of the year, Taylor heard from his client that he thought the property needed many more than that. Taylor did not disagree, but shot back alluding to the season, "I never intended to put on any more than the 7 I mentioned to you untill the first of November for I seldom run risks that I can avoid & never will sport with another mans property."[29] Another manager replied to a client's instructions to put on additional slaves, received during the storm season, with similar caution. "I approve very much of your determination to put on 15 New Negroes for two Successive years . . . ," he answered. "I shall let the next month be Over before I purchase any, then the fear of Storms will be Over for this Year."[30]

Quantity was also a factor to take into consideration. Simon Taylor often cautioned against putting too many new slaves at once on a property. Sometimes he articulated such warnings as general prudence. After buying thirty-two slaves for a client's cattle pen, Taylor admitted that the place still needed twenty more able bodies to get the property into proper shape. It would not do, however, to simply add to the place all at once. The additional strength should be built up "by & by" contended Taylor. It would be "the best way to pay for these first."[31] There was, he appeared to suggest at another time, a clear relationship between the number of new slaves settled onto a plantation at one time and a manager's ability to keep them alive and working. So, after purchasing an already seasoned gang of black laborers, he advised the absentee owner for whom he worked, "we must not buy anymore Negroes for some time, but take care of these we have."[32]

At moments, Taylor was clearer on the consequences of bringing on too many new Africans at once. Because Jamaican slaves supplied a great deal of their own provisions by raising staples when not laboring in their owner's cane fields, newly arrived slaves were in the precarious position of being fed either by their owners or by other slaves until they got established in grounds of their own. With such arrangements, attempting to settle too many slaves at once could very well strain a property's capacity to provision itself. So when Taylor told his friend Arcedeckne that the latter's pen and sugar plantation "both want strength," he was quick to add that the task "must be done by degrees, the Negroes put on shall not be starved."[33]

Managers' ideals and actions concerning the provisioning of prospective new purchases informed a set of decisions with tremendous consequences to the seasoning of newcomers. The ideal was straightforward: "it would be the height of Imprudence to buy Negroes to put on the Estate until there is something for them to eat."[34] Acting on this ideal, however, was not always so straightforward. The need for additional hands and their availability did not always coincide with a property's access to provisions, so the determination managers demonstrated on actually meeting the conventional wisdom was very important. Sometimes the cycle of provision agriculture put slaveowners in the position of deciding whether to put off purchases until foodstuffs ripened. If provisions were available but there were no Guineamen on the coast, the call was whether to preserve some of the present harvest for slaves not yet on the property.[35] At other moments, the vagaries of weather complicated matters, as when a storm during the previous season jeopardized provisions on Chaloner Arcedeckne's Golden Grove property a full half year later. Simon Taylor explained the situation as follows: "We cannot put on Negroes just now. there are not Provisions anywhere. the Plantain Trees were blown down the 1st Septm. The Negroes were obliged to live upon their Yams untill [sic] Christmas when they spring & is the time for Planting them since that they have been entirely on their Cocos & tho there is a great Appearance of Plantains they will not come in before we get the May rains to fill them & then there is no trusting to them. about Nov. will be the time [to put on negroes]."[36]

For months in 1790, Joseph Barham's attorneys wanted to acquire additional laborers but were at a loss to acquire a commensurate amount of additional provision grounds. The managers understood full well that "provisions should be had in forward . . . for the intended purchase of Negroes," but they could never secure title to a suitable tract of land. Ultimately they decided that the best way to proceed, perhaps, was "to order out an additional twenty puncheons of pease or split beans, and two puncehons of kiln dried Oatmeal from Glasgow," and perhaps "Six Barrells English flour" because "that article has already become scarce and high priced here." Absent sufficient provision grounds, in their opinion, all of this would be necessary to tide over any new purchase.[37]

Beyond Jamaica, matters relating to the imperial politics of Great Britain and the pressing issues of Anglo-Atlantic society affected the purchasing behavior of slaveowners and thus something of the circumstances in which newly arrived Africans found themselves. States of war between Great Britain and other powers in the hemisphere operated powerfully in this regard. Chiding a Jamaican business partner who desired to take a wartime interest in a few slave ships, Bristol merchant and slave trader William Miles alluded to the choking off of the sea lanes that typically followed the declaration of hostilities between European powers. "Do you begin to forget," Miles chastised John Tharp, "[that] there are Spainiards, Frenchmen & Americans your Enemies that you wish to have two or three Guinea Ships more?"[38] It was a truism in Jamaica that "Negores are always scarce in Warr."[39]

A solid peace after a long conflict could generate the opposite effect. In itself, for instance, the end of hostilities in the American war was not enough to send Simon Taylor headlong into the slave markets. But after the armistice was formalized he made plans accordingly: "I would upon the Presumption of a Peace have bought you a doz. of Negroes lately, but I conceived that Sugars would sell very low indeed for the first year, did not know on what terms the Peace was to be made, and was very diffident what to do, but now thank God that Blessed Event has happened we can with ease and Safety with prudent management go on Improving every year and adding to the Strength yearly."[40]

Also Atlantic in scope, the progress of the British abolition movement could have an equally pressing effect on planter conduct. Inasmuch as news about and the actual progress of the abolition movement affected the price of African slaves, this too affected the way slaveowners approached the question of adding workers. So, Charles Rowe pointed out to his employer that "the present value of Negroes seem to be daily on the rise from the General opinion formed as to the Expected abolition of the Slave trade" and then asked whether it would not therefore be prudent "to have a further purchase made whenever a suitable Opportunity presents itself."[41]

Sometimes the progress of the abolition movement persuaded slave-owners to go beyond an immediate assessment of their labor needs when considering the purchase of additional slaves. In 1793, when Caribbean slaveowners and British Guinea traders feared the imminent demise of the slave trade, the result was "a very great many Guinea Men now at Kingston, indeed a great many too many." Because of the glut, Simon Taylor predicted, "some People will be Idle enough to buy without having food & Houses sufficient for them & consequently will loose them."[42] In 1794, Taylor himself partly justified putting on more laborers as all he could do "to put of[f] as farr as I possibly can the Evil day that must infallibly come on us, should Mr. Pitt and Mr. Wilberforce be able to compleat their Scheme of destroying the West India Colonies by their Mad Schemes of Abolition."[43] Six years earlier Taylor's assessment of the abolition movement, one probably shared by others, had inspired a less dramatic posture, and thus a different approach to the market. At that time, he wrote, "I was much embarrassed respecting the buying [of] Negroes for the Penn but concluded at any rate that there would be nothing done in the Negro business this Year and therefore bought 31."[44] Had Taylor concluded that the movement would generate greater immediate momentum, presumably he would have added many more slaves.

Come an actual purchase, all of the ideals shaping slaveholder thinking on *why* and *how* a planter should put on additional labor—how many to buy at a time, what tasks to assign them, how to feed them, et cetera—determined a great deal of what initially became of enslaved African immigrants to Jamaica. How planter ideals played out in plantation practice reveals in finer detail the world to which newly arrived Africans had to adjust, and the important role planters and their underlings played in its formation.

For the most part, Jamaican planters purchased additional Africans because they required additional laborers. It was an open question, however, whether newly arrived slaves went immediately to the work, or even to the place plantation owners ultimately envisioned for them. How slaveowners followed through on the intentions they harbored for the new people on their properties was of tremendous consequence to their slaves' initial experience. The life chances of recently purchased Africans, Simon Taylor believed, were not helped by throwing them headlong into the arduous labor

basic to raising sugar—planting cane, tending fields, taking off and distilling a crop. On the plantation he managed for Chaloner Arcedeckne, and on
his own properties presumably, when Taylor put on new people he thought
it best to "season them in making & clearing Pastures & light work for the
first year untill they are settled & then work them on the Estate, by that
means we will keep them alive to work for you & yours & not kill them."[45] It
was not uncommon that the island's largest slaveowners operated cattle pens
as well as sugar plantations, and Taylor thought it best that new people, initially at least, spend about 40 percent of their week working around a planter's pen, and 60 percent of it establishing provision grounds and building
houses for themselves.[46] The evidence Taylor pointed to in support of this
approach was purely anecdotal. Still, what he had seen with his own eyes,
and for many years, convinced him that there was a difference between how
newly arrived Africans fared at the pen versus the sugar plantation: "the
last New negroes put on there at the Penn," he once observed to Arcedeckne
"are doing very well, and those at the Estate are not turning out well."[47]

If it could be helped, the economy and physical geography of the places
to which planters sent new workers to season were not to be discounted.
From long experience, Taylor thought Chaloner Arcedeckne's Batchelors
Hall pen a better place than Arcedeckne's Golden Grove plantation for the
seasoning of new slaves. But the years had also taught him that even the pen
had its drawbacks. It was a "Wett Place," and there were moments when
that condition, along with a concomitant fear of disease, cautioned Taylor
from sending slaves to the property.[48] Places subject to cold also gave him
pause. Speaking of a plantation called Swamps, Taylor once opined that
the place desperately needed more hands—"there are not Negroes to do
the work of the Estate, much less to take the least care of the Penn"—but
warned that the property was "so caol [cold], that it is one of the Worst
places in the Island to Season New Negroes in." If more Africans were to be
put on the property, it would be prudent to season them elsewhere first.[49]

Occasionally, talk of the importance of keeping Africans away from the
cold and wet gave way to allusions to what was perhaps the fundamental
problem of seasoning slaves at sugar plantations, regardless of their geography. Sugar planters required slaves to raise sugar, and the work basic to sugar
plantations habitually risked the imminent destruction of newly arrived
slaves (as it likewise continually diminished the vitality of workers long-
established on the plantation). Taylor appeared to admit as much when con-
cocting a scheme to ensure that the total labor required by a certain sugar
plantation did not fall too completely on the plantation's own slaves. Of a
pen and sugar property he managed, Taylor thought the laborers "thrived

better" at the cattle pen than on the plantation and wondered therefore whether he should raise and season a gang for the plantation at the pen.

Such a gang, Taylor imagined, could plant canes in the fall and spring on the sugar property, but would not "Cutt Canes, take off the Crop, [nor] clean the Estate." At other times they would work at the pen, tending the cattle and keeping up the pasturage. The plan would keep the new slaves from a good deal of the sugar work, but it would also reduce the load, theoretically, for the slaves then living at the plantation.[50] Yet even when pushing his imagination to its limits in thinking of ways to season slaves so they lived to work, Taylor would admit to a certain amount of folly. He could and did manage many of the conditions of black life on the plantations under his supervision. But even when the Africans Taylor bought *seasoned kindly,* as he liked to put it, he understood quite well the difficulty of achieving such results in the long term. To "say that they will keep up their Population," Taylor once admitted of one hundred Africans he recently purchased, "I know as well as that I shall die, I cannot without fresh Importations."[51]

Despite this pessimism, all the more powerful because it was also realistic, planter decisions about the management of their properties affected the circumstance of how Africans were received and how they adjusted to their life and labors in Jamaica. Negative examples, accounts of plantation management where slaveowners, attorneys, and overseers compromised plantation ideals nearly to the point of rejection, illustrate just how important plantation management was to the seasoning experience and continuing livelihood of Africans in Jamaica.

Ironically, we can depend a great deal on circumstances at Golden Grove plantation and Batchelors Hall pen to make the point. Simon Taylor was not always the sole attorney for these properties. Before the end of the American war, Chaloner Arcedeckne depended on a Jamaican planter named John Kelly as the prime overseer of his properties. Only after a dispute arose between Kelly and Taylor did Arcedeckne dismiss the former and make Taylor his sole proxy. The assessments Taylor made of Arcedeckne's properties after his promotion illustrate how different management styles could shape African life on a property.

Under Kelly, Golden Grove was an ideal property in terms of the production of sugar and rum. Even during the American war, when provisions were often scarce, and force and supervision on plantations lax, Kelly squeezed from the property more than three hundred hogsheads of sugar and two hundred puncheons of rum at a harvest.[52] Such feats earned him a great reputation and no small amount of wealth. But the effects of these accomplishments on the slaves who made the crop, coupled with other of Kelly's managerial habits, made Golden Grove a particularly hard and difficult place for newly arrived Africans and long-settled slaves alike.

When Taylor visited Golden Grove after Kelly's dismissal, he found the slaves there a "very feeble Set indeed." In his opinion the workers had been nearly annihilated. Taylor was far from a friend of slaves. Consummate with his station and the times, he thought little of blacks in general, perceiving them as human beings like himself but of a lesser sort, either rascals to be subdued or wretches to be pitied.[53] He nevertheless sensed in the workers at Golden Grove a misery and dejection that went beyond their material circumstances. The Golden Grove slaves, he informed Arcedeckne, would "require a deal of good nursing, their hearts have been broke."[54]

The origins of their abjection, thought Taylor, lay in how hard Kelly pushed them, "driving every thing to the Devil to make a great Crop to get himself a Name."[55] Taylor was of the mind that there was a point on any plantation—depending on its strength and the acreage in sugar cane—where making a great crop exacted more than an ordinary toll on the strength of the property's black laborers and other capital. This was Kelly's folly, thought Taylor, for "it signified nothing to make Sugar to loose Negroes and Cattle."[56] Of the Africans seasoned under Kelly's watch, Taylor wrote: "you have been really ill used indeed, for had the Negroes you have bought been taken Care of, you would have nearly enough for every purpose, but it is too late now to repine and will not mind matters."[57]

Things on Golden Grove reached such a state not simply because the slaves worked too near their limits too often. Driving slaves hard produced devastating ancillary effects. Most importantly, planters inordinately concerned with sugar production could not help but to neglect slave provisions. At a most basic level, keeping captives fed required owners, attorneys, and overseers to allow slaves ample time to tend their provision grounds and gardens on evenings and weekends. To guard against famine and other catastrophes, slaveowners had to go even further and direct selected gangs to plant ground provisions for the use of the entire estate in case of emergency—this in daylight working hours during the week.

On properties where the volume of sugar and rum produced in a season drove the entire management of the plantation, the provisioning of the estate necessarily suffered. Slaves worked daily to their limits in the cane fields had little left when the time came to tend their grounds, and the planter concerned only with the amount of sugar and rum he could ship would be loath to put slaves to work on provisions during his own time. So under Kelly's attorneyship, apparently, even though those working under him understood the consequence of such negligence, feeding Arcedeckne's slaves became a secondary concern.[58] Kelly exacerbated his ordinary neglect of provisions, charged Taylor, by siphoning off for his own use whatever rations Arcedeckne thought to send to the plantation as supplements. While the blacks at Golden Grove "were Starving," ranted Taylor to Arcedeckne, "every Store you send for the use of your Estate is Consumed at his own House, your Negroes wanting real Necessaries to Support Life in your Hothouse, while his Negroes are in the Same place & supplied from your Stores."[59] Only after Taylor obtained sole proxy for Arcedeckne's properties and worked the estate for some time could he write, "you have now what never has been on the Estate, which is a very fine parcel of Ground provisions, so that there will not be any danger of your Negroes wanting a belly full." This was of consequence for the property's prospect of supporting additional labor, and on this score Taylor continued that there was now "plenty for New Negroes as soon as any Guinea Man from a good country arrives."[60] Before this, the prospects for recently arrived Africans were dismal, as there was little for them to eat and they were "killed by overwork & harassed to Death" in the day-to-day grind of the properties' hard-driving routine.[61]

The disposition of one or two white people on a property could make a significant difference to black life. Taylor was convinced that Golden Grove would have never supported "a Gang of Negroes while he [Kelly] had any thing to do with it." As the years unfolded, Arcedeckne would have found himself in possession of "Land without Negroes."[62] Taylor exaggerated to make a point, and given the animosity that developed between he and Kelly, it would be unwise to trust his word on every matter regarding his antagonist's management of Golden Grove.[63] We can be sure, however, that there were in Jamaica planters who fit Taylor's description of Kelly all too well. Taylor admitted as much, writing once that it was Kelly and managers like him whose practices provided continuous fodder for abolitionists back in Britain. It "is certainly owing to these sort of People," fumed Taylor, "that such stories are propagated among the People at home to our disadvantage."[64]

The portrait Simon Taylor painted of John Kelly, regardless of its veracity in every particular, was true in general of a not insignificant proportion of Jamaican planters. Despite what abolitionists had to say about slavery in the Caribbean, there was evidence enough from Jamaican slaveowners themselves. For years, for instance, Joseph Barham thought that his Island estate was well off in general for provisions. In particular, he thought this was the case with any new people put on the plantation, as he always heard as much from those who managed the property. In the fall of 1794, however, when Barham directed a new attorney to the estate, the news he later received was quite the opposite. "There has been no provision previously made for the last Twenty New Negroes that were purchased," reported the attorney. To be sure, the Africans were not in the best of health when first brought from the ships, but even the resident overseer admitted that the plantation's white people squandered all chance that "they *might* have made a shift" by not having grounds or rations ready for them when they arrived.[65]

To make matters worse, slaves long-resident on the property were not much better off than those just arrived. "Most of the Old Negroes were Scarce," reported the attorney to Barham, and the reason for their frailty lay squarely with the plantation's managers. The property's provision grounds were near the place where an adjacent landowner grazed his cattle. There was no fence between the two plots. Consequently, cattle from the property next door routinely destroyed the slaves' provisions. The likelihood that they would never benefit from what they planted compelled the enslaved blacks to neglect their grounds in general, or as the property's attorney put it, "made them become Nearly careless of themselves." All that was needed to secure the slaves' grounds was a barrier of about three quarters of a mile. The previous attorney was not ignorant of the problem, he had simply not acted to correct it. The total effect of this neglect on new people and settled slaves alike was chilling: "There are now 49 Negroes that must (to preserve them) be regularly fed untill they have got grounds of their own. Thirty of them are either Meagre, Bloated, taken to eating dirt, or with most dreadful ulcers." None of these maladies, admitted the estate's attorney, could really be addressed until "the best generous Nourishment was plentifully given."[66]

The Swamps estate was in a similar condition as Barham's property. Owned by a absentee planter named Mrs. Cowell, in the spring of 1789 rumor was that the property's blacks were "allmost [*sic*] all dead."[67] In the lean, hurricane years of 1780–1781 and 1783–1785, Simon Taylor remembered running across blacks from Swamps "hunting about in the Savannas for Sweet sops who told me they were starving."[68] They certainly were. During those particular years, slave provision grounds failed in general throughout the island, and owing to ignorance, poverty, callousness, greed, or some combination of all of these, the managers at Swamps "would not buy anything" to ensure that the slaves had rations.[69]

When Taylor made it up to the estate in the spring of 1791, what he found was not as bad as he had feared, but it was quite bad enough. The fields were in ruins, the plantation's blacks were "scarce of provisions and all the Old Stock dead." Under these circumstances, taking off the present crop and tending to the next presented something of a conundrum: The number and strength of the slaves presently on the plantation was not enough to accomplish the work at hand, but there was not enough sugar in the fields to justify hiring help to accomplish what needed to be done.[70] Knowing something about the succession of attorneys who had charge of the place, Taylor had strong ideas as to how the property came to such a state: "how could it be otherwise from the Choice of Attorneys that both Mr. as well as Mrs Cowell had had, first Kelly, who used to keep it as a place to break in his Young Irish Overseers, then Phil Pinnock, who never knew any thing about an Estate, but to keep Expences on one, the next French, who I turned away myself from it for Lying, and not taking care of it, and now George Scott, a Young Man with out knowledge or experience on life. In short if it does not gett into very different hands, it must sink alltogether."[71]

Attorneys and overseers who considered the preservation of capital a goal commensurate to the produce of the estate could, through their decision-making and follow-through, establish a different context for black life on their properties. Even on plantations where black laborers could count on the customary time to tend their grounds and gardens, it took slaveowners and managers attuned to the precarious season-to-season nature of slave provisioning to ensure that the blacks on their property experienced no more than the hunger ordinary to Jamaican slaves.

The island, or a part of it, could count on a punishing drought, a strong gale, a hard rain, or a full-blown hurricane almost every year, and the gardens and grounds of Jamaican slaves were particularly vulnerable to every kind of severe weather. Because the amount of time they could count on to feed themselves was limited no matter the regime under which they worked, plantation blacks tended to concentrate on crops that required very little attention. In Jamaica the plantain fit this bill very well, but plantain trees were as susceptible to severe weather as they were easy to cultivate. So even on a property whose slaves worked assiduously in their grounds, a stroke of bad weather could materially affect the plantation's ability to feed itself. And in Jamaica, in the late eighteenth century, strokes of bad weather were as dependable as the arrival and departure of Guineaships: It was impossible to know precisely when they were coming, but that they were coming was a surety.

Given Jamaica's climate, arranging for the import of rations and order-ing gangs of slaves to plant provisions for the benefit of the entire property were together the only way to ward off famine. Simon Taylor understood this from experience, and when he acquired sole charge of Chaloner Arce-deckne's Golden Grove plantation and Bachelors Hall cattle pen he ordered his overseers to supplement whatever produce the properties' workers raised for themselves. Noting slaves' inclination toward plantains—"as they require so little trouble"—Taylor wrote to Arcedeckne as follows on the matter: "I will myself see that the Overseers put in a large quantity of ground provisions of Cocos, yams, Cassava &c. on every Estate I have anything to do with and kept as the Estates property, exclusive of what the Negros, who would plant nothing but plantains if left to themselves, put in."[72]

From London, the once resident but now absentee owner of Phillipsfield plantation and Boxford Lodge pen, Nathaniel Phillips, instructed his attorney along a course similar to Simon Taylor's after a recent storm. Not completely satisfied with his attorney's response to the storm—as outlined in a letter his proxy sent to London soon after—Phillips sent a letter peppering him with all the things he had left undone. It was one thing to tend to the plantain walks and provision grounds after such a storm, wrote Phillips, but even more attention was necessary. Thus Phillips asked his attorney whether he had indeed been following his previous orders "to plant early Potatoes & Guinea corn at the Pen." Further, he directed him, "In such an emergency you ought to fence off 50 to 80 Acres . . . or as much as might be wanted for Guinea Corn &c, to furnish you with early provisions for the Negroes of both Estates, which would give great plenty in a few months." To tide the slaves over in the meantime, Phillips wanted to be certain that his attorney buy sufficient provisions from North America to put the slaves on an allowance. Lastly, regarding the blacks on his properties, Phillips ordered his proxy to "encourage them as much as possible to repair their losses by assisting them in rebuilding their houses & giving them a few days to put their Grounds in good order."[73]

Clearly, white attorneys and overseers affected the basic parameters of black life on their properties by virtue of their power as planters and the theories of plantation management to which they subscribed. Sometimes, perhaps, slaveowners overestimated the effect of their decisions on the disposition of their labor force. There was not, as one Jamaican attorney once implied, an axiomatic relationship between the demeanor of a particular overseer and the health and well-being of the black workers he ostensibly supervised: An efficient overseer, committed to the preservation of his owner's capital, did not make for happy, contented slaves.[74] All the same, however, slaves laboring on an encumbered property held by a planter with little credit and no cash could not help but feel the difference.[75]

The dialectic between ideal and practice in the management of a property materially affected the circumstances that newly arrived Africans—and long-settled workers alike—confronted on an estate. In turn, to the extent that slaveowners, their attorneys, and overseers affected the context

of black life on a property, they shaped as well some of the basic circumstances of black society. Because of the nature of the evidence available for
reconstructing Afro-American life on eighteenth-century Jamaican sugar
plantations and on the cattle pens sometimes associated with them, the argument has thus far proceeded indirectly. Whites on Jamaican plantations
did not write often about the details of black society. The market for sugar
and slaves, the progress of the present crop, and other such matters were of
greater interest to them, and in any case they had but limited opportunity
to observe the particulars of black life—outside of black labor—that took
place around them.

Nonetheless, salient aspects of black life are implicit, if only by induc-
tion, through considering the ideals and practices of plantation whites. It
is not difficult to imagine the kind of society encouraged on a plantation
where the managers thought very little about slave provisions or housing,
and where the making of a great crop was the overarching aim of management's every decision. Likewise, a place where the managers made a show of
preserving the life and health of the blacks they enslaved would encourage
quite a different kind of society. Along other lines, attorneys who routinely
added additional slaves to plantations already struggling to feed themselves
went a long way toward determining the kind of reception such new people
might receive.

These are not far-fetched conclusions. Sometimes, nonetheless, we are
spared having to draw them because the consequences that planter decisions held for black society emerge unequivocally from eighteenth-century
materials—demonstrating explicitly what a preponderance of the material concerning planter decision-making and black life only implies. On
Chaloner Arcedeckne's Golden Grove sugar plantation and Batchelors
Hall cattle pen, as we have seen, Simon Taylor spoke directly about the
effect of a previous attorney's management on the nature of black society
on the properties. When John Kelly looked after Arcedeckne's properties,
and made great crops, he supplemented Arcedeckne's labor force with a
gang of his own slaves. As mentioned earlier, one of the charges Simon
Taylor subsequently made against Kelly had to do with the latter's habit
of appropriating for his own slaves stores originally sent out for Arcedeckne's. This alleged larceny was reflective, evidently, of other prejudices
sowed between Kelly's gang and the people enslaved by Arcedeckne. In
addition to being better fed than the people held by Arcedeckne, Kelly's
gang occupied the choicest habitations, living in parts at the hospital
and at the plantation's main house.[76] Together, these material biases resulted in a peculiarly stratified black society on Arcedeckne's properties:

The workers for whom he held a title scratched away for provisions and lodged in inferior housing, "while a few favourites"—a gang not even native to the properties—"dominnered at pleasure" over them. Apparently, similar kinds of stratification were a consequence on properties where attorneys and overseers, for different reasons, decided to sow differences by the way they provisioned, housed, and worked the various black laborers on their lands. Thomas Barritt, attorney to Nathaniel Phillips, made this point indirectly when praising a particular overseer. Among the man's qualities was that the blacks on the estate were "all treated alike."[77]

On properties that people like Simon Taylor would have considered well managed, a different aspect of black society could develop: insidious paternalistic ties between enslaved blacks and the whites for whom they toiled. According to Philip Morgan, paternalism developed out of a more authoritarian ideology of patriarchalism over the course of the eighteenth century. "Patriarchalism," writes Morgan, "rationalized the severity that lay at the heart of the slave system. True, the patriarch was obliged to provide for his slave, but in return the slaves had to obey. When they did not, they could expect the swift retribution of a wrathful and unforgiving father figure." Patriarchalism stressed expected obedience and necessary punishment of dependents as much as it did the obligations of the patriarch. Beginning in the late eighteenth century, though, and owing among other things to "the rise of evangelicalism, romanticism, and humanitarianism," patriarchalism gave way slowly and unevenly to paternalism, an ideology that stressed "greater softness, more reciprocity, less authoritarianism." The paternalistic-minded slaveowner imagined his slaves contented and expected a certain amount of reciprocity for the ostensive indulgences that punctuated his relationship with his slaves.[78]

In the historiography of slavery, though, analyses of slave culture and society in the Caribbean do not usually notice the importance of paternalistic ties to the shape of black society. Slave societies in Africa, in general, in the antebellum South, and in parts of nineteenth-century Brazil are considered clearer illustrations of the phenomena, while the West Indies have been presented as a kind of counter example.[79] Trevor Burnard has argued that the "shift from patriarchalism to paternalism never occurred in Jamaica":

> It remained a patriarchal rather than a paternal society through-
> out the eighteenth century. Moreover, it remained a society with
> a particular variant of patriarchalism, derived from its peculiar
> demography and unusual social relationships. Patriarchalism was

very raw in Jamaica. White men there were less concerned than white men elsewhere in the British world with making sure that their authority was tempered by an understanding that patriarchs had to recognize mutual obligations between household heads and dependents. Jamaican men refused to accept any constraints on their freedom to act as they chose, least of all constraints placed on them by dependents. Patriarchy was not shaped by concepts of stewardship but was "the manifestation and institutionalisation" of raw male dominance, with scant regard to the duties men owed to others.[80]

For late eighteenth-century Jamaica, though, there is evidence that on plantations where property owners and managers recognized enslaved blacks as individuals and cultivated the disparity of power that existed between them, a kind of paternalistic clientship developed within the property's black society. On the properties he managed for absentee owners, Simon Taylor surely behaved in such a way as to encourage the development of paternalistic connections between himself and the blacks whose labor he directed. To an employer he pledged to treat his "slaves as human Creatures." When requesting that an absentee owner send out new cloth for the blacks who raised his sugar, he once promised as follows: "you may depend on it your Negroes are & have been lately better taken Care of than for some years past, and that they shall be taken Care of, I Know the value of Negroes too well to let them be Neglected when I can help it."[81] On another property, the absentee proprietor sent an annual "Negro present" to demonstrate his beneficence upon enslaved blacks.[82] These kinds of expressions, if regularly personified among a property's blacks, encouraged slaves to cultivate personal, if far from stable, bonds with powerful whites, incorporating them into the details of black society regardless of their distance from the lived exigencies of black existence.

On Phillipsfield, and Boxford Lodge, for example, even though the proprietor was an absentee, the fact that Nathaniel Phillips had lived on Jamaica previously made a critical difference to the nature of black society on his properties. Phillips, it should be noted, left a colored family in Jamaica. But even if we discount the consequence of blood relations, and approach black society from the vantage of the slave villages instead of from the proprietor's house, the place Phillips occupied in the public manifestation of black society on his properties was profound. In the letters that passed between Phillips and his managers during the time he lived in Britain, it is clear that he and the blacks whom he kept enslaved both cultivated in the other a client-patron relationship. Phillips was clear on this point to his attorneys and overseers, once writing, "Nothing will give me more pleasure than to hear at all times, that the management of the Estates goes on with the greatest harmony . . . & satisfaction to yourselves, as well as to my *Black Friends,* many of them have been faithful servants, & deserve every encouragement to be thrown out to them."[83]

The blacks on Phillipsfield and Boxford Lodge addressed Phillips, though he was far away, with a level of deference commensurate to the measure of interest he displayed in their material well-being and the power he had to affect their circumstances. Peppering the letters Phillips's overseers sent to Britain were greetings and compliments from black workers. Sometimes the salutations were general, as when an attorney reported that blacks on Phillips's various properties "often enquire of me how their master do, and tell him 'how'ye Grandee.'"[84] At other times they came from specific quarters of Phillips's plantation or pen. The women sometimes sent word specifically. At another moment, it was the "head men on the different properties" who asked to be remembered to Phillips and wondered when he would again visit the property.[85]

The rationale at the base of these greetings, and something of the circumstances of black life on Jamaican plantations, is apparent in a salutation relayed to Phillips in the spring of 1793 when workers on his properties entreated the attorney to "tell Massa howd'ye." The attorney continued the greeting, now as if imparting a secret, "I have heard say that they think it is worse since you went home."[86] In other missives, black workers' intentions in cultivating public ties with the people who owned their labor is clearer. On one occasion, as part of their compliments, the women on Phillip's properties requested of the attorney that he would entreat the proprietor to order "out Blue Blanket to their coats, instead of the Linsy woolsey as it last much longer."[87] At another time it was, "Your black friends says I must tell their Master howdy for them. And the women hopes you'll not forget their blue blanketing."[88]

For their parts, owners, attorneys, and overseers on Jamaican properties cultivated client-patron relationships with enslaved blacks for the very reasons that their black laborers did: to meet their own particular interests and improve their own circumstances. Without question, planter paternalism was a shield for slaveowners in their ongoing transatlantic skirmishes with British abolitionists. More than once, Simon Taylor characterized Jamaican slaveowners as responsible stewards in response to one abolitionist charge or another. Of the activists, Taylor "wish[ed] to God they would . . . be quiet with their Negroes business, they know nothing about it." In years past, unfeeling brutes may have comprised the body of Jamaican planters, but at present, things were quite different. If the abolitionist "Stop at home where they are, they will have done a good deal of Service," argued Taylor, "by making many people use their Negroes better than they did before."

But even where abolitionist pressure did not effect such a shift, interest did:

> the Price of Negroes must make them do it, and I assure you that there Never was so great an Attention in any thing, as in the different treatment of Negroes now, and when I first came here, and the Minds of People are softening every day more and more in that respect, and as Most of the Overseers and Bookeepers are now people of decent Families and Connexions, they would not on their own Characters Acct. ill use any poor Wretch under their Care, and the greatest part of the Banditti that used to be here, and employed on Properties, are either dead, or left the island for want of Employ.[89]

There was also the fact that paternalistic management could reap for planters very important returns. As the attorney Charles Rowe wrote to Joseph Barham in England concerning supplies the latter recently sent for the use of the blacks on his property: "The Articles of cloathing sent for your Negroes proved most acceptable and I really must say they seem by their Conduct to have every due sense of your goodness towards them, and cannot but ultimately, I am persuaded prove beneficial to your Interests."[90] John Vanheelen, writing earlier about many of the same blacks as Rowe, made an even more telling point about the ends of paternalistic planter ideas about provisioning the black laborers on their properties. It was important for slaveowners to be generous concerning provision grounds and rations because by so doing they cultivated in the blacks on their lands "an Attachment to the property where they find themselves so well provided for."[91] According to Taylor, for all of the reasons that it was in the interest of planters to behave as stewards and fathers to their slaves, he "never knew the Negroes happier & better disposed[,] poor things."[92] Indeed, if it were not so, if Jamaican planters were "the Inhumane Race" abolitionists were fond to portray, "would not our Negroes have cut our throats long ago, and have they not had every encouragement from home to have done it."[93]

Of course, what Taylor and his colleagues would never admit was the fact that their paternalism, because it was paternalism indeed, contained alongside the beneficence to which they loved to point a complement quite the opposite of what they would own publicly. "Violence," as Frederick Cooper has pointed out, "was part of paternalism," and it is clear from the correspondence and actions of Jamaican planters—if not from their public pronouncements—that force and the threat of force sealed the bonds of clientship that existed between slave and slaveowner.[94]

During times of extreme crisis, Jamaican whites would admit as much, at least to one another. When a town of Jamaican maroons revolted against the colonial government in 1795, for instance, slaveowners depended in part on the sharper edge of their paternalism to ensure that a smallish revolt of maroons did not erupt into an island-wide conflagration. The renegade maroons definitely pushed the matter, calling on plantation blacks to join their revolt and holding out to them "that it is only the Whites" with whom they were at war. In response, on Joseph Barham's Jamaican estates the attorney made a point of showing himself more frequently among the property's slaves, counting that their perception of his power to help and to harm would help to keep the peace. "I go often among them," he reported of his routine among Barham's blacks during the conflict, "that they may see the Eyes of a Master is attentive to their Movements."[95]

From the mouths of slaveowners, this kind of straightforward allusion to the cutting edge of paternalism is rare. More often we are privy only to the penultimate exercise of paternalistic planter violence: when property owners and their attorneys pondered whether to sever captives from the hard society of sugar cultivation and condemn them again to the ordeal of the slave trade, this time the interregional version operating between the Caribbean islands and the various colonies of mainland America. White managers and plantation owners knew that shipping a slave from their estate did as much to aggrandize them in the eyes of those who remained as it did to punish the particular culprit. Accordingly, when a number of just arrived Africans became "a good deal troublesome" and were always running away, Charles Rowe saw the influence of a Jamaican-born slave called Island. From his infancy, thought Rowe, the young man was "given to every imagineable Vice that can be conceived & has long been accounted by me as irreclaimable." "As an example to the others" concluded Rowe to his absentee employer, "I am under the necissity of desiring your Sanction for shipping him off the Country."[96] Likewise, when Simon Taylor desired to ship off two blacks from Chaloner Arcedeckne's properties—one of whom he was afraid would one day "sett the Estate on Fire"—his reasoning was that "these two examples would really be of service to all the Negroes."[97]

Planters' gestures of violence and beneficence and the initiative of enslaved blacks within their white managers' paternalism combined sometimes to illustrate quite clearly the relationship between white power and black society on Jamaican sugar plantations. On Elizabeth Haughton

Taylor's Haughton Court, the proprietor's departure for Britain in 1786 gave rise to just such a situation. Haughton Taylor's leaving and the contemporaneous placement of a new overseer on the property encouraged among the blacks there a conspiracy against the new manger based on their understanding of their now absentee owner's sense of paternalism. So soon after the arrival of the new overseer, Haughton Court blacks began to slack off the tasks required on the property. Further, to their master's relations— knowing word would reach her in Britain—Haughton Taylor's slaves began to express a clear contempt for the new man. At moments, evidently, they even went so far as to goad the overseer into breaking Haughton Taylor's instructions concerning how her slaves were to be treated. Their thinking, apparently, was to test the new man's temper, to attempt to push him toward a kind of rage that their owner would not brook in others toward her human property, and then, having gotten him to cross Haughton Taylor's boundaries, to get word to their owner about his transgressions, leading ultimately to the man's dismissal.[98]

In the end, if this was indeed their plan, the scheme did not unfold exactly as the property's blacks intended. Nonetheless, Haughton Court's slaves did manage to accomplish many very useful ends. Their complaints to Haughton Taylor's relations—Simon Taylor, to be exact—moved Jamaica's richest planter to lecture and cajole the new overseer concerning how he must treat the slaves. Indeed, the pleas Haughton Court blacks made to Simon Taylor moved him to exert no small amount of authority over the new overseer himself. Taylor relayed to his sister-in-law, "I have spoke and wrote to Stewart [the new overseer] the same as if he was my own Son to take every Care of the Negroes, and treat them with Humanity, and that no Cruelty of any kind be used to them."[99] That the blacks on his plantation— who were slaves under his orders—operated too in the world of his ostensive betters must have made no small impression on the new overseer. The experience, no doubt, went a long way toward seasoning Stewart into the world in which many Haughton Court blacks were already old, worn hands.

Paternalism, William Dusinberre has warned, is a particularly tricky term for analyzing relationships between slaveholders and slaves because it is often used in several rather distinct senses to refer to "(1) the slaveholders' ideology (2) their motives, and (3) the system of punishments, allowances, and privileges which the planters imposed on their bondsmen and women."[100] Moreover, the term is troublesome because its connotations are generally benevolent, which creates particular dissonance when the expectations and obligations that characterized master-slave relations are the subject (because the description of the transition from patriarchalism to paternalism among American slaveholders turns mostly on what transpired in the heads of slaveholders themselves). Thus Morgan's description of paternalism as "a more enlightened patriarchalism," as reflecting "greater softness," and as "Austere, rigid patriarchalism slowly" giving "way to warm, mellow paternalism" certainly reflects how planters like Simon Taylor may have seen themselves and how they distinguished themselves from their planting forebears, but it cannot adequately encompass how slaves experienced the transition in question.[101]

Dusinberre counsels against employing the term paternalism at all.[102] Trevor Burnard agrees that planter paternalism was largely an ideology and argues that it was one that did not prevail on Jamaica. Of the Jamaican planter at the center of his study, Burnard writes that Thomas Thistlewood "was no paternalist. He did not see himself as a 'beneficent master,' nor did he attempt to mask the exercise of his authority through psychological inculcations of his racial and moral superiority." Thistlewood, advances Burnard, "did not appeal to his slaves; he threatened them." Burnard is certainly right about Thistlewood, and he is also certainly correct that "The principal method of controlling slaves in Jamaica was through terror. . . . Terror, or naked power, was at the core of the institution of slavery."[103]

Still, the habits of planters and attorneys such as Simon Taylor and Charles Rowe underline that in late eighteenth-century Jamaica, terror, violence, and the threat thereof were also central aspects of the practice of paternalism. Paternalism as an ideology was certainly not so well developed in Jamaica as it was in the American South. When the attorney John Vanheelen sent to the Spanish Main Jaffray, "a Young Man very Worthless" who "would never Stay Home," and Mamie, a young woman who showed signs of pica and who refused to work, he did not even bother to get his employer's permission, let alone go through any of the rhetorical contortions that Walter Johnson has shown to be central to ways that Louisiana planters cast their forays into the slave market as being in the very interest of slaves themselves.[104] Nevertheless, in the period after the American war some Jamaican slaveowners cultivated paternalistic relationships with the slaves they owned. Moreover, their practice offers a clear-eyed view of planter paternalism in action and thus good glimpses of how it was actually experienced by enslaved blacks. This is key, because as a definitional matter, how paternalism was experienced by enslaved blacks is just as important (if not more so) to how the term should be understood as how the idea of paternalism was variously articulated by slaveholders. And as experienced by Jamaican slaves, terror and the threat of terror were at the heart of the kind of paternalism then developing on the island.[105]

The ideals, practices, and power belonging to white planters and their managers determined a good deal of the context of black life and the shape of black society on Jamaican plantations and cattle pens. In part, the extent to which white decision-making affected enslaved blacks has to be surmised. We cannot be absolutely certain of the effect on black society of planter decisions concerning such matters as the season to buy slaves, the number to put on a property at a time, and the kinds of preparations to make beforehand. We can be sure, however, that such decisions mattered, even if attending to their particular consequence requires further research. Further, there *are* matters relating to the power and decision making of white planters of which we can be sure—the importance of crop conditions to the shaping of slave society, the kind of black community encouraged on properties with hard-driving owners or managers, the stratification that might result on plantations where white decision-makers materially favored one group of blacks over another, the basic social conditions determined by mangers' approaches to such matters as provisions, and—perhaps, most dramatically—the kind of client-patron relationships created by interracial interaction that bound black society to white on some eighteenth-century properties. The upshot of all of this is a point that cannot be taken for granted when considering the passages in store for newcomers to Jamaican sugar plantations: in ways that cannot be ignored, white power intersected black society.

FOUR

ROUTINES OF DISASTER AND REVOLUTION

The stage on which freshly arrived Africans worked out new lives in Jamaica was formed in large measure by the whims and desires of a small number of white planters and their managers. Moreover, in the late eighteenth century the context and rhythm of slave seasoning was further shaped by peculiar environmental circumstances. In the years surrounding the American war a handful of storms ravaged the principal islands of the West Indies—killing in the process, either directly or indirectly, thousands of the Caribbean's most vulnerable inhabitants.[1] The disasters of the late eighteenth century and their consequences helped form, to no small extent, the society of a generation of enslaved Afro-Jamaicans. For these blacks, disaster was as certain as work. Hunger and famine, deluge and drought, disease and death were all routine. Consequently, in the years following the American Revolution, bound Jamaicans constantly contended not only with their enslavement and the work it entailed, but also with cataclysm, which could be counted on regularly to jeopardize their already precarious access to food and shelter, while imperiling their tenuous physical well-being. Hurricanes in 1784, 1785, and 1786, gales and tropical storms in 1783, 1788, 1790, and 1791, and drought that sometimes settled into the spaces between storms made late eighteenth-century Jamaica a particularly hard terrain.[2] The outer edges of the society slaves formed under such circumstances, and thus the communities into which newly arrived Africans seasoned, could be just as hard and difficult.

But the late eighteenth century was also a moment of profound social and political upheaval in the British Atlantic empire, characterized by a series of imperial wars (hot and cold), a slave revolt at St. Domingue, and the climax of British antislavery action against the slave trade itself. As surely as newly arrived Africans on Jamaican sugar estates had to adjust to the demands of work, provisioning, and disease, they seasoned also to a series of remarkable political events that became central to how enslaved migrants at the heart of Great Britain's American empire fashioned their world. In negotiating the demands of environmental disaster, the constraints of slavery, and the peculiar openings offered by the late eighteenth-century political landscape, black migrants and settlers in Jamaica responded in profoundly

human ways to the confounding complexities of a social setting characterized by deepest tragedy but tinged also with remarkable individual and
collective possibility.

We must start first with yams. And cocoes. And plantains. To begin to
understand the disaster at the heart of the experience of enslaved migrants
and settlers in eighteenth-century Jamaica, it is critical to grasp what was—
among blacks—perhaps the most important aspect of their lives: their
provisions.[3] On properties with relatively diversified grounds, enslaved
Jamaicans depended on yams from September to February, cocoes from
February to May, and plantains from the summer months through the end
of the year.[4] This is, it should be pointed out, a generous calendar. Even
on properties where blacks tended a variety of food crops, their harvests
were never enough to meet their needs through the span outlined above. So
although there was a yam harvest on Jamaica in August, to say that slaves
depended on it from September to February is not to say that it sufficed.[5]
Further, on many properties the harvesting of slave provisions did not span
at all the cycle drawn above. There was an inverse relationship between the
attention slaves paid to their provisions and the amount of rum and sugar
made on an estate. So, on properties where the yearly bottom line drove all
else, black workers made do with fewer food crops, and of these they depended most on those that required the least of their attention: plantains.

The upshot is that even on the most liberally managed plantations,
where slaves tended a number of different food crops and had more or less
ample time to see their work to fruition, it was part of the normal state of
affairs that blacks annually suffered acute periods of hunger. Surveying
material from throughout the British West Indies, Robert Dirks concluded
that "Periods of scarcity severe enough to attract attention from chroniclers
recurred frequently, on some estates weekly, on most islands annually." In
general, the months following mid-year were the toughest.[6] As an upbeat
December missive from an attorney in Jamaica to an absentee planter in
Britain read, "Am happy to say," went the report, "we have got over the
Hungry times."[7]

In late eighteenth-century Jamaica, hurricanes quite often came right
on top of the hungry times, and not without consequences for slaves' food
crops and their prospects for subsistence. The hurricane that visited the island on July 30, 1784, for instance, "committed horrid devastation; its bane-
ful influence having extended in a great degree over the whole face of the
country."[8] Admittedly, this official description from the lieutenant governor
was something of an exaggeration. The initial reports concerning any storm
were always the most alarming, and it turned out later that the brunt of the

hurricane fell on the leeward and southern sides of the island.[9] Neverthe-less, the consequences of the storm were extraordinary for a great many Ja-maican slaves who were, as the storm struck, nursing along their provisions.

At Golden Grove plantation, in consequence of the weather, the overseer believed that not a plantain tree in the neighborhood remained standing. At Holland estate, in St. Thomas in the East, a witness to the destruction went even further: "There is not a Plantain Sucker left," he wrote, "even the Trees are blown up by the Roots." At estates with ground provisions—which were less susceptible to destruction from high winds—the storm still left much to worry about, as what was planted was hardly enough to sup-port the whole property. This was the case at Amity Hall, where the prop-erty's overseer admitted that in time provisions from abroad would "keep the Negroes from Starving." On properties that depended a great deal on plantains, fears were perhaps more acute. On one such estate, the overseer feared that in three weeks' time "One half of the Negroes will not have a Morsel to Eat." On another, the agent admitted that what was left of the trees would not "be more than a Melancholy respite" from sure famine.[10]

Another tempest washed over the island on August 27, 1785—the fourth such storm in five years. The 1785 hurricane approached the island at dusk and raged in places for more than twelve hours. At Joseph Barham's Island estate, the people, buildings, and crop "Suffered very little by the Wind," but the rain and storm surge compensated for their good fortune by over-flowing "Almost the whole of that Country" around the property. Slave provisions necessarily suffered, though not to the same extent as during the previous year's hurricane. So, planters worried about the effects of the storm in their particular area, but the lieutenant governor, for his part, was satisfied that what Jamaicans feared most in the wake of a hurricane would not, in this case, follow: famine. At the moment the storm struck, "The Island was," to the relief of the lieutenant governor, "fortunately, full of Provisions."[11]

The next year, it looked for a while like the island would escape what had become an annual misfortune. Toward the very end of what residents knew as the storm season, however, another hurricane rolled over Jamaica, this one clipping the island's western edge. The storm began on the evening of October 19 and continued into the following morning. In Westmoreland, it was reported, "most of the buildings have been destroyed and the Canes and Plantain walks (upon which they principally depend for provision-ing) rendered useless."[12] In others parts of the island, the storm was not so severely felt. In St. Thomas in the East, the ever vulnerable plantain trees showed the effects of the wind. Simon Taylor reckoned that the storm "destroyed about half the Plantains in generall," in the area and admitted that on two estates with which he was concerned there was "hardly left a Plantain tree" standing. But he also knew of places where the plantain walks were sheltered to the southeast and weathered the storm, consequently, as if none had passed.[13]

From 1783 to 1795, when hurricanes bypassed the island it seemed that some other meteorological phenomenon was sure to compensate. In 1788, although the island escaped a general hurricane, parts of Jamaica wrestled with a series of gales, storms, and then drought. Before the hurricane season, five days in March produced "the most ferocious North wind that ever was known at that time of the year," which did no small damage in the cane fields and leveled "most of the Plantain Trees" in and around Golden Grove estate.[14] Come May, more than two days of constant rain resulted in what Simon Taylor called "the severest & heaviest flood that we have had for these 23 years, indeed infinitely higher than in any of the Hurricanes."[15] By the end of August, blacks on Golden Grove were still working on repairing damage done to the plantation—not to mention their grounds—by the March gale and the May flood, when they found themselves in the middle of a "Cruel spell of dry weather" that "destroyed the canes every where but about the river" and parched all other vegetation, presumably, that was not similarly situated.[16]

In 1789, there was again no hurricane, but that hardly meant that the effort slaves put into their grounds and plantain walks went unchecked. A blustery day in June turned into a "severe squall" that did "considerable damage to the plantain walks" about Joseph Barham's properties in the western part of the island. The storm, it turns out, was an ambiguous reprieve from a long period of dryness begun months earlier. In April, John Weddernurn observed from Westmoreland that "For this considerable time past, we have had exceeding dry Weather, lately a little Rain but not much." As a result, the cane fields had gone from green to brown (and doubtless much of the slaves' ground provisions as well).[17] To the south and east, Simon Taylor was more emphatic, complaining from Kingston at year's end that "such a dry year I never saw before." And in case anyone mistook his claim for hyperbole, Taylor elaborated:

we have hardly had a Shower that has done any good since the beginning of Augt. there is not a sign of any thing Green than upon
a Brick yard, the Ponds are all dry, the Cattle must be removed, or
they must perish, the Corn all burnt up and lost, and I never saw
any thing like it in my life, it [is] as nearly as bad as it was in April

and May 1764. and the Drought Extends all the Way from St. Davids down, to all the Low lands in Clarendon, and what is worse there is no prospect of our having rains untill the Month of April or May.[18]

There was no general drought the next year—though some parts of the island continued for some time in the same dry vein while other parts were good and green.[19] Come September, however, the island felt the effects of a storm that relieved the previous drought, in some places, too much. At Joseph Barnam's Mesopotamia estate, the overseer thought the September storm was "equal in its consequences as to canes and provisions, to any we have ever experienced."[20] Another witness, writing from the same quarter of the island, claimed that in strength, though not in direction, the wind from the storm approximated a hurricane and had "totally destroyed the plantain Walks" in the area.[21] The storm was not as strongly felt on the eastern quarter of Jamaica, but still, there too in St. Thomas in the East the wind "did a very great deal of Mischief" blowing down "all the Plantain Trees in the Parish."[22]

The next year—1791—at least along the southeastern rivers, misfortune heaped upon misfortune in the form of a storm that began on September 26. What began as a steady downpour turned a day later, if only for a few hours, into a squall. In the short time that they lasted, gusts from the storm leveled plantain walks, tore through fields of sugar cane, and ruined buildings in the eastern part of the island. And after the wind died down, the rain continued—pushing rivers in the area out of their banks and across nearby estates. At Holland the waters carried "4 or 5 foot waste over the greater part of the estate." At other properties both provision grounds and cane fields suffered from the deluge—so much so that overseers downplayed expectations concerning the coming crop and placed orders in Britain for provisions to tide over their slaves in the months to come.[23]

After the floods of 1791, three seasons passed before extreme weather again visited the island. But the period cannot be counted as any kind of respite from the calamities recounted above. The island and the provision grounds of the island's slaves were not during those three years materially injured by flood, drought, fire, gale, or hurricane. But true to the calamities that seemed to plague the island since the end of the American war, slave provision grounds failed all the same during these years—for political and economic reasons rather than environmental ones. In 1791 a slave revolt at the French sugar colony of St. Domingue crippled what was then the world's largest producer of sugar, resulting in a sugar boom in Jamaica as that island and rest of the Caribbean ramped up to fill the void—opening new lands and putting on more slaves.[24] In 1793, in the midst of this boom, Great Britain and France went to war. The combined effects of these two events resulted in the same kind of crisis of provisions that usually attended storm and drought.

The effects of the war with France were immediately perceptible on Jamaica's ability to feed itself, as the Atlantic and it constituent seas became too dangerous for ships laden with provisions and bound for Kingston, Montego Bay, or some other Jamaican port. The state of affairs on the island from April to July 1793 is instructive on the effects of world war. In the spring, the declaration of war detained the fleets that regularly sailed from Ireland and England to Jamaica with food and supplies, as it also deterred ships—contraband and legitimate—from North America.[25] By summer the effects were unmistakable. In June, most of the island's estates went without the supplies of salt fish meant to supplement the slaves' diet, and very little of the American corn that the island counted on to augment its own crop had arrived.[26] From Kingston, Simon Taylor complained to Jamaica's agent in London that "the Negroes are starving all over the Island for the want of the usual supplies of Fish . . . & the White people in the Country are in the same situation for want of Beef Pork & Butter. . . . Our Supplies from British America & the united States" he ranted "is cut of[f] by 2 French Frigates and some Privateers who range along the whole Coast of America."[27]

The Irish ships arrived not long after Taylor's complaint, but other factors ensured that Jamaica did not move easily out of scarcity.[28] For one, Jamaica counted continually on provisions from Britain and America to meet its needs. War fractured this system, and supplies arriving from one station were not enough to make up for what was usually expected from others. Further, since the rise of a competent abolitionist challenge in Britain and the 1791 collapse of the sugar industry in St. Domingue, Jamaican planters had embarked on an expansion of their properties and a concomitant increase in their slave purchasing that simply outstripped the capacity of then developed provision grounds. Of this, one Jamaican observed as follows: "so long as the notion continues that the trade will be abolished, people will buy at any price, even to their own ruin; and the destruction of half the negroes, for want of provisions."[29] The Assembly of Jamaica, when trying to explain the very tight market in provisions, figured that in the year running from June 23, 1792, to the same date in 1793, more than twenty-three thousand African slaves landed at Jamaica. The figure represented, on average, almost a 100 percent increase from the number of Africans landed on the island during each of the two previous years.[30] Said one planter, perhaps unfamiliar with these precise numbers but cognizant nonetheless of the buying frenzy then going on around him: "the late very great Imports of New negroes give us much uneasiness for [the] consequences."[31]

To make matters worse, the revolt in St. Domingue resulted indirectly in a spike in Jamaica's black population as British planters scrambled to fill the void in the world sugar market created by the loss of the world's greatest sugar-producing island. Moreover, the revolt resulted in a stream of French refugees to Jamaica who also had to be fed. Further, when a British expeditionary force made for the former French colony, the invasion created a British market for provisions and supplies in St. Domingue that rivaled Jamaica.[32] The prices that could be fetched in St. Domingue made it that much more difficult for Jamaica to attract shipping to the island or to maintain its stores. The lieutenant governor phrased this difficulty rather simply, "We at this moment are obliged to feed some thousands of french besides our own Troops at Saint Domingo."[33] Those not in government put the matter more indelicately. "We are in genrall in the Utmost Want of every thing, what ever is ___ to sale, is instantly bought up for Hispaniola, . . . I never knew Matters managed so ill as everything has been uniformly so."[34] Matters worsened in 1794, when the United States placed an embargo on the shipping of supplies and provisions to Jamaica.[35]

So throughout the period 1792–1794, when Mother Nature was kinder to Jamaica, the combined exigencies of the market in slaves and provisions ensured that keeping the island in food was no small task. Many were convinced that only the periodic flouting of restrictive British trade conventions—the opening of Jamaican ports to all neutral shipping, which the lieutenant governor and council felt compelled to do whenever provisions became too scarce or prices to high—was all that kept the island from moving from precipice to disaster as far as its food supply was concerned. Such was the case in August 1793 when the lieutenant governor opened the ports for four months, justifying his decision, in part, as a vital step toward keeping the island's slaves supplied. "At present," the lieutenant governor explained his decision, "I can venture to say that the Negroes throughout the Island are happy and have no wants, but should their provision Grounds be destroyed they would have recourse to plunder which might eventually tend to a Revolt."[36] "We must have starved," Simon Taylor later noted, "had not the Ports been opened for American Grain to be brought in"—suggesting that the part of the lieutenant governor's justification for opening the ports that related to slaves and slave provisions was perhaps more pressing than he was willing to let on officially.[37]

On top of these continuing political and economic difficulties, natural disaster returned to Jamaica in the form of ten months of bone-dry weather, stretching from the winter of 1795 to the end of 1796. In January of 1796, Jamaicans counted thirteen weeks without anything resembling a shower. By April, parts of the island had received small rains, but nothing of much benefit. Across the island, it was reported, "the Cattle, Mules, & Horses are dying almost every where for want of Fodder, the Crops of Corn have failed, and the Plantain Trees are drying up, and weathering [sic] away for of Moisture, & Young Canes are mostly dead, there has been no rain to plant ground Provisions." Fires were common. Around Pleasant Hill plantation, according to the attorney, "There is not a week passes, but there are three or four Alarms in the Neighbourhood of fire, Shells blowing." In April and May of 1796, fires raced continually through Jamaican cane fields, slave villages, and provision grounds, with little relief until winter.[38]

So, for more than a decade after the American war there was almost annually on Jamaica a catastrophe to exacerbate the seasonal privations that sugar island slaves counted on even in the best of times.[39] For enslaved Jamaicans, the personal, physical consequences of these disasters, and the scarcity they engendered, were especially stark when considered in light of the disease regimes normally prevailing on Jamaican plantations. Just as there were hungry times across the island, there were sickly times as well. Whenever black laborers from Joseph Barham's Island estate set out to harvest their provisions, for instance, debilitating outbreaks of fever and gastrointestinal distress followed almost without fail.[40] What are now thought of as childhood diseases ran a regular and dangerous course through the younger slaves on a plantation.[41] Further, there were times when enslaved workers on a particular plantation succumbed in numbers to some malady or another—sometimes a kind of pox, sometimes a localized outbreak of venereal disease, sometimes dysentery, and sometime some general ailment or combination thereof that was only described as "The Negroes have been Sickly for sometime and a great many of them laid up wth. different complaints."[42] In addition to these local, seasonal afflictions, epidemics periodically blew through the island. Scarcity, natural disaster, and morbidity overlay and reinforced one another in late eighteenth-century Jamaica.

In the wake of the hurricanes that struck the island following the American war, official Jamaica went to some lengths to document the medium-term consequences of these kinds of disasters for the island's slaves. "By these destructive visitations," claimed the Jamaica House of Assembly about the successive storms, "the plantain walks, which furnish the chief article of support to the negroes, were generally rooted up, and the intense droughts which followed, destroyed those different species of ground-provisions which the hurricane[s] had not reached." For Jamaica's slaves, further claimed the

House of Assembly, the storms of 1784, 1785, and 1786 were made into more perfect tragedies by the restrictive, postwar trade policies that governed intercourse between the British Caribbean and the new United States.

The House of Assembly's argument concerning the consequences of successive Jamaican hurricanes and British trade policy is worth following. After the storm of 1784, the lieutenant governor lifted the restrictions then in place on intra-American trade, allowing American ships to bring foodstuffs to the island. The term of the reprieve, however, was short, and thus the number of ships that heeded it was small. Consequently, "the small quantities of flour, rice, and other provisions" that were allowed into the country remained at an "exorbitant price" and thus out of the reach of many. According to the House of Assembly, when the ports were closed again following their four-month liberty, "the sufferings of the poor negroes, in consequence thereof, for some months afterwards, were extreme."[43]

By the summer 1785, Jamaican blacks had come a long way toward recovering from the previous year's storm and the island's markets looked to be returning to normal. Soon afterward, however, another hurricane slammed into the island. Though provisions were not, at first, at all scarce, the destruction done to crops then in the ground and the fact that the lieutenant governor refused, following this storm, to fortify the island further by opening the ports meant that scarcity and worse followed as "the productions of the country soon exhausted" and the island's blacks were again backed into a "scanty and unwholesome diet." Consequently, in the spring and summer of 1786, according to the House of Assembly, what contemporaries called "dropsies and epidemic dysenteries" prevailed on plantations across Jamaica and "proved fatal to great numbers of the negroes, in all parts of the country." And once these medium-term effects of the previous year's storm began to wane, there came another hurricane in October 1786.[44] The attorneys and white functionaries who made a living on the island's plantations described the slow carnage around them with a language that was both awful and imprecise. All the same, the magnitude conveyed by descriptions on the ground is very important. In a country where long-standing demographic realities meant that whites had developed a very high tolerance for black death, their shock at what was transpiring around them is quite telling. "It is a Truth indisputable as it is horrid, however little it may be known or noticed on your side [of] the Ocean," went one such account, "that many Thousands of Negroes perished this year in Jamaica by Famine, And as we have had a Hurricane, if a Drowth [sic] should follow, as happened after the preceding ones, many Thousands more will inevitable perish next year."[45]

On top of the morbidity and mortality directly related to the storms of the late eighteenth century, epidemic disease sometimes followed or preceded natural catastrophe in fairly quick succession. So even when the relationship between the disaster and disease was not direct, the hardship created when the two nevertheless reinforced one another was enormous. On the Bogue estate, when an outbreak of measles came four months on the heels of the hurricane of 1784, former relief that the property had fared fairly well in the aftermath of the late storm must have dissipated quite quickly once it became clear that infection would tend to the work that the hurricane had missed.[46] These kinds of coincidental hardships were especially prominent in the span following the island's successive hurricanes. In 1789, in the middle of that year's tremendous drought, a strain of influenza ran through, some thought, almost the entire population of Jamaica—debilitating those who were in possession of a good portion of their health when the bug struck, and killing quite a few who, for one reason or another, were already weak come the outbreak.[47] The following year, right on top of the rains that turned every street in Kingston into "a great river," there was an outbreak of smallpox on both north and south sides of the island.[48] In 1793—in the midst of the general scarcity that for various political and economic reasons prevailed across the island—an influenza epidemic again swept Jamaica. At the height of the outbreak, the disorder enervated up to one-quarter of the blacks at Mesopotamia.[49] Adding fuel to this particular fire was a simultaneous outbreak of scarlet fever at Kingston, supposedly brought to the island with refugees from St. Domingue.[50] The influenza and scarlet fever both struck during the dry season, prompting Simon Taylor to describe the scene with no small amount of foreboding: "The Thermometer is constantly up at 90° in the middle of the day & putrid sore throats & Scarlett Fevers are destroying People daily & it is no uncommon thing for a Man to be about one day & buried the next."[51] In the midst of the drought of 1795–1796, both yellow fever and measles held various parts of the island under siege—the former mostly laying hold to the island's ports from July 1794 through May of the following year; the latter seizing the countryside and alternately tightening and relaxing its grip for eight months from January 1795.[52]

Despite regular, successive disasters that had catastrophic effects for black society in late eighteenth century, Jamaica's slaves were able to establish, maintain, and develop human and humane relations. Indeed, Jamaica's slaveowners sometimes counted on the love and affection black mothers demonstrated toward their children to bring their own plans to fruition. When the attorney and doctor on Golden Grove sugar plantation

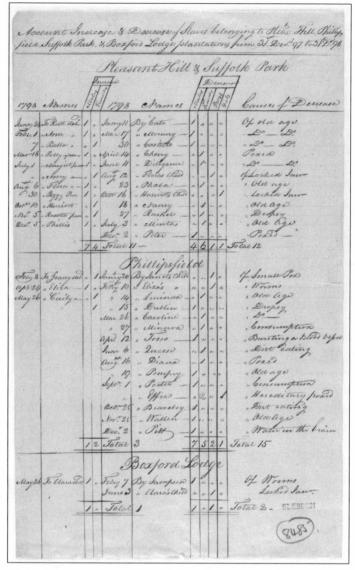

Figure 5. A yearly toll on a Jamaican property. Note the "Causes of Decrease," and the extent of child mortality. "Account Increase & Decrease of Slaves belonging to Pleast. Hill, Phillipsfield, Suffolk Park, & Boxford Lodge plantations from 31st Decr. '97 to 31st D. '98," n.d., Slebech Papers and Documents, MSS 8485.
Source: By permission of Sir Edward Dashwood and Llyfrgell Genedlaethol Cymru, The National Library of Wales

constructed a lying-in house on the property for new mothers and their children, the two knew that black mothers' initial reluctance to discard some of their previous birthing customs and take advantage of the facility could eventually be overcome by the aspirations slave mothers had for their children.[53] Along similar lines, when another attorney was informed of the death of "a valuable breeding woman named Cocoa who has left Five children the oldest not more that Nine Years and the Youngest about four Months," he knew that he could count on the departed woman's family to ensure that the newly orphaned children—who were valuable to him in the short term as ammunition against abolitionist volleys, and who would grow to be very valuable to him in other ways—had a committed guardian. Wrote the attorney to the deceased's former owner: "I have directed [the deceased woman's] Mother to take charge and care of rearing her Grandchildren assuring her that on due performance of that it is the only labour you will ever require from her."[54]

Further, enslaved Jamaicans formed strong, familial-like relations with fellow slaves who were not necessarily kin. Thus, it was not an uncommon occurrence for newly arrived slaves to forge relationships with captives with whom they had survived the voyage from western Africa to Jamaica. In the consciousness of Jamaican planters, such relationships became clear too often in the context of small rebellions, as when "two or three of the last purchased" Africans forced onto a Jamaican sugar estate by Charles Rowe "were foolishly led away by a discontented shipmate of their[s], and absented themselves for a few days from the property."[55] Newly arrived captives and long-established slaves likewise connected to and forged familial ties based on language and memory. So when the attorney for Nathaniel Phillips's Jamaican holdings settled forty Gold Coast Africans on two properties, it turned out, as the buyer put it, that "most of the old people here, such as Winson, Cooper Ben, Frank, etc. are of the same country, And by interpretation that were done, most of them says they have had the Yaws . . . . The old people are glad to see them."[56]

Enslaved Jamaicans—as some of the examples illustrate above, and as the current literature demonstrates irrefutably—constituted viable families, organized strong associations, formed committed friendships, and established vital recreative outlets.[57] But these connections were (and this point needs to be stressed) constantly tested and not infrequently perverted or broken by the circumstances of plantation life. Consequently, for each area of Jamaican life for which there is evidence of slaves' ability to craft and maintain society in spite of the pressures under which they lived, there is also evidence that these same accomplishments were never complete and were quite often chimeral—again, because of the demands under which enslaved Jamaicans lived. Accordingly, one does not have to dig very deep into the source materials to find that the *general* constraints and personal disaster defining enslavement and the *particular* disasters that colored black life on Jamaican in the late eighteenth century all had an effect on the society of enslaved Jamaicans. For slaves, late eighteenth-century Jamaica was lean, uncompromising, exploitative terrain. Slave society, particularly for those who experienced it only within the confines of the properties on which they were bound, was very often the same.

So although Jamaican slaveowners, especially after the abolitionist movement gained momentum in the 1780s, made a great deal of the fast fraternal connections that formed between slaves already settled on plantations and newly arrived captives, this was all probably as much propaganda as it was reflective of any broad Jamaican reality. Stephen Fuller, who was the agent for Jamaica in London, characterized the relationship between new people and old as instantly supportive and celebratory. This was a point of view in line with what slaveowners presented publicly as the good society to which the slave trade and subsequent slave seasoning process were vital. From the ostensive perspective of old people in Jamaica, Fuller decried abolitionist successes as events that would "certainly add to the distress of the Negroes already in the Island, whose greatest Joy is in frequent arrivals of Negroes from Africa."[58]

There is a great grain a truth in Fuller's point, but it cannot be rescued from planters' public perspectives. Rather, when slaveowners were completely candid, it is clear that the relationship between new people and old—the joy Stephen Fuller maintained that settled slaves expressed when new people were brought to their properties—was quite often grounded in base exploitation, grown up from the enormous physical demands placed on already-settled slaves and the scarcity with which they lived. For slaves already settled on a property—worked to their limits, quite often starving, and suffering regularly from extraordinary disasters—new people represented, potentially, hands to lighten their loads. On late eighteenth-century Jamaican plantations, as in contemporary prisons, those already established on a property often looked to those just arrived as exploitable commodities. So obvious was this propensity toward abuse that attorneys and overseers thought that it was in their interest to develop remedies.

Simon Taylor prescribed several seasoning regimes meant to dampen the kind of exploitation that already-established slaves often had in mind for newcomers. Thus, after purchasing fifteen new slaves for Chaloner Arcedeckne's Jamaican estates, Taylor laid out a plan for their seasoning that included keeping the group, particularly during their critical first months on the island, as independent as possible from those already established on the property. Of this plan, he wrote as follows to Arcedeckne: "There was plenty of Plantains at Golden Grove & in consequence of the absolute necessity there was for it, I have bought you 15 new Negroes, and must buy as many more as soon as possible, these Negroes are employed three days in the Week cleaning your Pastures, and 4 in making their own grounds and preparing Houses for themselves, by this means they will I hope season kindly and by being by themselves not be destroyed by the old Negroes making them their Slaves."[59]

As it concerned the interaction of women and men on a property, Simon Taylor was more specific on the kind of sexual violence and exploitation that could follow when a proportion of the new people brought to a plantation were women. The slave village, apparently, was a particularly dangerous place for newly arrived slaves (and not just because of the well-documented sexual exploitation white attorneys, overseers, and bookkeepers visited upon enslaved women who lived within their reach). Thus Taylor thought it risky practice to settle on a estate female slaves of a certain age. If "the Girls are bought to[o] Young," it was his experience that the men on a property "play the very devil with them."[60]

Older women were not by virtue of their age and maturity exempt from the kind of sexual violence, potential and real, that could follow their addition to a property. Consequently, even when Taylor added older women to an estate, he knew it was in his interest to provide for them some degree of independence. When Taylor purchased an already seasoned gang of enslaved workers from a former business associate and provided them with wives—women presumably purchased from the island's African slave marts—he knew his investment was safest if the women in question were not too completely tied to their so-called husbands. To this end, he instructed the women to make provision grounds for *themselves* (providing time and additional hands for this task). Further, when their grounds were complete, he knew the next task was "to help them to make Houses, so as to be independent of their Husbands, should they quarell."[61]

Similar kinds of violence affected other aspects of slave society on Jamaican plantations. The evidence presented above, for instance, suggests that the black family in slavery—often interpreted as a kind of refuge against the calamities of servitude—was itself hardly immune from the pressures of the institution in which it developed. So, in late eighteenth-century Jamaica—though no doubt earlier as well—there is suggestive evidence concerning how the conditions of servitude might permeate and embitter relation's between enslaved kin. On the Golden Grove estate, an incident between a son and father—Quashie and the blacksmith Guy—illustrates the point. In the week of September 4, 1791, Quashie began petitioning his father for money to buy drink. His father refused repeatedly—appreciating, apparently, that his son took too much refuge in alcohol and spending. After days of asking and then, no doubt, begging for coins, Quashie decided that he could no longer brook his father's refusal nor the continued absence of the numbing that followed strong drink, so he decided, evidently, to kill the old man by fire. The son set fire to his father's house and ran away. His blacksmith father survived the attempt on his life, but the plantation nearly did not. The fire completely consumed several outbuildings, and "the Works might have been burnt for he sett Fire to the two Houses about 3 O Clock in the Afternoon and the Fire was not extinguished untill one the Next afternoon."[62]

The Golden Grove attorney had the rebel tried, but in the end the case against him turned out to be mostly circumstantial, consisting of the fact that the "Overseer, Bookkeepers and indeed all the negroes agree in belief of his guilt" and that the plantation's attorney did "not think it safe to send him back to the Estate."[63] The most damning evidence against Quashie is at the same time the most telling concerning a side of black slave society deserving of close attention: testimony that he was seen before the fire turning over nearly a full pint of rum and heard to say that he intended "to make his Father as poor as himself."[64]

Months after the failed patricide, Golden Grove's attorney arranged to have Quashie sold from the island (he had spent the interim in the Kingston workhouse). His father, reportedly, "was glad to find he was not to be returned to Golden Grove. he said his son would not mind, and it would be dangerous to the Estate (particularly to him) were Quashie to be sent there."[65] There were, no doubt, many precipitating factors to Quashie's homicidal outburst, and we can know very little about any of them. But given the young man's rage, his apparent alcoholism, and his quick recourse to tremendous violence, it is safe to reason that at least part of his apparent arson was an outgrowth of the violent and desperate conditions under which he lived.

Vice and tragedy infiltrated every aspect of black society, even the areas of slave life ordinarily thought of as proving the opposite. There is evidence that the plays and dances that contemporary planters bemoaned, and that historians have rightly pointed to as examples of captives' rich social life, cultural independence, and recreative imaginations, were not simply incubators of what slaves managed to salvage from their enslavement, but also crucibles in which the same kinds of abuse, excess, and suffering that defined black servitude was ground as well into black society.[66] Blacks on the Phillipsfield estate, for instance, had easy recourse to a river than ran through the property and thus frequent intercourse with the boatmen and other travelers that ran up and down the waterway. They exploited these connections in ways that expanded their society and made their lives more bearable than those of workers who were more isolated. That the white man charged with extracting and organizing their labor continually complained about their interactions with passersby, their continuous wandering off the property, and the lost labor that both entailed is strong proof that the Phillipsfield blacks worked out more room for themselves than did many sugar workers.[67]

At the same time, however, a significant number of these same slaves used their connection to the waterway to facilitate better access to strong drink, and the refuge it provided from their reality. Their recreation was quite often a form of escapism that took a mental and physical toll of its own. At Phillipsfield, complained its attorney to its proprietor, "the males become Drunkards & Runaways, and the females disordered and feeble, so that the Estate looses much of their Labour." He was certain that it took three blacks at Phillipsfield to do the work done by two at another of the estates he managed. The former and once again head driver on the estate, according to its attorney, was proof of the pervasive effects of alcohol on the property. Pera, the driver in question, was at one time apparently a very efficient supervisor, "But when he took to Drinking," reported the attorney, he became quite "faulty, and when punished, he got dejected, and was very impudent to the Whites!" Further, Pera's embrace of drink seemed to coincide with a similar turn across the entire property: "It was then noticed, that the Negroes did not work in their usual way, and many of them took to Sculking, and others to drinking, wch. occasioned much loss of Labour!"[68]

The particular material exigencies of Jamaican slavery were reflected, no doubt, in other areas of black society. At Mesopotamia, a small gang of slaves who made something of a living by looting the homes of fellow captives and plundering others' provision grounds were very likely encouraged in their behavior by the sheer desperation of their circumstances. The fact that they stole from people who were themselves poor and hungry sheds light on how human responses to slave society could make black servitude that much harsher.[69] Further, in addition to larceny, there was murder. It was not unheard of for the governor to seek the king's pardon for the slave of a Jamaican gentleman forced to murder in order to avoid being murdered himself.[70] Overseers and attorneys sometimes alluded to struggles between

slaves ending in the ultimate form of foul play. So, when a driver at Mesopotamia lost his life through an "accidental fall," the property's attorney
had strong reason to believe that "his Death must have been occasioned
through some unfavourable events not yet arrived to our Knowledge and
of which my Suspicions against the fellow Plato are still very strong and
presumptive"—these suspicions probably existed within the slave village as
well, where the attorney must have received the information that made him
doubt the original cause ascribed to the driver's demise.[71]

Jealousy, subjugation, addiction, murder, larceny, and sexual violence,
all of this and more defined black slavery in late eighteenth-century Jamaica, and thus all were also definitive aspects of black society. But in
addition to these kinds of malignancies—which were all affines to the general exigencies of black slavery—there was too, it seems, a social challenge
peculiar to the generation of black Jamaicans that was formed in the decade
after the American war. The successive environmental tragedies and disasters that overlay the general disasters and tragedies of Jamaican servitude
during this period formed themselves into a gauntlet that all slaves had to
run, whose effects inflicted a significant portion of this generation with a
fatalism that went beyond that of mere enslavement.

As far as enslaved blacks are concerned, the first hints of the social
consequences of the disasters that frequented Jamaica during the period
in question appear indirectly, in the form of their consequences for white
society, where they induced combinations of paranoia, desperation, and
helplessness. The correspondence of Simon Taylor is replete with examples
of how the threat and actuality of hurricane, drought, storm, epidemic, and
famine affected whites across the island.

In terms of sheer sentiment, the disasters enforced a general resignation.
There "really seems to me to be a fatality attending this unhappy Country,"
Taylor opined in 1794. "This has been the most difficult year I ever remember." But these kinds of sentiments were not materially different from those
expressed and implied across white society from the end of the American
war, when Jamaican whites, for very good reason, never thought themselves
far from calamity. There "is no Year or Season that does not bring some
Calamity to us," Taylor had written ten days before Christmas eve in 1786.
It was this learned foreboding that moved him never to count a sugar crop
until it was shipped. Despite his efforts to encourage the natural increase of
his enslaved labor force, the same apprehension always brought him back
to the conclusion that his goals on this head were an impossibility. Slaves
were born, and new negroes were landed to die. So acute was the anxiety
of the time, an enigmatic horizon, sea breeze, or tide was enough to bring

on a palpable dread. "We have very odd Sort of Weather here just now," he admitted in 1786, "a dead Calm and gloomy Sky for these four days past with every Appearance of Rain but none falls, the Sea is very quiet which makes me hope it will wear off, but we have had so many Storms that every thing frightens us just now."[72]

It is rare that the sentiments of enslaved Jamaicans are on any matter documented with the clarity with which Simon Taylor wrote of the paranoiac gloom that affected, for a time, white society on the island. Nonetheless, from the circumstance, actions, and words of black Jamaicans that have survived, it is clear that the effects of Jamaica's late eighteenth-century disasters were not unique to the island's whites. Indeed, if anything, hurricanes, storms, drought, and the pronounced hungry seasons and famine that followed prompted even greater degrees of dread and desperation from Jamaican blacks. Property owners and plantation whites fretted over loosing crop time, hogsheads, and money to the disasters that seemed always upon the island. To enslaved blacks, what their owners thought of as sugar not made or capital lost was understood and experienced by them more directly as sickness, starvation, and death. Thus Simon Taylor, no doubt, came very close to expressing the sentiments of those whom he held in captivity with a lament from the end of 1786, in which he observed, "there is no Year or Season that does not bring some Calamity to us, very great numbers of Negroes especially in Trelawney St. James's Hanover & Westmoreland [have] perished for real want."[73] The number the Jamaica House of Assembly put to these black deaths gives further context to the pressures on black plantation society during the period in question. Considering the effects of the hurricanes of 1784–1786, and adding to these the effects of storms that overran the island in 1780 and 1781, the House concluded, conservatively they thought, that some 15,000 blacks perished on Jamaica owing to "famine, or of diseases contracted by scanty and unwholesome diet[s]" relating to one or another of the island's late hurricanes.[74]

As far as black plantation society is concerned, the actions and words of enslaved Jamaicans throughout the ordeals of the late eighteenth century confirm what is suggested by their very context: desperate times demanded from black society much of the same. So along the edges of Golden Grove plantation in 1792, there were groups of blacks who staved off starvation by pillaging the property's cattle, "by setting rasres &c in the Bushes."[75] That the times demanded this kind of contest between slaves and property owners is perhaps to be expected. That conditions on the island fomented similar, and in cases much more intense, struggles among slaves is even more telling. Across the island as a whole, one observer estimated that hundreds of blacks had lost their lives either defending their provision grounds from other slaves or as marauders who saw such plundering as necessary for their own continued survival.[76] Speaking to both sides of this desperation—and illustrating in the process that the disasters of the late eighteenth century had as palatable an effect on black Jamaican society as it had on white—was the response of a group of black workers when entreated to tend to their provision grounds in the fall of 1786: "what does it Signify," they asked, "Storm come and blow down every thing, or them Run away or hungry Negroes come steal every thing." Despite this example that there was a "a general Ruin covering the County" and that "people seem to give themselves up to it as a matter of Course, indeed the very Negroes seem to give themselves up," the planter who elicited the preceding response from the blacks who lived on the property he managed was optimistic that the slaves would return to their grounds soon. It was then October, very near the time when "there never was Known any general Storm."[77] It is likely that quite a few blacks on the property took their passage into the middle of October as proof of safety, and therefore returned to their grounds. For those who did, we know for certain that their efforts were wiped out in a matter of weeks by a hurricane that covered the island on October 20—a storm remarkable for just how late in the season it appeared.[78]

Disaster and subjugation formed the greatest part of the plane on which enslaved Jamaicans worked out the substance of their lives.[79] Consequently, to answer for black slave society the question Michael Craton once posed concerning the material conditions of servitude across the British Caribbean, relations between slaves on Jamaican sugar plantations in the late eighteenth-century were particularly Hobbesian.[80]

The principal forces operating on slave-worked properties on Jamaica were centripetal. Combined, the ideals and actions of Jamaican planters, the exigencies of slave labor, prevailing regimes of mortality and morbidity, and the abiding scarcity that characterized slave life all weighed on blacks in ways that constricted and compacted their existence so as to work them into societies whose center was nearly constant struggle and disaster. For black captives whose existence revolved around their owners' property, this was the nature of the world.

But not all plantation slaves lived lives so effectively circumscribed. Physically and psychically, some were seasoned to and inhabited much larger domains. Consequently, though the coarse society of Jamaican slaves described thus far was pervasive, it was not total. Beyond the local demands made of slaves, and beyond the local contexts into which they were initially settled, there was a world comprised of events and ideas that both joined and transcended the properties on which slaves worked, contributing to an aspect of black society and socialization that must be folded into the one already depicted.

The work of Julius Scott depicts and analyzes this larger world in some detail by calling attention to "The Common Wind" of news, rumor, and revolt that blew across Afro-America in the late eighteenth century—creating connections generated in part by black mobility and making the discrete lives of enslaved Americans a little less so—from the southern colonies of British North America, to slave-worked outposts along the Gulf of Mexico, to plantation settlements on the northern coasts of South America.[81] Here, focusing on how enslaved Jamaicans responded to ideas, and events relating to major currents in the system identified by Scott, I want to argue that the world beyond the properties on which enslaved Jamaicans were bound very often impinged on captives' local circumstances, and when enslaved Jamaicans engaged this larger world they engaged as well the forces that tended to render black society on the island a society defined largely by constraints of disaster, desperation, and the power of slaveowners.

The result of this engagement was not necessarily to blunt or to deflect the late eighteenth-century miseries that beset so many blacks on the island (though they could and did). The result, rather, was to establish a dialectic to the facts of life that conspired to make the world of Jamaican slaves so small. This is important, because the smallness of the worlds in which enslaved Jamaicans were originally confined both framed and intensified the hardest consequences of their society, and inasmuch as slaves pressed the boundaries of the properties onto which they were initially settled, they were seasoned, too, to circumstances beyond the basic exigencies of their enslavement and servitude. For the late eighteenth century, the results of this second seasoning are of consequence for the way scholars think about black society and culture on American plantations.

Mobility was the ingredient sine qua non of enslaved Jamaicans' second seasoning, and in late eighteenth-century Jamaica there were many opportunities for slaves to escape their owners' domains. Physically, for instance, it was quite common that black laborers moved beyond the properties of their owners. Indeed, basic realities of Jamaican slavery demanded as much. The system of local provisioning by which slaveowners required black laborers to feed themselves contributed to networks through which slaves vented at market produce not consumed locally. The practical workings of the system—best described by Sidney Mintz and Douglass Hall—encouraged and normalized significant amounts of slave mobility as slaves moved back and forth from their villages to their grounds for cultivation—whenever circumstances permitted or demanded—and from village to market, to buy and to sell, on occasional Sundays.[82] The resulting, regularized mobility could be vast. On market day at Montego Bay, for instance, it was not uncommon to find the roads toward town choked with hundreds of blacks.[83]

There were other routes off pen and plantation. Sometimes the very labor slaveowners demanded of their slaves contributed to black mobility. Slaves, for instance, carried letters and messages from one part of the island to another.[84] Further, in Jamaica, as throughout plantation America, there was a tradition of black canoe men who worked various coastal and river trades.[85] Outside of work, other circumstances allowed for slave movement. Though it was undoubtedly not common, valuable blacks—not unlike Jamaican whites—might go to sea if it was thought that such a voyage would be beneficial to their health.[86] Of course, blacks were constantly deserting (and returning to) their owner's properties. Thus sprinkled in the correspondence of plantation managers are references to the actions of "runaway people," and sometimes the details of their reclamation.[87] Lastly, and perhaps most regularly, slaves so inclined quite often traveled off their various plantations during the night for camaraderie, drink, and dance at plays where blacks from many properties milled and congregated until the small hours of the morning, even "till day light."[88]

There were also psychic and indirect mobility—the latter in the form of interactions between plantation slaves and others not similarly situated, and the former consisting of ideas and communication that reached enslaved blacks about the world beyond the particular properties to which they were bound. Both represented a kind of vicarious movement, and because Jamaica was an imperial crossroads, instances of this kind of mobility were as vast and complicated as the thousands of foreigners and new arrivals on the island at any one time. In the aftermath of the American war, the four thousand or more slaves from the former thirteen colonies who ended up in Jamaica with their loyalist owners represented just one such opportunity.[89] There were Jamaican slaves who left the island for England and returned again.[90] And there were the many foreigners on and about the island with whom Jamaican slaves interacted. The Spanish presence on and about Jamaica, for example, was pervasive. Indeed, real mobility often resulted of the vicarious mobility represented by the intercourse between enslaved Jamaicans and Spanish sojourners on the island. There was, as a result of news about Spanish policy that passed through Jamaica, a small stream of Jamaican slaves who deserted their owners and set themselves toward Cuba, where authorities were adamant in offering a kind of asylum—a different kind of servitude really—to blacks who made the island and professed a desire to practice the Catholic faith.[91]

The point I want to make now is that the varieties of actual and vicarious mobility exercised by Jamaican slaves gave them entrée into many worlds beyond the ones to which they were bound upon their arrival on the island. In the late eighteenth century, moreover, black mobility brushed enslaved Jamaicans against three particular phenomena that for much of the period in question expanded and tested black society perhaps more than any other interregional events: the imperial contests of Great Britain as they played out in Jamaica; the back and forth of the British abolitionist movement; and the massive slave revolt and revolution in the French colony of St. Domingue, combined with its reverberations across the region. Each of these, by themselves and together, impinged on black society across Jamaica in peculiar and sometimes profound ways. Enslaved Jamaicans could not help but notice these larger events, and at moments the phenomena themselves and blacks' responses to them could not but alter the dynamics of black society.

Great Britain's wars and near wars, as played out on and around Jamaica, were apparent to slaves and pushed and pulled at black society in several important ways. We have already seen how real and threatened belligerency between Great Britain and her rivals both created and reinforced the kinds of disaster that were omnipresent aspects of black society on Jamaica in the late eighteenth century. In addition, however, it is important to note that war and the threat of war could inject potentially meliorating forces and opportunities into prevailing local circumstances on Jamaican pens and plantations. During the American war, for instance, though secondary aspects of the conflict undoubtedly resulted in the deaths of thousands of Jamaican slaves, for the living the war affected the nature of slave labor and the force of white power on slave-worked properties in ways that gave enslaved Jamaicans greater control over aspects of their lives and work.

To shore up the island's defenses when invasion threatened, Jamaican slaves were quite often drafted from the plantations regardless of the work required of them by their owners. The labors to which they were put, no doubt, were intense. But there was hardly any harder work in the Americas than the labor demanded by the cultivation of sugar. Consequently, for some slaves, wartime offered a kind of respite, as they moved from being put to some of the most taxing labor imaginable to assignments that as taxing as they might be were not sugar work.[92]

The demands of war also had more direct consequences for black society by profoundly shifting power relations between slaves and their overseers.

Whites were few on Jamaican plantations and pens, but their presence and power, as shown above, could hardly be dismissed. During wartime, however—especially during martial law—the requisites that transferred, multiplied, and made real the power of interested whites on a property could fade to insignificance. War, as one attorney described it at the height of the American war, could hobble the regime required on plantations. He wrote: "The continuance of Martial Law prevents the business of Plantations from going on with the usual regularity: the Overseers and white people being often out on duty; and a very considerable number of able Negroes calld [sic] to the Fortifications in this Parish, Kingston, and Port Royal."[93]

It is commonly understood that in plantation societies such as Jamaica—where blacks so greatly outnumbered whites—that slaves labored a good deal of the time independently of white supervision. The disintegration of plantation discipline that occurred during wartime, however, reinforces the point made earlier concerning just how pervasive and effective the power of white mangers could be in organizing and affecting the lives and labor of slaves. As long as white managers were present *somewhere* on the property, the power they could command was never far from the minds of blacks. There was, therefore, really no such thing as slaves laboring independent of white supervision. This is important because the consequence of wartime conditions in the slave quarters and cane fields provides a contrast to the ordinary running of slave-worked properties, which itself suggests how slaves' coming to terms with imperial conflict could lead to quick shifts in black society. Especially during martial law, when the few whites who did oversea black labor on a property might be called away for militia service or some other duty, a defining aspect of black society was loosed. During wartime, the kind of labor regimes that ordinarily shaped slave society could very nearly fall away.

On this point, one white manager offered during the American war that "at times Estates are left without one white person and the business going on at the Mercy of the Negroes." This was owing to the fact that "the Governor being still of opinion that we shall be invaded" had ordered nearly half the whites from the interior part of the island to the towns as militia. For short spells he would allow them back to the interior to see to their other responsibilities, but even then they were largely ineffective in reestablishing discipline on their respective properties because "they are so fatigued from the inconvenience they experience that they are not capable of attending to their usual occupation."[94]

The result was that the work ordinarily ordered and accomplished on their properties slacked off. The manager who owned that the island's sugar properties were being run during the war at the discretion of their slaves informed his absentee employer that "under these circumstances the Crops will be somewhat shortened."[95] From another estate, letters from Jamaica to Britain spoke even more directly to the opportunities offered plantation slaves by war: "for the want of white peoplle on the respective propertys, Estates have suffered very much, as the business has for days and Weeks been left intirely to be executed by and intrusted to Negroes only, in course and unavoidable a great deal of Sugar and Rum has been made away with."[96]

Slaves surely availed themselves of the added space war sometimes allowed them. The question remains, however, whether there was a relationship in the minds of slaves between the course of imperial conflict and their consequences on Jamaican properties. Did slaves only dimly understand the imperial machinations going on around them, but grasp fully the opportunity imperial conflict offered? Or did slaves reason from understandings of such conflicts to the kinds of opportunities they might provide? There are probably no pure answers to these questions. Afro-Jamaicans, we could guess, undoubtedly did both. But to the degree that slaves turned over and assimilated information about the larger world and then acted accordingly—rather than simply responding to obvious local opportunities—it can be argued that the world beyond the properties onto which slaves were initially bound was indeed the site of a second seasoning with important consequences for the effects of the first.

Given the movements of whites off and on Jamaican properties during the height of the American war, and the drafting of plantation slaves for work on island fortifications at the same time, it would be remarkable indeed if Afro-Jamaicans did not calculate the seriousness of the matters then occupying the minds of their masters when responding to the conditions the war wrought on Jamaican plantations. This is only conjecture, but there is very good circumstantial evidence in the period after the American war concerning exactly this—the ways that slaves assimilated themselves to the state of affairs beyond, sometimes well beyond, the properties to which they were bound. From a particularly tense moment in 1790 when Great Britain and Spain threatened war, it is evident that enslaved Jamaicans followed imperial conflict—impending in this case—and acted with one another in ways that took world and regional events into account.

In the spring of 1790—though no state of war formally existed between the two countries—two Spanish warships captured several British vessels off the coast of North America. A flurry of activity on both sides of the Atlantic resulted as officials in London encouraged their charges in the Americas—as quietly as they could—to prepare for the worst.[97] By early summer, officials in Jamaica knew that the secretary of state, still reacting to the state of relations with Spain, had dispatched to the island a major general with orders to cooperate with the present governor in civil matters and to serve as commander in chief to military forces in the region.[98]

By June, if government had been previously successful in keeping preparations for hostilities with Spain as quiet as possible, word was now out. White Jamaicans worried out loud to correspondents in Britain about the prospect of war, and by mid-summer one would not have to be white, privy to official conversations, or even literate to appreciate the now potentially volatile state of affairs.[99] In response to the threat of war, an embargo was laid on Kingston in July of 1790 to guard against infiltration of the island's principal town. Afterward, for all who cared to notice, impending war was evident almost everywhere. On plantations that depended on Kingston shipping to send sugar and rum to Britain, slaves would not have had to have seen the embargo firsthand to know that it was on. One of the consequences of the quarantine was to back up plantation work on properties that shipped their produce through Kingston. So slaves on many parts of the island made sugar and rum, but it left Jamaica only slowly.[100]

Enslaved Jamaicans who failed to notice the impact of the embargo on the productions of their owners' properties would have come to know another of its consequences—a further tightening of their already tight access to provisions. On some plantations, managers depended on a coastal trade from Kingston to bring supplies and supplemental provisions to their properties. In the summer of 1790, even when the lieutenant governor ostensibly took off the embargo, he would not allow custom officers to clear vessels from Kingston that were carrying any kind of provisions. From the perspective of the colonial administration in Jamaica, in case of war, provisions would be as important to the island as arms, and once functionaries cleared a vessel containing foodstuffs, whatever the vessel's ostensive destination, officials really had no control over where it sailed. So to ensure that the island did not loose food to other markets, no ships containing provisions were cleared at all, though in the interior this diligence had the precise effect government was trying to avoid. Parts of the island were then "burnt up to a degree unconceivable to any person that does not see it," and so actions seen as precautionary at Kingston elsewhere looked as if they were designed to court famine.[101]

From the late summer of 1790 to the summer of the following year, Jamaica was, it was evident throughout the island, in "a Strange Situation . . . between Warr and Peace." News would arrive at moments signaling that hostilities with Spain had been averted only to be followed afterward by information or events suggesting exactly the opposite.[102] This state of affairs is important as it concerns black society on Jamaica because of longstanding intercourse between slaves on the north side of the island and the Spanish possession of Cuba. In a memorial to the king, aggrieved Jamaican planters described the intercourse as follows: "the vicinity of the Southern Shore of Cuba to the North side of Jamaica" and the fact that "the navigation between the Islands is Short, and so secure as to be performed without risque in fishing Canoes" are the primary reasons why slaves—too frequently and "without the possibility of Prevention"—fled by water from the one island to the other.[103]

During the moment of tense Anglo-Spanish relations spanning 1790–1791—and in the immediate aftermath—enslaved Jamaicans' ideas about Cuban refuge and relations between Great Britain and Spain were important factors in the shaping of black society on Jamaica, at least for some slaves. During the period in question, the significance of imperial conflict in the lives of Jamaican slaves is best captured in the initiative of a group of six blacks from the north side of Jamaica who fled to Cuba in 1789, the response of their owner to their desertion, and the larger political context to which both events contributed, and in which both transpired.

In April of 1789, six blacks fled St. Ann's Bay, Jamaica, for Cuba. Spanish officials called the runaways Juan Baptiste Hypolito, Panter, Guillermo, Juanico, Cupide, and Maria. The particular story of their flight and the larger story of which their actions became a part are quite revealing. Upon reaching Cuban waters, the runaways expressed a desire to be baptized, a rite "which they had many times before wished for but never had an opportunity till now."[104] What baptism meant to these English slaves, is not clear. Whether the runaways meant that they fled Jamaica simply to practice Catholicism, or whether they imbued baptism with more expansive meanings—as being a relative of emancipation, for example—we cannot know. What is more certain is that of the six escapees, Hypolito had been a Catholic adherent since infancy, and the estranged owner of the runaways thought his particular influence over the others was a prime catalyst in their desertion.[105]

Hypolito had been born free and worked on a privateer—apparently during the American war—until the ship was captured. He was thereafter sold into slavery, and after several transactions ended up on Jamaica as the property of one Captain Greenland, passing upon the captain's death to his widow. He described himself and was referred to in Jamaica as a Frenchmen or French negro—Jean Baptiste Hypolite—and when questioned in Cuba was "Sworn according to the Rites of the Romish Church" (whereas his coconspirators were simply given oaths "in the manner that is administered to those who are not Christians").[106]

Without question, Hypolite was very well seasoned to the world beyond the particular site of his Jamaican servitude. More important to the point pursued here, however, is the fact that enslaved Jamaicans did not have to possess résumés similar to Hypolite in order to be likewise assimilated to the exigencies (and opportunities) of imperial politics as they played out off Jamaica. This is a point partly proved by the five English slaves who joined the French negro in his escape to Cuba. It is further, and even more clearly, indicated by what transpired in Jamaica in the aftermath of Hypolite, Panter, Guillermo, Juanico, Cupide, and Maria's flight from St. Ann's. The man who held title to the six runaways doggedly pursued them to Cuba, unsuccessfully pressing the matter of their return with the Spanish governor. When he failed there, he continued to pursue the matter through diplomatic channels in Great Britain itself, resulting in the matter being discussed, ultimately, at the Spanish court.

Apparently, by the time the fate of the six slaves had been determined, the details of their flight had become, at least on the north side of Jamaica, something of a cause célèbre. When the British secretary of state informed Jamaica's lieutenant governor that the matter had been resolved in general if not specifically, he suggested that even British ministers—probably because of their interactions with Caribbean governors, West Indian agents, and absentee sugar planters—knew something of the potential expansiveness of slave discourse on Jamaica. Spanish officials on the continent agreed to no longer enforce, though not rescind, the forty-year-old decree whereby Cuban governors had justified offering refuge to English slaves who sought baptism. Coming to this arrangement had taken many months, and in sending word to officials in Jamaica, the governor tellingly assumed that word had already reached Jamaican slaves and would affect their ideas about Cuban refuge accordingly. "No formal communication has yet been made by the Court of Spain of the Repeal of the Edict [by] which protection has been hitherto afforded in the Spanish Colonies to fugitive Slaves; but as the measure appears now to be generally known among the Slaves, it will I have no doubt, have the good effect of checking their desertion in the future."[107]

Proof of the dedication with which enslaved Jamaicans followed and assimilated themselves to the turns of imperial conflict is illustrated even more decidedly by events in the aftermath of the Anglo-Spanish brinkmanship of 1790–1791. In the winter of 1791, for instance, come the conflagration at St. Domingue, enslaved Jamaicans hearkened back to the state of affairs a few months previous when reflecting on the present situation on the French island and considering the consequences of that rebellion for Jamaica. Consequently, not long after the revolt at St. Domingue, slaves on the Orchard estate in Hanover conferenced about the future turn of events, saying "that they expected the Spaniards were to assist them in getting soon their Freedom." Indeed, at least some thought Spanish assistance was imminent. A little girl who half-listened as blacks at Orchard discussed the matter later reported to her owner that although "She had not heard the time" at which Spanish forces could be expected, she understood that they were already "then in the Pass coming."[108]

Overall, the response of Afro-Jamaicans to the rebellion in the French colony further illustrates how regional events insinuated themselves into black society on Jamaica. Apparently, as soon anyone on Jamaica knew of the goings-on at St. Domingue, the island's slaves did, and not at all on a selective level. By September of 1791—but weeks after the rebellion got under way—blacks on the island had incorporated news about the revolt into popular songs.[109] Further, as months and years passed and the revolt on the French colony turned into a war, ever more palpable examples of and information about the troubles in St. Domingue made themselves plain in Jamaica. In the early months of fighting on the French colony, among white Jamaicans' most desperate fears was that blacks from St. Domingue, whether French loyalist or not, would make their way to the island and infect enslaved Jamaicans with the lessons of their presence. Thus rumors abounded in the early months of the revolt—some of them reaching London—that blacks from St. Domingue had landed on Jamaica.[110]

As the months and years rolled on, this fear became an undeniable reality as refugee planters, slaves, and people of color from St. Domingue became obvious throughout Jamaica. When French planters began to flee the destruction at St. Domingue, Jamaica was a prime destination. Kingston and environs became the refuge of once well to do French slaveowners, and they were anything but inconspicuous about the town. There was something of a steady stream of displaced Frenchmen calling on the governor's house in Spanishtown, and even the interior parts of the country were no strangers to the refugees.[111] Their coming and going at some estates apparently had neighbors on other properties on the lookout to ensure that the visitors kept their distance.[112] On properties in the interior where French refugees frequently called, their visits could generate charges of conspiracy or treason against their Jamaican hosts.[113] By the spring of 1795, there were, according to official counts, more than two hundred families on Jamaica who were formerly of St. Domingue. Together these families probably amounted to more than six hundred people.[114] Simon Taylor complained of them, "The People that had Properties in Hispaniola are not very fond of going [back to St. Domingue], but rather to sculk here, & lett us fight for them."[115]

Whether slaves and free people of color were included in the official counts presented above, I do not know, but that both sets of people were indeed on the island is an absolute certainty. When making for Jamaica, refugee French planters brought what slaves they could, sparking in the process grave concern at their asylum about how to ensure that "there is no communication between the french servants, & the english slaves."[116] But it is also very likely that there were slaves from St. Domingue who landed on Jamaica as part of the island's contraband regional slave trade and were therefore inserted into various Jamaican slave communities straightway and far from the watchful eye of officials whose duty it was to prevent such things. Against these newcomers there was very little that could be done.[117] As far as free people of color from the affected areas were concerned, two declarations from 1791—one meant to expel from Jamaica free people of color from St. Domingue already presently on the island and another intended to make it very difficult for additional ones to land—suggests there were not only slaves and planters from the French colony on Jamaica but also a few of the class of people whom slaveowners from other parts of the Caribbean most despised as the prime fire starters of the present chaos on one half of Hispaniola.[118]

Jamaican slaveowners and their allies understood quite clearly that the rebellion at St. Domingue was "a very bad example to all the Islands in their Neighbourhood." Consequently, they fretted over French refugees, slaves, and others from St. Domingue because their conspicuousness posed a spate of problems, ranging from quite practical concerns about potential espionage and subversion to worries relating to the lessons Jamaican slaves might take from the presence of defeated French planters or rouge French blacks. This latter worry about the inspiration that French refugees and slaves might offer their Jamaican counterparts was especially chilling, as far as the island's slaveowners were concerned, in light of the running battle the island's planters had fought for at least three years against the efforts of British abolitionists.

From the time the first petitions to Parliament against the slave trade began in the winter of 1787 and news of the petition campaign first reached Jamaica in the spring of 1788, the island's slaveowners struggled to cordon off enslaved workers from the idea that black servitude and their masters' way of life was under attack at home.[119] They failed miserably. Whenever printed reports detailing debates and examinations in Parliament over the trade arrived in Jamaica, for instance, the news invariably made it to the ears of the island's slaves.[120] It was, Jamaican slaveowners admitted, simply impossible to insulate blacks from such news, and over the long run the effects of slaves' engagement with British abolitionism was the provision of aid and comfort to any among them who could imagine a black society unencumbered, in general, by the power of white slaveowners.

Before the advent of the abolition movement, complained Jamaican planters, the rebelliousness exhibited by the island's slaves stemmed mostly from "accidental and local Causes"; was to be expected, in the main, from newly arrived Africans; and was aimed, by and large, at simply separating slaves from the power of their individual owners. Under the circumstances encouraged by British abolitionism, however, slave-fomented disturbances gained the potential support of "general pervading Opinions." The consequences of the synergy between black aspiration and Atlantic-wide ideas of abolitionism could be profound. Indeed, Jamaican slaveowners thought the difference engendered in the direction and purpose of slave recalcitrance a stark one: "That the Object in former Times was simply the persons of the Whites, but in the present the total destruction of both their property & persons: that the first was of small national Import and to be easily repaired, but that one at present would be of the very first consequence as a National Object since if attended with the possible Success it may not only greatly embarrass Great Britain but may overturn all present Systems."[121]

Enslaved Jamaicans spent significant portions of their daily lives in two realms whose scope and circumstances differed markedly one from the other: the relatively small world of the sugar plantation or cattle pen, and a more expansive world of Atlantic and regional ideas and politics. It is not necessary to subscribe to the argument that slaves' engagement with regional and transatlantic movements transformed fundamental aspects of black society in order to see this point. It appears that one domain offered some melioration to the worst consequences of the other, and inasmuch as enslaved Jamaicans engaged issues, ideas, and people beyond the sites of their particular enslavement, they practiced a kind of self-defense.

It appears this way, and this indeed might have very often been the case, but the reasonableness of the argument, on its face, is probably a result of considering the matter in isolation when Afro-Jamaicans most certainly did not and could not live their lives in this way. Jamaican plantations were not all peopled with worldly, multi-lingual, well-informed captives, nor were they filled with hundreds completely given over to both the harsh circumstances of their servitude and the power and paternalism of their masters. Most slaves, undoubtedly, not only lived lives in between these

two extremes, but lived also, as lives are, in flux. For Jamaica in the late
eighteenth century, there is a small body of material that illuminates this
point: reports from committees of secrecy and safety established in the
wake of the revolt at St. Domingue and in anticipation of the first Christmas following the rebellion.

It was thought on Jamaica that if there was to be an uprising on the island of the sort then under way in St. Domingue, it was most likely to occur
at the end of the year. The committees of secrecy and safety established
in several of the island's northern parishes were designed to discover and
check any such intrigue. In retrospect, but perhaps only so, the sedition,
schemes, and conspiracies the committees uncovered ultimately led to
very little. A particular case from the reports generated by the committees,
however, offers a glimpse into the ways that blacks, in their daily lives,
at once negotiated exigencies relating to both worlds in which Jamaican
slaves often found themselves—pointing, in the end, to a conclusion that
illustrates the significance, and potential necessity, of examining the lives
of American slaves in relation to both local and regional contexts.

For a moment in the heady, paranoiac days of fall 1791—according to
one of the most developed cases from the island's committees of secrecy
and safety—the peace of Jamaica appeared to turn on what two enslaved
Africans said or did not say about a revolt then broiling in St. Domingue
and the prospect of a similar conflagration erupting on their own island.[122]
Duncan and Billy, the Africans in question, had traveled from their quarters near Anchovy Bottom estate to buy provisions from the property of a
carpenter named Dent. Dent not being home when they arrived, the two
entered into small talk with three other slaves about mutual acquaintances:
Had Duncan and Billy, asked the others, seen Tom and Quo? They were
runaway for some time now. Duncan replied that he had not seen his
countrymen—apparently Duncan and the runaways of whom he spoke
had arrived in Jamaica on ships from the Gold Coast—but he expected
that they would make themselves plain quite soon. There was to be a rise
at Christmas, a rebellion of the slaves. No doubt, they would "tand in the
Ring with dem cutlass in dem hand." For their part, Duncan and Billy
continued in boast, they too would gladly "lick off Boccara head" when
the time came.

This sedition, uttered too loudly to remain a confidence, pricked the
ears of Dent's housekeeper, who came to investigate. "Cui Miss Diana da"
started Duncan, but the woman was already sure of what she heard. Miss
Diana—a woman of color no doubt, perhaps previously a slave, and in
any case known to the white people of the island, more formally, as Jenny

Reid—upbraided the men for their apparent treason and promised to inform Mr. Dent when he returned. At this threat, Duncan, swore that he would not do any harm to his *own* master come the reckoning (but backed off not at all concerning his intentions for other whites on the island). Billy recanted altogether. "When the Negroe rise," he pleaded with Miss Diana, "me will tand with Boccara."

Despite these retractions, Miss Diana remained true to her word and informed Dent of the cabal that gathered while he was away. The news shocked the carpenter, but he had good reason to pause before sounding an alarm. Astounded at the vividness of his housekeeper's account, the bold talk of the slaves, and the prospect that there was a plan abreast to slaughter the island's whites, the carpenter was nonetheless reticent to inform on Duncan and Billy directly. He was anxious about the slaves' connections and worried over the prospect of insulting their master should his charge prove overblown. So Dent only slowly made up his mind to contact Duncan and Billy's owner, and then did so only through an intermediary.

As Dent had feared, Duncan and Billy's owner dismissed the charges against his slaves as ignorant exuberance, promised to punish them accordingly, and then simply carried on as usual (though perhaps not without some prejudice against the carpenter whose charge had just endangered his property). Unsatisfied, Dent then took his indictment public, making a report to the parish Committee of Secrecy and Safety (parish bodies bolstered in the wake of the slave revolt at St. Domingue to ensure that similar troubles did not erupt in Jamaica). The committee organized examinations to get to the bottom of the matter, and at the hearings Duncan and Billy eventually confirmed and added to the details originally brought forward by Jenny Reid and Dent.

There was nothing sacred about the Christmas date, confessed Duncan. The revolt was not planned for the holidays per se—when the island's slaves were traditionally excused from labor and the time of year Jamaican whites always suspected some mischief. Rather, the conspirators had settled on Christmas as one of several dates when the island's ports and the naval station were thinned because of the fleet's having sailed. Rising at a moment of relative isolation, they reasoned, would be key. As to the rationale behind the coming slaughter, the obvious was left unsaid (though the ordinary instigations no doubt applied). Rather, to the horror of the Committee of Secrecy and Safety, when members pressed Duncan as to the exigencies behind the plot, he intoned succinctly, "to be sure Massa when one Country fight against another Country every body stand for him own." Thus Duncan framed his participation in the plot using language that could be taken to refer to the imperial politics of the Caribbean, the recent slave revolt in St. Domingue, and the cultural politics of Jamaica itself, where social and racial divisions were quite often addressed in a kind of nationalist cant. These were very wide terms, and for the committee their breadth was part of what made Duncan's disclosures so troubling.

The intrigue involving Duncan, Billy, Ms. Diana, and others illustrates how Jamaican slaves negotiated at once the local and regional circumstances comprising their world. Exigencies relating to the small worlds of the island's plantations and pens remain obvious, even though the officers of the committees of secrecy and safety were most interested in uncovering how Afro-Jamaicans acted in relation to regional and transatlantic affairs. Duncan and Billy's trip to Anchovy Bottom, for instance, where they started bold talk about the forthcoming slaughter of the island's whites and spoke even more boldly about their place in the coming rebellion, all took place in the context of the two Africans' search for provisions. In this case, the exact relationship between their hunger and their intentions is not clear, but it probably fanned the flames of both their rhetoric and their designs. This was certainly the case with other Jamaicans suspected of conspiracy in the aftermath of the revolt at St. Domingue. At Lawrence's Pen at Long Bay (like Anchovy Bottom, also in St. James), the head penkeeper, named Yoru, and a slave from off the property called Cuffee came under suspicion for a conversation that began with Yoru declaiming, "Thank God I and all of us will soon [be] done with this damned Famishing," to which Cuffee replied, "Not you fret for is it any more than two weeks, this every damned Sould of them shall go."

Also obvious in Duncan and Billy's apparent plotting, oddly enough, is the power and influence of their owner. Up to a point, this is not at all surprising. Given the seriousness of Duncan and Billy's designs and the range of their owners' power, Billy's quick retraction at Ms. Diana's threat to inform on their cabal is entirely to be expected. More interesting still, however, is Duncan's response to the same threat, because it suggests how slaves could accommodate a hatred for their servitude, designs on the lives of the island's whites, and still show themselves within the realm of their owners' paternalism. It was a line similarly walked by a group of blacks at Brampton Bryan estate, investigated by a committee in St. Ann, who "said they were ill treated by their overseer Mr. Sutton and unless their owner returned and did them Justice they would fly to the woods and join Brutus [a runaway and alleged conspirator]—that they would rise against the Whites."[123]

Violence, privation, alienation, despair, and the power of slave traders and owners (in Africa and the Americas alike) all powerfully shaped the migrant experience at both the greatest source and the most frequent destination of captives forced across the British Atlantic world. The movements of black migrants under such conditions changed them. The social relations migrants cobbled together and the societies they built in motion always reflected the particular pressures of their captivity. Ironically, these were the same pressures—violence, privation, alienation, despair, and the power of slave traders and owners—that shaped too the migration of free blacks across the British Atlantic.

PART II
VOYAGERS

FIVE days after the commissary—a man called Gustavus Vassa—handed in the last of the embarkation lists, the *Atlantic*, the *Belisarius*, and the *Vernon* got under way. The small convoy was charged with ferrying some four hundred black Londoners, Vassa among them, from the English capital to Sierra Leone, where the migrants were determined to found a free colony in western Africa. It was February 1787, the very height of the British slave trade.[1]

Shortly after getting under way, the transports' escort, the HMS *Nautilus*, struck a sandbar. Already, more than one hundred days had passed since the first colonists boarded the ships. While the transports were loading, the migrants had waited at Gravesend, outside London. After the transports dropped down the Thames to Spithead at Portsmouth, the ships lingered again. So with the *Nautilus*'s early mishap, it must have looked to the departing settlers as if their waiting was about to begin all over. Captain Thompson, however, was able to "wore off without any damage" and the ships subsequently made good time from Spithead into the English Channel. Three days into the voyage the "Fresh breezes" that had facilitated the initial journey gave way to more unruly winds, which whipped up strong seas. Once again the whole voyage was in jeopardy, and all still within sight of England. The gales and choppy waters proved too much for the *Vernon* and "carried away her fore topmast." Knowing that he could not weather the storm, Thompson ordered the three transports to fall in behind him and directed them to make for the safety of Plymouth Sound.[2]

So five days after leaving Spithead for the channel, the expedition to Sierra Leone came to an inauspicious halt. Having been separated from the others and unable to make it to Plymouth Sound, the *Nautilus* and *Vernon* anchored at Torbay to make repairs, while the *Atlantic* and *Belisarius* did the same at Plymouth. Not until March 18 were the ships at Torbay fit to join the others at Plymouth, and when they did, the expedition all but unraveled. Tensions that had long been simmering between the expedition's conductor and its commissary—Joseph Irwin and Vassa, respectively—came to a full boil, and the migrants themselves approached a state of a rebellion. In the tumult that followed, Vassa was dismissed.[3]

The ships repaired and the punctilious Vassa expelled, the convoy set sails for Sierra Leone yet again on April 9, 1787. Considering the many weeks they were aboard the transports to cover only the distance between London and Plymouth, the settlers spent relatively little time at open sea: It took only thirty-one days to sail from Plymouth Sound to the Sierra Leone River. Still, if there were those on board the transports who suspected that the troubles they faced when first leaving England were a portent of things to come, they would not have been comforted by circumstances at Sierra Leone after the ships anchored and moored on May 10, 1787. With nightfall and the convoy finally settled into the river, "At 11 PM came on a tornado from the SE with heavy rains, Thunder, & lightening."[4] Portent or not, within thirty months of their landing most of the four hundred settlers were dead, debilitated, or had deserted.

When Lydia Jackson stumbled into Halifax, Nova Scotia, after a daring flight from an adjacent county, she hoped for refuge, finally, from disaster. Deserted and left destitute by her husband at Manchester, on Nova Scotia's eastern edge, some three or four years earlier, Jackson had indentured herself to a white settler as a servant to his wife. As fearful for her freedom as she was desperate, she agreed to a contract of only one year—long enough to allow her to get her bearings and to plan how to find her feet, short enough so as not to jeopardize her liberty too recklessly. Soon after she placed her mark on the indenture, however, her new master informed her that she was to serve out her term with a physician in Lunenburg, on the western half of the peninsula. On her arrival there, she learned "to her great astonishment, that she had been articled out" not for one year but for thirty-one years.[5]

Compounding this ruse, the Lunenburg man and his wife were cruel employers. For missteps real and perceived, the doctor beat his new servant unmercifully, with his wife "by no means backward to lend him her assistance on these occasions." The abuse led Jackson to protest to a local attorney, who filed a complaint against her overbearing master. The doctor used his influence with the court to quash the charge and in response promised to sell his too bold servant to the West Indies as a slave. In the meantime he banished Jackson from his home, sending her to his farm some three miles out of the town limits, where he gave "authority and sanction to his servants, to beat and punish her as they thought fit."[6]

From the farm, Jackson plotted and then executed the escape she was unable to effect legally while at the doctor's town house. She fled through the woods surrounding the country estate and made her way to Halifax, probably by schooner, where she filed another complaint against her master in the form of a memorial to the colony's governor and an application to the chief justice. While waiting in Halifax for replies that never came, she noticed the city crowded with blacks and abuzz with their intentions to quit Nova Scotia altogether. By the hundreds they filed into the city, all with complaints of their own, each determined to settle in west Africa under the auspices of a recently capitalized London firm and a trustworthy-enough agent lately arrived in the colony to arrange the affair. The settlers would replenish a colony planted by black Londoners some year previous. This was a way out, Jackson reasoned. So nearly eight years after first falling on hard times and after some three years of being in the power of a sadistic physician, she decided to start over and join the exodus then forming. This was on the cusp of winter in 1791.[7]

Ultimately, the vagaries of her case prevented Lydia Jackson from departing Nova Scotia. But she is in many ways representative of twelve hundred or so of the province's black residents—perhaps one-third of the colony's total black population—who did take up the offer made by the London-based Sierra Leone Company. Jackson's story and the stories of her cohort offer another point of departure for studying the nature and consequence of the Atlantic crossing.[8]

Like Africans from the Biafran interior sacrificed to the slave trade and the adventurers from London who cast their lots for Sierra Leone in 1786–1787, black emigrants from Nova Scotia to west Africa did not begin their journey from a standing start. Lydia Jackson and other potential Nova Scotian migrants were people in motion before they became a movement of peoples. In this case, Nova Scotia's black migrants for Sierra Leone were originally part of the same post-war emigration from the former thirteen colonies whose ranks swelled the black population of London; only at war's end this part of that larger black decampment settled in small communities across a rugged North American peninsula rather than in the hemisphere's largest metropole. The nature of their initial migration to British Nova Scotia and their intervening years in an unforgiving rural context helped to produce, by 1791, a group of potential migrants who differed significantly in temperament, resources, and opportunity from the

London adventurers who preceded them and the enslaved Africans whose movements we have tracked thus far. These distinctions initiated in Nova Scotia a kind of Atlantic crossing—a black exodus; a mass, centralized, communal migration—materially different from the slave trade from the Biafran interior and divergent as well from the adventure to Sierra Leone undertaken by black Londoners only a few years before.[9]

Taken together, though, these movements of people to Sierra Leone represent a black antithesis to the massive forced emigration from the Bight of Biafra and the enormous enslaved immigration to and settlement on British Jamaica. Examining the movements not only makes clear their differences—from each other as well as from the British empire's larger forced migrations—but it also calls attention to some of the underlying similarities between all kinds of transoceanic black British migration in the late eighteenth century. For free black voyagers their Atlantic crossing was also a gauntlet, and the social consequences of their migrations were extraordinary.

FIVE

SOCIAL MOVEMENT AND IMAGINING
FREEDOM IN THE BRITISH CAPITAL

Why did hundreds of blacks depart London to hack out a British colony in Sierra Leone? An item in the *Public Advertiser* during the first month of 1786 starts toward an answer. The notice in question asked the city's well-heeled merchants and gentry to focus their attention on the plight of "Asiatic Blacks"—i.e., South Asian sailors—who, dismissed from their ships, were stranded in London with little or no means of support. The missive encouraged the formation of a public subscription to attend to the needs of these mariners. Within two weeks of its establishment, the "Committee of Gentlemen" organized to give aid and comfort to London's stranded lascars realized that the issue they set out to address was broader and more complicated than they originally envisioned. In one of their early canvasses, the committee discovered only thirty-five lascars in need of their benevolence but encountered more than one hundred black sailors of African or American origins, all in dire need. Thus the philanthropists learned that the condition of London's East Indian sailors was the smaller part of a more general predicament faced by nonwhite seamen throughout the metropolis.[1]

Blacks—Asian, African, and American—were no strangers to the alleys and street corners of eighteenth-century London; nor were they uncommon in the city's mansions or around its fashionable meeting places. Britons' long participation in the Atlantic slave trade, their extensive planting interests in the Americas, and the island nation's wide-ranging imperial concerns ensured that the capital captured a noticeable population of black servants, slaves, sailors, paupers, and performers. Social historians and demographers have only just begun to quantify the population of black London, but recent surveys suggest that as many as seven thousand blacks may have lived in the capital during the latter part of the eighteenth century, that black London was overwhelmingly male (perhaps as high as 80 percent), and that the vast majority of black Londoners (perhaps 90 percent) were immigrants, not long arrived from someplace else.[2]

For the immediate benefit of the destitute among the city's blacks, the newly renamed "Committee for the Relief of the Black Poor" dispensed loaves of bread, meals of broth, blankets and bedding, shoes and stockings.

A hospital was set up in Warren Street on the edge of Bloomsbury, and for some of the impoverished, the gentlemen of the committee provided sea passage home.[3] Before long, moreover, the committee turned its attention from providing for the immediate physical needs of their beneficiaries to striking out at the very heart of the problem of black poverty in London. For the committee, the heart of the problem was this: a majority of the capital's destitute blacks landed in London with few prospects from someplace else.

To the members of the committee, the solution to the capital's present humanitarian problem seemed obvious. It was explicit in the appeals a number of blacks made themselves to the committee—that they be returned to their former homes in the Americas. Soon then, the larger object of the committee became to transport London's blacks "to such places as may put them in a condition of getting their bread in freedom and comfort."[4] The committee successfully enlisted the British Treasury to help underwrite this mission, and so what began as a winter relief effort turned slowly into an emigration scheme.[5] This slow turning allows a good view of the ways in which the movements preceding a transatlantic voyage could be decisive. In the case of black Londoners bound for Sierra Leone, two particular types of movement were critical in articulating and shaping key aspects of their society: the migrations that had brought them to London in the first place, and, second, the very considerable social movement and debate surrounding their decisions to quit London for western Africa.

From January to April, the notion to settle London's blacks in Nova Scotia remained only that. Over these four months, newspaper accounts concerning the actions of the Committee for the Relief of the Black Poor mentioned little in the way of actual emigration planning. Moreover, it appears that the committee did not begin sending its minutes to the Treasury Office until May 1786, indicating that the government took little formal interest in the emigration portion of the overall relief effort until that time.[6] In the beginning, then, black Londoners desiring the committee's assistance did not have to consider any substantial plan for their resettlement. A physician and naturalist named Henry Smeathman soon altered this state of affairs.

Dr. Smeathman lived and worked at Sierra Leone and on the Banana Islands for almost four years during the early 1770s, and he had sought support for a plan to establish a colony in western Africa ever since his return. For years his efforts were famously unsuccessful, but in the winter of 1786 he rightfully interpreted the "problem of the black poor" as an opportunity for his ideas on African colonization. Smeathman introduced himself to the committee in February 1786; by March he provided them with a general outline for a settlement at Sierra Leone; and by May he drew up, for the committee's approval and for the approval of the Treasury, a detailed blueprint for transporting the black poor from London to Sierra Leone and the establishment thereby of a British colony in western Africa.[7] The committee was persuaded. Shortly thereafter members ordered that a handbill be printed "to inform the Blacks of the Intentions of providing for them."[8] So from May 1786, monetary and in-kind assistance to London's poor blacks from the committee and the government came attached to a specific contingency: emigration to Sierra Leone.

There is evidence that London's blacks may have first heard of the proposal for Sierra Leone from Smeathman himself. From the moment the committee began offering in-kind and monetary assistance to London's blacks, quite a congress gathered weekly at each of three disbursement centers: the White Raven in Mile End on the capital's eastern edge, the Yorkshire Stingo in Marylebone, and at the committee's hospital in Warren Street.[9] Smeathman, it appears, in addition to working to convince the committee of his idea, took advantage of the crowds drawn to the Yorkshire Stingo and the White Raven to make his case among the potential emigrants themselves. No record survives of the arguments he marshaled for emigration in the East End, in Marylebone, and to those who undoubtedly approached him in the street. But a version of the doctor's plan that was printed for the benefit of London's blacks sometime in the spring of 1786 gives a good sense of the case made for emigration during the previous winter.[10]

Apparently, Smeathman began his pitch by drawing a stark contrast between black Londoners' present circumstances and the situation that awaited them in Africa. At Sierra Leone, émigrés would be granted as much land as they could cultivate, and when future circumstances warranted additional acreage it would be provided. The land itself, with only moderate labor, could be easily transformed into something of an Eden. All the cash crops of the Americas—rice, indigo, cotton, and tobacco—could be raised there with relative ease, and other produce—fruits and spices especially— grew in the wild, needing only to be gathered. The place was congenial not only to planting, but to hunting, fishing, and the raising of small livestock. Deer, fowl, hogs, goats, sheep, and fish were prolific at Sierra Leone in ways that British husbandmen, fishermen, and hunters could scarcely imagine. Land so rich required only the slightest labor: set a man down at Sierra Leone with an ax, a hoe, and a knife, and he could very soon make himself quite a comfortable life.[11]

To black Londoners at the Warren Street hospital, or to those lining up for broth, bread, and six pence on Lisson Green and at Mile End,

Smeathman's overtures must have provoked polite interest, at the very least. "Locked up" in the metropolis, hundreds of black Londoners were starving, sick, harassed, and cold. On the streets, they were harried by parish officers who disciplined them as vagrants. The poorest among them pawned their shirts for spare change. Others struggled continuously with disease, injury, exposure, and hunger.[12] To Londoners living under such hardship, Smeathman's Sierra Leone must have sounded a bit like paradise. Yet the doctor's obviously idyll descriptions piqued more than interest; his remarks initiated heated debate concerning the doctor's intentions and the fundamental merits of his proposal.

Black Londoners did not accept Smeathman and the committee's proposal whole. The journeys that slaves, runaways, refugees, and free people made to the capital and the lives that they lived there ensured a preoccupation with the preservation and expansion of liberties they made en route to London and liberties they made within the city. So even enslaved blacks from Great Britain's Caribbean colonies who were slaves in the city would have weighed carefully the differences between being a slave in London and free in Guinea. Afro-American slaves were notorious for executing in England prerogatives long harbored but kept in check in the slave societies of the Caribbean. Complained one Londoner of the slaves who traveled to the capital from the Americas, "they cease to consider themselves as slaves in this free country, nor will they put up with an inequality of treatment. . . . It is therefore highly impolitic to introduce them as servants here, where that rigour and severity is impracticable which is absolutely necessary to make them useful." When Nanny, Polly, and Jemmy departed with their owner from Jamaica to England in 1786, the attorney who oversaw their former plantation feared that they would undergo just this kind of transformation. Thus he lobbied for their return before Britain ruined them for slavery. It would not necessarily have occurred to such slaves that being free men and women in western Africa, in daily view of passing slave ships, was to be absolutely preferred to living as slaves in London so near to a kind of liberty unknown to them in the Americas.[13]

Former slaves who gained their liberty en route to London or within London, and who struggled daily in the metropolis to preserve it, had even greater reason to approach Smeathman's plan with a critical eye. Such Londoners had made great sacrifices and followed long paths to their present status. James Somerset was one such Londoner, and before his life became a subject of deliberation in Great Britain's highest courts, what little we know about him exemplifies the kind of route many of London's blacks took to the capital and their eventual liberty. Before coming to England, Somerset belonged to a Scottish civil servant named Charles Stewart in Boston. In 1769 Stewart left Massachusetts for London, taking Somerset with him. After some two years in the city, and for reasons that have gone unrecorded, Somerset absconded. Numerous slaves before him transformed the anonymity of London's streets into a successful course to freedom. Somerset, to his misfortune, however, was quickly apprehended by agents of his estranged master, imprisoned upon a ship then in the Thames, and bound over for Jamaica. Before the ship's master could get under way, Somerset's case was taken up by a set of English abolitionists hoping to prove chattel slavery illegal in Great Britain.[14]

After no small struggle, Somerset achieved the right to remain in London. This was, granted, only a kind of liberty. But it was not slavery; it was hard fought, and blacks who inherited because of Somerset the right to run away when on English soil would have been fools to gamble it indiscriminately. Indeed, because slaveowners who lost their human property in London often did not respect the law that gave blacks the right not to be detained by their ostensive masters, living in the capital as fugitives could only make such blacks more vigilant about their freedom. No doubt, all of black London knew stories—such as the one Olaudah Equiano told about John Amis—of erstwhile slaves stalked in London by their former masters and reenslaved, in spite of English law and all of their precautions.[15]

The most conspicuous of the capital's late eighteenth-century black residents were fugitives and evacuees from Great Britain's war in America. These new Londoners—including many who served with the British army and navy, who gained their freedom through such service, and who later found their way to the seat of Britain's empire—would too have been extremely jealous of the difference between their former status and their present one.[16] The routes that some of these immigrants took to London, by indicating the price they paid for their current liberty, suggests as much. Benjamin Whitcuff, for instance, was born into a free black farming family on Long Island. When the war began Whitcuff's father joined the rebels. Whitcuff himself remained loyal and about two years into the war joined British troops at Staten Island. He claimed to have worked as a spy for the forces of British commander Henry Clinton, an occupation that earned him a death sentence in New Jersey and probably encouraged his subsequent immigration to England's first city.[17]

Samuel Burke and John Twine took even more circuitous routes to the capital. Burke was free-born in Charleston, South Carolina. During the war he served with British forces on the Mississippi and "married a Dutch Mulatto Woman at New York" with whom he kept a house, presumably before and during the British evacuation. Further, Burke swore he was christened in Ireland (whether before the war or during his journey to London he did not say). Twine's journey to the capital was just as complicated. He lived as a free man in Petersburg, Virginia, when "the troubles broke out" and served as a teamster for the Americans. After about a year in the service of the rebels, Twine crossed over to the British side, where among other duties he acted as a personal servant to a British officer.[18]

How would blacks who lived in and had come to London under such circumstances respond to proposals to emigrate? Some of the reservations voiced by black Londoners were reported by contemporaries. Many more, however, are obvious from the different emphases apparent in two versions of Smeathman's colonization plan: one penned in 1783 and directed toward a Quaker abolitionist and the previously cited proposal printed in May 1786 and "intended," according to the title page, "more particularly for the service and happy establishment of Blacks and People of Colour."[19] When Smeathman's two proposals are read in conjunction with the earliest surviving minutes of the Committee for the Relief of the Black Poor, the voices of London's blacks are evident: Right off, some disputed Smeathman's description of the landscape in that part of western Africa; others wondered out loud about the intelligence of settling a colony of blacks at a river known to be a center of French and British slaving and where the disposition of the natives was unknown; yet others questioned whether the emigration plan was a thinly disguised attempt at transportation and enslavement.

Granville Sharp recalled that very soon after Smeathman made his proposal known among London's blacks, groups of them—"sometimes they came in large bodies together"—would gather at his door to discuss the merits of the plan. Apparently, there was talk that the Sierra Leone Smeathman painted could hardly coincide with the country as it really existed. "Upon inquiring among themselves," the skeptics and Sharp found several among them who worked or lived near Sierra Leone previously and who confirmed that "there was much fine wood-land unoccupied in that part of the coast."[20]

Potential voyagers were even more concerned about the effect of emigration on the state of their liberty. Likely migrants must have peppered Smeathman with numerous questions on this point, for one of the most striking differences between the emigration plan the doctor wrote in 1783 and the one printed in 1786 was the attention paid in the latter to the status of the settlers. In the version of the Sierra Leone plan that Smeathman wrote in 1783, the author was ambiguous about the legality of slavery at the proposed settlement. Although the 1783 proposal was addressed to an ardent abolitionist, Smeathman admitted that slavery would not *necessarily* be prohibited. Further, in the 1783 document he was not afraid to acknowledge that his circle of friends included at least one British merchant engaged in the African slave trade.[21]

In the 1786 version of the proposal, Smeathman allowed no such ambiguities. Four times in the twenty-four-page *Plan*, the doctor stressed that the settlement at Sierra Leone was to be founded strictly upon the surest principles of liberty. The cover of the pamphlet declared that emigrants were "to be shipped as freemen." Later, concerning land tenure, the booklet pledged that settlers would hold their tillage "in security and freedom." And in case potential migrants suspected that the *Plan*'s references to laborers and hirelings hid something more sinister, the author laid out stringent guidelines on the nature of paid labor at Sierra Leone: "Only eight hours of fair labour each day will be required, in Summer or Winter; and on Saturday's [sic] only six hours. Sunday, being the Sabbath, will, as among all christian nations be set apart as a day of rest, instruction, and devotion."

Toward the end of the *Plan*, Smeathman guaranteed the emigrants' liberty with a phrase that would have resounded with great meaning among London's former slaves and veterans of the recent war in America: "An opportunity so advantageous may perhaps never be offered to them again; for they and their posterity may enjoy perfect freedom."[22]

In the version of the Sierra Leone proposal that Smeathman wrote in 1783, the doctor made little mention of his ideas concerning what was to be the nature of settler society. In the *Plan*, the matter was given pride of place, and each point the doctor made in this regard sheds light on a question asked or a preference expressed by London's blacks. As for the Africans already living at Sierra Leone, Smeathman dismissed as myth and stereotype prevailing notions about their temperament and customs. "The Africans in the neighbourhood of Sierra Leonea," Smeathman chided, "are sagacious and political, much beyond what is vulgarly imagined." Indeed, he argued, "the peaceable temper of the natives" was one of the reasons the proposed settlement was destined to succeed.[23]

To the charge that western Africa was an unhealthy place for settlement, a notion that the many sailors among London's blacks would have held quite firmly, Smeathman answered with the kind of mind-numbing detail required when addressing experts. "The cause why it has been so fatal to many white people," said Smeathman of residence in western Africa, "is that they have led the most intemperate lives." For one, the diets of sailors and traders to west Africa were unwise, consisting mainly of "dried, salted, rancid, and other unwholesome provisions." In addition, voyagers' tendency toward the excessive use of alcohol only exacerbated the effects of poor diet. Second, he argued that one of the main causes of mortality in western Africa was the fact that sojourners there tended to spend their time "cooped up in ships, small craft, or factories, stationed for the advantage of trade in close rivers or creeks, not choosing healthy spots, as by the proposal before us is to be done." Lastly, the fact that the present set of British doctors were "generally ignorant" about treating tropical diseases and were in most cases not "sufficiently supplied with medicines" meant the causes behind a great deal of African mortality were avoidable. Speaking in the authoritative voice of one who lived and studied in the region, the doctor asserted that all of the above mentioned pitfalls could be carefully avoided.[24]

Smeathman's 1786 *Plan* stressed the proposed settlement's communal and democratic society in ways absent from the 1783 version. Such a tack would have been engaging to black Londoners fresh from the war in America who were loyalists, yes, but jealous of their freedom all the same and versed in the language of rights tempered during the American conflict. The settlers' town at Sierra Leone was to be "run up by the joint labour of the whole" and the land on which the town stood was to be the "joint property" of the "Community of Settlers." The settlement would include a clergyman "in order to promote Christian Knowledge," and two teachers would join the voyagers "that those who have children may have them instructed." The cost associated with these employments was to be borne equally by all of the migrants. Perhaps most important to potential settlers, the law of the land, by and large, was to be their law. "With respect to disputes relative to property, or offences committed among themselves," claimed Smeathman, "these will be settled by the laws, which are judged of by their own peers, that is by a Town Meeting, according to the custom of the country, which is invariably fair and equitable." Such points concerning the law, community property, community labor, and the instruction and improvement of the settlers' progeny, though rather subdued in earlier incarnations of Smeathman's plan, were highlighted in the 1786 version. Indirectly, the contrasts tell us a great deal about the wants and desires of impoverished black Londoners.[25]

Though potential migrants among London's blacks no doubt expressed an affinity for the kind of society laid out in Smeathman's *Plan*, come the spring and summer of 1786 there remained a formidable distance between their hopes and their convictions. The earliest surviving meeting minutes of the Committee for the Relief of the Black Poor reveal that potential emigrants continued to nurse a healthy skepticism as to whether a settlement at Sierra Leone could indeed live up to their expectations. Remaining foremost in the minds of potential emigrants was the question of their liberty,

and the minutes reveal that black Londoners explored both direct and indirect means of guaranteeing their freedom should they decide to migrate.

On May 10, Smeathman reported to his philanthropist employers "that
the Black Poor are earnest in their request" for "Fire Arms and a propor-
tionable quantity of Ammunition agreeable to the custom of the Inhabitants
of the Grain Coast of Africa." Knowledgeable about the dangers of raising
up a settlement in an area frequented by slave traders, potential emigrants
thought firearms an important guarantor of their safety. The committee
agreed to this request, or rather agreed to support it with officials in government. Nevertheless, in the following weeks the reticence among London's
poorest blacks remained apparent in the dry reportage of the committee's
occasional expenses. On May 17, 1786—well into Smeathman's personal
campaign of recruitment—the doctor assured the committee that "at least
130 of the Black Poor would go with him to Africa." Yet during the previous seven days more than 300 had lined up for sustenance and six pence.[26]

Distressed by the story such numbers told, the chairman of the Committee for the Relief of the Black Poor, Jonas Hanway, visited the distribution sites on Lisson Green and at Mile End during the first and second
weeks of June. He chastised the gathered paupers for their apparent skepticism, saying that "he must be the worst of all the wicked on Earth" if he
and the committee were out to deceive or to enslave them. His audience
responded to his presence by requesting even further guarantees of their
freedom. Earlier they asked for arms, now they called for "Instruments
insuring their Liberty"—some kind of official writ that would guarantee
their status as free men and women upon landing in Africa. Hanway agreed
to produce such a document.[27]

At a subsequent meeting with representatives from the crowds Hanway
harangued previously at the White Raven and Yorkshire Stingo, the chairman produced the draft certificate. Eight delegates pronounced themselves
pleased with the document, though they revealed something of their deep
distrust of white Britons even as they expressed their approval of "the fair-
est and most just Agreement that ever was made between White and Black
People." One delegate remained unmoved altogether by the legal imprima-
tur of Hanway's guarantee: A "Ninth Man, said to be a Person of weight
among the Blacks," excused himself from the meeting, saying simply of
Hanway's document that "he would consider of it." For this unnamed Londoner, a paper contract promising "Freedom without Let or Molestation, or
any Violation thereof whatsoever" was simply not compelling enough when
one considered its source and the plan now at hand.[28]

Immediately following Hanway's meeting with the black poor, the absolute number of people calling at the committee's distribution centers fell dramatically. Two days after the Hanway rendezvous, 208 people accepted the committee's assistance, whereas 347 claimed payment only three weeks earlier. About thirty blacks refused the committee's benevolence altogether, answering the pay clerk in the same manner as the unnamed "Person of weight" addressed chairman Hanway earlier, "that they wished for time to consider." Others desired assistance but did not wish to commit themselves for Sierra Leone, stating instead "that they were ready to go to their respective Homes in America and the West Indies."[29]

The absolute number of blacks calling on the committee's resources soon rebounded in the wake of Hanway's conference with likely migrants, and the emigration scheme seemed to pick up steam. The committee redoubled its publicity effort, ordering an additional 500 copies of Smeathman's *Plan* and 750 copies of the recently drafted agreement. The documents and their distribution, according to the committee, were "indispensibly necessary to inform the intended Settlers of the nature of the Offer made them." In addition to printing handbills and a prospectus, the philanthropists investigated how they might transform Hanway's "Instrument of Agreement" into a legally binding indenture so as to persuade more potential settlers of their seriousness and sincerity. The committee expedited concrete plans concerning the actual departure and put in place precautions to keep minors and slaves from journeying to Sierra Leone.[30]

Most important, the committee widened the channel of communication between black Londoners and themselves, naming the eight blacks who met earlier with Hanway official representatives of the would-be emigrants. Included were James Johnson and Aaron Brooks, farmers originally from New Jersey; John William Ramsay, a domestic from New York; John Lemon, a cook and hairdresser from Bengal; John Cambridge, a net maker and domestic born in Africa; John Williams, a seaman last sailed from Charleston, South Carolina; William Green, a servant from Barbados; and Charles Stoddard, a cooper born in Africa. On nearly all fronts, then, things appeared to be progressing apace. But on Saturday, July 1, 1786, Henry Smeathman, the prime mover of the plan for Sierra Leone, "died of a fever."[31]

In all probability, Smeathman was struggling with fatigue and a long-standing illness for months before his actual death. Yet previous to his demise there is little evidence that his condition raised any significant doubt in the minds of his philanthropic supporters. But after July 1, incredibly, Smeathman's plan became all but untenable to the members of the committee. Less than four days after the doctor's death, the committee began soliciting alternatives to Sierra Leone.[32] Only days after Smeathman's death, the philanthropists entertained and then endorsed a prospectus for creating a black settlement on Great Inagua in the Bahamas archipelago.[33]

As quickly as the committee came to this decision, the black poor began agitating against the idea. The committee discussed the Bahamas option at meetings on July 5, 10, and 12, voting at the last conference to recommend the plan to officials at the Treasury. But at the assembly following their vote, the committee was reminded that they could not carry on in a vacuum. The philanthropists' second order of business on July 15 was to attend to a petition signed by fifteen delegates of the black poor. The signatories introduced themselves as the proper representatives of "upwards of 400 persons" and informed the committee "that a Report has been circulating for some Days relative to a Design of sending them to the Bahama Islands." These rumors, reported the delegates, were the source of "considerable uneasiness." They were decided on Sierra Leone—"no Place whatever would be so agreeable"—and since they came to their decisions only after a great deal of inquiry and negotiation they were puzzled by the sudden change of plans. They reminded the committee that "after the fullest investigation" they had "every reason to believe" that the plan for Sierra Leone "met with Your Honour's approbation." Anticipating that the committee might be reluctant to follow through with immigration to west Africa because they perceived the plan now lacked proper leadership, the petitioners continued that they reposed supreme confidence in the late Mr. Smeathman's lieutenant, Joseph Irwin. If the committee saw fit to appoint Irwin as their "Agent and Conductor," they would be "ready to embark with him whenever they are ordered so to do."[34]

The committee responded to the petition by stating their continued adherence "to their Resolution of the 7th July concerning the Settlement of the Black Poor." Minutes for that meeting have not survived, but we can suppose with confidence that the resolution in question laid out the committee's rationale for scrapping the plan for Sierra Leone, for in a subsequent order of business the committee provided a letter of introduction to the two merchants who were then proposing to transport the black poor to the Bahamas. These new agents, the committee told the Treasury, appeared "to be well qualified to take Charge of conveying the Black Poor abroad."[35]

London's would-be black emigrants did not let the charity's wavering intentions deter them in the least. A week and a half after the committee recommended the organizers of a proposed Bahamas settlement to officials at the Treasury, five delegates from the black poor appeared before the committee and "represented that the Blacks in general were not inclined to go to any of the Bahama Islands, apprehending that they cannot find a support there." Apparently, the would-be migrants knew full well that Great Inagua was little more than a great desert isle flanked by foreign powers, intelligence probably gathered from the good number of sailors among them. The delegates remained confident that they could coax a sustenance from the land at Sierra Leone and that those already there would support them. To sustain these claims they offered to bring before the committee "a Person residing in London who is a native of that country and gives them assurance that all the natives are fond of the English & would receive them joyfully." At this, the committee appeared to relent, resolving that they would reconsider the plan for Sierra Leone if the evidence brought before them at their next meeting was convincing, otherwise they would continue working toward a settlement at the Bahamas.[36]

If the delegates of the black poor brought a native of Sierra Leone to the committee's next meeting, the minutes are silent on the matter. Nevertheless, the record clearly indicates would-be emigrants' continued insistence on Sierra Leone. To a proposal read at the July 28 meeting suggesting that the blacks be settled along the Gambia instead of at Sierra Leone, the representatives of the black poor answered in terms used in the past to express a certain disregard for the question at hand: they would, according to the delegates, give the matter their "consideration."[37]

What the black poor meant by giving the matter their "consideration" must have been clear to the committee, for the philanthropists began to show signs that the efforts of the black poor in behalf of the Sierra Leone proposal were having the desired effect. The committee's minutes from late June incorporated a primary point made by potential migrants in their previous petition: "The foundation of the Compact with the Blacks and people of Colour having been to embark and form a settlement in Sierra Leona under the Direction of the late Mr. Smeathman, tho' he is dead the Blacks and people of Colour appear to have the same Prejudice in favour of that Spot."[38]

In the minds of the committee, passion and prejudice may have been the chief causes behind the blacks' insistence on Sierra Leone, but it is clear that the gentlemen duly considered and were moved by the perspective of the settlers. A primary contention of the black poor in favor of Sierra Leone was the simple, elegant fact that the committee and the would-be settlers had entered into a contract.[39]

In the week to come the committee made several more last-ditch attempts to persuade the black poor to settle for a destination other than Sierra Leone. On July 31, the committee laid before representatives of the black poor a plan to settle them in Canada. With their usual circumspection, the delegates promised that they would confer with their constituents and report their sentiments at the next meeting. These assurances aside, their opposition to the plan was palatable, as a committee member reported to the Treasury just after the Canada proposal was made: "The Committee approved the Plan; but the Blacks are very averse to it; and I am afraid will hardly be prevailed upon to go to any other place than Sierra Leona."[40]

Jonas Hanway—the chair of the committee and one who championed Smeathman's proposal when many among the black poor were reluctant to sign on—made one final effort to convince would-be emigrants to change their minds about west Africa. During the first week of August, the committee's pay clerk read a memorandum from Hanway to an assembly of prospective settlers. In the letter, the chairman retracted every material point made during his previous speeches at the White Raven and Yorkshire Stingo. They could not and should not go to Sierra Leone, Hanway told them, because their freedom could not be guaranteed if they did. There was "no place on the whole coast of Africa" he argued, "where there can be any solid security against Slavery." Indeed, given Smeathman's ambiguous abolitionist credentials, Hanway even doubted the intentions of the doctor himself on this point. "What his real Designs were when he should have landed in that Country and had nothing further to hope or fear from the Committee," Hanway fretted, "will be a subject for strong suspicion in the Breast of every Man concerned as long as they live." Further, the chairman trailed out a litany of objections about which would-be migrants were already satisfied. With the demise of Mr. Smeathman, Hanway warned, there was no one available to guide the settlement who was both familiar with the area around Sierra Leone and unattached to the slave trade. The implication was clear: the migrants' choice of an agent was a dubious one, Joseph Irwin having never in his life even laid eyes on western Africa. Lastly, Hanway cautioned the assembled blacks that there was "another great ambiguity respecting the Coast of Africa." Smeathman proclaimed that with due care Sierra Leone was as healthy as any spot on earth; yet the doctor himself, Hanway pointed out, "brought from thence a Constitution which lasted him but a little while."[41]

The assembly received the chairman's words politely enough. The clerk reported "That the Blacks seemed very well pleased and satisfied with the justice of the Remarks." But upon a count of whom was committed to Sierra Leone and whom to Canada, "those inclined to go to New Brunswick was comparatively small, being only 67 of whom 5 afterwards retracted." The vote forced the committee to a resolution officially reaffirming their support for a free black settlement at Sierra Leone. "Resolved," began the committee's about-face: "That from the general view of the Disposition of the

Blacks it is not probable that any decision will be come to, unless they are permitted to go to Sierra Leona carrying with them such a number of Arms as the Lords of the Treasury shall think proper to entrust them with."[42]

So eight months after black Londoners first began lining up for medicines, soup, shirts, six pence, and other assistance offered by the committee, it appeared that Henry Smeathman's migration scheme, which the black poor made into their own, was now under way. It had been a long road, and one that would probably have been abandoned except for the opinions and persistence of the black poor themselves. The process was so long because the black poor behaved as we would expect men and women who were former slaves, who lived among the complex of opportunity and vulnerability that was late eighteenth-century London, and who came of age during the Anglo-American crisis and the war which followed: black Londoners were careful of their liberty and jealous of their rights. This habit all but exhausted the Committee for the Relief of the Black Poor. Gathered in a room at Batson's Coffeehouse, the gentlemen members complained in their minutes of August 4 that this business had "trained out to a tedious length." There was no way of knowing then, though some may have suspected, that this business was really only just begun. The capital's black poor would be many more months leaving London.

SIX

MIGRATION AND THE IMPOSSIBLE
DEMANDS OF LEAVING LONDON

By the fall of 1786, potential emigrants and their Samaritans had come to terms. Eight months of plans, proposals, and counters were slowly turning into something of actual substance. Before this time, black Londoners were obliged only to decide whether they agreed with the proposals before them. Now, they faced the harder question of whether they would put their lives behind what they had bargained for. In the end, most of black London, even many who earlier pledged themselves for Africa, decided not to take the risk. The contemporary narrative record—newspaper accounts, the memoirs of participants, minutes of the Committee for the Relief of the Black Poor, and the records of government—all suggest that the affair was doomed by the emerging conditions of embarkation, conditions that made London look more sufferable than the ships on which blacks were to travel to Sierra Leone. This is a point of consensus in the historiography of the black poor.

Material conditions, however, do not fully explain the unfolding debacle. As the migration to Sierra Leone got under way in earnest, the vast majority of black London was simply unable to meet the demands that the movement made of their society. The idea that had emerged from negotiations between black Londoners and their benefactors was for a settler colony. It was not clear at the time, but this was a kind of migration for which black London was uniquely unsuited.

In late August, the Navy Board began the actual process of organizing materials and resources necessary to realize a settlement at Sierra Leone. In early October two transport ships, the *Atlantic* and the *Belisarius,* were hired to load passengers in the Thames in order to meet the Navy Board's target embarkation date of October 31. Not long after preparations were under way with those two ships, it was determined that a third transport might be necessary to accommodate all of the emigrants who were likely to present themselves. Consequently the admirals and their administrators cast about for a third transport to convey the projected overflow.[1]

Government also appointed to the expedition a general commissary responsible for rudimentary record-keeping while the transports were still in port and accountable for the management of stores and provisions once the expedition disembarked at Sierra Leone. A man whose life experience resembled that of a sizable cross section of black poor was selected for this position: Gustavus Vassa. Vassa was a former slave and deep-sea sailor who had purchased his freedom and was now a devout Christian, ardent abolitionist, and one whose life journey left him among London's several thousand black residents.[2]

For its part, the Committee for the Relief of the Black Poor rushed to tie up loose ends of its own. The philanthropists sent Mary Latouch and Mary Harris—white women married to black migrants—to the City of London Lying-in Hospital for brief training so that the expedition would have recourse to a set of certified midwives. To meet would-be migrants' previous demand for written assurances of their freedom, the committee applied to the Lords of the Treasury for "some kind of certificate bearing his Majesty's Arms, or some other conspicuous Mark of Authority," anything that would show that the migrants were "Freemen, going of their own Accord" and thus "protect them from insults."[3]

Among black Londoners themselves, interest in the expedition appeared higher than ever. On September 20, 715 people lined up for the government's weekly allowance, and during the first week of October that number plus twenty-one more made their way to the committee's disbursement centers. In general, the allowance is an imperfect index with which to judge interest in the expedition. In this case, though, the suggestion it makes is justified by the fact that as the transports contracted by the Navy Board settled into the Thames to prepare for passengers, about 675 Londoners placed their names on a contract declaring firm intentions to embark for Sierra Leone as soon as the ships were ready. Moreover, delegates from the prospective emigrants were stepping up their own preparations. Meeting with the committee in October, William Green, John Mandeville, Abraham Elliot Griffith, George Sealey, and a Mr. Johnson inquired into and suggested the procurement of additional supplies for the voyage. At that same gathering, an anonymous group of black Londoners, through an unsigned petition, asked the committee's support in procuring the release of a number of incarcerated colleagues, so they too could embark for Africa.[4]

By the last day of October 1786, the *Atlantic* and *Belisarius* transports began to load passengers at Deptford, a village and shipyard below London on the south side of the Thames. Yet after three weeks of taking on emigrants, and in the wake of all the previous activity and apparent excitement, the two transports held between them a mere 259 passengers. This was considerably short of the 500 the two ships were expected to carry, and it was nowhere near the throng of more than 700 that organizers previously expected to vie for places aboard the first two ships.[5]

Puzzled and troubled by the slow rate of embarkation, the committee considered how they might encourage on board, at the very least, the nearly 700 people who signed the "Memorandum of Agreement," thus pledging themselves for Africa. Announcements were placed in a London paper calling on those who received the bounty of government to make their way to the waiting ships and informing others who met the committee's criteria that they could still join the expedition. The frustrated committee chairman, now Samuel Hoare, even warmed to a suggestion first made by the Treasury: that those who received the charity of government but were not yet aboard the ships should be arrested and deposited at Deptford.[6]

During the two months after officials prepared the first embarkation lists—counting 259 people on board the *Atlantic* and *Belisarius*—167 more passengers boarded the transports. A month later, though the convoy itself was now completed at three ships—the *Atlantic*, the *Belisarius*, and the *Vernon*—only twenty-eight more people joined the expedition. So after four months of embarkation, not 500 people stood ready to sail to Sierra Leone. Of this number, at least forty were white passengers unrelated to any of the blacks on board—mostly clergy, doctors, and artisans. Thus, come February 1787, the number of black emigrants ready to sail fell far short of the nearly 1,000 Londoners who stood in line, at one time or another, to receive the government's daily payment of six pence. It was also conspicuously shy of the 675 people who ostensibly committed themselves as settlers by signing October's "Memorandum of Agreement."[7]

Material and social conditions on board the transports during the first two months of boarding go some way toward explaining the expedition's failure to attract a full complement. For those black Londoners who decided to take a wait-and-see or wait-and-hear approach to the expedition, seeing or hearing anything about conditions aboard the waiting transports would have been far from inviting. The *Atlantic* and *Belisarius* began boarding in late autumn, a precarious time of year in London as far as sickness was concerned. The same pathogens that attacked London in general at this time of year made themselves felt aboard the confined spaces of the *Atlantic* and *Belisarius*. It is not known whether there was great mortality as the two transports waited first at Deptford and then at Gravesend. It is apparent, however, that the ships were extremely sickly in general and that the emigrants endured an outbreak of fever during November and December. A white surgeon's mate aboard the *Belisarius* became so ill from the complaint that "he was obliged to be carried on shore for advice and assistance." Few among the *Atlantic* and *Belisarius*'s destitute black passengers would have been privy to the kind of shore-care afforded the suffering sailor; indeed, as sickness enveloped the transports, Gustavus Vassa, the expedition commissary, complained vigorously that the ship's officers were neither inclined toward nor equal to the task of caring for the transports' ailing emigrants.[8]

We know that at least fifty black emigrants perished before the ships left England. Undoubtedly, a good number of these fatalities originated in the deteriorating shipboard conditions of November and December 1786 as the *Atlantic* and *Belisarius* waited outside London. Years later, Vassa described the situation of the emigrants in terms that could have been used to describe the conditions of poor blacks in London itself. Accommodation on the transports, reported Vassa, was "most wretched." Many of the emigrants "wanted beds, and many more clothing and other necessaries."[9]

For a people who made much of preserving their "liberty" while debating the merits of Smeathman's original emigration scheme, the situation aboard the transports left much to be desired on this head as well. Embarkation meant surrendering certain freedoms. As black emigrants and their families began to board the *Belisarius* and *Atlantic* during November and December, the committee and government officials took pains to address what the philanthropists described earlier as the blacks' troublesome dispositions and obvious "want of discipline." Foremost among the government's concerns was the back-and-forth movement of black emigrants between the ships and the shore. Consequently, after a month of embarkation the Navy Board asked officials shipboard to restrict the mobility of prospective emigrants. A similar request was made in the weeks to come, signifying that the question of mobility was a matter of contention between black migrants and their supervisors throughout preparations for Sierra Leone. It is obvious that this was a battle in which the emigrants did not fare well, for both detractors and supporters of the expedition would later point to migrants' strict confinement as a factor in their subsequent mortality.[10]

Life aboard the transports also included restrictions concerning what emigrants might do to pass the time or to make themselves comfortable through the English winter. When passengers burned fires and candles through the night—apparently for warmth and light, but probably as part of shipboard revelries as well—the ships' masters bemoaned the migrants' "want of Order" to officials at the Treasury and cast about for a solution. The committee suspected that alcohol was behind the "disorderly behaviour and irregularity" and thus recommended that the rum allowance be cut until the ships arrived in Africa.[11]

There is evidence that the expedition's titular superintendent, Joseph Irwin, withheld from emigrants supplies more necessary than rum. Beginning in January, migrants complained that they were denied proper provisions and that, when supplies were handed out, their quality and quantity left much to be desired. Vassa complained that the emigrants were continually "plundered and oppressed" and that the whites on board the ships meant to use "the blacks the same as they do in the West Indies." As far as the last matter is concerned, the commissary no doubt exaggerated in order to make his point: The shipboard hierarchy was hardly accommodating and in addition was shot through with no small amount of racial chauvinism.[12]

As further discouragement, there was a great deal of confusion in the London press concerning the relationship between the expedition to Sierra Leone and the simultaneous outfitting of the first convict ships for Australia. In the public mind the two schemes became hopelessly intertwined, to the point that newspaper accounts reported that London's most hardened criminals were intended for western Africa while more tractable convicts from the country at-large were being sent to Botany Bay. Such misinformation-cum-news encouraged would-be emigrants to reconsider the whole matter of Sierra Leone, particularly the intentions of the government. It could not but occur to the city's blacks that the same government that was loading its convicts aboard prison hulks for banishment to Australia was ostensibly providing for their own conveyance as free people to Sierra Leone. John Stuart, a literate black Londoner born Ottobah Cugoano and a staunch critic of the Sierra Leone expedition, put a finer point on it: Could the same government that supported the transatlantic slave trade *from* Africa really intend to plant a free black settlement *in* Africa? Lest such ironies materialize into more sinister realities once in Sierra Leone, migrants who were apparently committed to the expedition in early October became much more hesitant. The *Public Advertiser* reported that confusion about whether Sierra Leone was really to be a free settlement caused a number of October's signers to seek the counsel of Lord George Gordon—namesake of London's worst eighteenth-century civic disturbances and an opponent of convict transportation. To be safe, Lord George apparently advised them that they should remain in the capital.[13]

From what can be gleaned from the documentary record—the London press, the meeting minutes of the Committee for the Relief of the Black Poor, and the published accounts of protagonists—black Londoners studied the question of whether to depart for Sierra Leone with the same critical faculties they applied earlier to Smeathman's original plan. Would-be migrants asked themselves whether they might protect and expand their liberty through immigration to Sierra Leone, and ultimately the vast majority of those who were involved with the scheme from January through September of 1786 decided in October, November, and December that the answer to that question was a resounding "No." Of the 973 Londoners listed in the committee's records as having "received the Bounty from Government," only 242 were shipboard in February 1787 as the transports made sail for Sierra Leone, an embarkation rate of roughly 25 percent.[14]

Without doubt, blacks avoided the ships for Sierra Leone because their sensibilities as former slaves and sailors and their present predicament as Londoners in tune at street-level with the turns of British politics persuaded them it was safer to remain where they were than it was to venture to Sierra Leone. Yet there are bits and pieces of evidence outside the narrative record indicating that a major factor behind the expedition's poor embarkation rate may have also stemmed from the social demands of migration and black Londoners' inability to meet them. A close look at eight lists of potential and actual migrants for Sierra Leone indicates that a collision between the demography of black London and the demographic exigencies of the kind of migration proposed to and embraced by the black poor was as much behind the adventure's failure as anything else.

The eight lists in question were compiled between November 1786 and February 1787 (see Figure 6, for example). For the most part they contain simply the names of Londoners associated at one time or another with the expedition to Sierra Leone. In addition to names, the registers sometimes give sex and "marital status," and when these are not given outright it is often possible to infer them. The largest list, "An Alphabetical List of the Black People who have received the Bounty from Government," is fifteen pages long and names about 973 people. A nine-page list drafted in October 1786 is a contract entered into by 675 Londoners who agreed with Joseph Irwin to join the expedition to Sierra Leone once the transports were ready. Two lists compiled in November 1786 note the names of emigrants then embarked aboard the *Atlantic* and *Belisarius* transports; combined they contain the names of 259 emigrants. Four more lists drafted in February 1787 give the names of 455 passengers then parceled out between the *Atlantic*, *Belisarius*, and *Vernon* while the transports were anchored at Spithead in final preparation for their departure to Sierra Leone.[15]

When the 973 names on "An Alphabetical List of the Black People" are compared to the 675 Londoners who contracted with Joseph Irwin to embark for Sierra Leone, a number of insights follow. Simply glancing at the totals on the two lists gives the impression that some 30 percent of those who received alms from the government could not be persuaded subse-

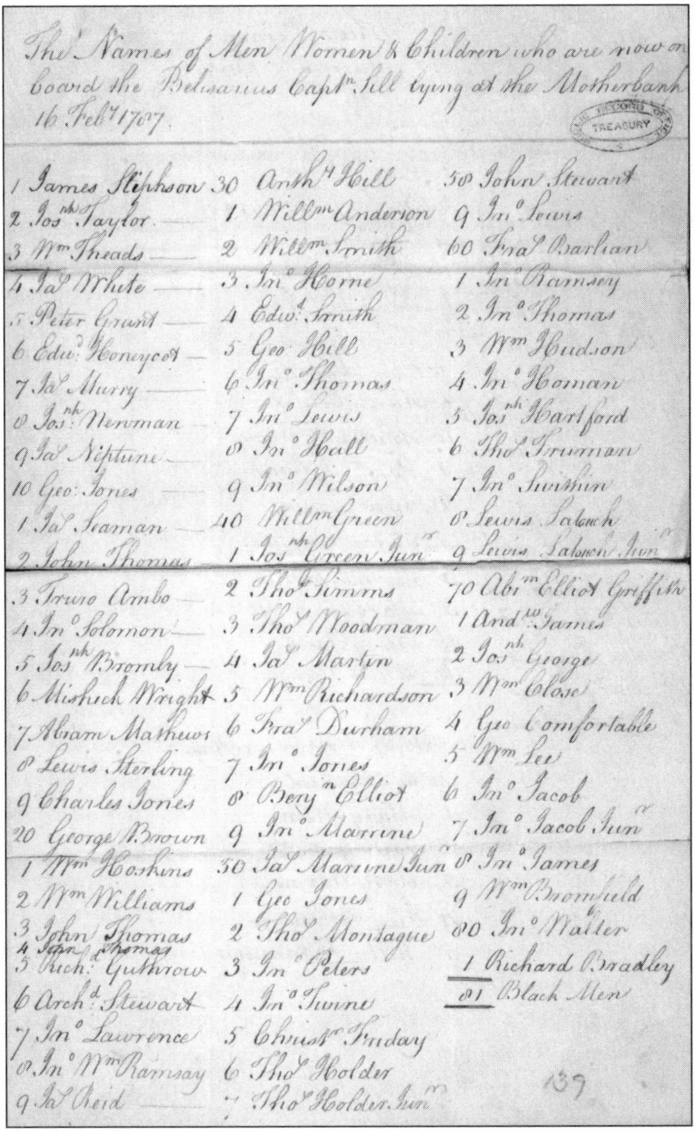

The Names of Men Women & Children who are now on board the Belisarius Captn. Sill lying at the Motherbank 16 Feby 1787.

TREASURY

1 James Stiphson	30 Anthy Hill	58 John Stewart
2 Josnh Taylor	1 Willm Anderson	9 Jno Lewis
3 Wm Theads	2 Willm Smith	60 Fras Barlian
4 Jas White	3 Jno Horne	1 Jno Ramsey
5 Peter Grant	4 Edwd Smith	2 Jno Thomas
6 Edwd Honeycot	5 Geo Hill	3 Wm Hudson
7 Jas Murry	6 Jno Thomas	4 Jno Homan
8 Josnh Newman	7 Jno Lewis	5 Josnh Hartford
9 Jas Neptune	8 Jno Hall	6 Thos Truman
10 Geo: Jones	9 Jno Wilson	7 Jno Swithin
1 Jas Seaman	40 Willm Green	8 Lewis Salouch
2 John Thomas	1 Josnh Green Junr	9 Lewis Salouch Junr
3 Truro Ambo	2 Thos Simms	70 Abrm Elliot Griffith
4 Jno Solomon	3 Thos Woodman	1 Andw James
5 Josnh Bromly	4 Jas Martin	2 Josnh George
6 Mishick Wright	5 Wm Richardson	3 Wm Close
7 Abram Mathews	6 Fras Durham	4 Geo Comfortable
8 Lewis Sterling	7 Jno Jones	5 Wm Lee
9 Charles Jones	8 Benjn Elliot	6 Jno Jacob
20 George Brown	9 Jno Marrine	7 Jno Jacob Junr
1 Wm Hoskins	50 Jas Marrine Junr	8 Jno James
2 Wm Williams	1 Geo Jones	9 Wm Bromfield
3 John Thomas	2 Thos Montague	80 Jno Walter
4 John Thomas		
5 Richd Guthrow	3 Jno Peters	1 Richard Bradley
6 Archd Stewart	4 Jno Twine	81 Black Men
7 Jno Lawrence	5 Christr Friday	
8 Jno Wm Ramsay	6 Thos Holder	
9 Jas Reid	7 Thos Holder Junr	139

Figure 6. Closely read, lists like this one allow insight into the individual human movements comprising the migration of black Londoners to Sierra Leone in the late eighteenth century. Gustavus Vassa, "The Names of Men, Women & Children who are now on board the Belisarius Captn. Sill lying at the Motherbank 16 February 1787," enclosed with George Marsh to Secretaries Treasury, 27 February 1787, T1/643. *Source:* Courtesy of the National Archives-Kew

quently to sign on for Sierra Leone. Actually cross-indexing the names on the two documents suggests that the drop off was somewhat higher. Of the 973 names on "An Alphabetical List of the Black People," only 556 occur on October's agreement, indicating that 43 percent of those who sought the support of the government could not be convinced afterward to sign Irwin's contract.

By itself this "desertion rate" means very little because it offers almost no insight into why particular Londoners did or did not sign the agreement. Of the 418 names that occur on the list of those who received government support but that do not appear on the agreement, some may have positively refused to sign the contract to migrate. Others, for any number of reasons, may not have had the opportunity to sign. The rate only becomes meaningful when used comparatively as a benchmark for inquiring more carefully about the people who received alms but did not sign the agreement.

A close comparison of the two lists suggests that some groups of black Londoners did indeed make positive decisions not to sign the contract. The number of black female adults with no apparent male partner on the "Alphabetical List" dropped off by some 62 percent in October's "Agreement Between Mr. Jos. Irwin and The Black Poor." The number of black female adults with an apparent male partner dropped by only 23 percent between the two lists. The number of single black males between the two lists dropped only as much as would be expected—44 percent, almost exactly the same reduction as the global drop off between the lists. The number of black male adults for whom a female partner is apparent hardly budged at all between the two documents, dropping by a mere 8 percent.

Clearly, Londoners deciding whether to commit themselves to Sierra Leone did not simply study circumstances pertaining to the expedition itself; they simultaneously gave serious consideration to their own personal circumstances in relation to the proposed expedition. Unattached black women, for example, avoided Irwin's contract at rates higher than the average. The women who appear as single on the list of government payees may have been rooted in the capital by virtue of having children or other dependents. We know from the minutes of the committee that some of the female payees who appear single on the "Alphabetical List" were in fact connected to men who at the moment were absent from London. In May 1786, the committee paid support to fifty-seven women described collectively as "Unmarried Women or whose Husbands are at Sea." Black women with husbands working outside of the city would have been reluctant to leave London without them.[16]

All the same, most of the decline in the number of single black women on the agreement can probably be explained by the fact that the expedition offered them very little except the opportunity to take enormous risks with their livelihood. In London itself, unattached black women were susceptible to a range of physical abuses, and their opportunities for gainful employment were sparse since the demand for black domestics was largely a demand for black manservants. In the short term, at least, the expedition to Sierra Leone promised only to exacerbate this condition. For single black women adept at making their way through what was already a very dangerous capital, the prospect of being confined on the Thames and then at sea with a cross section of black London may have simply looked like the opportunity to live an intensified version of their already trying experience.[17]

Examining the set of Londoners who did choose to sign Irwin's agreement is revealing in its own right. One hundred and twenty of the signatures on the agreement belong to people who did not previously receive the support of government. They were new recruits and consisted of seventy black men, thirty black women, nine black children, and eleven white females. This list of people willing to sign on for Sierra Leone, though apparently not previously involved with the scheme, foreshadows related trends that became more important following the start of actual embarkation: married Londoners' apparent attraction to emigration and male voyagers' apparent recruitment of female passengers.

If the 120 new recruits on the agreement had signed on at the same rate as those who went from the government rolls to the contract, we would expect the party to have consisted of a greater number of males and proportionally fewer females and children—namely, ninety-four black men, eighteen black women, six black children, and only one white female. The difference in the actual composition of the group suggests that the new recruits were not drawn to the agreement for the same reasons as were those from the bounty rolls. An analysis of the "marital status" of the newcomers confirms that a significant portion were probably mustered onto the contract by a previously involved spouse or signed the agreement as a couple, as all of the white women and half of the black women among the new recruits were married. Moving behind the statistics and examining the agreement and the roll more carefully reveals that twenty-two of the new recruits were indeed joining partners who were previously involved in the emigration scheme: twenty women apparently recruited by their husbands and two men apparently recruited by their wives.[18]

The abysmal embarkation rate that ensued once the *Atlantic* and *Belisarius* transports began boarding has already been discussed. Though 675 Londoners signed the agreement in early October 1786, only 259 passengers were on board the transports come the last full week of November. Again, the problem with these numbers in absolute terms is that they do not relate anything of the complex decision-making process of would-be emigrants. In absolute terms it appears as if around 38 percent of those who contracted with Irwin actually boarded the ships. The reality was both far worse and somewhat less troubling all at the same time.

Of the 259 migrants on board the *Atlantic* and *Belisarius* in late November 1786, only 190 were on the agreement. Fifteen more, however, were previously listed on the bounty rolls, so the general embarkation rate was somewhere around 28 percent (not 38 percent, as the unanalyzed list totals might suggest). But here again, subsets of would-be emigrants embarked at significantly different rates. Dramatically, of the seventy-two apparently single black females who signed the agreement, only three were on board the transports in November, an embarkation rate of around 4 percent. Married black women who signed the agreement embarked at the higher but still unexpectedly low rate of 21 percent (in general, married couples embarked at a rate of around 45 percent.)

Submerged within the dismal overall embarkation rates between the agreement and the November ship musters is the decision by fifty-four Londoners previously unassociated with the migration plan to join the ships. As with the transition from the bounty rolls to the agreement, a disproportionate number of November's fresh recruits were married and women: Twenty-eight of the new enlistees were female, and of these three-quarters were married. Twenty of the new female recruits appear to have been joining spouses who were themselves already connected with the expedition.[19]

Gustavus Vassa, the expedition commissary, compiled the final ship musters in February 1787. By then, the two transports that commenced loading at Deptford in late October were now three, and all at Spithead with the navy sloop charged with escorting them safety to Sierra Leone and seeing to their initial settlement, the *Nautilus*. The *Atlantic* and *Belisarius* made for Spithead from Gravesend during the second week of January. The *Vernon* began the same course not two weeks later. Thus the embarkation lists made in February probably represent passengers taken aboard during the forty days between November 22, 1786, and the first week of 1787.

Comparing the lists compiled in February 1787 with those written in November 1786 reveals additional details concerning how Londoners made decisions about Sierra Leone. The absolute rise in embarkation is the most obvious difference between the two musters. In November 1786, only 259 Londoners were aboard the ships for Sierra Leone; in the weeks following the number of migrants rose to and steadied at about 455. As usual, however, this increase in embarkation tells only a small part of the overall story. As the number of migrants boarding the boats increased steadily from November to January, a significant number of prospective migrants departed as well. Fifty-six black men, eighteen black women, and nine black children who were on board the transports in November were not present on the subsequent muster. Together this group accounts for close to one-third of the initial embarkation.

Some of these departures must have been due to death, for there were a number of apparent couples on the November musters who did not appear together on the rolls from February. Thomas Demain, for instance, received the bounty of government and signed the agreement. After the ships began boarding in late October he embarked on the *Belisarius* with Elizabeth Demain. By February, though Elizabeth remained with the expedition, Thomas no longer appeared on any of the lists. The Provey family appears to have endured a similar tragedy. North Carolinian John Provey, his wife, Ann, and their daughter, Louisa Ann, each received government support throughout the first nine months of 1786. In the fall all three boarded the *Belisarius* planning to begin a new life in Sierra Leone. Come February, Ann appears to be the only surviving member of the family. We cannot be certain that these disappearances were due to death rather than desertion, but given conditions aboard the transports during the winter of 1786 it is likely that some, if not many, of the departures were due to mortality.[20]

There is also convincing evidence among married and related emigrants in the November register that a good number of the entire group of parting passengers did not die but rather reversed themselves, deciding to return to London proper before the transports sailed south and it was too late. "George Adams & Child" received the bounty of government during the course of 1786 and signed Irwin's agreement at the start of October. Both were among the initial embarkation and were aboard the *Belisarius* in November, which placed them among a committed group of emigrants who seemed determined to follow the emigration scheme through from beginning to end. By February, however, it appears as if the father decided for himself and his son that the trip was not worth the risk, for neither appears on the muster made at Spithead. Betsey and William Dover, Joseph and Maria Groves, Jacob and Rebecca Jackson, and Robert and Elizabeth Robertson all appear to have left the ship in a similar manner.[21]

There is no evidence that members of the committee understood that completing the ships was a complex matter of people both *coming* and *going*, but to their good fortune more than three times as many Londoners joined the transports between November 1786 and January 1787 as departed.

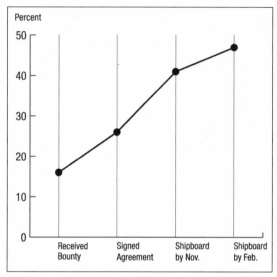

Figure 7. Married emigrants as a changing part of
prospective adult migrants, 1786–1787

Given the eighty-three prospective emigrants who disembarked, it took 279 enlistees to push the February muster to 455. Forty of the last recruits were white passengers, mostly artisans and their families, recruited by the committee with its friends and agents. In December 1786, for instance, a "very ingenious Engineer" named John Geçeau and his wife, Mary, were recommended by Granville Sharp to the attention of the committee. They both boarded the *Atlantic,* joining doctors, a baker, a mason, a tanner, a smith, and others who probably came to the expedition in a similar fashion.[22]

The vast majority of those who joined the transports after the November muster were not adventuring artisans and professional people but black Londoners and their connections. At least 113 of those who boarded after the initial embarkation could claim some previous contact with the emigration scheme either through receiving the bounty, signing the agreement, or both. Given conditions on board the transports, these latecomers probably considered it in their interest to delay boarding as long as they possibly could. One hundred and twenty-six of those who joined the transports after the November muster appear never to have been previously associated with the expedition, for they do not occur on any other list.

Comings and goings aboard the transports between late November and early January continued and intensified embarkation trends begun earlier—namely, a disproportionate number of married people persisted in joining the ships, and the recruitment of female partners by male emigrants already shipboard continued apace. Perhaps the most dramatic example of this trend was the embarkation of fifty-four white women who, although they were never previously associated with the migration plan as indicated by receiving the bounty or signing the agreement, joined the expedition between November and January as the wives of black migrants. The trend is illustrated more fully by comparing the rates of embarkation for single and married migrants from the time of the agreement to the February muster and by examining the steady rise in the proportion of married migrants committed to the expedition as it unfolded over time.

There was a regular increase in the proportion of married migrants involved in each stage of the expedition: from around 16 percent on the bounty rolls to nearly half of the total number who were aboard the transports in February (see Figure 7). This steady relative increase of married emigrants was due in part to a remarkable difference in embarkation rates of married and single prospective migrants, as on average married emigrants who signed the Agreement embarked at rates 3.5 times higher than single migrants. The steady rise of the number of married emigrants was also due to the fact that in the coming and going that defined the larger process of embarkation, married migrants made up an appreciably larger share of those coming and a significantly smaller part of those going.

The bounty rolls, the agreement, and the embarkation musters paint a dynamic picture of how particular Londoners came to join the expedition for Sierra Leone. The registers demonstrate that filling the transports and the decision-making of prospective migrants were incremental processes characterized by fits and starts, surges and reverses. The narrative record captures very little of this give and take and instead portrays preparations for sailing as simply a long, slow, one-way process.

Further, capturing the coming and going of potential migrants is not an end in itself. Its primary importance lies in the suggestion it makes for an enhanced understanding of the migration to Sierra Leone. The narrative record and by extension the bulk of the historiography ascribe would-be migrants' refusal actually to embark for Sierra Leone as a sign of black London's failure of confidence in white philanthropy and its mistrust of the British government. Most historians have judged this suspicion as justified; some have colored it unfortunate; all have ascribed it to their subjects' knowledge of and place in the larger eighteenth-century world.

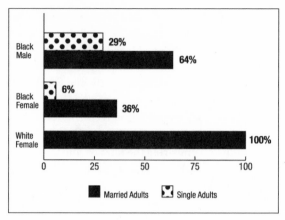

Figure 8. Adult emigrants who signed the agreement and
were on board the transports in February 1787

The registers and embarkation lists left by the government and the committee do not dispute this interpretation. They do, however, require us to tack on a corollary. Black Londoners may have refused to embark for Sierra Leone because they understood and in the end rejected the risks involved, but it appears as well that *who they were* informed this rejection as much as *what they knew*. From the lists it appears that the prevailing sex ratio of black London played a decisive role in undercutting immigration to Sierra Leone. The nature of the adventure to Sierra Leone encouraged would-be migrants who had or could acquire helpmates (see Figure 8). In this sense, the embarkation lists capture the convictions of black Londoners concerning the nature of freedom and the demands of settler society that have gone unremarked in the narrative record. Black Londoners recognized a fundamental relationship between their liberty, the prospects of settler society, and marriage.

The narrative record reveals just how concerned would-be emigrants were about protecting their freedom in Sierra Leone. The embarkation lists tell that migrants with partners were far more likely to decide that it was possible to protect and maintain their liberty in Sierra Leone and thus join the expedition. Indeed, it appears that the very prospect of emigration encouraged black Londoners to find mates with whom to migrate. Given that many black Londoners were former slaves, we should not be surprised by the apparent association they drew between forming a family and freedom. One of the hallmarks of American slavery was the dramatic instability it forced on black unions. In London, it looks as if former slaves took the converse as a central principle of liberty. In this regard, as the migration scheme wore on, the notoriously unbalanced sex ratio of black London and the city's attendant lack of black nuclear families could not but stifle emigration. The project of a settler society in Sierra Leone made demands of potential migrants that black London, being four-fifths male, could not possibly meet.[23] This would not be the case five years later. When the government agreed to transport black subjects then in Nova Scotia to Sierra Leone, a veritable exodus ensued.

SEVEN

FROM SLAVES TO FREE SUBJECTS IN BRITISH NORTH AMERICA

The men and women who comprised the mass migration from the Maritimes mustered an ironic influence over the reorienting tendencies of transatlantic migration. Whereas the transatlantic social experiences of captives from the Biafran interior and of black adventurers from London can both be largely comprehended as *communities made in crossing,* the migration from Nova Scotia is better understood as a *crossing undertaken by whole communities.* This is not to say that the Atlantic crossing did not have a profound effect on emigrants from Nova Scotia; it is to contend, rather, that it had a distinct effect. Ultimately, the black exodus from Nova Scotia did not so much refocus migrants' society and culture as much as it sharpened to a fine edge previously existing, if nascent, aspects of Afro-American community and self. This is clear from the end. In the beginning, however, the migrations that brought significant numbers of blacks to the Maritimes in the first place—the migrations during which many underwent the civil transformation from slaves to free British subjects—were crucibles indeed.

Unlike in cosmopolitan London, before the American war there were few blacks to speak of in British Nova Scotia (which then also encompassed much of present-day New Brunswick). For the most part, the colony's non-native population consisted of Yankee emigrants from New England, Protestants from the European mainland, and French-speaking settlers remnant from a time when the peninsula was part of another empire and called Acadia. In 1775, when Nova Scotia's non-native population hovered around twenty thousand, there were perhaps no more than several hundred black slaves, settlers, or sailors across the entire colony.[1]

This situation changed drastically toward the end of the American conflict, when Nova Scotia became a refuge for loyalist evacuees from the former thirteen colonies. If the British evacuation from its rebel provinces swelled an existing black population in London—as we saw previously—the same exodus created from scratch a series of hardscrabble black communities across the sparse landscape of Nova Scotia.

In the main, the Maritimes' black population resulted from the 1783 British evacuation of New York, when nearly three thousand blacks boarded government transports for Nova Scotia. The joint committee of British and American officials who oversaw the evacuation kept registers of basic data on blacks who left the city. The registers were meant to support future complaints should the time come when Great Britain would have to account and provide compensation for plundered American property—former slaves being the most valuable kind. The entries in the "Book of Negroes," as the registers came to be called, were terse, as in "Boston King, 23, stout fellow. [Formerly the property] of Richard Waring of Charlestown, South Carolina; [left him] 4 [years ago]."[2] Taken together, however, the information preserved in the registers provides important details concerning the parameters, nature, and effect of black migration to Nova Scotia.

Separately, Ellen Gibson Wilson and James St. G. Walker have combed the "Book of Negroes" to recover the geographical and statutory origins of the blacks who removed from New York at the British evacuation. According to Walker's reckoning, more than 70 percent of the blacks leaving New York were former slaves, now free for having taken advantage of British proclamations offering liberty to American slaves who deserted their rebel owners. Wilson has found that most of these defectors were black southerners: two-thirds of the refugee blacks hailed from Virginia, the Carolinas, or Georgia. Most important to grasping the nature of the passages such refugees took from slavery to liberty is the length of their journeys. For more than half of the blacks who departed New York at war's end, the commissioners who compiled the "Book of Negroes" approximated the year that the refugee cast his or her lot with the British. On average, the thousands of blacks who departed New York with the king's troops had trailed alongside royalist forces and/or maintained themselves within British lines for nearly five years.[3]

For former slaves, what were the consequences of these long journeys? Like Africans traded down the Biafran interior, most followed drawn out courses to their eventual debarkation in Nova Scotia, and just as the demands of migration from Biafran interior to littoral were transformative, so too were the wartime migrations American blacks made leading to their eventual settlement in the Maritimes. Indeed, the routes followed by black migrants to Nova Scotia primed them for as radical a transformation as one could make in eighteenth-century British North America: the transformation from slave—the most degraded of objects—to that of Free Briton, the most self-possessed of subjects.

Evidence from the "Book of Negroes" and from the surviving accounts of American blacks who settled in Nova Scotia suggests that several smaller shifts comprised this larger transformation. First, blacks who were former slaves developed during their time with the British powerful attachments to their newly won liberty. Second, alongside this sense of liberty, many blacks living and working with British troops or behind British lines simultaneously nursed a palpable and compelling loyalism to the king and his representatives. Third, the dislocations of the American war and the circumstances surrounding Afro-American life among British forces privileged and encouraged the growth of black Christianity. Consequently, religious practices and institutions that were of little significance across eighteenth-century southern plantations grew to enormous potential among blacks who departed with British forces at war's end, ultimately coloring Afro-American liberation and loyalism with a compelling sense of righteousness. Last, it appears that all of these changes were catalyzed in important ways by the physical contexts in which they transpired. Wartime entrepôts facilitated all of the just-mentioned shifts. Particularly important in this regard were the American cities where black refugees found themselves holed up with British forces over the course of the war.

The "Book of Negroes," with its compact entries, concentrates attention on the moments when American slaves chose to ally themselves with the British. The details in the registers, by alluding to the hardships blacks agreed to surmount in order to make British lines, indicate that slaves sought their liberty with great feeling and urgency. There were laborers—such as "Henry, 47, stout man"—who fled their former owners upon hearing British proclamations offering freedom to the runaway slaves of American rebels. There were families—sometimes from separate plantations and/or owners—who managed to gather themselves at the opportune moment, to keep together over the long course of the war, and to make for Nova Scotia from New York all at once, when the British finally quit the colonies. There were others who initially allied themselves with the American rebels but who over the course of the struggle realized their best interests, perhaps, lay not with the Continental Army but with the king and so, putting themselves at no small risk, deserted. There were, the "Book of Negroes" makes clear, networks of women who traveled together as domestics—carrying their children, some of these fortunate enough to have been "Born within the British lines" and thus always free. There were also children who traveled alone. On the frigate *London*, bound for Bremer Lee and leaving New York on July 16, 1783, was "Jeffery, 10, likely boy. . . . Says that he lived with Daniel Smith at Secaucus in New Jersey; that his father brought him to New York; that his mother was born free; that both of them are gone to Nova Scotia."[4]

The war and its attendant dislocations were not transformative in that they generated among blacks a desire for liberty. It is unlikely that before the war such slaves as "Henry, 47, stout man" were satisfied in their servitude and that the war shook them from their complacency. As it concerns Afro-American desire for liberty, the transformation wrought by the war was more subtle (but no less important because of its subtlety): it initiated among blacks action where before there was only desire.

The very simple entries in the "Book of Negroes" illustrate the point by virtue of the number of women contained in the registers. Enslaved women, in all American slave societies, were never as likely as men to run away from the plantations, farms, and families to which they were bound. Students of slave rebellion in North America, for example, have found that less than a quarter of the South's black runaways, in any period, were women. During the American war, in contrast, the entries in the "Book of Negroes" indicate that women comprised approximately 40 percent of black Americans who ran to the British.[5] This is a fantastic difference, and it calls attention to the particular transformative power of the American war; it calls attention to the ways in which the war encouraged enslaved blacks to realize their desire for liberty by making a life in liberty appear first practical and then necessary.

One of the reasons that comparatively few enslaved women ran away from their masters is because fleeing slavery was never just a matter of leaving one's owner. In many circumstances, fleeing slavery also meant striking off into the unknown, departing family, friends, and familiar places, and so it involved mounting enormous practical and psychological barriers that had little to do with slavery itself. Accordingly, historians speculate that women runaways appear in the record much less than men partly because women tended to subjugate their desire for freedom to the responsibilities they felt for their children and families.[6] In this sense, the "Book of Negroes" suggests that the opportunities of the American war turned many blacks from slaves who desired liberty into men and women who would no longer stand slavery.

The transformation is clear and compelling in the stories told by blacks caught up in the war. David George lived and worked as a slave around Silver Bluff, South Carolina, at the moment when British forces took nearby Savannah, Georgia. George's owner was, as George put it, an "Antiloyalist" and decided that the proper response to the British offensive was to flee—leaving all of his property, human and otherwise, behind. Subsequently, George and fifty other Silver Bluff slaves decided for themselves to seek out the very thing their former owner was fleeing; so they pressed toward Savannah and the British lines.[7]

David George was painfully ambivalent about this journey. He no doubt desired his liberty. Before arriving at Silver Bluff, George was something of a career runaway. All the same, he developed during his time at Silver Bluff sincere connections to his master—to whom George acknowledged he owed a great deal—to his home, and to his work.[8] So what transpired after the Silver Bluff refugees reached the king's forces just outside Savannah should not surprise: After the British ordered the refugees and other loyalist noncombatants to a nearby plantation, George balked, inviting the charge that he was conspiring to lead the Silver Bluff people *back* to their former homes instead.[9]

In his memoir, George neither denied the accusation nor explained his intentions. We can surmise, however, that his initial interaction with British troops was severe enough to convince him that whatever he felt about his former servitude, it was perhaps better to return to the people and places he knew best than to remain among liberators such as these. This reasoning earned George a month in prison. On his release—he was taken out by a British colonel—George and his wife worked inside the British lines raising corn, taking laundry, and trading meat. They saved all they could in the hopes of escaping Savannah. But by the time they were able to leave, George no longer intended to return to Silver Bluff. The Georges, rather, bought passage from Savannah to British-controlled Charleston, South Carolina.[10] Apparently, as the months wore on behind British lines, whatever impetus that had once convinced David George that the known was preferable to the unknown—even when the known was a life in slavery—faded away.

Implicit in George's account, and in the number of women listed in the "Book of Negroes" compared to their normal representation among American runaways, is the fact that even slaves who abhorred their condition nonetheless developed over the course of their lives attachments in slavery that made fleeing their conditions difficult. In this sense, the opportunities offered by the war and the courses blacks followed alongside the king's forces over the span of the conflict were important because each fostered among American blacks a grasp of and attachments to liberty that made their decisions to live no longer as slaves practical. After George's initial bolt for the British, it appears that it was the extended period he spent behind British lines working and living as a free man that normalized for him what before had only been a notion.

Boston King, in his memoir, made this point and process abundantly clear. King was a slave in South Carolina who achieved his liberty by gaining Charleston when British forces took the city in 1778. It was a decision fraught with regret and hardship, and there were moments when King wondered at the price of living free. "I was much grieved at first," he remembered, "to be obliged to leave my friends, and reside among strangers." In time, King conquered his brooding, and developed material and psychological attachments to his life in liberty that confirmed and reinforced his initial decision to run for the British lines. The extent of this change of mind became particularly evident when, after several years of service with the British, King was taken by Americans and reenslaved in New Jersey.

After his capture, King was quite relieved that he was not "confined in jail," and that his master "used" him as well as he could expect. Further, it is clear from his account that there were moments when such fictions all but convinced the former South Carolinian that to be a slave in a northern city was hardly to be a slave at all. Compared to what he knew at Charleston and environs, the life of an urban slave was only a hardship—not the utter and complete catastrophe he had known previously. Slaves in northern cities got "meat once a day, and milk for breakfast and supper," and it was not unheard of for masters to allow their blacks to study when not in service, so "that they may learn to read the Scriptures."[11]

Such reasoning notwithstanding, King could never delude himself for long. "Sometimes I thought, if it was the will of God that I should be a slave, I was ready to resign myself to his will; but at other times I could not find the least desire to content myself in slavery." So just as there came a time when Olaudah Equiano's travails in the Biafran interior convinced him that he would, perhaps, have to reconcile himself to slavery, Boston King's life as a free man behind British lines eventually moved him to the point where he found the prospect of enslavement completely untenable. Accordingly, when the time was right, he risked his life to get back to British lines.[12]

Formerly enslaved blacks who achieved their liberty among the British tended to develop in the process a potent allegiance to the king and the cause that made their manumissions possible. Boston King, for instance, was not particularly well treated when he first went among the British. When he and other blacks succumbed to smallpox, the British quarantined them and sometimes did not supply food or water for a day at a time. It was, as King later recounted, "a grievous circumstance to me and many others." Yet when King recovered, buoyed no doubt by a "happiness of liberty," it became clear very soon that the war and his time with the British had forged in him unequivocal loyalties.[13] Once, when King was separated from the main body of his regiment, a militia captain enticed King to desert by saying, "I have been long enough in the English service, and am determined to leave them." To this, King responded with indignation. Such was his loyalty that when King escaped from his would-be co-conspirator turned kidnapper, he quickly informed British officials about the man's treason, causing a troop of light horse to track the deserter and burn him out of house and home.[14]

On ground level, black loyalism often expressed itself in patron-client relationships that developed between refugees and the British troops among whom they lived and worked. Such relationships framed the travels of David George from the time he and his family departed Silver Bluff for the British lines. It was a Colonel Brown who fetched George from a British jail after he was imprisoned for conspiring to lead the Silver Bluff people back to their former homes. In Savannah, George's wife, Phillis, "used to wash for General Clinton," the British commander. When the Georges fled from Georgia to Charleston, South Carolina, David George apparently entered the service of the British major who commanded the town. Consequently, when the Georges moved from one British outpost to another, David George apparently smoothed his way with letters of recommendation from the officers he served previously.[15]

Boston King's memoirs give further evidence that patron-client relations were critical to the development and articulation of black loyalism. To the American militiaman who tempted King to desert by asking, "How would you like me to be your master?" it is telling that King replied that he was "Captain Grey's servant," at once asserting his liberty and calling attention to the personal ties between black refugees and British troops that helped define the nature of black liberty and loyalism.

After a year with Grey, King "entered into the service" of another soldier, the commanding officer at Nelson's Ferry. The 250 or so British troops stationed there were constantly endangered by the approximately 1,600 American forces who roamed the area. When writing about his experiences at this new post, King detailed further the kind of loyalism that developed among blacks who served with the British. When British troops at Nelson's Ferry were in particularly dire straits, the officer King served prevailed on him to set off across enemy lines with a letter begging for reinforcements, "promising me," King later recalled, "great rewards, if I was successful in the business." King was successful, and when he reached British troops near Mums Corner, the captain he met there received him with "great kindness," marveling at his "courage and conduct."[16]

This kind of interaction between blacks and British officers was definitive of black loyalism. King made the point especially clear, though by negative example, when he related how the Nelson's Ferry matter eventually concluded. When the captain who received King took him to the camp's commander to deliver his plea for reinforcements, the colonel in question earned King's disdain for his handling of the matter. "Colonel Small gave me three shillings, and many fine promises," King recalled before adding the rebuke, "which were all that I ever received for this service from him."[17] The loyalism blacks cultivated alongside their newly won liberty ensured that the latter developed into more than the erasure of their former bondage. By their loyalism, blacks infused their liberty with palpable senses of honor, propriety, and entitlement; through their loyalty blacks considered themselves enfranchised in the way of the king's other free subjects.

A small but significant number of black loyalists added Christian practice, ideology, and rhetoric to the way they expressed and articulated their liberty, and there is evidence that the war itself fueled this development. In the southern colonies, from where the majority of black loyalists hailed, most of the enslaved population "lived and died strangers to Christianity." In the main, slaveholders' general hostility toward instructing their slaves, and a High Church clergy ill equipped for catechizing even a captive audience, if faced with a cultural divide of any magnitude, ensured that Christianity and black southerners confronted one another hardly at all. So, though there were black Christians here and there across the southern colonies before the era of the American Revolution, there were no black churches to speak of and thus no viable institutions capable of making the faith matter to enslaved people at large.[18]

This state of things began to give way during the era of the American war, and largely as a consequence of the conflict itself. The faint collective biography that emerges from advertisements for runaway slaves during the period from the start of Anglo-American crisis to the war years suggests that the Revolutionary conflict accelerated the potential if not the force of black Christianity. On one front, quite simply, that the war offered surer hopes for freedom meant successful fugitives had a greater chance for the independent practice and development of their faith. Daniel—"has on his sides and back several large bumps like warts, occasioned by whipping"— who ran away from Chesterfield County Virginia in May 1781 "when the British troops were there" and who was "much given to singing hymns," surely had more room to maneuver as a Christian than did Hannah— "scarified under the throat from one ear to the other. . . . pretends much to the religion the Negroes of late have practised"—who bolted southward from Virginia in 1767 hoping simply to pass for free. The American war was important because the circumstances of conflict loosened, for a while, the constraints then binding black Christianity. During the war, as Sylvia Frey and Betty Wood have demonstrated, enslaved Christians took advantage of increased social space to develop, on their own terms, the inner workings of more independent churches.[19]

The life of David George and the history of the congregations of which he was a part offer a singularly important example of this process. George had "no serious thoughts" about his soul until the birth of his first child. It was sometime afterward that his spiritually ambiguous if not dissolute manner inspired a black itinerant laborer from Charleston to tell him that he "should never see the face of God in glory" if he continued living as he was. The words pricked George severely, and to counter his uneasiness he began to pray fervently, constantly repeating the Lord's Prayer that it, as he put it, "might make me better." But rather than subside, George's melancholy only deepened. He told chroniclers who listened to his life story years later: "I felt my *own* plague." So great was George's despair he could hardly work; he told his owner that he was ill.[20]

After reaching this valley and realizing that there was little he could do to save his soul or to will himself a better man, George surrendered in prayer, and as he put it, "now the Lord took away my distress. . . . I was so sure that the Lord took it away because I had such pleasure and joy in my soul, that no man could give me." This pleasure and joy turned to commission and confidence as George steadily grew stronger in Christ. He witnessed openly, began to pray publicly, and with others—white and black, free and enslaved—nurtured at Silver Bluff a steady Afro-Baptist congregation. He soon developed "a desire for nothing else but to talk to the brothers and sisters about the Lord." His co-religionists, recognizing his skill and calling, conferred with a white minister who earlier helped to form them into a church and asked whether George might serve as an elder, leading the hymns and encouraging the people.[21]

George "proceeded in this way till the American war was coming on, when the Ministers were not allowed to come amongst us lest they should furnish us with too much knowledge." Thus circumstances required that full responsibility for the church at Silver Bluff devolve slowly onto George until he had the "whole management" of the church. Spurred on perhaps by these new duties, at this time George also learned to read, taking lessons from the white children on the property. Obviously, the committed elder developed into a strong minister, for the congregation grew as George did. He "continued preaching at Silver Bluff, till the church, constituted with eight, encreased to thirty or more, and till the British came to the city Savannah and took it."[22]

At this, as we have already seen, the George family and about fifty other Silver Bluff blacks made for the coast. Once at Savannah, the church George had nursed in the interior maintained itself and perhaps even expanded while in exile. In Savannah, the Silver Bluff congregants commingled with other blacks then in the city to nurture among the chaos of occupation a viable, living church. Indeed, years after the war's end, former leaders of the Savannah church referred to the experience as something of a crucible. In 1791, George Liele—a Virginia-born black minister who preached at Silver Bluff before the war, ministered with David George in and around Savannah during the war, and came to the leadership of the Savannah church before the war's end—wrote the following recommendation for Hannah Williams, herself then bound for London: "We . . . do certify, that our beloved *Sister Hannah Williams during the time she was a member of the church at Savannah until the vacuation, did walk* as a faithful well-behaved Christian, and do recommend her to join any church of the same faith and order."[23]

Liele's recommendation for Hannah Williams, along with the rambling geography of his own vita, makes another point concerning what one scholar has called "The Priority of the Silver Bluff Church and Its Promoters": that the post-war dislocations of black Christians opened the way for the continuation and amplification of the wartime experience. David George, as we will see below, would be instrumental in turning Nova Scotia's black communities into thoroughly Christianized ones. George Liele—sometime preacher at Silver Bluff and pastor of the Savannah church—planted a thriving black Baptist congregation in Jamaica after the war. Andrew Bryan, another wartime Savannah supplicant, remained after the British evacuation to sustain and then significantly increase the church there. Jessie Peter (also called Gaulphin), who with David George was an original member of the church at Silver Bluff and later at Savannah, returned to the area around Silver Bluff after the war to reestablish and expand the church. Brother Amos, also a member of the Savannah church, departed for the Bahama Islands at war's end, where he founded a congregation at Providence (a church that by 1791 had three hundred members). We can only guess at Hannah Williams's post-war activities in England, but that she continued in London the kind of service that distinguished her in Savannah we can be fairly certain.[24]

The way the war pushed blacks into cities keyed and facilitated many of the social and cultural transformations that emerged from Afro-American wartime migration. The growth and conversion of the Silver Bluff congregation from a small rural church to an Afro-Baptist movement of hemispheric proportions, for instance, was clearly an urban phenomenon. The gathering of small, black Baptist congregations in Savannah during the war concentrated in one area a tremendous array of black Baptist leadership alongside a host of potential converts, and all outside the restrictive confines of chattel slavery. The result, as we have seen, was the nurturing and articulation of an Afro-Baptist faith and identity that would eventually make itself felt across North America and the Caribbean.

Similarly, the exigencies of urban life affected Afro-American notions of personal liberty and British loyalty. In this way, Savannah, Charleston, and New York functioned in ways not unlike Old Calabar, Elem Kalabari, and Bonny in the slave trade from the Biafran interior. In the American cities in which black refugees crowded for months and years at a time, hundreds of blacks whose previous communities were defined, in great measure, by their members' slave status worked out and practiced what it meant to live and work as free, loyal subjects of Great Britain. When Boston King ran to the British and had to confront his despair at having left friends and family, he was aided no doubt by the fact that Charleston was filled with hundreds of blacks in similar circumstances, erstwhile slaves scrambling to consolidate, articulate, and protect their liberty.

Black refugees clearly defined their liberty in relation to each other, and so blacks who were strangers to one another before the war formed themselves into self-conscious communities of free blacks over the course of the conflict. While living in British-controlled New York, Boston King married—a deed that for a former slave must have been a central part of defining his new condition but also a feat that was facilitated by the fact that King was pressed in a city with hundreds of potential mates also striving to consolidate their liberty. It is also telling that when Boston King wrote of his life in New York he made as much use of "we" as he did of "I," thus testifying in several places to the city's community of black refugees. When King escaped to New York after having been re-enslaved and trapped for a time in New Jersey, for example, he reported that his "friends rejoiced to see me once more restored to liberty, and joined me in praising the Lord for his mercy and goodness."[25]

Describing the termination of the war in 1783, King gave further evidence of the nature of the black community that refugees managed to build in New York. King wrote that the armistice "diffused universal joy among all parties, except us," by whom he meant those "who had escaped from slavery, and taken refuge in the English Army." At the end of the war a report ricocheted among blacks in New York that part of the British settlement would be to return to the Americans all slaves who had taken refuge within their lines. "This dreadful rumor," King later remembered, "filled us all with inexpressible anguish and terror, especially when we saw our old masters coming from Virginia, North Carolina, and other parts, and seizing upon their slaves in the streets of New-York, or even dragging them out of their beds."[26]

More than one freedman was dragged from Manhattan Island and forced back into servitude by former owners before Guy Carleton, the city's British commander, stood firm on the promises the king's forces held out during the war. In a meeting with George Washington, Carleton guaranteed the liberty of those slaves who had sought the protection of the British before the cessation of hostilities, and he later supervised the evacuation of these black loyalists to Nova Scotia—along with the city's other royalist refugees.[27]

Boston King welcomed the exodus and reported on it in a way that calls attention to each of the transformations the war and its migrations made possible among blacks: the bone-deep attachment blacks made to their liberty, the abiding loyalism and sense of entitlement they developed over the course of the conflict, and the nascent Christianity the war facilitated among blacks. While Generals Carleton and Washington wrangled over the fate of the black loyalists, the refugees pondered what had become an impossibility for them: returning to slavery. The very thought, wrote King, "embittered life to us." King recounted the Washington-Carleton agreement in terms that stressed the wartime precedents on which the slaves had acted, stressing therefore what was owed to blacks because of their loyalty to the king. The agreement, King held, imported, "That all slaves should be free, who had taken refuge in the British lines, and claimed the sanction and privileges of the Proclamations respecting the security and protection of Negroes." Of the journey he and thousands of others then made from New York to the Maritimes, King wrote: "We arrived in Burch Town in the month of August, where we all safely landed. . . . That Winter, the work of religion began to revive among us and many were convinced of the sinfulness of sin, and turned from the error of their ways."[28]

For the black southerners who were to become Nova Scotian settlers, the war years and their attendant dislocations were a kind of crucible, and the cities in which black refugees often found themselves were crucibles indeed. It was in the confusion and chaos of the Revolution, and in American cities in particular, that blacks who ran away to the British forged for themselves a peculiar kind of freedom. It was peculiar because unlike the freedom that would have been familiar to them in the slave societies from which they hailed—a freedom based from the bottom up on the exclusion, circumscription, and dependency of black prerogatives—the Nova Scotia settlers claimed for themselves liberty—liberty granted by the king and his servants and paid for by their own service. Accordingly, their wartime experience did more than erase their enslavement, it imparted as well a sense of independence and enfranchisement. In the parlance of the times, and as recorded in the margins of the "Book of Negroes" next to a good number of emigrants, these former slaves sailed to Nova Scotia on their own bottoms. Further, not only were they now free—as was recorded on the passes and papers many carried with them—through their service they had also proven themselves "good Subject[s] to King George." So they were loyalists, too.[29]

The war also helped prepare the ground for the planting and nascent development of an Afro-Christian identity among a population who were previously unreceptive, ill at ease, or simply unaffected by Christian ideology. To be sure, the conversion of David George and others like him was an anomaly. Yet because it was an anomaly that sprang, in important ways, from circumstances peculiar to the war years, its idiosyncrasy hardly renders it insignificant. Religious transformations such as George's planted among former slaves who had just become nominally free British subjects the means to engage and define their liberty across a wider terrain, an expanse once the exclusive spiritual and political domain of their masters. Once in the Maritimes, black settlers elaborated the political expectations and social potential generated during the Revolution into the foundational ideas on which they established black communities across Nova Scotia.

EIGHT

BLACK SOCIETY AND THE LIMITS OF BRITISH FREEDOM

Loyalist emigrants from the former thirteen colonies washed over Nova Scotia in a massive wave.[1] Coming first in great fleets of organized transports and then in steady streams of constantly shuttling ships, between April and late November 1783, more than sixteen thousand refugees from Britain's failed war landed in her last North American colony. In return for their allegiance during the late conflict, the government saw not only to the resettlement of these refugees but promised them all, black and white, land on which to remake their lives and provisions to tide them over in the meantime.[2] Only, in Nova Scotia, few of these assurances ever really materialized. Without land or provisions—especially without land—the scope of black liberty narrowed considerably, until it was in large part simply commensurate with poverty, wage labor, and the constant threat of racial violence. The limits of British freedom were hard. But the harsh reality of Nova Scotia refined, rather than wore away at, black loyalist society as it had been forged during the migrations of the American war. And in the end, the troubles and checks on their freedom that black settlers faced in the Maritimes primed them for yet another migration.

In and around Shelburne (the renamed Port Roseway), officials declared themselves satisfied in 1786 that all of the grants due the area's loyalists were properly laid out and surveyed. Conspicuously excepted from this declaration, however, were claimants settled at the all-black Birchtown. For them it would be two more years of landlessness until colonial officials completed their grants. Even then, only one-third of Birchtown's black men actually received farms, and the farms granted averaged just a little more than half the size of those allotted to white settlers living nearby. For black loyalists all over Nova Scotia—those living in all-black enclaves as well as those living within larger loyalist settlements—these kinds of discrepancies were all too familiar. As a rule, black loyalists granted farms in Nova Scotia made do with smaller tracts than their white counterparts. More often than not, however, black claimants received no land whatsoever.[3]

Exacerbating this landlessness was the fact that the provisions promised

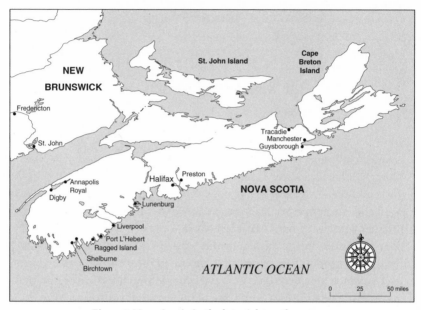

Figure 9. Nova Scotia in the late eighteenth century
Source: Map drawn by the Cartographic Laboratory, Department of Geography,
University of Wisconsin

black settlers for the periods during which their claims were processed suffered, in many instances, the same fate as their applications for land: They were delayed and denied. Without land, these new settlers were without prospect for securing independent livelihoods; without provisions, they tumbled headlong into destitution. In consequence, Nova Scotia's black immigrants often became wage laborers or indentured themselves in order to survive. Once in the labor market, black laborers and tradesmen found that the depth of their poverty and the discriminatory practices of white employers ensured that they commanded far less in wages than did their white counterparts. "It was this way it was," a Nova Scotian recalled generations later, "if you worked, you got whatever them that hired you thought was right and not very much o'that." Indeed, sometimes payment was not made in wages at all but in kind with pork or beef.[4]

White workers fumed at being undercut by this kind of cheap labor, and in consequence they sometimes resorted to violence. In Shelburne in the summer of 1784 a white mob rose against the area's black settlers in what a contemporary noted in his journal as "Great Riot Today." "The disbanded soldiers," he explained, "have risen against the Free negroes to drive them out of Town, because they labour cheaper than they—the soldiers" The mob, no doubt, was also frustrated with the snail's pace at which colonial officials parsed nearby land even for white settlers. In at least ten days of unchecked violence, the rioters razed about twenty black homes, forcing "the free negroes to quit the Town" altogether. David George, an object of the violence, recounted later that about "forty or fifty disbanded soldiers" reported to his property armed "with the tackle of ships, and turned my dwelling house . . . quite over." Because destroying his home, and the houses of others who lived on the lot, was not enough to drive the preacher out, the mob returned the following day and beat George into a nearby swamp. He and his family, like other black Shelburnites, retreated across the river to Birchtown.[5]

Across Nova Scotia, full-blown race riots like the one at Shelburne were rare. But violence on a smaller scale, both committed and threatened, was endemic. On occasion, black loyalists fortunate enough to receive grants of land were chased from their farms, their property appropriated by white settlers. Black day laborers and indentured servants suffered similar fates when their employers refused to pay wages, knowing blacks had little recourse to the courts. Even more chilling were incidents in which black working people who owned little besides their liberty lost even that when their employers "destroyed their tickets of freedom, and then enslaved the negroes for want of them." On occasion, such "unfortunate Africans" might then be "taken on board vessels, carried to the West Indies, and there sold for the benefit of their plunderers."[6]

For black loyalists, all of this—the abuses meted out by fellow settlers, and the poverty enforced by landlessness—was exacerbated by the often extreme physical conditions that prevailed across the Maritimes. Oral tradition from the largest of Nova Scotia's black enclaves suggests that for years after their arrival blacks struggled even to provide themselves with proper shelter against the elements. "I've heard grandfather tell about them," recalled a Birchtowner in the early 1930s when asked about the black loyalists and their habitations. "They just dug a hole in the ground and put a little peaked roof over it. They chose a hill for their purpose because the ground was drier. The peak roof would shed the water when it rained. There was a small trapdoor in one side of the roof and the negroes entered the house by dropping right down through. And that was the black man's home—a hole in the ground with a roof over the hole."[7] Suggesting that this rather dismal report may not have been far from the truth, preliminary archaeological work in the Birchtown area recently discovered an eight-foot by seven-foot subterranean living space, with no evidence of a superstructure, that was probably occupied from the early 1780s to the early 1790s.[8]

Black settlers were ill prepared on other fronts for the demands of the Nova Scotia countryside. The relatively well-to-do David George tells of returning to Shelburne from a mission trip to Preston when a winter storm blew his ship off course. George had no blanket and his clothing was unequal to the chill and wind of the North Atlantic (though by this time he had been in Nova Scotia some six winters). Consequently, before reaching Shelburne the preacher suffered frostbite in both of his legs and was unable to walk again in full stride until the spring (in the meantime, George's brethren carried him to preach on a wooden sled). In eastern Nova Scotia, the story was told of Tom Thompson, who while traveling from the lower part of Guysborough to the black settlement on the outskirts of town became faint with cold. Too afraid to ask for assistance at the homesteads of white settlers that he passed on the way, Thompson trudged on to Niggertown Hill. The journey cost him his feet, which had to be amputated.[9]

Black settlers across the Maritimes were continually denied the privileges due loyalists and the rights of free subjects, but under these conditions the social and cultural rhythms born of blacks' former migrations and central to the development of black loyalist society continued unabated. The more that circumstances in the Maritimes made it clear that black settlers were neither loyalists nor free subjects, at least not in the manner of their white counterparts, the more black society seemed to crystallize in defiance of such facts.

The situation of black settlers in and around Preston provides a telling illustration. The majority of the town's blacks were excluded from Preston's original grant because of the timing of their arrival in the area, or as the local surveyor put it, for "not being here when it was made." Only in March of 1785, probably some two years after their landing, were eighty-six Preston blacks able to lay official claim to a parcel reserved for their general use. Other settlers who arrived after this first award—around thirty-six in number—had to wait two more years for a parcel of their own. Even then, the land granted Preston's blacks were allocated in toto, and not divided into lots for individual families. The local surveyor protested that he was under no obligation to lay out the lots in greater detail without some remuneration from the settlers in question (perhaps a reasonable claim, given that the poor soul could hardly depend on the arrival of even his government pay). Many of Preston's whites—"& two or three of the Blacks" as well—thought the demand a sensible one and paid accordingly. The generality of blacks, however, refused.[10]

In recounting their refusal, Preston's embattled surveyor gave the impression that black intransigence flowed not from their poverty but from principle. "These People have all an Idea that government should have

Surveyed their Lands to them free of Expence, and this has been the Cause of Continual Murmur and Complaints." Preston's blacks remembered the promises made to them as loyalists and were hardly willing to compromise. Not only that, evidence from the affair suggests that blacks staked their claims as loyalists with no small measure of surety and belligerence, causing the local surveyor to admit as follows concerning their numerous complaints: He would continue, as had been his practice in the past, to exert himself for those blacks "who are in reality unable to pay. And who ask what they want without Threatening Demands." Only these kinds of supplicants, it seems, were not many.[11]

In similar fashion, disappointed, landless black settlers criticized, pleaded, threatened, demanded, and petitioned all across the peninsula. In western Nova Scotia the complaints of settlers Richardson, French, and Goding made their way to the governor after the three were evicted in 1785 from the common on which they squatted (being landless and without provisions or supplies since their arrival in Nova Scotia near two years earlier). Not until Thomas Brownspriggs and seventy-three other black families went public with their plight and petitioned for land in 1787 were blacks around Tracadie, in a northeastern corner of the colony, officially settled. For six years and to little avail, Thomas Peters and more than two hundred associates pressed their claims as loyalists on both sides of the Bay of Fundy, making "repeated Application to all persons" for grants of land they thought theirs by right.[12]

Afro-Christianity across the Maritimes, as it developed from a phenomenon perceptible only among handfuls of blacks into a wide-ranging aspect of Afro-Maritime politics and society, provided another space in which black loyalists asserted themselves as free subjects in the face of ever tightening constraints. Both the broader course and process of black Christianization and the details of black conversation illustrate the point, and the former circumstance is most clearly manifest in the ministries of the newly arrived Nova Scotian David George.

George arrived in Halifax from Charleston, South Carolina, in the winter of 1783. From Halifax, he made his way to Shelburne, where laborers, many of them black, were raising the town. On his first night at the embryonic settlement, George sang hymns at a local campsite. The response was overwhelming. "The Black people came from far and near," George explained, as the hymn singing and fellowship "was so new to them." Within a few days, George's vespers attracted such a following that he appointed a regular evening service "where those poor creatures who had never heard the gospel before" received his sermons with rapt concentration.[13]

When George settled temporarily on the lot of a white loyalist known to him from his days in Savannah, "the people came flocking to the preaching every evening for a month, as though they had come for their supper." And when he and his family had the good fortune to draw a lot of their own, they established the first black Baptist church in Nova Scotia when David and Phillis heard the experiences of four settlers whom the minister George later baptized in a creek running through the property. By the fall of 1784, when the Georges removed from Shelburne to the all-black Birchtown, the Shelburne congregation was more than fifty members strong and had raised its own meeting house. The Georges remained only a short time at Birchtown before returning to Shelburne in early 1785, but while there they established a church of around twenty baptized believers.[14]

Back in Shelburne, George began a series of mission trips that took him through much of the colony. At Ragged Island, about twenty miles from Shelburne, he ministered to whites and blacks alike. Across the Bay of Fundy he ministered to a loyalist settlement at St. John, where he helped to organize a small church comprising, among others, a cell of previously converted black Virginians. George worked at Fredericton in New Brunswick, helped establish a church at Preston, and preached at Halifax. George's errands were potent missions, as he attended many of these fields regularly and assigned elders from the church at Shelburne to live among and guide newly organized congregations.[15]

Across Nova Scotia, High Church Anglicans, Methodists, and Huntingdonians, practiced—to good effect—the Christianizing and church building evident in David George's Baptist missions. The Church of England baptized hundred of blacks at Halifax in the early days of loyalist immigration, and at Digby black loyalists quickly grew to a majority of the Anglican church. Methodist preachers, for their part, recruited black members in and around Halifax, Birchtown, and Digby until by 1790 more than a quarter of the colony's Wesleyans were black. Even the Countess of Huntingdon's Connection—an Anglican offshoot supported by an English noblewoman—planted a chapel at Birchtown and supported black itinerants.[16]

Figuring the effects of these Christianizing efforts in strict numerical terms is a difficult matter. But it is reasonable to estimate that by 1790 black Christians comprised around one-quarter of Nova Scotia's total black population. This is a remarkable proportion. Considering the Christian population of the regions from where black loyalists hailed—locales where Christians comprised from 1 to 5 percent of the total black population—it is clear that Nova Scotia's blacks, in the years following their settlement, participated in a revival of extraordinary measure.

Yet in some ways the absolute magnitude of black Christianity in Nova Scotia is beside the point, for the personal effects and institution building attending conversion lent black congregants a social and political influence out of all proportion to their actual numbers. The process of conversion, especially among nonconformist and Anglican offshoots, encouraged introspection, society, and action of a kind that under the right circumstances was particularly corrosive to ordinary assumptions and practices of social inequality. So as conditions worsened for black loyalists, the growth of black Christianity could not but strengthen the prospect of black resistance.

In this regard, the conversion and Christian walk of black loyalist Violet King at Birchtown, Nova Scotia, are instructive. King's previous life appeared in the "Book of Negroes" as "Formerly the property of Col. Young of Wilmington, North Carolina." She migrated to Nova Scotia with her husband, Boston, arriving at Port Roseway in the fall of 1783. That winter, while attending the services of black Methodist and former soldier Moses Wilkinson, King "was struck to the ground, and cried out for mercy," writhing for upward of two hours. So obvious and prolonged was her distress that others in the meeting sent for her husband to carry her home. She remained inconsolable for six days until "the Lord spoke peace to her soul."[17]

For nine months afterward Violet King "walked in the light of God's countenance," but she was unable to meet her Christian expectations much longer, and she "again gave place to bad tempers, and fell into great darkness and distress." Her husband "never saw any person, either before or since, so overwhelmed with anguish of spirit on account of backsliding, as she was." This constant worrying over the state of her soul, speculated her friends and family, took a toll on her body. Violet King fell ill and was confined to her bed for more than a year.[18]

Her convalescence was long, but "the Lord was pleased to sanctify her afflictions, and to deliver her from all fears," and in the wake of this long ordeal King emerged emboldened. She could not hold her peace and testified about her recent deliverance to all who would listen. Her message was lively and powerful, and her words convinced many of Birchtown's backsliders and skeptics of God's glory. Yet so potent was her delivery, so powerful her experience, and so overwhelming the response of Birchtown's sinners that some of the saints became wary, jealous no doubt of their privilege. "As she was the first person at Burch Town that experienced delivery from evil tempers, and exhorted and urged others to seek and enjoy the same blessing," remembered her husband, "she was not a little opposed by some of our Black brethren."[19]

Nevertheless, King persevered and continued her testimony. Indeed, the power of her conversion experience, and the fact that she "endured with the meekness and patience becoming a christian" the trials devised by her brethren, earned her the approbation of one of American Methodism's founding fathers. When Freeborn Garrettson organized Birchtown's blacks into formal classes during the summer of 1785, he praised and supported King's convictions, telling her "to hold fast her confidence, and cleave to the Lord with her whole heart." From their prominent place in Boston King's memoir, it is clear that Violet took Garrettson's interest and instructions as a kind of rebuke to her persecutors.[20]

Violet King's Christian convictions gave her leave to tread ground normally reserved for men. In similar fashion, black Christians throughout Nova Scotia used their faith to effect social intercourse of a kind to which white settlers might not ordinarily condescend. Thus when David George encountered resistance from New Brunswick settlers during his ministry in and around St. John, George was introduced to the lieutenant governor as a Christian and applied for and was granted leave to preach as one.[21]

Similarly, during his mission to Nova Scotia, Freeborn Garrettson found himself, much to his chagrin and amazement, embroiled in a theological dispute and contest of personality with the lowly John Marrant over the souls of hundreds of Birchtowners. During Garrettson's first visit to Birchtown in the summer of 1785, he organized a society of nearly two hundred believers. When he returned there less than a year later the fellowship was not half as large as he had left it. Garrettson blamed the reduction on "A negro man by the name of Morant, lately from England." Apparently Marrant lured these Birchtowners from one Anglican offshoot to another, and Garrettson was as angry about the trespass as he was put off by the trespasser's apparent credentials. "Surely if lady Huntington had him put into the ministry (as he gave this account) her ladyship was much deceived in the man; or else he has since become an amazing bad one." Frustrated and fuming, the pioneering Methodist returned to fields he thought already well plowed and planted: "When I went to their town, I called them together and informed them of [Marrant's] character. Many of them were convinced of their error, and returned to the society; so that in the whole we only lost about twenty persons."[22]

Through avenues provided by their embrace and articulation of Christian ideologies, black settlers asserted and practiced their credentials as free British subjects and loyalists. On the one hand, the Christianity practiced by Violet King and David George allowed them entrée and gave them influence across the larger Maritime society. To be sure, their influence was only the kind that clients have with patrons, but such relationships, as we have seen, were an important aspect of black loyalist society. In a time when loyalty returned very little as far as former promises for land and provisions were concerned, Christianity offered a space not dissimilar to the one that prevailed during the course of the American war. On the other hand, as is explicit in David George's missions and implicit in the actions of black settlers who deserted white preachers for black, Christianity in the Maritimes was also a place where blacks could exercise their liberty under terms increasingly denied them across the region at large.

For black loyalists, then, the peculiar circumstances of British freedom held peculiar consequences for the development of black community. In Shelburne, Birchtown, Guysborough, Digby, St. John, and other tracts across Nova Scotia, former southern slaves who landed in 1783 became in subsequent years passionate Christians and ardent loyalists—utterly convinced of their entitlement to the fruits of both kingdoms to which they now belonged: God's and George III's. Nothing about their subsequent experiences in Nova Scotia, however, suggested that their expectations would ever coincide with their Nova Scotian reality. Yet such disappointments only hardened their resolve. The more official neglect deprived them of their rights as loyalists, the more they claimed their due. The more that material hardship and white violence threatened their very existence, the more they banded together for survival, as in the fellowship and benevolence of their churches. The 1785 petition of New Brunswick settler and black loyalist William Fisher illustrates in one passage the hardships and attending transformations then affecting the generality of blacks in the Maritimes.

Having left New York in the year 1783 and come in the Ship Peggy Commanded by Capt. Wilson in July in the aforesaid year, we arrived here. I then joined Capt. Walker's Compy. At the Same time, [I] Came in as his Servant having Since got my freedom from his lady. I have, since I Came to myself, got no provisions or any sign of it, or any land, nor Neither have I recd. any one article that is allowed from government to poor indigent Loyalist[s]. Hoping your Excellency will take [my situation] into Consideration and Will grant me the same as is granted to all other loyalists. I have been this winter almost at Death's door both in sickness and in a starving Condition if it had not been for poor people that gave me relief. If your excellency will grant me some small pittance of land and provisions I shall Be forever bound to pray. . . .[23]

It is unknown whether officials in New Brunswick—which in 1784 was carved from Nova Scotia as a separate administrative area—paid any attention to William Fisher's petition. If he fared as well as the majority of black settlers north of the Bay of Fundy, then his plea fell on deaf ears. If his petition was successful and government took notice of his circumstances, then he may have joined the ranks of New Brunswick's propertied black settlers by being granted land in the backcountry of St. John or Fredericton—parcels later described as being "so far distant" from town "as to be entirely useless."[24]

NINE

THE EFFECTS OF EXODUS
Afro-Maritime Society in Motion

Sometime around 1790—some seven winters after the first black loyalists arrived in Nova Scotia—a domestic worker along the Bay of Fundy galvanized the frustrations of settlers like William Fisher and initiated among local blacks a discussion over whether they might better their conditions by once again choosing emigration. A remark batted about at a dinner party, the story goes, lit the spark. A serving man overheard a party of white settlers conversing about Granville Sharp's Province of Freedom and the hundreds of black adventurers—really Londoners as destitute as Nova Scotia's own blacks—who recently left the capital to found a country of their own. The name Sharp resonated with the server—had not he worked in favor of England's slaves?—and the notion of a black settlement at Sierra Leone intrigued him. He related the news to friends and associates, and before long the prospect that the African settlement might somehow figure in the relief of a segment of Nova Scotia's black loyalists animated settlers in Nova Scotia and New Brunswick.[1]

The name of the instigator in question, and whether he was from Annapolis or Digby, from St. John or Fredericton, or from someplace else altogether, is lost. What has survived is an outline of how settlers along the Bay of Fundy turned their Nova Scotian disappointments into a colony-wide discussion over their prospects in the Maritimes, how those discussions turned quickly to decision-making, and how the decisions of hundreds of black Nova Scotians spawned a colony-wide exodus. The narrative of these three moments underlines the consequences for black society of hundreds of black settlers considering, fomenting, and then executing a mass migration from the Maritimes to Sierra Leone. What becomes clear as the story unfolds are the ironic social forces generated by people in exodus. Each phase of black migration from the Maritimes counted on and thus reinforced aspects of Afro-Maritime society generated during the previous migrations of the American war. The efforts made by black settlers to insert themselves into the plans of the Sierra Leone Company beckoned to the kind of patron-client relationships between American blacks and British forces so evident during the late war. The process of decision-making and actual migration burnished black settlers' sense of British loyalism while reinforcing the practical bonds of black Christianity and community forged in the Maritimes. Yet, in the end, all of this apparent continuity led in exodus to fundamental shifts in the nature of Afro-Maritime society.

Far from any source of definitive information about the settlement at Sierra Leone, blacks along the Bay of Fundy could discuss the idea of emigration among themselves for only so long. After their conversations generated a critical mass of interest—more than one hundred settlers at Annapolis and about a hundred families in New Brunswick—they elected one among them to travel to London and represent their circumstances to the African colony's British organizers. Given the hazards that transatlantic travel posed for free blacks—for whom joining a ship was really to wager their liberty—this charge to travel to England was as dangerous as it was weighty. In the end, a formidable fifty-something-year-old former slave and soldier named Thomas Peters took up the task.[2]

Peters disembarked in the capital sometime in the winter of 1790, and his subsequent exploitation of the kinds of patron-client ties common among black loyalists guided his actions and ultimately resulted in a successful mission. On his arrival, Peters very quickly called on the captain of his former company, who provided him with a letter of reference vouching for his good character and service during the American war. He then tracked down the retired commander of British forces in North America, General Henry Clinton. Clinton remembered Peters as "a very active Serjt. in a very useful Corps," listened to the story of how the promises made to this former soldier were still unfulfilled, and wrote on Peters's behalf to the secretary of state for the home department concerning Nova Scotia's blacks who to his mind appeared "deserving the Protection of Govt. & who seem to be the only Loyalists that have been neglected. . . ." At the same time that Peters made inroads with military men known to him from the American war, he also connected with the group of abolitionist reformers and activists behind the Province of Freedom. Peters called on Granville Sharp, was in the company of Thomas and John Clarkson, probably met William Wilberforce, and made the acquaintance of scores of lesser lights in the abolitionist struggle.[3]

Combined, Peters's connections with old soldiers and his new relationships with British abolitionists ensured that the case of his Nova Scotian colleagues reached the highest levels of government. Before Christmas 1790, he presented a series of memorials and petitions desiring that government either provide Nova Scotia's black loyalists the land promised them in the Maritimes or procure for them "some Establishment where they may attain a competent Settlement for themselves and be enabled by their industrious Exertions to become useful Subjects to his Majesty."[4]

Peters was quick to get his story out, but it would be some months still before the matter of Nova Scotia's black loyalists reached official resolution. Most dramatically—there were more mundane reasons as well—this was because despite the stories of Sierra Leone that had brought Peters to London in the first place, it was not altogether clear in the last months of 1790 whether the Province of Freedom still existed. Owing to disease, scarcity, discord with nearby Africans, and conflict with local slave traders, the black settlement at Granville Town had all but disappeared some two years after its founding. So in the winter of 1790, upon Peters's arrival in London, the company of philanthropists who supported the original settlement—and who had evolved by then into a mercantile venture now called the St. George's Bay Association—were in the process of outfitting a ship for Sierra Leone to reconnoiter, report on, and reestablish the colony (for the directors were determined to continue as a business concern what had started as a philanthropy).[5]

Simultaneously, the association was preparing to lobby Parliament for articles of incorporation that would grant them power of governance and a monopoly of trade at the reestablished settlement—hardly a foregone conclusion given the disposition of the House of Commons, but an absolute necessity in the minds of the association if the venture was to have any chance at success. And if all of this was not enough, some of the prime movers in the Sierra Leone business were at the same time preparing to call a Parliamentary vote to abolish the British slave trade.[6]

Thomas Peters landed in London in heady times. Over the course of six to nine months, however, the complexities of his mission melded with the aspirations of the St. George's Bay Association, while folding nicely into the needs of the colonial bureaucracy he had petitioned on his arrival. In April 1791, opponents soundly defeated the bill to abolish the slave trade, prompting reformers to redouble their efforts on all other fronts. Drawing lessons from the abolitionists' recent failure, proponents of the St. George's Bay Association convinced the same MPs who had just voted down the slave trade bill that incorporating an association that was itself tainted by abolitionism was nonetheless in the national interest. By the end of May 1791, the association won this battle, clearing the way for its incorporation as the Sierra Leone Company. Further, by that same summer the expedition to reorganize the settlement at Granville Town was all but completed. Slowly then, things fell into place, and it became clear that Peters's original intentions might be realized after all.[7]

By late summer 1791, in the midst of all of this activity, Thomas Peters's recounting of the injustices suffered by black Nova Scotians convinced the directors of the Sierra Leone Company that they should depend on the Maritimes to reinforce their African settlement. The company's original intentions were to send out a small contingent of employees, a somewhat larger group of artisans and tradesmen, and a generality of white settlers. "Conscious," however, of the "many obvious reasons" for which blacks "were to be preferred to Europeans in the first plantation of a Colony in Africa," the directors decided against encouraging white migrants and instead applied to government to bear the cost of transporting Nova Scotian blacks who so desired to the company's lands in Sierra Leone (a creditable proposal, thought the directors, given that the blacks in question had "bled in the service of Great Britain" but were denied in Nova Scotia the fruits of their previous service).[8]

Having already received Peters's memorial and petition outlining the sufferings of Nova Scotia's blacks, secretary of state for the home department Henry Dundas, who was a little taken aback by Peters's charges, agreed to the company's application. Consequently, Dundas directed officials in the Maritimes to inquire into Peters's accusations. After conducting a proper enquiry, Dundas further ordered that those black loyalists who were not yet in possession of their promised lands be settled immediately "& in a situation so advantageous as may make them some atonement for the injury they have suffered by this unaccountable delay." Further, colonial officers were to make the blacks two more offers. Those who did not want to continue in Nova Scotia, even if finally granted the promises held out to them seven years ago, were to have the option of emigrating to Africa under the auspices of the Sierra Leone Company, and at government expense, a decision that Peters had already made for himself and his family. Lastly, Nova Scotia's blacks were also to have the option of joining British forces in the Caribbean as part of a black corps the secretary desired to establish.[9]

So it was nearly settled. Thomas Peters secured the support of the company, and the company and Thomas Peters secured the support of government. From London, all that was left to do was to procure an agent willing and able to manage the emigration. For this, the company turned to John Clarkson, brother of abolitionist Thomas Clarkson. Stirred by Peters's accounts of black life in the Maritimes, Clarkson agreed to travel to Nova Scotia as the company's agent and conductor. Thomas Peters departed ahead of the company's man, as Clarkson put it, "to appraise his countrymen of my intended visit." Peters arrived in Nova Scotia in early October, having executed the entire mission with which he had been charged almost a year earlier. That his success was due in large part to his loyalist connections and the confidence with which he presented himself as a free British subject is apparent in the comments of one of the objects of Peters's lobbying, who wrote: "Never did [an] ambassador from a sovereign power prosecute with more zeal the object of his mission than did Thomas Peters the cause of his distressed countrymen."[10]

Given the disaster that occurred following the 1787 settlement at Sierra Leone and the broken promises that succeeded the government-sponsored immigration of black loyalists into Nova Scotia in the first place, as far as the Sierra Leone Company was concerned the recruitment of black emigrants was not to go very far beyond what Dundas laid out himself in his letter to the Maritime governors. On his voyage from Britain to Nova Scotia, John Clarkson agonized over the moral consequences of aggressive recruitment should the present Sierra Leone settlement, like the last, flounder. In the end, he "decided upon not soliciting any person to go with me, but to explain to All the views of the Sierra Leone Company and those of his Majesty's Government, and to leave them to make their own choice; for I considered them as men, having the same feelings as myself, & therefore I did not dare to sport with their destiny." Officially, all of the company's employees—Clarkson, Thomas Peters, a physician recruited to attend to the recruited migrants named John Taylor, and a Halifax merchant named to assist them both, one Lawrence Hartshorne—took this line.[11]

From mid-October 1791, blacks along the southwestern shore of Nova Scotia—first at Halifax, then in succession at Dartmouth, Preston, Shelburne, and Birchtown—received visits from official agents of the Sierra Leone Company. At Preston and Port L'Herbert, black families awoke on different mornings to find white strangers among them—John Clarkson and Dr. Taylor—desirous of speaking about the condition of blacks in Nova Scotia and wanting to inform them of the opportunity to migrate to Sierra Leone. Black families at Port L'Herbert invited the visitors into their modest homes—Clarkson called them huts—where conversation proceeded casually from one topic to another until hitting finally and carefully on the subject of emigration. At the residence of Thomas Shepherd, Dr. Taylor studied the deathly ill Mrs. Shepherd and promised to send from Halifax medicine he thought would comfort her before informing the family of the opportunity held out by government and the company. In a similar fashion, black Prestonites invited the roving whites into their homes where they listened attentively to the company's offer and bent Clarkson's ear with stories of the difficulties they had suffered since their arrival in Nova Scotia. Their testimony and the evidence of their persons convinced him that "there cannot be a doubt but that their complaints were founded in facts, for they have certainly been very much oppressed and are now in a deplorable state."[12]

Black Nova Scotians took hold of news about Sierra Leone gathered from the company's agents and from the colonial press and fanned it along their own networks. So at moments—because Thomas Peters's and Dundas's letters to the governors of Nova Scotia and New Brunswick reached the Maritimes before Clarkson and Taylor—the company's agents, rather than always seeking black settlers to recruit, found that Nova Scotia's black settlers were just as prone to seek them out. At Birchtown, Nova Scotia's largest black enclave, potential emigrants read of the company's propositions prior to the arrival of the company's agents. So even before Clarkson and Taylor regained their land legs and set about recruiting in and around Halifax, Birchtowners and black Shelburnites were already deliberating on the matter. Having read and reread, considered and reconsidered the plan as presented on paper, they were at a loss concerning a few important points and so fired off a letter to Halifax, under the signature of Stephen Bluck, requesting further information. There were, Bluck wrote, "various reports" as to how would-be emigrants would be provisioned on their arrival in Sierra Leone. To address this confusion, he asked the agents to forward further information regarding "provision and transportation as the Directors furnished for the encouragement of Adventurers."[13]

If the black Baptists of Birchtown and Shelburne were part of the group who requested Bluck to write to Halifax, they soon grew impatient waiting for a reply. Having discussed the matter among themselves since the company's advertisement began circulating but having heard nothing from the company's agents, the Baptists voted to send their minister, David George, to Halifax to gather firsthand information on the proposed emigration scheme. But George never made his planned trip. On the morning of October 25, while preparing to embark for Halifax, he encountered at Shelburne the very men he was on his way to find. The company's agents, having already been at Halifax, Dartmouth, Preston, and Port L'Herbert, were come to the demographic center of black Nova Scotia to inform would-be migrants of the company's proposals.[14]

Shelburne's black teacher carried to Birchtown news that agents of the Sierra Leone Company would visit the settlement the following afternoon. The next day, a throng of more than three hundred blacks waited under heavy clouds to meet the two white men who had just made the short trip from Shelburne to Birchtown. Before the agents could describe the company's proposal and before those gathered could ask a single question, it began to rain. The assembled blacks moved the meeting inside one of their chapels. Pressed indoors, they invited John Clarkson to speak.[15]

Clarkson took the floor with a spate of papers in his hand. He was in church, and though surely no one expected him to preach, there were few, certainly, who thought that he would begin to read. But read he did, loud enough to be heard over the rain: "Sir, I transmit to you here with a Memorial of Thomas Peters, a Black, who served with the King's Troops in America during the late War . . . complaining that he and his Associates have not obtained the Allotments of Land promised to be granted to them . . . . If what the Petition represents be true, they have certainly strong grounds for complaint. . . ." This was the letter the British secretary of state had sent to the governor of Nova Scotia more than two months earlier. Clarkson repeated it word for word to the assembly, laying out in general the three options before them. They could continue in Nova Scotia and the promises of seven years ago would be fulfilled; they could remove from their present homes and join one of the West Indian black regiments that government was intended to form; or they could, at government expense, leave the Maritimes for a "Settlement on the River Sierra Leona" lately put forth by a cadre of London gentlemen. This last option, read Clarkson quoting Dundas, would be "attended with expence to the Public," but, and these words must have struck a chord among a people so self-conscious of their status as loyalists, "His Majesty in consideration of their Services, is anxious that they should be gratified, and that measures should be taken for that purpose."[16]

After finishing Dundas's rather long letter to Nova Scotia's Governor Parr, Clarkson turned the leaves of another document and began reading yet again: "The Sierra Leone Company willing to receive into their Colony such Free Blacks as are able to produce to their Agents Lieut. Clarkson of His Majesty's Navy and Mr. Lawrence Hartshorne house of Halifax or either of them satisfactory Testiments of their Character (more particularly as to Honesty, Sobriety & Industry) think it proper to notify in an explicit Manner upon which Terms they will receive at Sierra Leone those who bring with them written Certificates of Approbation from either of the said Agents which Certificates they are hereby respectively authorized to grant or withhold at Discretion." This was a version of the company announcement with which the audience was familiar. In the main, it outlined the amount of land emigrants would be granted in Sierra Leone and spoke to the nature of civil society and governance at the new settlement.[17]

After Clarkson completed the company's announcement, he addressed the audience directly, saying that the entirety of the company's present offer was due to the labors of Thomas Peters while in London. Then Clarkson attempted, in his own words, to summarize the details he had just read in the letter from Dundas and in the advertisement from the Sierra Leone Company. But here the monologue ended, for as Clarkson began to expound on the salient points of the government's offer of transport and the company's offer of settlement, members of the audience shouted out questions.

What did it mean, the parenthetical note in the company's proposal that land grants in Sierra Leone would be "subject to such changes and obligations (with a view to the general Prosperity of the Company) as shall hereafter be settled by the Company in respect to the Grants of Lands to be made by them to all settlers whether black or white"? Those assembled had been promised free land before, only to be told that it could not be granted unless they paid to have it laid out. Was this a similar ruse—a fee, or worse, a rent in disguise? Clarkson assured them that the stipulation, vague as it was, "was by no means to be considered as an annual rent." Rather, the passage in question referred to a tax, a benevolence really, to be applied to "charitable purposes such as for the maintenance of their poor, the care of their sick, and the education of their children."[18]

Others in the audience called out questions concerning their transportation to Africa. Many must have remembered their initial voyages to Nova Scotia and the poor treatment they received at the hands of the crew who piloted them to the Maritimes. And on their arrival, black settlers, as we have seen, were constantly on guard for unscrupulous sailors bent on enticing them aboard ship and enslaving them. In their advertisement, the directors of the Sierra Leone Company had promised would-be emigrants a settlement free of slavery and characterized by equal protection under the law for both blacks and whites. So some in the audience wanted to know whether they would or could be afforded such protections while gathering aboard the transports and while at sea. As a matter of course, replied Clarkson, masters would have to depend on the labor of those shipboard when circumstances required. But for all intents and purposes emigrants would travel as passengers, and as such "no compulsive methods would be adopted towards them nor would a white sailor upon any account be suffered with impunity to lift up his hand against them."[19]

Back and forth it went on like this for some time. But as the afternoon and the rain wore on, the assembly appeared more and more satisfied with the offers and assurances put forth by the company and government. Before standing down, Clarkson, according to his determination to recruit as passively as possible, asked the assembly to give all three offers their utmost consideration, not just the proposal of the company. In any case, the company's agents would not begin interviewing potential emigrants until tomorrow afternoon. With this, the assembly broke up.[20]

As the people drifted out of the chapel, the black farmers, mechanics, day laborers, and washerwomen of Birchtown and Shelburne responded to Clarkson's plea for judiciousness by buttonholing him on their way out and justifying individually the crowd's general response to the Sierra Leone proposal. Phrasing their explanations in as many ways as there were people present, together they told Clarkson that "their labour was lost upon the land in this country, and their utmost efforts would barely keep them in existence." Consequently, they were determined to quit the colony; they would rather wager their lives, said some, than remain in Nova Scotia.[21]

Over the course of the next eleven days—before Clarkson and Taylor returned to Halifax—blacks from Birchtown, Shelburne, and environs came in the hundreds to sign on for Sierra Leone. In others parts of Nova Scotia and New Brunswick, where potential migrants negotiated with agents appointed by the colony as opposed to being in direct contact with company representatives, the same kind of enthusiasm prevailed. In less than three weeks after the October 25 meeting at Birchtown, nearly eight hundred settlers announced themselves for Sierra Leone. And when these would-be migrants had to prove their intentions by actually making for Halifax in preparation for embarkation, they came in even greater numbers: on the cusp of winter 1791, more than a thousand men, women, and children sailed, rode, and marched into the city.[22]

This is an amazing number. For the period in question, conservative estimates place the black population of New Brunswick and Nova Scotia at about thirty-five hundred. But even if there were five thousand black settlers across the Maritimes in late 1791, the decision of more than one thousand of them to quit the country en masse represents a population movement of enormous proportions. Consider, for example, that throughout England from 1773 to 1776, about eighteen hundred voyagers per year, in a territory whose population hovered around 6 million, chose to remove to the other side of the Atlantic. For migration from England to British America during the period indicated above to have matched the intensity of the exodus that later transpired in Nova Scotia, more than 1 million souls per annum would have had to decide to make the voyage to the North American mainland (a number five hundred times greater than the two thousand emigrants a year who actually did depart). This rather outrageous contrast suggests that the sheer mass of what was to happen in the Maritimes made it more than a simple migration.[23]

In New Brunswick and Nova Scotia, whole congregations, workgangs, neighborhoods, and hamlets, even entire towns, decided together to attempt to replant and reproduce themselves in a new land, and to do so under the guidance of a single conductor—John Clarkson—who wielded significant authority over the process of their coming resettlement. The migration from the Maritimes became, in fairly short order, an exodus.

As an exodus—a mass, centralized movement of entire communities—black emigration generated peculiar repercussions for the migrants involved. As the exodus grew in potential, it tempered to a hard edge tenets that had come to define black society across the Maritimes; but as the exodus gathered actual mass, the circumstances of its realization dulled the consequence of these same aspects of Afro-Maritime society. The exodus sharpened expressions of black loyalism and Christianity, as it compromised their effect as bulwarks against white authority and as expressions of Afro-Maritime independence. Following the decision-making process of black settlers across the Maritimes—paying special attention to obstacles to their enlistment and how they justified, nonetheless, their intention to emigrate and then watching how they began the voyage to Sierra Leone—brings this paradox into focus.

Blacks responded enthusiastically to the company's planned settlement at Sierra Leone, but because detractors of the plan obstructed would-be emigrants in every conceivable way, actually volunteering for the colony was no easy task. At one level, the same network over which black settlers transmitted news of the company's planned African settlement carried as well rumor and innuendo fashioned by the plan's critics. Fearful that a full-scale black exodus from Nova Scotia would prove the charges Thomas Peters made in London and strike a blow to the economic interests of those who depended on black labor, officials in the colonial government and the region's principal men whispered constantly about mortality along the west African coast, raised doubts about the company's intentions, and wildly fanned any bad news that might arrive from Sierra Leone.

In the first official announcements about the offer of the Sierra Leone Company—notices composed in Nova Scotia prior to the arrival of the company's employees—colonial officials played word games in order to give pause to potential emigrants. The notices made conspicuous use of a term for western Africa preferred by slave traders, offering that the government proposed to provide black settlers with free passage straight to "Guinea." In and around Shelburne and Birchtown, helpful whites harped on ambiguous passages in the company's offer, claiming that the settlement plan meant to make serfs out of those credulous enough to sign on.

Others passed around material from the proceedings of the Society for the Propagation of the Gospel in Foreign Parts in which the divines lamented the failed settlement made in Sierra Leone by black Londoners some three years previous. A minister the Society sent out to the colony was "much injured by the undertaking," and though it had been many months since failing health obliged the missionary to return from there to London, he had "not yet found the blessing of a perfect restoration."[24]

A similar kind of dissuasion took place in the colonial papers, where a Nova Scotian writing under the name Philanthropos highlighted weaknesses in the company's proposal. Philanthropos warned blacks to steer clear of the scheme lest they "fall victims to the mistaken principles of commerce" at its base. On top of all of this, as early as October 1791 word reached Halifax concerning what had become of Sierra Leone's first black colonists: a local big man recently routed the settlement. With this news, even the governor himself predicted the plan's failure.[25]

Opponents of black emigration did not confine themselves simply to talking against the plan. Quite often their opposition rose to violence. In and around Shelburne, the chief magistrate and other principal men visibly displayed their contempt for blacks considering the plan and the agents who publicized it. Such men threatened David George, suggesting that he would leave the Sierra Leone business alone if he knew what was good for him. This kind of intimidation worked to a point: It did not convince George to drop the matter, but it put him in fear of his life, persuading him to be as circumspect as possible in his support of emigration.[26]

At Digby, opponents of emigration made good on the kinds of threats and insults David George suffered farther south: Thomas Peters took a beating for his recruitment efforts. In New Brunswick, colonial officials and white settlers detained would-be emigrants for debts and contracts real and forged. At St. John, for instance, detractors fabricated notes and indentures in the names of prospective migrants and their dependents, saying that they would prosecute any who tried to leave. Similar kinds of deterrents obtained at Shelburne, where a potential emigrant had to steal his indentured son from a butcher who was decided on taking the boy to Boston, where he intended, according to the father, to sell him as a slave.[27]

Potential migrants negotiated a series of less serious official obstacles as well. The company's directors iterated in their communications, both public and private, that only volunteers likely "to become profitable Members of the new Community" should be enrolled, and officially would-be emigrants were to produce certificates of good character before being signed on. In practice, this was a stipulation that company officials on the ground were often willing to overlook, but in ways in which the qualification could still prove itself something of an impediment. So when local whites refused to write out certificates and attest for themselves to the character of a black emigré, applicants could prove their worth beyond a doubt by virtue of what they had been able to eke out, year after year, during their time in the Maritimes. A house "in decent order," land, if a family had any, "cultivated as well as it can be," and signs of having acquired even "moderate property, such as several bushels of Potatoes &c &c" were, in lieu of a certificate, all the character testimony Clarkson required.[28]

Stephen Bluck, prominent among the black settlers at Birchtown and Shelburne and very formal in his correspondence, had the disconcerting habit, as far as the company's agents were concerned, of omitting key terms in the certificates of character he issued to potential migrants. Whereas the company was interested in the sobriety, honesty, and industriousness of volunteers, Bluck routinely omitted one term or another from his recommendations. Abigail Godfrey—who with three generations of her family in tow had run from Norfolk, Virginia, when she herself was over seventy years old—according to Bluck was sober and industrious but, apparently, insufficiently honest. Job Allen—not much over thirty years old and who during the war had run to the British from the eastern shore of Maryland—was, according to Bluck, honest and industrious but perhaps not very sober, as that description did not appear on his certificate.[29]

In all, Bluck described more than twenty potential migrants using only two of the three qualities required by the company. The various omissions prompted one of the company's agents, Dr. Taylor, to write and ask whether there was any rhyme or reason behind Bluck's notations. Given the number of settlers clamoring for Sierra Leone, Bluck sarcastically replied, Clarkson and Taylor "cannot be surprised to find so few are destitute of the character demanded by the worthy gentlemen of the Sierra Leone Company." "Permit me," Bluck continued in a postscript, "to recommend the honest and industrious, in the liveliest terms to the Agent, the others are in his power to keep sober."[30]

Emigrants' final bureaucratic hurdle was to convince the company's agents that they came to their decision to migrate after serious reflection. When a comparatively well-to-do black sharecropper traveled the fifteen miles from his farm to Halifax to sign on with the gathering exodus, he found himself, instead, engaged in a kind of debate with the agent over whether it was really worth his while to make the trip. The man complained, like so many other would-be voyagers, that he had not received "the least proportion of land to which he was entitled from Government." Yet unlike so many other black settlers, he had managed over the course of the last few years to avoid the poverty so common throughout the province. By way of what the agent called "indefatigable perseverance and industry" the man was now among the most comfortable blacks in the colony. So when this farmer asked for his name to be included among the other emigrants, instead of being allowed to enter it straight away, the agent asked him to consider all that he had to lose by choosing to start his life over. Eventually the sharecropper agreed that he would be better off accepting the government's renewed promise of land in Nova Scotia than signing on for Sierra Leone.[31]

Stories of hardships to come did not deter Nova Scotians with less to lose. Armed with a powerful critique of Maritime society, the poor came to company agents thoughtful and optimistic about an African future. According to them, after so many years of struggling with "small allotments in a soil so over-run with rocks and swamps" or, in other cases, cultivating "the lands of a white man, for half the produce," it was too late to reap any real benefit from the king's renewed promise of land in the Maritimes. Answered one emigrant to an agent bent on testing his resolve by underlining the other options open to him: "we should certainly perish, even if the best land were given us now, before we could clear it & receive the benefit of a crop." Similarly, an African-born settler who heard the details of the Sierra Leone plan only in passing responded in creolized English to the agent's warnings about the dangers of emigration by pointing out that though he was a free man, he worked like a slave in Nova Scotia and so imagined that he could do no worse, come what may, in any other part of the world.[32]

For a few, the opportunity for emigration reinforced an impulse to evangelize. By 1791, Boston and Violet King had managed to build a certain security around themselves and their family. Boston worked for a local man who allowed him two shillings per day and provided for his food and lodging. These wages, real and in-kind, placed King, as he put it, "in a comfortable way." When he first applied to emigrate, the agent with whom he spoke was reluctant to accept him, saying that King and his family were really "under no necessity of leaving Nova Scotia." King responded that "it was not for the sake of the advantages I hoped to reap in Africa" that he desired to try Sierra Leone, but, rather, the hope of "contributing to the best of my poor ability, in spreading the knowledge of Christianity in that country." Persuaded, the agents relented.[33]

The majority of enrollees, according to the company's employees, justified their desire to emigrate in terms of what the move might mean for their families. These applicants understood that making new lives in western Africa would be difficult, perhaps even deadly, but it was a trial with a promise, whereas Nova Scotia was simply a trial unending. In Sierra Leone, their hard work and sufferings had the potential to establish their children "upon a better foundation." After more than seven years in the Maritimes, it was clear that Nova Scotia and New Brunswick would never deliver as much. John Coltress, a slave, testified directly to the strength of this belief when he accompanied his wife and children, who were free, to see them enrolled for Africa. He wept as he gave them up but said that in the future he knew that his grief would give way to a kind of happiness. Once his family arrived in Sierra Leone he would "cheer himself with the pleasing reflection that his wife and children were happy." For others, enrolling for Sierra Leone *enforced* rather than *reinforced* familial affections and ties. Single women, according to the policy of the company's agents, had to negotiate with an also emigrating man or family and acquire a pledge of support before being allowed to enlist.[34]

Obstacles, external and official, required black Nova Scotians to weigh carefully the potential costs and benefits of emigration (indeed, the potential costs and benefits of even being seen to consider emigration) and then to express themselves unequivocally on the matter. Inasmuch as the discourse and drama of the process concentrated the minds of would-be migrants on the injustices they suffered in Nova Scotia and required them to articulate and justify a vision of their future, this decision-making buttressed prevailing values regarding the nuclear family, loyalism, and Christianity. Such notions were not new to black Nova Scotia (this chapter has argued that it was over the course of black loyalist settlement in the Maritimes that they came into their own). Nonetheless, the gathering exodus and the decision-making it entailed fortified these foundational ideas by requiring a public adherence in ways central to the migration at hand. In this sense, the suspect black settlers whom Stephen Bluck enrolled despite his misgivings about their character and the single women signed on only after they had inserted themselves within a larger family highlight how the sheer mass and ritual of the exodus lent itself to a kind of social and cultural conservatism, supporting in the process the more complete hegemony of a set of already operative ideas.

In stages, the weight of the exodus devolved onto Halifax, where preparations for migration encouraged further shifts in the nature of black society. Settlers who met John Clarkson while he toured the peninsula's southern shore repaired to the capital as soon as transport was arranged and their belongings gathered, the same with blacks along the Bay of Fundy who signed on either with Thomas Peters or with sundry other agents around the Maritimes. Throughout, blacks from central Nova Scotia came into the city for intelligence about the exodus and returned again with family and belongings after deciding to join. So by mid-November, the company's employees were preparing for an onslaught of some nine hundred voyagers, who according to their expectations would arrive in the capital in great groups. By mid-December, more than seven hundred of the predicted migrants were in the "neighbourhood of Halifax," a number that would in just weeks grow by hundreds more.[35]

The courses some of these migrants took to Halifax were absolutely harrowing. In New Brunswick, around St. John and St. Ann, Richard Crankipine, William Taylor, Sampson Heywood, Nathaniel Ladd, and another, though they were all small landholders, decided to try their fortunes in Sierra Leone. But colonial agents in charge of transporting emigrants from New Brunswick to Halifax denied them certificates. Under pressure from opponents of the plan, colonial agents withheld passage to any applicant who could not produce his or her Free Pass, a paper issued to black loyalists, in many cases as they left New York for the Maritimes some seven years earlier. Many blacks had misplaced these passes. Some had retained theirs, but they were "so worn out as to render them unintelligible," and thus unacceptable to the agents in charge.[36]

Undeterred by such schemes, Crankipine, Taylor, Heywood, Ladd, and another simply set out to walk to Halifax. The trek took them around the Bay of Fundy, across the isthmus joining New Brunswick and Nova Scotia, and through the middle of the Nova Scotian peninsula—an overland journey of more than two hundred miles, which took them fifteen days to negotiate and which lamed one of them.[37]

Most migrants came to Halifax in coasting schooners. Thomas Peters and more than ninety others arrived all at once from Annapolis, followed later by perhaps two hundred more also from around the Bay of Fundy. A convoy of eleven sail took five days to ferry more than five hundred from Shelburne and Birchtown, some ships stocked with only two days' rations and all "very much crowded." In and around Halifax itself, more than two hundred blacks filed into the city, interested in passage to Sierra Leone.[38]

The resulting scene was a crowded pell-mell of sound, smell, and movement as would-be migrants disembarked at the capital dragging their lives' possessions, stuffed into chests and bundled in packages, from the ships that had carried them. Those who marched into the city portaged lighter loads on their heads while pushing heavy cooking pots, beds, and other furniture through the snow on sleds and carts. And whether by land or by sea, not only did people and their movables make for the rendezvous, but the people's small stock came as well: So tens of dogs, flocks of small fowl, and perhaps a pig or two (although these were strictly forbidden) arrived in Halifax as just one more kind of migrant.[39]

This concentration of people and their belongings produced and transpired amid a constant murmur of confusion and distress. Some arrivees, having left property or unfinished business whence they came, had to leave or consider leaving Halifax not long after having arrived. Others arrived only to find that circumstances would not allow them actually to join the exodus. There was likewise a small backwash of migrants who changed their minds about Sierra Leone as the affair really got under way. Gathering in the capital managed even to divide a few families, stranding them somewhere between staying in Nova Scotia and leaving for Sierra Leone. John Martin of Shelburne signed on for Africa even though a local man claimed Martin was indebted to him for almost £4 and thus could not leave. Martin made for Halifax anyway, via Liverpool, but did not leave clear instructions for his wife and children—perhaps to protect them from his creditors. In any case, he trusted that they would follow as the general convoy from Shelburne to Halifax got under way. When the Shelburne ships did sail, Mrs. Martin refused to go along (despite the best efforts of a company employee to persuade her otherwise). She would not depart for Halifax, she said, "because she did not know"—or perhaps more accurately was not sure—"where her husband had gone."[40]

Conditions in Halifax were daunting for those who did make the trip. Black migrants moved themselves and their belongings into spaces hired for them by the company. These were mostly storehouses transformed into barracks, and as the weeks wore on they were prone to overcrowding. Further, it was a cold winter and hundreds pushed into Halifax without sufficient clothing, prompting employees of the company to write to the governor concerning "the miserable plight a great number of them are in for want of clothes, several of them are literally naked." The older people among the migrants suffered most, and some took deathly ill while in Halifax. But the young were also affected: A woman from the Shelburne-Birchtown area miscarried aboard ship on the way to the capital and died from complications a few days later once in Halifax proper.[41]

Underlining these harsh conditions was the fact that the kind of intimidation and violence that hovered over migrants while they had decided whether to take up the company's offer continued once they made it to Halifax. Opponents of the plan, as was their custom, continued to resort to rumor and innuendo to discourage migrants and to prejudice the city against them. Enemies of the gathering exodus claimed "that an Epidemic disorder prevailed amongst the Blacks" then gathering in Halifax and that some of the migrants were conspiring "to set fire to the Town." There were more direct threats and obstacles as well. Former Virginian Nathaniel Snowball, who with wife, Violet, son, Nathaniel Junior, and daughter, Mary, had claimed their freedom at the very start of the Anglo-American conflict and made it out of New York together at war's end, would not, it appeared, make it to Sierra Leone as a family: A white settler claiming Nathaniel Senior was in his debt tracked him to Halifax and called him out of the exodus.[42]

Similar predicaments prevailed with families who signed on for Sierra Leone and made for Halifax only to find that a loved one would not be able to make the trip because they could not be extricated from a contract or indenture. Prince Murray found himself in this impossible position, poised to make the voyage to Sierra Leone but denied his child. The Smith family, who had been forced to indenture a daughter to the Hughes after a fire consumed their home and property some five years back, found as they prepared for Africa that no sum of money could convince their daughter's new guardians to return the girl. The Smiths knew that if they settled in Africa with their other children, the Hughes would sell the daughter who remained into slavery: They would not be able to return or send for her later.[43]

Through all of these pressures, black migrants maintained a certain coherence and society in Halifax. There is evidence that between their gathering in the capital and actually boarding the ships, some emigrants supported themselves and their families by taking work in and around town. Religious life and community thrived. The blind preacher Moses Wilkinson held evening prayer services among migrating Methodists, and David George's Baptists were known to repair to the roof of their barracks to sing hymns and receive from George their daily bread. The settlers continued to exhibit something of the independence and skepticism distinguishing their brand of loyalism. They came to Clarkson continually with questions about the company's various assurances and wanting further details about the upcoming voyage, their concerns prompting the agent to write that "many of the free Blacks were very particular in their enquiries about Sierra Leone, and the promises made to them." Specifically, noted Clarkson, "they wished to know, if they should be prevented performing their worship on board a ship, as they said they knew that Captains & sailors were not very religious, and made many other suitable observations relative to their future prospects, all of which were gratifying to me."[44]

In some respects, billeting in the capital may have prompted prospective migrants to hold former community bonds and relationships in greater esteem than they did ordinarily, allowing the migrants gathering in Halifax not only a certain sense of normalcy but creating a kind of hyper-normalcy. The exodus was certainly organized in a way that encouraged migrants to hold fast to regional identities. In the main, blacks arrived in Halifax after having gathered previously in a regional port closer to their former settlements. From there, they sailed to the capital and were housed according to their place of embarkation. So, as far as the company was concerned, the migration was less a movement of particular families than it was an exodus of communities defined by their port of departure. This was how the company's agents organized barracks in Halifax, and this was how the company interacted with migrants in the aggregate. Thus John Clarkson addressed the "Annapolis and Digby people" or made arrangements for the "Preston people" or the "Halifax people." And Clarkson was not beyond noting (or perhaps ascribing) character and virtue based on where migrants hailed. The migrants from Preston and Halifax, according to Clarkson, were clearly "the flower of the Black people."[45]

Exigencies of emigration sometimes required emigrants to take concerted action on just these terms. Migrants from Birchtown-Shelburne pooled their meager resources to pay the debts of people from the area who otherwise would not have been allowed even to travel to the capital. The short trip to Halifax to join the exodus appears to have made migrants from Preston not only ultracognizant of their own bonds of community but a bit wary of their fellow travelers as well. Preston heads of household forwarded the following to the company's agent: "The Petition of us whose names are under written humbly sheweth That your Petitioners hath lived [as] neighbours in the Township of Preston between six and seven years, and come all united together and well aquatinted with each other, and our Petition is that you will be pleased to settle us altogether on our Lands at Sierra Leone, without being intermixed with strangers."[46]

There is in this draft from Preston evidence of a sensibility somewhat at odds with the signers' main sentiment of self-reliance and tight-knit community. That the Preston heads of household understood that petitioning John Clarkson was central to securing the future of their clan suggests that as the exodus progressed from recruitment across the Maritimes to actual billeting in Halifax, emigrants' impulse to exploit relevant patron-client ties—long a basic aspect of their loyalism—came to encourage shifts in the nature of Afro-Maritime society: Ironically, in the context of exodus, black loyalism encouraged the transformation of black loyalist society.

In the seven years since their arrival in the Maritimes, black settlers of Nova Scotia and New Brunswick were, on the colonial landscape, little more than a disenfranchised, yelping minority. In the wake of Thomas Peters's mission to London and the attention of government and the Sierra Leone Company that followed, these same settlers became, in a moment, pivotal to Maritime public life and debate. Where once they were isolated and ignored, now, with the option of emigration before them, even what the poorest among them said or did regarding Sierra Leone was of consequence. Further, with John Clarkson, of the Sierra Leone Company and His Majesty's Navy, black settlers could claim a patron in their Maritime struggles, and one who was not adverse to seeing them as they saw themselves: as loyalists, as free British subjects, as Christians.

For some, this change of fortune, over time, became centered on the person of Clarkson himself. Evidence of this shift in black politics is subtle at first. Following Clarkson's tour of the southern coast of Nova Scotia and his return to Halifax, groups of free blacks gathered at the docks to welcome him back into the city and, as Clarkson put it, "to congratulate me upon my arrival." When opponents of emigration took to the colonial press, blacks in Halifax responded dramatically and with Clarkson as their audience. The agent wrote in his journal: "many of them in a body called upon me with a present (as they termed it) which they delivered to me in a contemptuous way telling me it was a paper which the Whites had been circulating amongst them at Preston, and which they had brought to me, to make me sensible how much they despised it. . . ." The paper in question contained the piece signed by Philanthropos cautioning blacks against leaving for Sierra Leone.[47]

As Halifax began to brim over with migrants, settlers of all stripes sought to establish personal bonds with the man designated to conduct them out of the Maritimes. Documenting these interactions became an almost constant refrain in Clarkson's journal: "All this morning employed taking down the names of people having complaints, giving advice, writing letters, &c. . . . perplexed all this morning with complaints of one kind or another. . . . received many complaints respecting the manner the people had been sent from Shelburne. . . . It is impossible for me to walk the streets three yards without meeting some one who is in great distress, asking me to lend them money, to give them a Shirt, Shift, &c. . . . Could not get out of my house till near one o'clock from the number of people continually coming in. . . . Employed all this morning in hearing disputes and deciding upon them."[48]

Clarkson retreated from the practical strain of such interaction, recognizing captains among migrating blacks and attempting to work through them. Thomas Peters, David George, and John Ball served as kinds of deputy superintendents in this regard, and Clarkson desired "them to inform the people at the different Barracks, not to come to me with their particular complaints but to inform me through them."[49]

Ultimately this innovation was to no avail. But it is doubtful whether Clarkson would have truly welcomed its success. Though the agent recoiled from aspects of his role as arbiter, confidant, and patron, he more than encouraged the formation of such relationships in the first place. In fact, he insisted upon them. In his interviews with prospective migrants Clarkson asked them to "reflect upon the change they are about to make," and on deciding for Sierra Leone required them "from that moment [to] look up to me as their Guardian and Protector, and that in return I shall expect their obedience [and] good behaviour." And the agent knew full well how to spin strands of patronage in order to bind migrants to him. When Rose Murray came to Clarkson to ask whether her daughter, a "girl who had been unsteady for some times past," could sign on for Sierra Leone, Clarkson refused to give an answer on the spot, intimating instead that he would allow the girl's conduct in the weeks to come to form his decision.[50]

Clarkson's paternalism was not always this naked. He worked tirelessly, even selflessly, in the interests of those gathering in Halifax. He negotiated on behalf of families trying to recover apprenticed or enslaved members. He met the obligations of those in debt. He hounded colonial officials to ensure migrants had proper provisions, shelter, and clothing. He agonized over every detail of the upcoming voyage that bore on the health and comfort of his passengers, particularly matters relating to the condition of the ships slated to carry them to Africa.[51]

For their part, black migrants evinced a profound gratitude and personal loyalty to Clarkson for the efforts he made on their behalf. Something of the level of their commitment is evident in the honor they paid him on New Year's day 1792, when a company of migrants, each with a musket, paraded to Clarkson's lodgings, bid him to the door, and prepared a public salute. Clarkson, aware of the symbolic import of the gesture and thus quite cognizant of the effect it might have on the city's principals, desired the group "to go down to the Wharf where my Pendant was hoisted on board the *Lucretia,* where they might salute there." On Clarkson's part, such patrimonial displays and his whole experience in Nova Scotia worked to bind him emotionally to the needs and posterity of those he was to conduct to Sierra Leone: Just as there were migrants who thought they would rather die than remain in the Maritimes, John Clarkson came to think he would give his life, if that was what it took, to ensure their safety.[52]

The exodus's patrimonial tendencies encouraged small but basic shifts in the nature of black society. Before even leaving Halifax, for instance, Clarkson called on his position to inculcate migrants with a different understanding of the relationship between freedom and labor, telling single women that they must abandon what had become in Nova Scotia their principal employment and the basis of their independence: the taking in of washing. Having already inserted such women into larger black families as a condition of their emigration, Clarkson intimated that they must in Sierra Leone continue to earn their bread in such groups by agricultural labor. To men who had likewise made their living in service, Clarkson ordered that they must not attempt to do the same in Sierra Leone.[53]

Clarkson took a keen interest in the religious practices of black migrants, observing that "the majority practice what they preach," but he remained somewhat troubled, nevertheless, by their enthusiasm. He was committed, as he wrote to his superiors in London, to "getting them in our way of thinking." There is some evidence that migrants were aware of Clarkson's intentions on this head. Though it is impossible to know whether they moderated their practices for his benefit while in Halifax, it is clear that Clarkson believed such a shift might occur. Once, after a visit to the Birchtown barracks, Clarkson stole into one of David George's prayer meetings on the roof of the building. Afterward, he admitted to his journal that he had "left them sooner than I wished, fearing that David George if he had seen me might have been confused." That migrants tended to draft Clarkson into the intricacies of their religious affairs is telling as well. In mid-November, a lone migrant petitioned Clarkson, asking the agent "to ordain him as Preacher to a particular sect." In early December, Hector Peters, Simon Collvill, Thomas Sanders, Robert Harrison, and Richard Richards—all Baptists—wrote to Clarkson asking that they be *allowed* to nominate teachers and preachers among themselves.[54]

Thomas Peters, a prime mover in instigating the migration and once a principal in organizing the affair, felt keenly this shift in black society. In late December, as Clarkson was preparing ship musters, Peters met with him to speak about how "to arrange the people on board the vessel he intended to go in." The confab turned into a test of wills, with Clarkson stressing the importance of "regularity and subordination on board the ships" to strike down Peters's intentions. Clarkson "went to bed much indisposed." Peters, no doubt, returned to his barracks feeling likewise, but with the added burden of knowing John Clarkson's new place in black Maritime society.[55]

If Peters, or any one else, was unsure of this shift or its importance, it was all abundantly clear by the second week of January after those assembled in Halifax were aboard their respective ships. Just before the convoy pulled out of Halifax harbor for Sierra Leone, Peter Richardson wrote Clarkson about a matter then brewing aboard the transport *Mary:*

> Dear Sir the Ill behaviour Of Some Of the people that Went Against Orders Not Agreeable to the Rules of the Law for One Of Our Woman Goes by the Name Of Sally Pone Mentions Some Expression that Other People May take Some holt And do As She has Done And Said for She Says that she do not Care for You and I Nor for Any of the laws thatt Is made by Your Orders for Sir this Morning There was some Of the People thatt did not behave And did what was not Agreeable to the Rules of Our Law and we was Exammining of them and this Woman Sally Pone came in when we was Exammining them And She say what I have mention Obove And not Only but Call us a pack of Deavils And Mention many Expressions that was very Scandilous And we Egreed to lett you know thatt She may be Justifyed According to the Rules of the Law.[56]

The paradoxical effects of exodus on Afro-Maritime society are clear in this confrontation aboard the *Mary.* Sally Pone—jealous of her rights and the rights of her fellows, dismissive of authorities who took them lightly, and unsparing to those who did not meet their obligations to her—was a settler very much in line with the way black loyalist society had developed over the course of the American war and in the Maritimes. In her dismissal of John Clarkson, his orders, and his cronies were echoes of Boston King's reproach of the commanding officer at Nelson's Ferry, of the self-confidence with which Thomas Peters conducted himself on his mission to London, and of the righteous intransigence with which black settlers at Preston demanded that the government surveyor lay out their lands at no charge.

Peter Richardson's apparent commitment to John Clarkson and his orders was also very much in line with the development of black loyalist society. It was, after all, a society that developed in a context in which part of being a loyal subject meant obeying and serving British officers and expecting certain considerations in return. The confrontation aboard the *Mary*, however, underlines how the circumstances of exodus turned these long-standing aspects of black loyalist society from an instance of continuity to an instrument of transformation. Before Clarkson, black loyalists' exploitation of patron-client relationships tended to serve the expansion of black liberty. In Halifax, the loyalist impetus toward patronage served to weaken long-developed aspects of black independence. Under the exigencies of transatlantic migration, even apparent continuities among migrants could lead to the eventual alteration of migrant society.

TEN

ARRIVING IN SIERRA LEONE
Catastrophe and Its Aftermaths

The prospects of black voyagers bound for Sierra Leone were not so grim as those faced by captives from Africa destined for Jamaica. But prospects are only that, and the realities black colonists confronted upon landing in western Africa were nothing short of calamitous. The Londoners who disembarked in Sierra Leone in 1787 faced and then succumbed to one catastrophe after another, and for the Nova Scotians who arrived in 1792, the disaster of the previous expedition reflected quite plainly the demands they would continue to face during their own early experiences in western Africa. The two sets of black colonists wrestled with material conditions as harsh as those faced by any migrants in the Atlantic world. Thus it makes sense to ask a hard question of their society: How did their being free affect how they seasoned at Sierra Leone, and how did their seasoning affect the nature of the communities they strived to build? More pointedly, when the black poor suffered horribly and died in droves at the hastily erected Granville Town, did it matter to the substance of their society that they did both in perfect possession of their liberty?

It did. Those who survived in Sierra Leone built amid an utter disaster the rump of a free society that was arguably as enlightened as any in the eighteenth-century Anglo-Atlantic world. Their society, however, was both remarkably democratic and incredibly fragile. In the end, the London adventurers who set out for western Africa in 1787 could not withstand the exigencies of slavery, both local and hemispheric, that pulled and pressed at their colony until it all but collapsed. Moreover, the social, economic, and political forces that heralded the demise of Granville Town all but ensured that Sierra Leone's second wave of settlers, though they might suffer as much, would never be as free as they had hoped nor as independent as the Londoners who preceded them.

During the early evening hours of February 23, 1787, after more than three months of preparing for sea—first in London, then at Gravesend, and later still at Spithead—the hundreds of London's black poor determined to resettle themselves in western Africa finally stirred toward open water. At

Captain Thomas Boulden Thompson's command, the HMS *Nautilus*—the settlers' escort—fired two guns as a signal for the three transports packed with migrants to weigh anchors and steer out of Spithead. "In working out of St. Helens," though, on the western edge of the Isle of Wight, the convoy's flagship "Struck upon the Horse sand," and the routine navigation of the banks, wrecks and buoys into the English Channel threatened to go awry. Fortunately, the *Nautilus* was able to "wore off without any damage" and the convoy settled into a westerly course that would eventually lead the ships into the Atlantic.[1]

Still, from the very beginning of their sea voyage the black poor were never far from disaster. On the evening on Tuesday, February 27, when the migrants had progressed just beyond Plymouth, things began to fall apart. The *Vernon, Belisarius,* and *Atlantic* were each under the *Nautilus*'s stern when "Strong gales" and "A heavy sea" came on from the southwest. In a matter of hours, the little fleet for Sierra Leone was swamped. The gale crippled the *Vernon,* carrying away "her fore topmast," and Thompson ordered the *Atlantic* and the *Belisarius* to seek refuge in Plymouth Sound. The *Nautilus* made for the safety of Torbay, as did the *Vernon.* In the teeth of the storm, the relatively short journeys to both shelters were punishing. Hard gales, a heavy sea, and reduced visibility considerably slowed each ship's retreat. The transports and their escort labored "very hard" for every mile gained—taking on water and losing rigging and sight of each other all along the way. The black colonists aboard the transports—though not flung about as easily as the hogsheads and puncheons on the upper decks of the *Nautilus* that were tossed overboard by the winds—were hard battered nonetheless.

By mid-morning on March 1—after almost three days of suffering through the storm—the migrants aboard the *Vernon* and sailors on the *Nautilus* finally made it to Torbay, with the settlers aboard the *Atlantic* and *Belisarius* having already made it to Plymouth. With the ships all in harbor, the winds died down considerably, though occasional squalls punctuated the improving weather.[2]

The black poor, their ships in disarray, were again stuck in England. At Torbay work began immediately on the *Vernon.* Carpenters from the nearby HMS *Druid* were drafted for the effort, and the workers soon discovered that the transport's topmast was so rotten as to be "unserviceable." Captain Thompson sent twenty feet of oak plank to the *Vernon,* and for the next ten days or so both the *Vernon* and the *Nautilus* made repairs. Not until March 13 were the two ships ready to make for Plymouth Sound, but even then they were delayed, as the *Nautilus* found that it could not weigh its anchor.

It would be another day, some trial and error, and no small amount of broken rope and tackle before Thompson calculated that it was necessary to weigh with the tide. And so on March 14, at high tide, the *Vernon* and *Nautilus* navigated out of Torbay. By the seventeenth, the two ships had joined the *Atlantic* and *Belisarius* in Plymouth Sound.[3]

Not long after the two ships' arrival, however, yet another storm broke. Weakened by months of waiting in the Thames, Gravesend, and Spithead, and recently tried by heavy weather in the channel, the sheer physical strain of the expedition began to show. At Plymouth, blacks confined aboard the transports died at rates that could not be ignored. In a complaint published in the *Public Advertiser,* one of the emigrants, Abraham Elliot Griffith, lamented that "The People in general are very sickly and die very fast indeed, for the doctors are very neglectful to the people, very much so." Contemporary estimates suggested that as many as one in ten migrants perished over the three weeks the convoy stood in Plymouth Sound.[4]

This physical toll sowed and exacerbated social tensions and mistrust among the expedition's black settlers and their mostly white overseers. Since January, Vassa had complained of how the voyage was provisioned and of the conduct of the expedition's white conductor, Joseph Irwin, in attending to the basic needs of the emigrants. While the convoy was delayed, these previous tensions mounted into a full-scale dispute as Vassa was more and more vocal about alleged misappropriations. From Plymouth, Vassa charged that "many of the black people had died for want of their due," and called Irwin a "great villain." The migrants themselves also rebelled, complaining to Captain Thompson in late March and early April that Irwin was not providing for them as it was laid out in their agreement, a charge Vassa himself made before Irwin and the captain at least four times during the same week.[5]

From Captain Thompson's vantage point, continuing the voyage as it was presently organized was completely untenable. The conductor was incompetent and the black commissary, in Thompson's mind, was irritatingly overzealous. Further, as Irwin and Vassa dueled, the general body of migrants displayed "a Spirit of Turbulence and dissatisfaction" with the whole state of affairs. As many as twenty-four migrants were forced from the ships for mutinous behavior. A like number stormed off of their own accord. The Navy Board in London, which in conjunction with the Treasury had done a great deal to get the emigration scheme under way, caught wind of the expedition's unraveling and, fearing a general exodus from the ships, suggested moving the entire convoy to Torbay, where the migrants would not have such a ready egress.[6]

Irwin, who was feeling the heat from Vassa in particular and the migrants in general, vowed to quit the expedition and to return to London. Thompson interpreted this promise as an ultimatum. In consequence, he attempted to settle the discord in Irwin's favor. Thompson wrote the Navy Board: "I am sorry to be under the necessity of complaining to you of the conduct of Mr. Gustavus Vasa, which has been since he held the situation of Commissary, turbulent, and discontented, taking every means to actuate the minds of the Blacks to discord." Unless, the captain continued, "some means are taken to quell his spirit of sedition, it will be fatal to the peace of the settlement, & dangerous to those intrusted with the guiding it." Accordingly, Vasa was dismissed.[7] A week after the putsch, the black convoy rearranged itself in Plymouth Sound and set sail, yet again, for Sierra Leone.

Thompson charted a course that would take the colonists from the English Channel to Tenerife in the Canaries. Once in the Canaries, the ships sailed from Cape Barbas to Cape Verde, and from there to Cape Sierra Leone. Upon getting out of Plymouth, the trouble with leaving England so late in the season hardly made itself felt at all. The storm that forced the convoy back to Plymouth and Torbay was the most dramatic weather the colonists had to face during the entire journey. So as the ships headed south, the danger of sailing for the African tropics during the wet season was far from evident. There were a few days of heavy seas and just enough cloudy weather to warn of the wet season, but far and away the journey was characterized by hardly any rain. It was more marked by productive "fresh" and "moderate" breezes that moved the ships along at a nice clip. But if the weather was cooperative, life was far from ideal in other ways.

At sea, life for the colonists was close and regimented. While loading the transports in London, the would-be settlers had often chafed under the control of the Committee for the Relief of the Black Poor, and while waiting on the south coast the regulations of the Navy Board proved something of an irritant. Once out of Plymouth Sound, there was no chance of egress and the power of Captain Thompson, Irwin, the new commissary George Harvey, and the masters of the three transports to shape and order the routines of the black colonists would have only multiplied. There was no more going back and forth from ship to shore for recreation, companionship, or sustenance. Instead, Vassa's replacement doled out salted meat and other provisions—whose quality was not always certain—and the daily routine for all unfolded over very limited ground (as one of the organizers of the expedition later described conditions on the transports, the migrants were "rather too much crowded between decks").[8]

Still, all of this was to be expected at sea, and the ships were making good time. Moreover, the fact that the colonists organized daily prayer services and schools for their children while on board the transports suggests that the migrants managed to nurse at sea aspects of their society as it had developed in London and during the late war.[9] Still, what may have been unexpected, and in any event must have been very disconcerting, was the rate at which the settlers continued to die while aboard the ships. It only took the transports thirteen days to reach Tenerife in the Canary Islands, but in that period at least fourteen black settlers perished at sea. A death of one of the would-be colonists punctuated every single day of sailing since the ships had departed Plymouth.

The captain of the *Nautilus* fished around for an explanation for the mortality and settled on diet. "As they have been some time on salt provisions," wrote Thompson to the Navy Board, "I have thought it necessary to purchase for them a bullock to each Ship." Three young bulls, with forage, were moved from Santa Cruz to the three transports by boat, and George Harvey dutifully recorded receiving them "for the use of the Black Poor."[10] The fresh meat was no doubt welcomed, and Thompson's efforts on behalf of the colonists must have been much appreciated by those who helped and watched as the steer were hoisted aboard the transports. That Thompson could call upon the resources of the British Treasury for the protection and benefit of the colonists for Sierra Leone would not have been lost on the settlers. That the sixteen-gun *Nautilus* later took on six bullocks itself, when each of the colonists' transports only received one, would not have been lost on them either.[11]

Throughout the journey, the little convoy was beset by the benefits and ambiguities of imperial dominion. Captain Thompson and the *Nautilus* ordered the movements of the transports throughout the voyage, regularly firing his guns and sending signals to direct the course the ships were to follow. Moreover, Thompson was fastidious in projecting a sense of British power over the group. As the convoy passed south of Cape Barbas and not long thereafter Cape Blanc, and the transports began to share waters with slavers, the irony at the heart of the journey made itself keenly felt in the form of potential danger. Thompson certainly kept an eye on the horizon for strange sails: "Several strangers in sight. . . . At day light a strange sail to Eastward. . . . passed a large Ship standing to the Westward. . . . At 9 AM saw a strange Sail to the westward."[12] Black colonists on the *Vernon,* the *Belisarius,* and the *Atlantic* no doubt made their own mental notes, and as the convoy neared Sierra Leone they saw Thompson and the *Nautilus* more resolutely begin to announce and project British power in the region where the black settlement was to be made. On May 8, as the convoy turned two miles off Cape Sierra Leone, Thompson shifted to a noticeably more active posture. Early that morning when the captain "saw two strange sail in the NE" he wheeled the *Nautilus* around, ordered the transports to continue on their course, and set after the unknowns. Within an hour and a half, the *Nautilus* had closed on the ships and "fired two guns shotted to bring the strangers to." The pair turned out to be a French ship based at the Isles de Los with a sloop, her tender. The Isles were a way station for French slavers, and these two ships were bound for Gambia. It is impossible to know for certain whether the larger of the two French ships was indeed a slaver. But it probably was, and if black settlers who spied the sails earlier in the morning assumed as much, they would have been both encouraged and disheartened by their escort's actions. Passing merchant ships, of all stripes, had to answer to the *Nautilus*. Their escort, and thus they themselves, presented a force that could not be ignored. But still, the *Nautilus* bore no special animus toward slavers. In any case, His Majesty's Ship was certainly raising its profile as the convoy approached its destination. In the days and weeks to come, the two French ships would have announced the arrival of hundreds of free black settlers and a British war sloop to every ship they spoke with between Cape Sierra Leone and points north.[13] In the meantime, Thompson ordered the men on the *Nautilus*—once the sloop was back in the company of the convoy and only miles from the Sierra Leone River—to exercise the ship's small arms.

The journey from Plymouth to Frenchman's Bay calls explicit attention to many of the factors that would shape and define black life once the colonists landed at Sierra Leone. In many ways the voyage from England to western Africa was the beginning of the black poor's seasoning to their new land. In several instances, the *Atlantic,* the *Belisarius,* and the *Vernon* certainly mimicked what the settlers would face once they left the ships. The weight of endemic sickness, the prospect of daily mortality, and the lack of provisions and comfortable shelter characterized much of the voyage to Sierra Leone. These conditions would continue and worsen in the months to come. At sea, too, the settlers had to contemplate concretely what was more of a debater's point back in London: How would they manage a free black society in an area thick with Guineamen and slave traders? Among the settlers, every strange sail on the horizon must have hammered this question home with greater urgency. The voyage underlined as well the settlers' ambiguous relationship with the British state: The *Nautilus* was the settlers' benefactor, but did the sloop's captain consider himself *their* captain, too?

All of these social questions and conditions would intensify once the settlers disembarked in Sierra Leone. In addition, matters that were more or less moot during the sea voyage would become salient again—especially

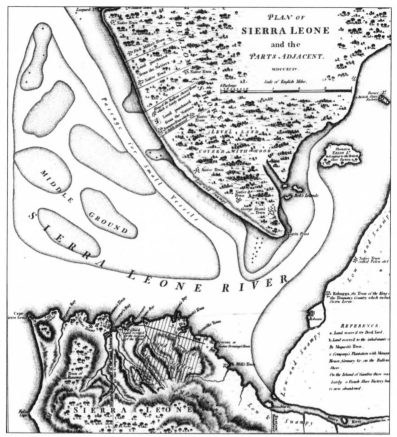

Figure 10. B. Baker, "Plan of Sierra Leone and the Parts Adjacent"
(London: J. Phillips and George Yard, 1794), MPG 1132
Source: Courtesy of the National Archives-Kew

the social consequence of the relationship between the settlers and the London philanthropists who had helped to facilitate the expedition. And new factors bearing on the continued development of settler society would become increasingly apparent—in particular the various ways those already settled in Sierra Leone would receive and respond to hundreds of mostly black newcomers.

For their part, the settlers at sea gave mixed indications of what would guide them and how they would respond to such factors in the building of an immigrant society in Sierra Leone. Without question, the concern for posterity that had skewed the expedition toward families and couples continued and would continue to guide the settlers' behavior and ambitions. That the colonists' managed to organize prayer services and lessons for the children amid the less than ideal conditions that obtained aboard the transports speaks to this point. But what politics would prevail among the settlers was suddenly an open question. In London, Plymouth, and in between the black poor certainly displayed a good deal of the radical spirit of former slaves who had won their freedom in a revolutionary age. But there had been a steady culling—through discharge and desertion—of some of the most "mutinous" settlers, and what effect the steady deaths at Plymouth and at sea would have on the spirit of the people remained to be seen. Certainly the settlers Thompson described while the transports were at Tenerife bore only a small resemblance to those who continually tested his patience in the south of England. The settlers, Thompson wrote from the Canaries, "have hitherto conducted themselves remarkably well."[14]

Whether the body of black settlers who would disembark in Sierra Leone was in character and disposition essentially the same body of settlers who were on the ships before the convoy was delayed in the channel by the late storm remained to be seen. But all interested in such questions would soon have an answer. On Wednesday, May 9, 1787, the *Nautilus* carefully approached the estuary of the Sierra Leone River—commanding the three transports carrying the settlers to fall in line behind her and ordering the sloop's pinnace ahead to sound the way. For several hours the ships maneuvered first into and then within the river, with the *Belisarius* nearly running aground during the process. By evening, the transports moored one to the other and all sails were loosed. Already in the river were "an English merchant ship and three French Vessels." The black poor had finally arrived, and with them arrived too a sign of the season to come: Their first night in the Sierra Leone River there "came on a tornado from the SE with heavy rains, Thunder, & lightening."[15]

It did not take long for the convoy to gain the attention of the local powers that be—the transports entered the Sierra Leone River with the *Nautilus's* guns firing out commands, and in any case the arrival of four ships at once must have piqued the interest of every trading man who had eyes to see. The day after the ships' anchoring in Frenchman's Bay, Captain Thompson went ashore to begin negotiating for an establishment on the black poor's behalf, treating with a local ruler whom Europeans called King Tom.[16] This process would go on for several months (and even after Thompson's departure another round of negotiations opened the following year).[17]

At their arrival, however, the settlers did not wait for the promulgation of any formal agreements. Four days after the meeting with King Tom—on a clear, breezy day—those settlers who were able spilled out of the transports and began the work of building their colony: hacking a passage from the river to the summit of a nearby hill, hoisting the English colors, and calling a meeting of "the body of people . . . on purpose to choose, their officers."[18] The migrants selected Richard Weaver "to be their chief in command."[19] The work of beginning a free black settlement at Sierra Leone, it must have seemed, was well started.

But the next day it rained. And it rained the day after that, and the day after that. And the day after that it rained too. Four straight days it rained. Then came a brief respite. The following week, it rained only twice, and the week after that, the last in May, it rained only twice again. Then came June and it rained almost daily. When the crew of the *Nautilus,* and no doubt some of the settlers, too, celebrated King George's June 4 birthday, it rained. The day that King Tom, Chief Pabongee, and Queen Yammalouba made their marks on a treaty transferring about twenty square miles of "Land, Wood, Water etc" for "the sole Benefit of, the Free Community of Settlers . . . lately arrived from England," it also rained heavily.[20] All told, there were only ten days in June that did not see rain of some sort. The following month, a week of fine weather in the middle of July limited the rain total in this stretch of the calendar to fifteen of thirty-one days. In August, however, it rained twenty-one days out of thirty-one (nine days straight at month's end). And during the first sixteen days of September, it rained every single day but one—Thursday, September 6, which though cloudy must have looked to the settlers as fine a day as any.[21]

The disastrous consequences of arriving at Sierra Leone at the start of the wet season did not take long to make themselves felt. The rains underlined the importance of what must have already been the newly arrived settlers' number one priority: erecting shelter. At the same time, however, the ever-present but highly variable precipitation—light rains, heavy rains, thunderstorms, frequent showers, slight showers, tornadoes, and squalls accompanied by rains—made the building of shelter a near impossibility. The settlers set tents for cover until the time that they would be able to build proper houses, but these, as one migrant put it, were of "little or no help to us, for the rain was so heavy it beat the tents down."[22] So those who left the ships to build Granville Town lived, for all intents and purposes, in the open. The rains also exacerbated what would soon develop into the settlers' chief problem, that of finding adequate provisions. Not long after their landing the colonists began to experience real scarcity, and so although they arrived prepared to plant various crops for the maintenance of the settlement, they were soon disappointed. Complained Richard Weaver of the dire circumstances in which the migrants found themselves: "we came too late to plant any rice, or anything else, for the heavy rains washes all out of the ground."[23] Writing after about three months in his new country, Abraham Elliot Griffith described a situation in which the settlers were forced to depend on a then undependable provision trade for their sustenance. "There is nothing to be got in the place but fowls; and as to any other food, it is next to nothing. Rice is the best thing they have."[24] Food, lamented James Reid in a letter to London penned more than a year after Griffith's, is "scarce to be got—no not one mouthful sometimes."[25]

Chronic shortages characterized the migrants' settlement well into their first year at Sierra Leone. Fish might have been relied upon as a source of protein during the wet season, as several times during the *Nautilus's* sojourn in the river the crew hauled a seine net and brought up considerable quantities—fish which the captain later shared with "such of the black poor as were sick."[26] But the incidents that suggest the provisioning possibilities of the river also point up another of the settlers' problems: the fact that a significant number of them landed in Sierra Leone sick from the very start or were incapacitated soon after their arrival. From their time at Plymouth, a series of illnesses crippled the migrants, and arriving at Sierra Leone in the wet season did not make things any better.[27] The settlers thus faced a hard reality. Although there was a great deal that needed to be done in order to provision and build the new colony, there were not always a sufficient number of able bodies to do either. Even "the Natives dies very fast," observed Abraham Elliot Griffith—writing of either the Africans among the migrants or their new neighbors at Sierra Leone, but stressing in any case that "it is quite a plague seems to reign here among us."[28] Given the surviving records, the plague or plagues in question are difficult to quantify. But it is likely that nearly a quarter of the migrants perished during their first four or five months in Sierra Leone, with many more being disabled at any given time during the same period.[29]

For the black poor, the conditions they encountered in Sierra Leone were certainly as challenging as those faced by enslaved Africans then arriving on the other side of the Atlantic in the British colony of Jamaica. But the black migrants who disembarked from the *Atlantic,* the *Belisarius,* and the *Vernon,* as desperate as they were, were not slaves. Thus they possessed choices in the building of their new society that slaves could not so easily make concerning theirs. Unsurprisingly then, from the moment the transports arrived in the waters of Frenchman's Bay and the demands of the new settlement began to bear down, many who were able quickly decided that it was in their best interests to take no further part in this experiment. So the free settlers' first days, weeks, and months in Sierra Leone did not so much form the background for the building of a new society as it began the nearly complete unraveling of the community the settlers had built for themselves to date. As soon as they could, the majority of the colony fled the disaster that everyone saw looming on the horizon. Some deserted the fledgling colony to work in slave factories along the river, others left to earn their bread aboard slave ships. Some decided that it made more sense to work their way to the Caribbean in departing English Guineamen than to try to make a living in Sierra Leone—an admission that they would rather wager their liberty in the West Indies, the very center of British slave society, than risk it in the so-called Province of Freedom.

By September 1787, of the roughly 400 settlers who had departed for Sierra Leone, about 270 remained attached to the colony.[30] By March of the following year, death and desertion had further reduced the colony to about 130 persons, a number that no doubt reflected more the hopes of those in London doing the calculating than it did the reality in Sierra Leone.[31] Six months after landing, then, the black poor's free settlement was less a colony and more a camp. Abraham Elliot Griffith had been prophetic, though not exactly prescient, when he wrote in July of 1787, "I do not think there will be one of us left at the end of a twelvemonth."[32]

Among the small number of colonists who survived and decided to make lives in Africa, the tragedy into which their settlement quickly sank significantly shaped the society and community they developed at Sierra Leone. The survivors, unsurprisingly, built a social world characterized by animosity and distrust, social conditions constantly stoked by the material scarcity, physical insecurity, and sheer uncertainty of their new lives. Consequently, the peace that had apparently distinguished the greater part of the settlers' voyage from Plymouth to Frenchman's Bay did not hold. The black settlers' distrust of and contempt for white authority that had been typical of the expedition both during the planning stages and during the colonists' ill-fated first departure for Sierra Leone very quickly returned upon their arrival in western Africa. The bulk of the colony's black settlers—when pushed to respond simultaneously to the dire conditions of their settlement-in-the-making and the commands of Thompson, Irwin, and others—made fast policy of ignoring the expedition's white officialdom. The settlers' suspicion and independence of Joseph Irwin's apparent authority so frustrated the conductor of the black poor that he "declared, soon after his Arrival at this Place, his determined Resolution of not settling with them."[33] The settlers likewise frustrated the officer in charge of the *Nautilus*. Captain Thompson was used to being obeyed by inferiors. So "the licentious Spirit which prevails amongst the People" offended him more than a little. Still, he began his assignment in the river sure of his ability, by persuasion or punishment, to bring the settlers to heel "in a little Time."[34]

This confidence, it turned out, was no match for the settlers' determination to keep primarily their own counsel. In the first week of July, George Harris's intransigence earned him an unrecorded punishment—probably stripes.[35] Still, the body of settlers were hardly cowed by the example. A little more than a week later, a settler simply called Dominick responded to Thompson or to some other official in a way that resulted in the captain having him, too, punished for "for insolence & misbehaviour."[36]

Just as Thompson did not record the exact punishments meted out to Harris and Dominick, it is impossible to tell the exact nature of the settlers' offenses, but the language of the ship's journal—the similar but slightly more detailed ways that Thompson recorded his punishment of the sailors and marines under his command—leaves little question that insubordination was the issue. Thompson and other white officials expected a certain obedience from the black settlers that the settlers themselves thought unearned. So when white officials, in the midst of the colonists' desperate strivings to stave off oblivion, requisitioned labor and other assistance from the black colonists, the settlers balked.[37] And they balked, no doubt, in ways not calculated to minimize giving offense. The main body of settlers, wrote Thompson, "shewed no Attention or Deference" to their white superiors.[38] So a little more than a month after expressing confidence that the settlers would soon obey him as did his crew, Thompson all but gave up on forcing the issue. "Remonstrance, persuasion, or Punishment" had not been sufficient to date, and things were unlikely to change.[39]

This state of things is noteworthy. For most of the voyage to Sierra Leone, a delicate order had prevailed. Given their experiences in readying the expedition, the main body of black settlers were certainly unconvinced that the white officials among them shared their interests, and for their part, the expeditions' white managers and craftspeople did not, no doubt, implicitly trust the larger body of blacks with whom they had cast their lots. Nevertheless, the two apparently achieved a certain modus vivendi during their weeks at sea. The expedition's white chaplain reported from the voyage that "all the jealousies and animosities between the Whites and Blacks had subsided, and that they had been very orderly ever since Mr.

Vassa and two or three other discontented persons had been left on shore at Plymouth."[40] This is too rosy of a description, but it was an optimism shared by Captain Thompson in his letter from the Canaries. So although these accounts do not and cannot reflect the perspectives of the black migrants themselves, they do portray an atmosphere at sea that differed significantly from that which previously prevailed.

During the voyage from Plymouth to Sierra Leone, the black settlers aboard the *Atlantic, Belisarius,* and *Vernon* were probably far from contended with their white overseers, but they were certainly less discontented than they had been. There was a chance, the sea voyage seemed to suggest, that the parties on board the transports, with their quite different expectations concerning class and racial privilege, could nevertheless work out a multiracial free society in the midst of the transatlantic slave trade. At sea this looked possible, and had conditions in Sierra Leone only been as trying as life aboard the *Atlantic,* the *Belisarius,* and the *Vernon,* perhaps the settlers would have continued their compromises and established a truly remarkable society at Granville Town and environs. But for the settlers, conditions on the ground at Sierra Leone were beyond trying, and the first causality of the rain, the hunger, the sickness, and the death that dogged the colonists was hope that the racial politics that had prevailed out in the Atlantic would be continued in Sierra Leone proper.

The broad multiracial society envisioned by some of the colony's staunchest supporters was not to be. But as already noted, given the conditions that prevailed at Sierra Leone, it was never clear that a coherent black settler society would emerge either. The black poor were as impoverished in Sierra Leone as they had ever been in London. Their provisions were insufficient. The "English seeds" they brought with them were more or less useless.[41] To trade for food, many were reduced to selling their clothing. The overwhelming majority of their number perished or deserted the colony altogether. Those who remained contended with waves of illness. Predictably, the same creeping dystopia that characterized interracial community at the Province of Freedom marked the colony's developing black society as well.

Upon landing, the black settlers were, in general, united in their opposition to Joseph Irwin's direction of the colony, and this opposition no doubt worked among them as a useful centripetal force. It was a force quickly spent though. Irwin's estrangement from the colony, then his death from one of the "Fevers, Fluxes, and Bilious Complaints" that ravaged the settlement, and the later desertion or demise of the colony's other white functionaries were probably not without effect on the main body of black colonists. The settlers did not need white direction—indeed, they spurned it—but their opposition to white managers had provided their embryonic society with an important raison d'être. So, as the colony's white functionaries died or drifted away, the social adhesion their presence had encouraged among the generality of black settlers gave way as well (to say nothing of how the settlers filled key skilled positions left vacant by the death and desertion of the majority of the white colonists). The splintering of the colony along racial lines, held Captain Thompson, "was followed by much Confusion" among the black settlers.[42] No doubt it was. But the confusion of which Thompson wrote was less a collective state of mind, as he no doubt perceived it, than it was a social phenomena. The colony's black settlers, under enormous stress and privation, had to reconsider the principles, conditions, and purposes of their association, and in some instances this collective reconsideration resulted in a collective reworking of the ideas and ends of their settlement at Sierra Leone. The process tended to splinter black settler society (just as conditions on the ground encouraged interracial fracturing). From Captain Thompson's quarters aboard the comparatively well-ordered HMS *Nautilus,* it must have all looked very much like chaos.

Among the black settlers themselves, it no doubt all felt very chaotic, too. Scores of survivors separated themselves from the main body of colonists and settled in smallish camps, micro-colonies of their own making. Others moved up river and joined themselves to slave factories. Some, to stay alive, worked aboard slave ships. A few attached themselves to African towns. In a letter to Granville Sharp from July 1787, Griffith illustrated what this general unraveling looked like through his own experience. Since Irwin's death, wrote Griffith, everything "was out of its order entirely." Griffith himself was weighing whether to enlist on a ship for the West Indies or to accept an offer from a local ruler. "The King," relayed Griffith, "has offered to build me a large house for a school, for me to teach those who would wish to learn; but their manner of living is so very bad and poor, that I cannot accept of the offer."[43] Henry Demane's decision making illustrates a route taken by others. Demane—once saved from re-enslavement and a life in the West Indies by the timely arrival of a writ of habeas corpus while his ship was passing out of the Downs—decided in Sierra Leone that it was in his best interest to move to the Bulam Shore, where he became a trader who counted among his merchandise enslaved Africans.[44] As a body, the settlers had negotiated hard in London to make sure that they did not fall prey in Sierra Leone to slave traders. Once cast into the swirling chaos of their new settlement, however, many decided that working the slave trade was their best chance to stay alive. A few, like Demane, did more than latch on to the trade as a lifeline. They became, rather, full participants in the slave society that thrived along the river, and they prospered because of it.

Most of the black poor, it must always be remembered, perished in Sierra Leone. Of those who staved off death, a large proportion decided that their continued well-being depended on their deserting the physical prospect of the colony as it then existed, or at the very least abandoning the idea of the colony as it had been envisioned from London. There remained, though, a group—much embattled and their numbers in constant decline—who struggled to build in Sierra Leone a Province of Freedom. Their efforts and society, though, were as prone to debilitating schism, were as generally troubled, and were as subject to confusion as the circumstances of their landing would suggest. A pall hung over them. The fact that so many others had died or fled "occasioned great discouragement to those that remained."[45] Captain Thompson and others were quick to portray this remnant as indolent, lazy, and intemperate.[46] Such reports were more defamation than description. Still, that a not insignificant number of the remaining settlers were physically battered and psychically stunned by what was happening around them cannot be denied.

As this small group worked to establish the parameters of their new society, these types of strains showed themselves in abundance. James Reid and Richard Weaver's accounts of the settlement's arms and what transpired after the *Nautilus* left the river in September 1787 illustrate how the colonists' unceasing material difficulties bred suspicion, distrust, and intrigue among the settlers. For reasons known only to him—but not difficult to guess—Captain Thompson had refrained from sending ashore the settlements' guns and powder until just before he took his leave of the colony.[47] The able-bodied men of the settlement each claimed what they could carry, but after enduring four months of illness, scarcity, and death along the Sierra Leone River, for many in the colony the guns and powder represented not simply the better part of their defense but a mercantile windfall and thus a possible solution to some of their most pressing current problems. So some immediately converted their arms into "strong liquors." For settlers hoping to eke out a living as traders, the move made perfect sense, and alcohol was a more promising commodity than many.[48] For others, the most damaged and despondent at the colony, trading their guns for alcohol was, no doubt, a way to numb the pain and suffering each day brought. The social consequences of these transactions, whatever their rationale, were noticeable. For those colonists who had argued forcefully in London for the provision of arms, the selling off of the colony's muskets sapped their hopes of what was going to be possible in Sierra Leone. The guns were a central means of asserting the colony's liberty and a powerful symbol of the migrants' collective enterprise. That the settlement's surplus guns—about eighty of them—were also soon broken out of the colony's makeshift storehouse and disposed of further reflected how desperate conditions were in the province. The larceny also added to the settlement's spiraling chaos as factions among the settlers implicated one another for the theft. Subsequent recriminations eventually sent one of the settlement's first captains flying from the colony to protect life and limb (either chased by a mob or stealing away on his own accord, depending on whose account you believe). It was also after the arming of the colony that small bands of settlers set out against Africans and slave traders to get their daily bread by stealth, convinced that strict self-reliance was impossible under the conditions in which they had landed.[49] And among all of this, there was also murder: A young man was "found shot, lying in the woods, but [it was] never found who was the person that did it."[50] Black society as it was developing among those committed to remaining in Sierra Leone was, in respects too many to count, a dismal one.

Still, what was remarkable about black settler society at Sierra Leone was not the nearly unceasing strife and desperation that characterized social relations and action at the settlement. What was most remarkable was that both in reaction to and in spite of conditions that prevailed at the colony, the surviving settlers constantly strived for, and at moments achieved, a society marked by extraordinary levels of democracy and cooperative action. At the present remove, it is impossible to uncover great detail about the settlers' administration of the new colony. The evidence that remains concerning the discourse, institutions, and habits of public life at Sierra Leone makes it impossible to doubt, however, that the settlers did indeed raise a fragile but functioning government and civil society.

During the time that Captain Thompson observed settler life from the *Nautilus,* he dismissed as ineffectual nearly all of the colonists' efforts at establishing themselves. Within some of his most caustic observations, however, lie evidence that a cadre of the survivors was animated by a spirit of cooperation that did not bode ill at all for the evolution of colonial governance. Thompson wrote as follows of the situation on the ground in September 1787: "The Mode of Government, which they had adopted was choosing Chiefs every Month from amongst themselves; but as little or no Respect was paid to these, of course there was and must be much Confusion amongst them."[51] There is no reason to doubt Thompson's observation concerning the general level of social confusion that prevailed at the settlement. It is also not out of order to give considerable weight to his description of the efficacy and reach of settler governance some seven months after their arrival at Sierra Leone. Still, what is extraordinary in Thompson's complaint is the fact that a significant number of settlers, through a formidable commitment to order, organized themselves against the disintegration of the colony. In his comments, Thompson meant to highlight what he saw as the sheer ludicrousness of the settlers' situation. His audience at Whitehall probably did not need much prodding to see things from his vantage. But those who joined in Thompson's mocking missed a larger and no doubt unintended point evident in his missive. In the midst of great hunger, disease, desertion, mortality and all of the social confusion bred by these conditions, bands of black settlers remained remarkably committed to projecting a sense of normalcy, and to erecting, exercising, and protecting nascent institutions of self-determination.

In this light, the developing commercial life of the colony is also important to consider. In response to the nearly complete failure of the colony's agricultural pretensions, and thus the collapse of the foundations upon which the colony was to be built, the remaining settlers gave serious collective thought to the reordering of the economic bases of the settlement. Even following his banishment—for his alleged involvement with the missing surplus muskets—James Reid reflected as follows to Granville Sharp concerning rejiggering the colony's economy: "There is one thing that would be very helpful to us: if we had an agent or two out here with us, to carry on some sort of business in regard of trade, so that we could rely a little sometimes on them for a small assistance, until our crops were fit to dispose of, and then pay them. it would be of infinite service to all the poor settlers, as provisions are scarce to be got."[52] The colony, it seems, turned most of its economic energies to trading and to the development of several service sectors. The slave factor at Bance Island described the activity as being a mix of legitimate commerce and larceny. The settlers, he wrote, "go over the Country, some of the industrious, to pick up poultry, or any other refreshments, to sell to the shipping that frequents this river, but the greatest part for no other purpose but to rob and plunder."[53] In addition, the colonists sometimes contracted to provide shore care for sick sailors from ships trading in the river.[54] They also levied anchoring and watering fees on ships desiring provisions and potable water from within their jurisdiction (and perhaps beyond as well).[55] The agent at Bance Island was perhaps writing of this practice when he complained of the settlers in early 1789, saying that "there have been several masters of ships stopped by them, and obliged to pay five or six hundred bars before they released them."[56] When the settlers considered, after a couple of years in Sierra Leone, what their friends in London might provide that would be most helpful for the colony, they settled on a sloop "to help in their trading and communication."[57] The request well illustrates how the first survivors searched out and then adapted a series of niche activities in support of the colony's collective survival.

The colony's interactions with slave traders and slave factors in the Sierra Leone River—sometimes symbiotic but more often strained and violent—offers some of the most detailed evidence concerning the path along which government and civil society developed in the province. In the colony's earliest days—even before all of the settlers and supplies had been unloaded from the transports—it appears that the threat of enslavement catalyzed the articulation if not the development of civil cooperation and basic civic institutions. The information, for instance, that the master of the *Belisarius* transport, upon completing the terms of his agreement, was attempting to leave the river with two settlers on board probably originated among the settlers and was passed expeditiously on to Captain Thompson. Thompson sent an officer to the transport to demand that the master of the *Belisarius* deliver the two men. When that proved ineffectual and the transport attempted "to drop down the river," the *Nautilus* fired a warning shot that rather quickly changed the master's mind about making a run for it. He returned the two men to the settlement, a victory for the colonists' watchfulness.[58]

After the departure of the *Nautilus*, the settlers developed their own police power and other institutions and practices in support of justice and self-defense within the colony. Their interactions with slave traders continued to add particular urgency to this work. Both African and British slavers constantly challenged the community of free blacks, and any difference between them could result in what for many of the remaining settlers had to be considered the ultimate punishment: slavery. During their first year in Sierra Leone, King Tom captured and sold two of the colonists over some disagreement while making very clear his intention to sell others who crossed him.[59] A Captain Campbell once took four colonist as slaves, and another slave ship master imprisoned six more.[60] The body of settlers complained in the fall of 1788 that the Liverpool slave traders were apparently fanning fires of conflict between the settlement and nearby Africans, who "were very intruding, by sending repeated challenges to our senit, and endeavouring to aggravate us, as much as possible, to break the peace with them."[61] The remarks sum up the difficulty faced by the colonists, as it cast light on the settlers' growing institutional capacity—through the settlers' senate, for example—to respond to such challenges.

An incident from the summer of 1788 illustrates both the determination of the slave traders and the growing capacity of the new settlement. When slave trader James Bowie, the agent at Bance Island, found that a storehouse on the property had been broken into sometime in the early morning hours of June 17, he quickly determined that "it was the new settlers, and immediately sent a canoe well manned with some of our most active people, offering 100 bars reward, and on their finding out the thieves, desired them to tell the heads if they did not deliver them up, I would stop and catch every one belonging to the settlement that passed the Island; on which they delivered them up."[62] At least this is what Bowie wrote his superiors in London, clearly giving the impression that he browbeat and cajoled the colony into compliance.

The testimony of John Lucas and Charles Stoddart in the affair suggests, however, that the settlers were anything but strong-armed into delivering the suspects. Further, though it is far from clear that anything approaching due process prevailed in the matter, where a semblance of order and process did prevail it was more evident among the settlers than among the involved slave traders. Lucas, then the governor of the colony, testified that he called on Robert Moore early in the morning following the alleged break-in at Bance Island. The governor claimed that he had no suspicion of any specific wrongdoing on Moore's part. He was well aware, however, that Moore and others had been on the river in the small hours of the morning and had returned to the colony around dawn. Of Moore, after some small talk, Lucas inquired "if he had nothing else to tell me." When Adam Sab, another of the men out on the river during the previous evening, came too into Moore's house, the governor asked, "You went out yesterday and returned very early—where did you go?" Following such questions, Moore inexplicably made the governor "a present of a couple of pipes" to give to his wife, and soon afterward Amelia Moore, Robert's wife, rushed to make the governor "a present of two rings." Lucas then took his leave, but before he made it home Amelia Moore set after the governor and asked if he would like to buy some earrings and showed him one of a pair. The governor said he would give Mrs. Moore one iron bar for the two earrings. He took the one she had in hand and desired her to bring the other when she could.[63]

When the posse from Bance Island arrived, they called on Lucas. One of their number spied an earring on the governor's table that he recognized as from the stores of Bance Island. The head of the Bance Island party, a Mr. Smart, then informed the governor of the recent theft and asked for his assistance in searching for the culprits. Lucas called a counsel of the settler's together—Charles Stoddart, John Cambridge, and a Mr. Richardson—to discuss the matter, and Smart requested from Stoddart, the chief justice of the settlement, a search warrant. Stoddart put the matter before a body of settlers, who, acting as a kind of grand jury, "gave it as their opinion, that it was very proper to endeavour to apprehend them who had committed the robbery." "They all said," according to Stoddart's statement, "they would endeavour to discover the offenders, for the sake of their own characters, that it should not be thought that it was a general plan of the people of the settlement." The settlers eventually arrested Lewis Sterling, Robert Moore, John London, Richard Bradley, and Adam Sab for breaking into the Bance Island storehouse. Eventually all five were delivered or delivered themselves to Mr. Smart.[64]

Evidence in the affair was taken by an audience of seven area slave traders and five of the new settlers. The number gathered looks remarkably like a jury. If that was the original intention, it is not at all surprising that the new settlers would have insisted on such a propriety and demanded, in any case, on being present and represented during the trial. When the verdict was handed down, however, it was not attested to by a single settler. Further, the conclusion of the makeshift court consisted of a punishment that any five black colonists probably could not have been persuaded to deliver: "banishment," which was James Bowie's artful term for delivering Sterling, Moore, London, Bradley, and Sab to a French slaver bound for St. Domingue.[65]

The Bance Island break-in and its aftermath offers an intriguing peek at the development of settler society at Sierra Leone. The affair clearly illustrates that some among the surviving settlers responded to their desperate situation with desperate plans and acts. Further, the affair suggests that colonial officialdom may have been implicated in some of the settlers' illicit adventures. The governor's very timely visit to Moore and others after their long morning out, his unspecific but potentially pointed questioning of them, and the round of reciprocal gift giving that the governor's queries and his interlocutors' responses seemed to prompt suggest that larceny—larceny winked at though not formally encouraged by the colony's leading men—formed a not inconspicuous aspect of the settlers' political economy. The Province of Freedom's tenacious hanging on in Sierra Leone may have been due in part to an official tolerance for thievery. If so, however, the pilfering connived at was the pilfering of people who, given the opportunity, would and did steal and sell the settlers themselves. In any case, what is conspicuous in the settlers' response to the incident is not the fact that a free black settlement in Sierra Leone hounded by disease and famine and surrounded by slavers threw up burglars and perhaps a few bandits. What is conspicuous is that out of social and material conditions that encouraged, if they encouraged anything, disorder and illiberalism the new settlers managed nevertheless to build a society that honored the forms and practices of enlightenment democracy. So although one or more of the settlement's leading men—and the settlement itself for that matter—may have benefitted from, if not encouraged, the robbing of slave traders, the colony was a place that also valued an idea of itself as an honest settlement and one committed to impartiality and justice for its people (even though it was not always possible to deliver either of these ideals).

Other encounters with slavers further document the ideological and institutional development of the colony and its colonists. Though it appears, for instance, that the colony could do little at the time to save Sterling, Moore, London, Bradley, and Sab from their outrageous punishment, it is equally clear that when the colony and colonists were at all able, the province and its settlers did not adopt a position of long-suffering where slave traders were concerned. When cheated or mistreated by slavers, the settlers often responded in kind.

The surgeon from a Bristol Guineaman who got into a dispute with the settlers—perhaps over care afforded to the ship's slaves or sailors—learned rather quickly that disagreeing with the settlers was not without consequence. When a settler named Smith found the Bristol doctor on Bance Island landing goods at the wharf, he drew his cutlass "and was going to cut him down" before the agent in charge of the island interfered. Restrained from assault—or perhaps manslaughter—Smith contented himself with insult and told the doctor within hearing of everyone that if the colonists "should catch him at the settlement, they would tie him up and flog him." The agent at Bance Island promised to arrest Smith for the threat. Smith responded by walking to his boat, retrieving his musket, and vowing that should the agent attempt to make good on his pledge Smith would have something for him. It took five or six Bance Island slaves to disarm Smith, whereupon Bowie had him "put in irons, where he was confined on the Island for some time."[66]

Granville Sharp may have been referring to this particular incident, or to another one altogether, when he wrote of a dispute between the settlers and a slave ship captain who declined to pay the colonists for nursing an ill sailor and for his subsequent burial (the death of the sailor probably being the reason given for the captain's refusing to honor his obligation). As a result of the disagreement, according to Sharp, the captain "afterwards seized a free man, and confined him in irons for three days." The settlers responded by arresting the captain and holding "him until he consented to pay a fine agreeably to their estimation of the injury committed by him."[67] At another time, at the request of an African trader with whom they were associated, a group of settlers traveled more than fifty miles to the Iles de Los to arrest a slave ship master who had cheated the trader in question. This was in all likelihood as much of a police action on the part of the settlers as it was a mercenary assignment. The captain whom the settlers captured at the Iles was also accused of having seized and detained six of the colony's free settlers.[68]

The colony's disputes with slave traders bring into focus what were perhaps the most important aspects of the settlers' developing political institutions and civil society, which were both characterized by a remarkable commitment to democracy, the rule of law, and the settlement's sovereignty. Further, in a manner unlike that of any other British settlement, the colony's settlers articulated a substantial commitment to racial equality. The settlers' commitment to antislavery was hardly categorical, but it was also, for a British outpost in the Atlantic world, arresting in the extreme. These latter two qualities of public life at Sierra Leone were apparent to all, and through their commitment to both ideas the settlers frustrated their friends as well as their enemies. Like very nearly every other white person with whom they interacted, the agent at Bance Island interpreted the settlers' insistence on their own personhood as insolence. The colonists, he observed bitterly, "looked upon themselves [as] better than any White people that came out or was settled in the Country."[69] Even Granville Sharp, though a friend of the colony, worried over the settlers' sense of independence, the utter certainty with which they expressed their sense of racial equality, and the depth of the colony's—if not every settlers'—antislavery. In a letter addressed to the "Inhabitants of Granville Town," and based on much more information about the settlement and settlers than historians are now privy to, Sharp all but pleaded with the colonists to tamp down considerably on expressions of the colony's antislavery and to not make too manifest their commitment to racial equality. Wrote Sharp: "be courteous and kind to all strangers that come to the settlement, even though you know them to be slave-dealers or slave-holders, provided they do not offend your laws during their stay. What is done beyond your boundaries you cannot help or prevent, except the offenders belong to your community; neither must you interfere with others in the least, except by kind and friendly warnings of God's impending vengeance against oppressors; and this only when you have fair opportunities of mentioning the subject, without giving personal offence."

Referring, no doubt to the party of settlers who traveled to the Iles de Los to arrest an offending slave ship captain, Sharp continued:

. . . I hope you will in future be more careful not to interfere in the least with any matter beyond the bounds of your territory; and be sure to maintain a friendly communication with all the neighbouring factories, and more especially with those that are most near, as the King of Rohanna's people, Bance Island, &c.; and avoid all disputes with masters of ships, about the fees for anchorage and watering. . . . I have no authority to interfere, but am only anxious that you may avoid disputes, and submit to lose your right in this matter, rather than contend for it, if it be refused. It is a point of public consequence, which Government will probably take into consideration in due time."[70]

Unfortunately for the settlement, as will become clear below, the colonists' conviction that they were indeed the equal of whites, their commitment to their superiority to most slavers, and the press of circumstances on the ground in Sierra Leone made it very difficult for them to take Sharp's advice to heart.

The colony's interactions with slave traders generated an amount and kind of documentation that allows the best available view of the early development of settler governance and civil society. As Sharp once wrote after describing one particular altercation between settlers and slave traders in Sierra Leone, "I must further beg leave to remark, that the whole proceeding of the settlers, on this occasion, proves that they really maintained some reasonable form of government among them, as well as an efficient civil power to support it."[71] Still, from the interactions of settlers and slave traders we are allowed only a glimpse at the settlers' society, and a glimpse from a certain angle, one stressing commerce and external relations. There is even less material documenting the settlers' attention to other aspects of family and communal life, but that which exists suggests that the settlers continued to work and aspire in these areas as well. When "the Old Settlers at Sierra Leone" wrote Sharp in September 1788 they looked forward to being able to construct a "church, court-house, and prison."[72] The latter two aspirations speak to priorities more than evident in the colony's dealing with area slave traders. The first, however, underlines an aspect of the community about which there is precious little additional evidence, but the desire speaks nonetheless to the fact that for some of the settlers nursing a spiritual life remained or became an important part of their existence at Granville Town. A religious mission was certainly evident in aspects of their internal politics, as was clear when James Reid, the former governor, was expelled from the colony. "After they broke me," Reid wrote of being threatened and chased of by a body of settlers, "they thought to have God's blessing, as they said."[73]

A query from Mrs. Lucas to Sharp on behalf of the women of Granville Town shines light on another aspect of settler life about which it is impossible to know much but which is perhaps the single most powerful illustration we have of the settlers' determination to carry on in Sierra Leone. Mrs. Lucas—very likely the wife of governor John Lucas—asked Sharp on behalf of the women of the settlement if he would procure from the Reverend Fraser a good roll of all the settlement's marriages.[74] The departure of Fraser for London apparently left the settlers without official records of unions at the colony, and perhaps without a witness whose word could be counted on as official. At one level, the request illustrates the kinds of social difficulties and confusion that abounded at Granville Town, where in the course of the journey to and early settlement at Sierra Leone couples whose unions had heretofore no legal sanction sought out Fraser to regularize their connections, and newer pairs did the same, but all at a clip and under circumstances that hardly encouraged meticulous record keeping. Fraser's illness and subsequent departure from the settlement could only have added to the ordinary difficulties surrounding the documenting of settler marriages.

But why would "the ladies of the settlement" require an official roll of marriages in the fall of 1789? Perhaps the very hard circumstances at Sierra Leone produced their fair share of equally difficult domestic consequences. Were the married men of the settlement avoiding responsibilities to help provide for their wives? Did the husbands of women debilitated during the journey and early settlement prefer to cast off a mate who had become a liability and to take another who could be more of an assistance? Perhaps. But the fact that the request to Sharp came from Mrs. Lucas suggests that the origins of the query may have had other motives as well.

There is no Mrs. John Lucas evident on any of the settler rolls taken before the ships arrived in western Africa, but by the fall of 1789 it is fairly clear that Lucas had wed. The new Mrs. Lucas was probably either one of the unmarried white women who joined the convoy in the early months of 1787, one of the few single black women who made the journey, or a widow of one of the settlers who did not survive in Sierra Leone. (It is unlikely that she was a local woman, but it is possible that other men pursued wives from the neighboring towns.)

The new Mrs. Lucas's short query, more than anything else, illuminates the dialectic that troubled and challenged settler society at Granville Town from the start: the heavy press of material conditions that encouraged the disintegration of the colony and the degradation of relations between the settlers, and the colonists' efforts to sustain and build social relations and civil institutions that, although they clearly reflected and were infected by their troubled context, represented the colonists' efforts to build promising, fulfilling, and free lives in western Africa. The settlers sickened and died in Sierra Leone, and they were constantly threatened by enslavement and destruction at the hands of slaver traders white and black. For a long time it must have looked like nothing would come of their efforts in Granville Town. And in the midst of all of this, they married. And not only did they marry, they worked to properly document their unions in ways befitting free British subjects. Thomas Thompson, had he known of the request the women of the settlement made of Granville Sharp, would have called attention to the sheer folly of it all. Sharp, for his part, promised that he would "attempt to procure a proper register of all the marriages." It was a difficult request with which to comply, though, as he could not, despite having "made earnest inquiry," locate the Reverend Fraser.[75]

Disease, disorder, famine, death, and despair characterized a good deal about black society at Sierra Leone. But the colony was distinguished by nearly equal measures of resilience, entrepreneurship, social cooperation, democracy, self-confidence, and hope. The internal dynamics of the colony—as much as we are privy to them—bear this out. But the social work of building the new settlement at Sierra Leone was not only the domestic labor of ordering and maintaining personal and economic relations among the colonists. It also involved navigating social relations largely external to the settlement. The point is more than evident in the glimpses of developing settler society presented thus far. But it deserves special highlighting. Sierra Leone was an active node in eighteenth-century Atlantic trade and commerce. Thus, for the colonists, part of building their world there involved negotiating webs of social and economic relations—interethnic, international, and British—long built.

When the *Atlantic*, the *Belisarius*, and the *Vernon* anchored at Sierra Leone, for instance, they did so in Frenchman's Bay. And until the arrival of the mostly black colonists from London the name was apropos indeed. Of the four ships that were in the river upon the convoy's arrival, one was English. The other three were French.[76] But Dutch and American traders were also active in the river, as were ships from Caribbean colonies and vessels based in western Africa—Gambia and the Banana Islands, for example—that conducted a coasting trade.[77] In addition to the largely maritime European and American establishments, there was, of course, the more settled presence of African towns and landlords. These relations were often fraught with difficulties, as is clear from the colonists' interactions with King Tom.[78] But they were not always so. King Tom's determination to find a tutor and interpreter from among the colonists suggests that he could be of two minds concerning the settlers.[79] The colonists' relationship with Rohanna, the town nearest the new settlement, was symbiotic if not friendly. Further, evidence taken in the jury-rigged trial of Lewis Sterling, Robert Moore, John London, Richard Bradely, and Adam Sab indicates that the settlers were quick to develop substantial trading relations with people and places all along the river. Bradley, for instance, testified that he had joined Sterling, Moore, London, and Sab on their early morning trip with the intention of paddling to Tomba to buy cloth. When asked what he had been doing on the river, Sab had answered that "He went no farther than King Nanbana's who was indebted to him, and he went to recover his debt, but did not receive it."[80] Whether their listeners believed Bradley and Sab is one thing. The Bance Island slave traders and many of their fellow settlers did not. That their alibis were plausible, however, speaks to the ways in which colonists had integrated themselves into the international and interethnic social and economic fabric of the river. The Sierra Leone at which the colonists arrived was the Atlantic world in small place, and the settlers, in a relatively short time, explored and inserted themselves into quite a few of its nooks and crannies.

Still, a part of the world the settlers encountered at Sierra Leone was particularly familiar. With their arrival, the colonists joined and jolted a small but long-standing British contingent that had existed in the region for some time. This small British diaspora was largely centered on Bance Island, about twenty or so miles from the mouth of the Sierra Leone River. From the late 1740s, the island served as a principal trading station—or factory, to use the contemporary term—for a group of London-based merchants active in the Africa trade. From the mid-1780s, the brothers Alexander and John Anderson were the proprietors. They kept on Bance an agent, several clerks, and more than two hundred slaves who did the work of the factory.[81] The Andersons sent their own ships to trade at the station, and they did business with other concerns as well. Consequently, when there were a handful of English slave ships and others in the river, the British population of the region could reach a hundred or so men.[82] When speaking of slave ship sailors and their officers, of course, "British population" is not a term of great precision. British ships in the Sierra Leone River were not manned solely by British subjects, and even inasmuch as they were, their shared Britishness did not so much bind them in purpose and agreement as it reproduced—on a reduced though perhaps more intense scale—the social fissures of British and British colonial society. But this is exactly the point. Though more than three thousand miles from London, how the settlers continued to relate to the world they left in Great Britain and how they addressed the version of British society they joined in Sierra Leone shaped what was possible at the new settlement and illustrated the colony's evolving sensibilities.

The principal British slave traders at Sierra Leone—those stationed at Bance and the ship captains that traded there—were a power unto themselves, and however precarious their position, they relished and guarded it. They traded at the sufferance of local African powers, but in the politics of the region they considered themselves big men too, and as far as was practicable made their own law. Probably reflecting a subdued sense of the self-righteousness exhibited by his employees and other British traders at Sierra Leone, the way Alexander Anderson answered questions put to him concerning the government of Bance speaks to how British slave traders at Sierra Leone conceived of and liked to carry themselves. When asked, for instance, under whose authority and law the five settlers who allegedly broke into a Bance Island storehouse had been tried, Anderson replied, simply, "I cannot answer." Incredulous, Anderson's Parliamentary inquisitor begged clarification: "Does the island of Bance belong to you?" When Anderson replied that the island indeed belonged to "our house," his questioner tried once again to get at the nature of authority at the station. "Is Bance Island," he continued, "under any government?" Anderson replied: "The Slaves that live on it are subject to the government of our agent; and there was an instance of one of our own people that was tried for a mutiny, before one of the Kings of the country who considers himself as the superior of that Island, and to whom we pay an annual tribute."[83]

Sensing that he was closing in on an answer to his initial query, Anderson's questioner then asked whether there were any Europeans at the island who were not in his employment—none really, came the reply—and whether he was familiar with the names of the men who pronounced sentence on the alleged Bance Island robbers—he knew some of them but others he did not. "Under what law," Anderson was then probed, "do those gentlemen live?" "Under the British government," replied Anderson, "sometimes subject to the laws of the Kings and Princes of the Country." And so after all of these peregrinations, Anderson's parliamentary questioner began his indictment: "Do you suppose that under the laws of this country, five freeman can be sold as Slaves?" "I believe not," stammered Anderson, "but I consider this was under the law of necessity." "Do you suppose," came the counter, "that under such a law of necessity a free Englishman, residing in Bance Island, can be sold as a Slave?" "I believe not," Anderson stumbled on, "but I consider that a Black man can—a Native of Africa can."

"State the distinction," came the response, "either in law or common sense, between the liberty of one free man and another, under the British government?"[84] Anderson would not have been able to answer the question (and in the end he was not required to do so). But his responses clarify that British slave traders at Sierra Leone fancied themselves lords of a kind of kingdom, as it makes plain that they also well understood the limits and fragility of their little kingdom. In this sense, the slave traders' banishment of the five black colonists was a display of their power, but it also hinted at the slave traders' very real vulnerabilities. As a defensive and not a little disingenuous James Bowie (the Bance Island agent) explained his actions to Anderson:

> I have some reasons to think that there my be some reflections on me for sending them off, particularly as they were sent out under the sanction of government. I first intended keeping them for a king's ship, but as there is but one called here these eight years, and the danger of keeping them upon the island, likewise their poisoning the principles of the people of the island, as well as to deter others from the like attempts, as it was the most daring one that ever was committed in this country, it was necessary to act with resolution in the suppressing of it; for where the people of this country see people afraid of them, they are constantly imposing upon them; but when they see a person not afraid of them, and will resent their insults, there is no danger of their being insulted.[85]

Thomas Thompson and the *Nautilus,* for as long as they were in the river, represented another aspect of the British world at Sierra Leone. Thompson, of course, held that he had little influence over the black colonists. This was not altogether true. He had influence. What he lacked from and over the settlers was the deference and control to which he was accustomed. Still, while in the river Thompson represented and projected the power of the British empire, which was formidable if not far reaching. The *Nautilus* created, first and foremost, a robust British physical presence charged with imperial imperative and martial potentiality. From the moment the *Nautilus* entered the river directing three transports and announcing the convoy's arrival through intervals of cannon fire, the sloop made itself a force to be recognized. The negotiations for the settlers' territory, for instance, were held aboard the *Nautilus,* and Thompson, through his showing respect for the African powers with whom he negotiated, made plain in the process the force at his command. Wrote Thompson on May 25, 1787, of some early discussions: "At 3 PM saluted King Anambayna with 13 guns on his coming on board to settle the purchase of the land."[86] The next day, he recorded of the king's leaving: "Saluted King Annambayna on his leaving the Ship with 13 guns."[87] When the parties signed the treaty formalizing the establishment of the colony, Thompson, demonstrating a knowledge of local political hierarchies then prevailing among the Temne, "saluted King Tom with 11 guns on the ratification of the purchase of the land for the free community."[88] Interestingly, on that very same day, the captain had the Articles of War read before meting out punishment to "Peter White, Rd. Matthews, Richard Quinton (seaman) & Robert Moore (marine) for staying on shore all night contrary to orders."[89] This was a naval rite meant to deter other sailors. Still, this particular display of Thompson's authority may also have been meant for King Tom, Chief Pabongee, and Queen Yammalouba (especially if the sailors had spent the previous night among Tom's people).

Throughout his stay in the river, Thompson's close adherence to the naval instructions regarding salutes created an audible, potential-filled British military and cultural presence. On May 29, 1787, the *Nautilus* fired nineteen guns "to commemorate the restoration of King Charles the second."[90] The following month, the sloop let go twenty-one guns in celebration of the birthday of the current monarch. At Irwin's funeral, Thompson ordered the firing of sixteen guns.[91] Further, the captain approvingly recorded in the ship's journal when traders in the river paid the proper respect to His Majesty's colors. "Arrived here an English sloop & schooner, the Sloop saluted us with 15 guns which we returned with 13. . . . returned the salute of an English merchant Ship with 11 guns. . . . Returned the salute of a merchant Ship with 9 guns. . . . Returned the salute of an English Schooner, and English Ship, & Dutch dogger with 11 guns."[92] And when a ship in the river neglected or refused to acknowledge the *Nautilus*'s presence, Thompson required fastidious compliance. "PM fired two guns shotted at a brig to make her pay due respect to His Majesty's colours. . . . Fired a Swivel shot at a Sloop to make her pay due respect to His Majesty's Colours. . . . Fired a Swivel shot at a Schooner for not paying due respect to His Majesty's Colours."[93] Once, when a cutter neglected to give proper consideration to the *Nautilus,* Thompson "Sent the Lieut. on board him to explain the 13th article of the Naval Instructions (under the head of salutes) as he pleaded ignorance, & ordered him to repass us & strike his topsail which he did."[94] On another occasion, when a French ship attempted to sail up the river without flying its flag, Thompson "Sent a boat on to her to make her hoist her colours."[95]

Thompson and the *Nautilus* presented a special variant of the British world at Sierra Leone—more representative of formal British imperial power, not to mention much more formidable than the British traders centered on Bance. Consequently, the masters and sailors of other ships in the river continuously sought the *Nautilus*'s guidance and assistance. When the French snow *Les Amis* came into the river, she put onboard the *Nautilus* two British sailors from a wrecked East Indiaman.[96] In July a Dutch dogger came down requesting the assistance of Thompson's surgeon.[97] The next day, Thompson was obliged to send his pinnace and cutter to tow a dogger that had gotten tangled up with the *Vernon*, perhaps the same Dutch boat that came down the river the day before.[98] At another time, Thompson sent a pinnace "to assist an English brig which had got on shore on the middle ground."[99] In late July, eleven men from the Liverpool slaver the *Brothers* took a boat and made for the *Nautilus* "to complain of ill treatment" at the hands of their master, James Clark. Thompson sent them back to their ship, and not six hours later Clark himself was on board the *Nautilus*, where he "complained of his Ship's company having mutinied."[100] Thompson took two of the alleged ringleaders on board, but the next day as the Liverpool slaver passed Thompson's sloop "two of her men leaped overboard & swam to us."[101] Thompson sent them back to the *Brothers* with an officer "to settle their disputes, & to demand Notes for the Wages of the two men received by us yesterday."[102] Thompson eventually put the allegedly mutinous sailors from the *Brothers* into the *Atlantic* as that transport prepared to leave the region.[103] When the *Vale* came into the river, three sailors deserted her and made for the *Vernon*, whereupon the master of the *Vernon* brought them to the *Nautilus*. A fourth man, who had joined the *Vale* in the Banana Islands as a passenger but was then "detained against his desire," came too.[104] Thompson returned the three "deserters" but allowed the passenger from the Bananas to go his own way.[105]

The London colonists fit oddly into the British world at Sierra Leone. They were not official extensions of the United Kingdom, like Thompson and the *Nautilus*, but they were, it was clear, under his nominal protection and armed by the government. Yet in spite of this apparent subordination, they exercised an independence and a will to power similar to that of the Bance Island traders. This combination only frustrated Thompson, who had nothing to fear from the settlers outside their disrespect. It much troubled, however, Sierra Leone's British slave traders, who with the arrival of the settlers were not only suddenly outnumbered but faced too the arrival of a dangerous ideology—a democratic antislavery—that did not bode well for the slave traders' continued work at Sierra Leone. The black settlement—as evident in the actions and complaints of Thompson and slave traders alike—gravely unsettled British Sierra Leone, and this troubling of British imperial and commercial waters along the river played itself out not only in and around the new colony but in a third space closely related but removed from the region: the world of letters and other communication between the river and London, and the public imagination fired by such connections.

The colonists, though beset by the remarkable press of day-to-day life in the settlement, fully recognized the importance, come what may, of establishing and maintaining reliable communication with the world beyond, especially with London. Though recovering from a near-death illness and working to get out of the colony, Abraham Elliot Griffith paused long enough to relay to Granville Sharp critical information about just how bad things were at the colony. The haste with which he penned the note underlined that he well appreciated the urgency of establishing and maintaining communication. "I had such short notice of the ship coming away," wrote Griffith, "that I have not time to give any further particulars of the country."[106] Further, Griffith and others strived to establish communication that, while bearing corporate news, was also personal. So Griffith, for instance, after closing the body of his note reminded Sharp, "I suppe you wil not recollect who I am. If you look over your papers, you will see that I am the young man that you lent the 1£ 6s to, for which I am in duty bound to pray for your goodness."[107]

When a body of settlers wrote Sharp in the fall of 1788, they likewise revealed the importance they placed on contact with London as well as the difficulty of doing exactly that. By September 1788, the settlers claimed that they had written no less than one hundred notes to the capital describing their situation. Their efforts, they came to learn, were "hitherto abortived, either from the rascality of the captains, as packet-bearers, who through some particular views have destroyed them, or otherwise through their indifference have lost them."[108] The September 1788 letter got to Sharp through some kind of subterfuge. It was postmarked Merazion in Cornwall and was written in the hand of Alexander Sanders, a name that does not appear on any of the lists of settlers. By way of explaining these anomalies, the settlers wrote in the body of the letter of their determination "ever hereafter, to use what policy we are possibly able to collect, in the conveyance of either packets or private letters; one specimen of which your great goodness will discover, when opening this packet."[109]

In London, the settlers' letters that did get through painted, for the most part, a distressing picture of the colony and set Sharp on a campaign to rescue the idea of the settlement from what was unfolding on the ground. In his correspondence to the settlers and to friends interested in the settlement throughout the Anglo-Atlantic world, Sharp followed Thompson in blaming the settlers themselves for the better part of their difficulties. For

Sharp, the colonists' appetites and work habits—their drunkenness and slothfulness—not the climate, the wet season, the disease environment, nor the way the expedition had been provisioned were to blame for the problems at the Province of Freedom.[110]

Outside of the particular details of each correspondence—the who, what, when, and where of Sierra Leone and London—what the body of letters that flew between the settlement and Britain points up more than anything else is the development, rehearsal, and consequence of the colony's transatlantic voice. Parsing the timbre of that voice reinforces what we know about black society at Sierra Leone from the actual actions of the colonists, but it also extends our knowledge of key aspects of black society at Sierra Leone. In this regard, the letters underline the settlers' sense of the obligations that bound and connected London and the new colony. The settlers' myriad complaints about their situation at Sierra Leone were not simply intended as points of information, they were also critiques of the combination of government and philanthropy that had helped them to Sierra Leone. So Richard Weaver's response to the outrages perpetrated on the settlers by the areas' slave traders represented not only the remaining colonists' growing resolve to resist such incidents, but was also a call to action and a testing of the network in London with whom they supposedly shared interests. "I think within my own breast," wrote Weaver of the settlers' traumatic first months in Sierra Leone, "that Government did not take the pains to send us here to be made slaves of."[111]

Granville Sharp, it seems, well understood that the letters he received describing conditions in Sierra Leone were not at heart laments but requisitions—requisitions furthermore wrapped around indictments, charges as pointed as the ones Sharp was prone to leveling at the settlers themselves. In the fall of 1788, Sharp responded by organizing a relief effort, sending out a small brig called the *Myro* laden with additional settlers and supplies. The expedition, in many ways, was a total failure. Sharp intended the brig to land 1,500 fowls, 450 head of small stock ("goats, sheep, and swine"), and more than a dozen large cattle ("twelve cows and two bulls"). He was convinced that "Nothing was wanting but breeding cattle, and tame fowls, to render life comfortable" at Sierra Leone.[112] In the end, the brig delivered no livestock whatsoever. The *Myro*'s master, one Captain Taylor, once at sea apparently balked at the impracticality of the contract. So when he paused to water at the Cape Verde Islands, where he was supposed to purchase the livestock, rather than turning the *Myro* into a kind of ark he instead carried to Sierra Leone "goods to the value of a certain number of cattle, and obtained a certificate from the settlers that they had received the value of so much cattle."[113] Sharp thought this a tremendous failure. The settlers who remained at Granville Town, because trade had become the lifeblood of the little colony, were probably less distressed over the matter. But in other ways the *Myro* failed quite unambiguously in its mission. Sharp originally angled for fifty reinforcements, but only thirty-nine actually sailed. Of these, thirteen perished on the passage, four refused to go any further than the Cape Verde Islands, and two others, once they arrived in Sierra Leone, could not be convinced to remain.[114] Of the twenty who actually landed at the settlement, within the year almost all were in the employ of slave traders (most if not all of the *Myro* reinforcements had been white men).[115] In this regard, Sharp's rescue was as much a boon to Bance Island as it was to Granville Town.

Still, the arrival of the *Myro* quite clearly demonstrated the potential power of the ragged band of settlers then hanging on at Sierra Leone. If the deaths and desertions that hamstrung the settlement in its first two years underlined the colony's many vulnerabilities, and the police actions and other examples of self-defense the settlers later mustered reflected something of the colony's ample internal resources, then the *Myro*'s coming, the aftermath of its visit, and the correspondence relating to both illustrates the range and consequence of the colony's developing public voice. From the perspective of African and Bance Island traders, the arrival of the *Myro* demonstrated that the colony could will itself from the brink of annihilation by virtue of its connections to and influence in London. In the months before the *Myro*'s arrival, the region's slave traders were, it seems, tightening a noose around the neck of the colony. Disputes over water and other local resources festered, and for at least eight very tense weeks in the fall of 1788, the people of Granville Town expected the settlement to be overrun at any moment. As the settlers themselves described their collective state of mind, they were "under constant apprehensions of being all massacred, for two months before the brig's arrival.[116]" Captain Taylor, who was careful to exploit to his advantage every commercial and economic exchange with the colony—not informing the settlers, for example, of the chalk sent out in the ship to assist the colony's masons until such time as the terms of Taylor's contract guaranteed him a windfall should the settlers claim it—nevertheless served as an effective deterrent to those who wished the settlement ill. Taylor and the *Myro*, it seems, were both carrot and stick helping the settlers and their neighbors come to terms concerning access to potable water and other essential issues. As the settlers put it, "to give Satan his due, he exerted himself more than what we might have expected; and the Natives have been pretty quiet since the arrival of the brig."[117]

Most distressingly, for those who felt the colony a thorn in their sides, the *Myro*'s arrival significantly reinforced the human resources available to the settlement (even if not in the way that Sharp had intended). Before the arrival of the *Myro*, Granville Town had been reduced to an effective strength of about forty. By the time the brig left in September 1788, the town had grown again to more than four times that size as settlers who had previously scattered streamed back—some hopefully, others perhaps more than a little selfishly, but back all the same. For neighbors who had not mourned when the settlement appeared well on its way to expiring, the colony's strong second gasp must have been as disconcerting as it was instructive. Unless dealt with quite decisively, the part of the black migrants most committed to an idea of themselves as a free, democratic society and most opposed to the region's slave traders—that hard center of the settlement—was not going to disintegrate on its own.

And at the start of the next dry season, the settlement was indeed shepherded into oblivion when King Jimmy, King Tom's successor, burned Granville Town to the ground. Details are sketchy and contradictory as to what motivated the torching, but the arrival of Captain Henry Savage and the HMS *Pomona* in the river in November 1789 set things in motion. Both the Bance Island traders and representatives of the settlers quickly bent Savage's ear with complaints about one other. The slave traders groused about the pilfering of goods to which the settlers were apparently prone, and the settlers lodged complaints about the kinds of bad behavior to which the traders seemed to be addicted (the selling of the settlers themselves, no doubt). According to Savage, however, both groups of Britons in the river enlisted his support in reining in King Jimmy, who was disconcerting the Bance Island traders and the Province of Freedom alike. Savage agreed to oversee a parley between the three parties, but when a group of marines was sent for King Jimmy, guided by several of the free settlers, instead of returning with the headman in tow the party came bolting back to the shore after having fired one of Jimmy's settlements—accidentally, Savage assured readers of his report on the incident. Other accounts are not so forgiving. In any case, King Jimmy's men felled three members of the party that was retreating toward the *Pomona,* and in response, over the next several days, Savage laid down a storm of cannon fire. Still, a strained calm returned to the river only when Jimmy was asked to stand down by his superior, the Naimbana (called King Anambayna in Thompson's log book, though Naimbana is more a title than a personal name). Once the *Pomona* departed, however, the settlers at Granville Town were given three days' notice to gather what they could and evacuate the colony. The place was then burned to

the ground and the settlers scattered, some to Bance Island, others to Rohanna, and a group of about seventy to a settlement more than ten miles
up the river.[118] Granville Sharp was convinced, probably because of details
provided through his communication with the settlers' then leader, Abraham Ashmore, that the burning of the settlement was encouraged if not
orchestrated by the Bance Island traders, who needed no more convincing
that it was in their best interest "that the settlers should all be dispersed."[119]

The razing of Granville Town came at a remarkably bad time for the
colonists. Communication surrounding the incident provided an important pretext back in London for an assault on a key idea of the settlement
itself—not by the colony's enemies but by its friends. In early 1790, Granville Sharp began working toward the establishment of a stock company
that would encourage the development of "an honest and honourable
trade with Africa, in order to discourage and supersede the detestable traffic in Slaves."[120] The work capitalized on notions that had been floating
in London for some time and was spurred no doubt by the high personal
costs Sharp had born in supporting the Province of Freedom through its
recent troubles. The company attracted a spate of prominent directors and
investors hopeful that a more moral trade with western Africa might prove
both good and profitable. Further, even before the company was properly
incorporated, the investors undertook to assist the burned out settlement
along the lines of Sharp's earlier *Myro* expedition. The small ship that was
dispatched to provide assistance, however, heralded the start of a new relationship between the settlers, their government, and their supporters in
London. The *Lapwing* was sent under the auspices of the then organizing
St. George's Bay Company, and as Sharp not so gingerly pointed out in a
letter to the settlers sent by the ship, the agent in charge of the goods was
"not empowered to give you the clothing and provisions now sent out, but
merely to supply them gradually, in return for such labour and assistance
as you may be able to afford him, or for such African goods of produce as
you may happen to have by you, or equal value in exchange.[121]" The *Lapwing*'s mission was not purely humanitarian, it was also commercial. If the
destitute colonists were bothered by this particular stipulation, they were
no doubt buoyed by a subsequent, and unmistakably clear, message Sharp
had for the Africans who had driven the settlers from Granville Town. The
master of the *Lapwing*, Sharp wrote the settlers, was empowered to negotiate with King Jimmy and the Naimbana for the return of their property
and for the right to return to the settlement. If they refused, a Royal Navy
ship would bring a harsh reply of his own from the king of England.[122]

As the St. George's Bay Company wound its way through the process of incorporation, the further commercialization of the enterprise and the alienation of the settlers' interests became ever clearer. The original agreements vested Granville Town into the hands of the settlers themselves and gave them the right to parcel out lots among the present colonists and among subsequent newcomers. The colonists, to put it simply, owned the settlement. Prior to the burning of Granville Town, both the actions of the settlers and their supporters in London left this point in little doubt. The signatories on the succession of treaties executed concerning Granville Town varied, but the point concerning ownership of land at the colony never did, and however the African landlords understood the agreements, the language could not have been clearer for those with even a slight grasp of English diplomacy and property rights. The treaties delivered the ceded land to "the sole Benefit of, the Free Community of Settlers, their Heirs and Successors."[123] Thus when Granville Sharp sent out new settlers on the *Myro* brig or desired to reserve lots in the colony for friends and associates of the Province of Freedom, the correspondences between London and Sierra Leone were clear where the prerogative to make such arrangements lied. Sharp could attempt to persuade on such matters, but he had no power to command. The settlers, where their rights were concerned and if they could help it, would neither be dictated to by their enemies nor by their friends, and on the matter of land, before the burning of Granville Town, this was a matter the settlers and their friends in London did not dispute. Thus the perceptive Sharp was careful not to mistake the settlers' deference toward him for fealty when asking that the *Myro* settlers be welcomed into the town as if they had been among the original colonists or requesting that lots be reserved for others then in England or other parts of Europe (including the abolitionists John and Thomas Clarkson, Peter Nassau, William Johnson, and Henry Martin Burrows—two former slaves and a free man of color—and "twelve Swedish gentlemen of rank, great learning and abilities").[124] Indeed, on such occasions Sharp mustered some of his finest rhetoric in attempting to move the colonists to decide in his favor. In requesting land for subsequent settlers, Sharp called the present colonists' attention to the great expense to which he had been put for the colony ("without the least view of any private interest to myself") and hoped that in light of his sacrifices the settlers would not:

> deny my earnest request to you, as a favour to myself, that you will
> readily admit all the persons that are now passengers on board the
> Myro, People of Colour as well as White, together with the captain,
> mates, and such of the seaman as desire it, to an equal share with

yourselves in the settlement, gratis . . . and (as the rainy season will probably be set in) that you will also receive them into your houses, and afford them the best accommodation you can give, with assistance to procure shelter also for their goods, cattle, and fowls, and to aid them in erecting houses for themselves as soon as the weather will permit.[125]

Sharp's appeal demonstrates that he understood how jealously the settlers guarded their rights and prerogatives. But his request also underlines a potential problem that must undoubtedly develop between the evolving St. George's Bay Company and the already established Province of Freedom. The settlers clearly understood themselves, at an individual level, as freeholders. Further, when it came to granting interest in the settlement, they saw themselves as empowered to operate at a corporate level as an executive council or as a board of directors. The ways the settlers had exercised power in Sierra Leone, and their conception of their powers, were incompatible with the authority that the new company of African traders had to claim for itself if it was to be successful in Sierra Leone. It should come as no surprise then that following the burning of Granville Town, as the new company moved from an idea to a reality, Sharp began to step differently concerning the nature of the colonists' establishment at Sierra Leone.

In his first letter to the prime minister upon hearing of the destruction of the settlement, after having had the opportunity of briefing Pitt in person, Sharp stressed the importance of returning the settlers to their rightful possession and underlined British interests in the region. He implored Pitt to send a war sloop with the *Lapwing* to help keep the settlers from being further dispersed (which he understood to be the intention of English slave traders in the region). But Sharp also had in mind keeping any foreign powers at bay. He favored sending out a sloop and marines "to retake possession of the settlement, and restore the settlers to their houses and cultivated lots of land, lest any foreign power should in the mean time purchase the same land as being now evacuated. Sharp argued that "If possession is not speedily regained, the Native Chiefs will conceive that the rights of the Crown of Great Britain are superseded by the evacuation; and the French, who have still, it seems, a factory in the neighbourhood, will probably be tempted to purchase the land." Indeed, Sharp had just received a pamphlet from an "eminent physician" in Paris urging his government to establish a "free settlement, on the coast of Africa, 'like to that . . . of the English as Sierra Leone'"[126]

Thus, in this first letter Sharp emphasized a strong relationship between reestablishing the settlers and reaffirming the lawful interest of Great Britain in the settlement. Sharp's next letters to Pitt toed similar lines.[127] Even the letter sent out with the *Lapwing*—though it made clear that the supplies aboard the ship were not to be doled out as charity—did not really challenge what Sharp and the settlers heretofore understood as the settlement's constitution. The master of the *Lapwing,* wrote Sharp, would "endeavour to treat with King Naimbana, and King Jammy, and the other Chiefs, for a restoration of your late settlement on the Mountains of Sierra Leone, which, having been twice purchased of them for the King of England, is now undoubtedly become English territory; so that if they delay to restore it, and should presume to deny the fulfilling the covenants they have signed (including their promises of being friendly to the settlers), they will draw upon themselves a very severe retaliation of vengeance from the King of England, as soon as any of the ships of war can be spared from their present destination."[128] Before Parliamentary debate over the incorporation of the St. George's Bay Company geared up in earnest, Sharp's thoughts on the constitution of Sierra Leone closely followed what had developed in practice since the founding of the settlement. For Sharp, the interests of the king and the interests of the settlers were one and the same. Thus, restoring the settlers to their settlement and possessions was what was required by the rights the king of England held in the territory. Conversely, denying the colonist their land and possessions was an affront to the king and his interests.

As the opposing sides ramped up in London over the incorporation of the St. George's Bay Company, the principles Sharp had long articulated concerning the parallel interests of the settlers and crown were necessarily set aside. Necessarily, because if the settlers were not somehow dispossessed of their former rights in the colony, it would be impossible for the new company to function. Thus, in a letter sent to the settlers with Alexander Falconbridge, the man selected to serve as the gestating company's commercial agent, Sharp suddenly took a decidedly different turn concerning the settlers' rights. Sharp had heretofore underlined the importance of returning the colonists to their land. Now, in the letter carried by Falconbridge he instead announced that "The present intention of the British Government is, to invest the general property of the King's land in the care of the St. George's Bay Company, that it may be better protected for the future; and the Company will grant free lots of land to all the settlers who will engage to support the British government according to the former Regulations, provided they will promise not to trade with any other merchants than the agents of the Company. . . ."

Sharp more proclaimed the change in logic than explained it. He came close to a justification, however, when he lectured the settlers that they "must attribute the loss of the settlement, in great measure, to that neglect of order and justice, and military discipline, which if you had maintained . . . the natives would not have dared to meddle with you."[129] Months later, after the St. George's Bay Company had successfully incorporated as the Sierra Leone Company, he was much clearer. The colonists, Sharp admitted (not without regret), were "no longer proprietors of the whole district as before, as the land has been granted, since they were driven out, to the Sierra Leone Company; so that they can no longer enjoy the privileges of granting land by the free vote of their own Common Council, as before, nor the benefits of their former Agrarian Law, nor the choice of their own governor and other officers, nor any of circumstances of perfect freedom proposed in the Regulations: all these privileges are now submitted to the appointment and control of the Company, and no settler can trade independently of it."[130]

In the end, the black poors' seasoning in Sierra Leone ended quite inauspiciously. The material manifestations of their survival in western Africa were pulled down or set on fire when King Jimmy razed the settlement. The ideological underpinnings of the world they had built—independence, racial equity, and antislavery—were severely compromised by the charge and power given to the Sierra Leone Company. There is little direct evidence that the settlers immediately understood their new predicament. If Sharp could be so frank about their changed circumstances, however, there can be little doubt that the settlers themselves were not slow to appreciate it.

The original settlement at Granville Town did not last even three years, and its entire existence was characterized by internal dissension, external threat, and near constant physical disaster. In the minds of its London supporters the settlement was a failure, a judgment that would have been shared, no doubt, by a good many of the original colonists (particularly those who fled for their lives during the settlement's first few months). In more recent times, most historians who have described the Province of Freedom have been similarly persuaded, and though students of the settlement have not portrayed Granville Town nor drawn its founders with quite the philippic that Sharp, Thompson, and their London contemporaries were prone to use, the eighteenth-century metropolitan critique of the colony has nevertheless profoundly, and understandably, shaped how scholars have analyzed the evolution of Granville Town and how they have framed its significance.

Consequently, although most historians now underline factors in the decline of the settlement that Sharp and his allies were loathe to admit, the eighteenth-century view from London still carries considerable weight. Thus, in his exhaustive study of the Province of Freedom, Stephen Braidwood has addressed both earlier work that tended to fault the settlers for the colony's demise and some later accounts that have more blamed the settlers' white patrons. According to Braidwood, "the determination of some writers to pin the blame for the settlement's failure on one or other racial group is . . . misguided. Instead, it can be argued that the great majority of both blacks and whites were overwhelmed by the harsh physical circumstances attending the foundation of the settlement, above all the prevalence of disease and the high mortality."[131] Braidwood is certainly correct to highlight the impact of settler mortality and morbidity on the development of the colony. Interestingly, however, even though material conditions in Sierra Leone explain a great deal about the colony's condition at almost any point in time, so weighty are the contemporary assessments of Sharp and others concerning the behavior of the settlers themselves that the principal explanation is still understood as deficient. So even Braidwood, after cogently outlining what he sees as the main factor in the demise of the settlement, goes on to treat what he understands as less important contributory factors in even greater detail than the ostensive chief cause. In the end, though he seems convinced that material conditions in Sierra Leone explain the degeneration of the settlement, the colonists' shortcomings nevertheless dominate his analysis of the settlement's decline. "The failure of the settlers," writes Braidwood "to establish a stable government was certainly a hindrance to the progress of the settlement and contrasts with the organization they had at first achieved in England."[132] Especially important, Braidwood contends, were the colonist's "unnecessarily bad relations with the slave traders and the nearby Africans," which he points out, at least as far as relations with the Africans were concerned, was really "the immediate cause of the destruction of the settlement."[133]

Focusing on the failings of the settlers in this way is not uncommon. In James W. St. G. Walker's trailblazing work *The Black Loyalists,* he writes that the London colonists "were not equipped by skill or temperament for a life as pioneer farmers: they squabbled, indulged in alcohol, and cheated each other."[134] In her wide-ranging work *Epic Journeys of Freedom: Runaway Slaves of the American Revolution and Their Global Quest for Liberty,* Cassandra Pybus counsels caution concerning the perspective of observers like Thomas Thompson, but in describing Granville Town is still prone to build on just such characterizations as the captain of the *Nautilus* was prone to make. Writes Pybus of governance at the Province of Freedom: "It was the case, however, that there was no structured form of government to regulate the settlement, such as Granville Sharp had proposed. . . . Neither civil nor clerical authority carried weight at Granville Town."[135] In his riveting *Rough Crossings,* Simon Schama gives full voice to the critics of Granville Town right beside cautions concerning the very same characterizations, but he never quite offers an assessment of his own. The fact, however, that Schama characterizes Sharp's subsequent relief efforts in Sierra Leone as rooted in a profound optimism suggests that he, like Pybus, is convinced that there was as much merit as there was animus in the descriptions of the black poor proffered by Thompson and others.[136]

This way of looking at the Province of Freedom suggests a particular narrative arc and analytical perspective. Thus, in much of the recent scholarship, the London colonists tend to be featured as an interesting backstory, a failed precursor to the more successful colony that the Nova Scotians would establish upon their arrival in 1792. Historiographically, the Province of Freedom has come to function, much as it did for John Clarkson while recruiting in Nova Scotia, as an object lesson. Not surprisingly, in recent histories of black migration to Sierra Leone it is the Nova Scotians, with their better documented protagonists—David George, Boston King, Thomas Peters, and Moses Wilkinson, among them—who become symbols both of the possibilities of Sierra Leone and of black life in the Age of Revolutions more generally. Granville Town and the Province of Freedom, in contrast, remain much as Sharp saw them, as "my poor little ill-thriven swarthy daughter, the unfortunate colony of Sierra Leone."[137]

Viewing Granville Town as a manifestation of Sharp's utopian hopes or from the vantage of Captain Thomas Thompson's idea of a good society certainly justifies the motif of failure that pervades nearly every recounting of the Province of Freedom. Further, without question, when viewed from almost any angle the history of the settlement is both tragedy and catastrophe. But when the story of Sierra Leone is viewed primarily as migration, and the struggles of the settlers to create their own society in western Africa are viewed first on their own terms, the appropriateness of failure as the story's key interpretive and analytical topos must be reconsidered, even as catastrophe and tragedy remain remarkably viable. The citizens of Granville Town had failings galore, but examining the progress of their colony and watching them season in Sierra Leone makes one thing abundantly clear. Granville Town did not so much fail. It was, rather, destroyed, and asking why it was destroyed, instead of why it failed, prompts an analysis focused, more appropriately, on the settlers than on the expectations of their patrons. Asking why the settlement was destroyed, while not covering the colonists' many failings, requires a recognition of the settlers' very real civil and institutional achievements, and demands too cognizant of the ideological developments that animated important parts of the colony's social and political life. When viewed in this light it is clear, to answer the question posed above, that Granville Town was destroyed because the settlers socialized toward a politics of antislavery that, although it was hardly unambiguous, was substantial enough when combined with the town's growing civil and institutional capacity to render the settlement noxious to prominent British and Temne traders in the region. Granville Town was not destroyed because of the colonists' failings in establishing a viable government and civil society. It was demolished precisely because of the colonists' achievements to date, and in fear of their growing potential.

The slave power in Sierra Leone demolished Granville Town and scattered its settlers for good reason. Ironically, it was the influence of the slave power in the British empire that ensured that the subsequent settlement would not and could not be rebuilt on its former terms. Of course, the West India lobby had no sway among the Sierra Leone Company investors, and they did not win their fight to keep the company from incorporating. But the slave plantations of the British West Indies framed the context in which the directors necessarily formulated the goals of the new company, and it was the necessity of emulating the economic success of the West Indians, whatever they thought of their actual chances of duplicating such success, that all but required the company to concentrate economic and executive power in ways that would significantly curtail the independence of subsequent migrants to Sierra Leone.

In many ways the migration of the Nova Scotians to Sierra Leone and their seasoning in the colony mirrored the experiences of the Londoners some years earlier. Their story has been ably and eloquently told by, among others, Fyfe, Walker, Schama, Pybus, and most recently James Sidbury: The voyage from Halifax was marked by both remarkable social tranquility and troubling mortality. More than sixty of the migrants died on the passage over, while many more than that took sick.[138] Though the Nova Scotians arrived in Sierra Leone at a more amenable time of year than had the black poor, mortality during their first months in Africa was also still considerable.[139] After the first rainy season, the Nova Scotians begin to achieve considerable success in raising houses and growing small crops.[140] Like the Londoners before them, many took to trading along the river for their livelihood.[141] The Nova Scotians—because of their numbers, their more balanced sex ratios, and the fact they traveled to Sierra Leone, in the main, in groups that had been formed in the Maritimes—established a richer community life sooner than the founders of Granville Town had been able. Freetown, the settlement the Nova Scotians founded to the west of the rebuilt Granville Town, featured a rich black associational life of Baptist and Methodist congregants. The Nova Scotians were notorious among slave traders for harboring runaways, but the power of the company over their external affairs ensured that they never became so troublesome in this regard as had the people at Granville Town.[142] In 1794, the settlement at Freetown was all but destroyed by a marauding French fleet, but unlike Granville Town in the aftermath of King Jimmy's devastations, the Nova Scotians had the wherewithal to remain together and to rebuild.[143] The Nova Scotians, backed by a kind of support from the Sierra Leone Company that, though it was far from perfect, was almost always more than what the Londoners could expect from England, built more with more in Sierra Leone. But they never achieved what they most wanted out of their lives in western Africa and what the black poor had managed, though under the gravest of circumstances, almost from the very start of their own settlement: self-governance.

So more than anything else, the story of the Nova Scotians' seasoning in Sierra Leone was the story of a constantly disappointing struggle for independence. The Nova Scotians were indeed granted land in Sierra Leone, but it took an inexplicably long time to come to pass, was not in the end as much as they expected, nor granted under the terms which they were promised.[144] During the first eight years of the settlement, consequently, the Nova Scotians struggled almost perpetually against the company's claimed right to impose an annual quitrent on their land: a fee, the settlers claimed, that contradicted their rights as freeholders and ensured, over time, that they would have little to pass on to their children.[145] As had the Londoners, the Nova Scotians selected hundredors and tithingmen and judged their peers in court. But for the governor and council appointed from London, the black representatives were merely to be consulted, and the black settlers, though no doubt happy with their positions on juries, did not accept that they must be necessarily barred from judgeships.[146] Harangues, threats, recriminations, and protests characterized relations between the Nova Scotians and the company's officers in Sierra Leone, and between the directors and the blacks' ambassadors on occasion when the settlers protested directly to London.

The Nova Scotians, as a group of them once petitioned John Clarkson several months after their arrival, were "all willing to be govern by the laws of england in full but we donot Consent to gave it in to your honer hands with out haven aney of our own Culler in it."[147] But this was also a point to which, in the aftermath of the settlement at Granville Town, the company could never consent in full. After years of recurrent frustration, in late 1799 the hundredors and tithingmen passed resolutions that all but declared the black settlers' independence. The subsequent uprising was put down forcibly, and the ring leaders either banished or hanged.[148]

MIGRATION AND BLACK SOCIETY IN THE EIGHTEENTH-CENTURY BRITISH ATLANTIC WORLD

An unceremonious death, this is what awaited so many black migrants, whether slave or free, on the other sides of their transatlantic journeys. But while they lived, the ways they moved (out of the Biafran interior, out of South Carolina, out of Georgia, out of New York, out of London, out of Halifax), and the consequences of their ocean voyages (some headed east, some west, others south through the Atlantic), and the nature of their settling (in Jamaica and in Sierra Leone), all of these things together present a neglected but vitally important view of the British Atlantic world.

It is a vantage, first and foremost, from which the logistical similarities between free and forced migration—the movements that engendered and sustained the eighteenth-century British colonial world—are made particularly apparent. Migrants to Sierra Leone, to be sure, were passengers not commodities, so at sea they did not so much travel as freight in the highly rationalized and impersonalized manner of slaves. But the larger movements of both slaves and free migrants were *largely* the same.[1] For both, their transatlantic journeys were framed by antecedent travels significant in their own rights. Captives at Biafran ports were not thrown suddenly into motion once the slave ships on which they were imprisoned weighed anchor for the Americas. Most had been weeks, months, even years in states of dislocation. Moreover, for African captives forced aboard a slave ship, the ordeal of waiting at the coast could be every bit the ordeal of the passage to come and every bit the ordeal of the passage already survived (and in any case the combined time it took captives to reach a slave port and the time they spent in the port almost always dwarfed time spent in transoceanic passage).

The arc of movement was hardly different for free black migrants. Sierra Leone's eventual black colonizers were years starting and stopping in the Americas, many launched from the temperate and semitropical Virginia and South Carolina of the future United States to the frigid north of Nova Scotia, others from this same rural vastness of the American South to the particular metropolitan logic of the largest city in Europe. And once in London and Nova Scotia, for free migrants, as for captives bulked at Old Calabar, Bonny, and New Calabar, their actual leaving was weeks and months in the making.

For enslaved and free migrants alike their passages were preceded by *passages* that must be understood on their own terms, and these processal correspondences are important to recognize because they form the main sites of comparative analysis for exploring the experience and consequence of being in motion for both free and enslaved migrants. It is from viewing people moving through the sites common to all kinds of transatlantic migration that some particularly important consequences of their dislocation become apparent, especially as far as matters of migrant society are concerned.

In the main, the historiography on migrations has given us two clear and relatively concise ways to judge and to speak about the consequences of Atlantic migration in terms of the social and cultural continuities migrants maintained in spite of migration and in terms of the social and cultural transformations wrought on migrants because of their movements.[2] Considered together, the passages of enslaved blacks within and out of the Biafran interior, the disembarkation and settlement of enslaved Africans on Jamaica, the movements of free blacks in the Americas and London, and the transport and arrival of the same in Sierra Leone illustrate the point with which Sidney Mintz and Richard Price began their essay theorizing the birth of African American culture: "No group, no matter how well-equipped or how free to choose, can transfer its way of life and the accompanying beliefs and values intact from one locale to another."[3]

There is a latent assumption in this point that people in motion *desire* to retain their former way of life. The assumption, of course, does not always hold. The peregrinations of slaves who cast their lots with the British during the American war were meant to undo the foundations of their former society. But even the American case speaks to Mintz and Price's larger point about the relationship between society and context by illustrating just how effective slaves' wartime migrations were in aiding the transformation of their lives and communities, in ways intended and unintended. The evolution of black loyalism provides a potent example. Though royalism is certainly an important theme in Afro-American history of the colonial period, there is little evidence that it inspired black action during the American war.[4] In the southern colonies, for instance, slaves did not make for British lines because they were convinced of the rightness of the king's cause. It was self-interest, rather, that spurred enslaved blacks toward British forces, and as the cases of David George and Boston King illustrate, the initial relationship between erstwhile slaves and the British army was particularly ambiguous. So, while it is true that the enslaved men, women, and children who used the war to free themselves were certainly not British loyalists. It is undeniable that through their movements with and service to British forces throughout the American interior, and through their pressing wartime urban experiences in places like Savannah, Charleston, and New York, and through their migrations out of the thirteen colonies at the end of the conflict, they were, by and large, well on their way to becoming British loyalists, a social change that would be refined by their stays in Nova Scotia and completed with their subsequent migration to Sierra Leone.[5]

The migratory transformation of plantation communities into black loyalist ones was a social change wrought largely through an opportunity of dislocation. It illustrates, still, the socially transformative tendency of being in motion. In the case of enslaved migrants, of course, dislocation hardly represented an opportunity, but it was transforming all the same.[6] For enslaved migrants, the conditions under which they were set in motion and the circumstances of their subsequent resettlement necessarily constrained their ability to reestablish themselves in the Americas as they once were, and thus more often than not resulted in significant changes in their former society and culture. Such shifts were largely owing to the constraints to social continuity inherent in migration (rather than the transformative opportunities of migration just alluded to). For the captives followed in this study, the most important transformative constraint was the tremendous violence and privation that characterized their movements.

As much as anything, the transatlantic dislocations of free and enslaved blacks were marked by extremes of suffering. From the late eighteenth century it is not possible, for instance, to distinguish the dislocations of free blacks from those made by slaves simply by the sheer physical misery entailed in their moving. The trails and rivers down which enslaved Africans were forced from the Biafran interior to the littoral were, to borrow Joseph Miller's characterization of the Angolan slave trade, ways of death.[7] But for black refugees of the American war tramping through Virginia and South Carolina boldly freeing themselves by fleeing to the British, their journeys too were perilous. They too suffered and died in droves, moving from plantation to camp and camp to port. Thomas Jefferson thought the number destroyed by smallpox ranged in the tens of thousands.[8] Similarly, though the transports that ferried the black poor from London to Sierra Leone were certainly not slave ships, this difference was not apparent from the rates at which free black passengers sickened and died while on board.[9]

For both free and enslaved migrants, the duress that framed their movements complicated their ability to reproduce their old societies in new lands as it likewise facilitated important social transformations. This is most clear in the case of black migrants from the Biafran interior. The process by which captives from this region were expelled from western Africa was violently transformative. Their migrations from the interior to the littoral and then from the coast into the Atlantic enfeebled their former society, forcing them to create new relationships. Following the stages of the slave trade from the Biafran interior reveals that the Igbo identity professed by and ascribed to enslaved Africans from this region was to a large degree a product of the violence and dislocation involved in the slave trade from the Biafran interior to the littoral. It could also result, however, from African urbanism at the littoral that was not necessarily related to the slave trade. There were Igbo in Biafran port towns who were never slaves, but most Igbo in the Americas who originated in the Biafran interior would have never known themselves as Igbo had the slave trade not made them such.

Put another way, Igbo slaves settled on east-side Jamaican plantations were not necessarily the same Igbo who arrived at Kingston, nor the Igbo who left slave ports such as Bonny, nor the Igbo of the Biafran interior whom slave traders forced to the coast. Migration mattered in ways that very often confounds social analysis bent on tracking transparent social relationships between migrants' former abodes and their new ones. Studying the movements of Atlantic migrants over the entire courses of their journeys—from their initial stirrings, to their transatlantic voyages, to the movements that defined their arrival, seasoning, and settlement at their destinations—makes this point clear, and it has important ramifications for how we understand transatlantic migration.

This book has been particularly concerned with the social significance of departures, voyages, and landings, and the social relations characterizing interaction between new immigrants and already-established settlers, and the examination suggests that the impact of the passages enslaved migrants made through Africa, across the Atlantic, and in the Americas deserve closer attention than has recently been the case. Over the last generation the historiography has come to downplay the transformative social significance of transatlantic migration. Thus Ira Berlin has argued that the linguistically dexterous, culturally plastic, and socially agile Africans (Atlantic creoles, he calls them) who arrived as slaves in seventeenth-century North America were probably not significantly affected by their enslavement and subsequent migration. "The transatlantic journey," writes Berlin, "did not break creole communities; it only transported them to other sites."[10] Berlin is cautious not to push his conclusions into the eighteenth century, but John Thornton believes that a similar argument can be made for this period as well. Of the ability of enslaved migrants to maintain fundamental aspects of their former culture in the Americas, he has written: "Whatever the brutalities of the Middle Passage or slave life, it was not going to cause the African-born to forget their mother language or change their ideas about beauty in design or music; nor would it cause them to abandon the ideo- logical underpinnings of religion or ethics—not on arrival in America, not ever in their lives."[11]

There is good reason to reframe, if not reject, similar analyses concern- ing the impact of the slave trade, at least as far as being and becoming Igbo in the eighteenth century were concerned. Igbo society and self-consciousness in the Americas began in the crucible of migration and depended first on captives coming to identify themselves as Igbo (a process that began first in Africa, as I have argued here, but that must have continued in other legs of transatlantic movement as well). To ponder the social origins of enslaved Africans is to recognize that in a critical sense their origins lie as much in the process of their enslavement as it does in the particulars of their previous domiciles.

In this sense, slavery studies has arrived at the same place as many con- temporary migration studies in the need to investigate more fully and theo- rize more rigorously the relationship between social origins, migrations, and destinations in ways that acknowledge the ironies and elisions that characterize these supposedly distinct categories. "Being grounded is not necessarily about being fixed; being mobile is not necessarily about being detached," is how the editors of a recent collection on modern migration allude to the analytical problem at hand.[12] An important strand of recent scholarship on the slave trade and its aftermath fully accepts the second half of this formulation. The first half of the pronouncement, however, is equally important.

Sara Ahmed, Claudia Castañeda, Anne-Marie Fortier, and Mimi Sheller argue that a present task of migration scholarship should not be simply "to categorize 'home' as a condition distinct from 'migration,' or to order them in terms of their relative value or cultural salience, but to ask how uprootings and regroundings are enacted—affectively, materially and symbolically—in relation to one another."[13] In interpreting the significance of the slave trade, a not uncommon oversight in slavery studies has been to treat African social and cultural categories and practices as necessarily and by definition native to African slaves, and to do so in ways that occlude the kinds of uprootings and regroundings that were prime consequences of enslavement. Claims that put the perseverance of African languages at the center of the argument concerning the perseverance of African culture and the negligible social and cultural consequence of the Atlantic slave trade illustrate this tendency. Thus writes John Thornton:

> Of course, the Africans retained their native languages, and African languages were widely spoken in eighteenth-century America. There were more first-language speakers of African languages in many parts of America than speakers of English, French, Dutch, Spanish, or Portuguese. Many of these Africans developed a certain neces-sary proficiency in the colonial language, the European language of their masters and other European or Euro-American settlers, after some years' residence, but it was always a second language, spoken with an accent. They were like the runaway woman, described in a late eighteenth-century Jamaican newspaper advertisement, who 'speaks not altogether plain English; but from her talk she may eas-ily be discovered to be a Coramantee.' She, like other African-born Americans, probably thought, dreamed, and communicated more often in her native language than in the colonial language.[14]

Likewise, Paul Lovejoy has suggested that "In determining ethnicity, the charter principle seems to have been based on common language."[15]

The argument neglects, though, the ways that the language spoken by any particular enslaved Africans in the Americas was not necessarily their native language, but a language bequeathed them by the vagaries and demands of their captivity. This is certainly the point that emerges from Vassa's account of the slave trade from the Biafran interior. The several languages that Equiano acquired while enslaved in the interior were very likely related to the language spoken in his own town and perhaps even mutually intelligible. But Vassa is very clear that these languages were not *his* language. Though intelligible, they did not carry for him the same social and cultural meaning as the language of his town, his true native tongue.[16] The conflation of intelligibility with language occludes the uprootings and regroupings necessitated by the slave trade in nearly every area of human relations, and results in under-interpreting the relationship between lan-guage, in its fullest sociolinguistic sense, and the slave trade.

The question that should be asked and not assumed about African language in the Americas is the degree to which they existed and func-tioned in the New World as they did in Africa. Vassa's *Interesting Narrative* suggests that linguistic differentiations even within what we might now consider a single language could nevertheless hold notable social, cultural, and ideological difference. Thornton brushes against the point but fails to engage it when he writes as follows of the development of African nations in the Americas: "Indeed, loyalties in their homeland were likely to be to a village, or perhaps one of dozens of independent, often hostile states, or to a leader of wealth and status—but not to a language group. Yet, in America these African distinctions *were put aside,* and linguistic loyalty formed a first order of contact and companionship."[17] What this argument neglects is the fact that important facets of language can and do, in the parlance of linguistics, index all of the social and political statuses mentioned above. The development of the kind of linguistic loyalty Thornton and others have outlined would have necessitated, for many, the alteration of heretofore critically important aspects of their native tongues. So if it is true that slaves spoke the colonial language as a second language and with an accent, it is probably also true that the so-called African language of their nation was a second language, too—spoken with accents that their masters could not hear but that were probably quite relevant among their fellow captives.[18] The impetus of all of this linguistic change, social change really, of course, was the slave trade.

The slave trade—especially its violence—was essential to the creation of the eighteenth-century versions of Igbo society and culture that existed in the Americas. The violence of enslavement was not something that Africans necessarily overcame during and following their captivity on the way toward leading the fullest lives possible. The violence of enslavement, rather, was a formative and fundamental part of captives' social and cultural lives. That there were Africans in the eighteenth-century Americas who claimed or accepted being Igbo is evidence, in and of itself, of the lasting and fundamental transformations effected by enslaved migrants' various passages.[19]

The transatlantic movements of free black migrants, as we have seen, were every bit as affecting. Those who set out for Sierra Leone from Nova Scotia became more community-minded, more Christian, and more loyal to Great Britain while in motion, and they did so in ways that transformed critical aspects of black community and independence. That their transformations were based on the multiplication of already salient aspects of Afro-American and Afro-Maritime society underlines the ways that people in motion catalyze significant social change out of apparent continuity as well as from obvious disjunction. The movement of free blacks from London to western Africa illuminates how migration can affect the basic character of people put in motion, but also how difficult it is to judge the society of a source population from the migrants it puts up. To assume, for instance, that the black poor who decided for Sierra Leone represented a social and cultural cross section of black London is, as we have seen, a leap indeed. On all fronts, migrants' transatlantic passages complicate the apparent social relationships between their points of departure and points of arrival.[20]

Together, the movements of free and enslaved black migrants speak also to the relationship between the African diaspora, the British empire, and the Atlantic world. The settlement of free blacks in Sierra Leone and enslaved Africans on Jamaica underscores the ways that British power operated at both sites. Black settlement in both colonies was framed by official and semi-official violence, and an ideology and practice of paternalism that severely checked black aspiration. Simon Taylor was as committed to slavery as Granville Sharp was to its destruction, but they both knew what was best for the blacks in their circle in ways that are as similar as they are disconcerting. Black migrants at both Jamaica and Sierra Leone lived in a realm of British power. This is not the same as saying that they constantly lived *under* British power. They did not. They did, however, live constantly within its reach. So, though one of the analytical benefits encouraged through study of the African diaspora is a focus on the particulars of black community and society, in black migration to Sierra Leone and Jamaica it is clear that the African diaspora and British empire overlapped in ways that made it impossible for migrants to occupy one without also occupying the other.[21]

And if the African diaspora to Jamaica and Sierra Leone were particularly British in ways too important to ignore, the converse is also true. The British Atlantic was definitively black. Its blackness—its deep and fundamental ties to African migration and labor—is what distinguished the British Atlantic world from other parts of Great Britain's worldwide colonial empire in the late eighteenth century.[22] Both enslaved and free migrants traversed and settled in worlds thick with British politics, imperial and domestic, and by their actions some also shaped those politics. Both the free man Thomas Peters and the enslaved would-be rebel Duncan were deeply steeped in the British political culture of the day, and the actions and ruminations of both were felt as far away as Whitehall.

Concerning the issue at the heart of the experience of those black slaves and free people, like Peters and Duncan, whom Ira Berlin has appropriately called "the Revolutionary Generation," it is clear that the difference of possibilities available to enslaved and free migrants could be profound.[23] In this sense, the accomplishments of the black settlers at Granville Town were remarkable. But the ways that the two kinds of black migration and settlement were similar were tragic indeed. When she was a slave, Elizabeth Freeman said that she would have traded her whole existence for a moment to breathe free. For former captives who risked their liberty on transatlantic voyages to Sierra Leone, their wagers turned out just so. In this way, life as an enslaved settler in Jamaica and a black colonist in Sierra Leone was not so different. Blacks who pressed too hard toward liberty in both places were hanged or transported. In the late eighteenth-century British empire, black freedom with all of its opportunities yet entailed some of black slavery's most grievous challenges.

NOTES

INTRODUCTION

1. "Captain's Log *Nautilus*," March–September 1787, NA-Kew, ADM 51/627, ff 14, 22 (At the beginning of the log, Captain Thomas Thompson of the *Nautilus* is ambiguous as to whether ships traversing the river on his arrival are actually slavers. Later in the journal he is less circumspect.); Rodney, *A History of the Upper Guinea Coast;* Brooks, *Landlords and Strangers; Free English Territory in Africa.* In reality, these "black" settlers were a congregation of Africans, East Indians, Afro-Americans, and white Britons who landed as free men and women and took possession of the land ceded them—cutting pathways and erecting shelter—within view of hundreds of captives who passed intermittently out of the Sierra Leone estuary confined aboard European slave ships. Five years later, the survivors from this initial settlement would be buttressed by more than a thousand more immigrants—mainly former Virginians, Carolinians, and other refugees of the American war—arrived most recently from Nova Scotia.

2. On the 1787 voyages of these four ships, see Eltis et al., eds., *The Trans-Atlantic Slave Trade,* voyage id 17990, 17998, 82156, 83178.

3. Morgan, "British Encounters with Africans and African-Americans, circa 1600–1780," 162; Eltis, *The Rise of African Slavery in the Americas,* 9. Beginning in 1580, African migration to Americas exceeded European migration. Only after 1820 did European migration begin once again to outstrip African immigration. (Eltis, "Free and Coerced Migrations from the Old World to the New," Table I, 62.

4. Braidwood, *Black Poor and White Philanthropists,* 147–148 (number in the 1787 expedition); Wilson, *The Loyal Blacks,* 228 (number in the 1792 expedition); Eltis et al., eds., *The Trans-Atlantic Slave Trade* (figures for the slave trade from the Bight of Biafra). Of the 250 Guineamen calling at the Bight of Biafra, the British share of this total was 189 ships forcibly embarking more than 64,000 Africans.

5. Fyfe, *"Our Children Free and Happy,"* 37.

6. For the relationship between British abolitionism and the colonization of Sierra Leone, see Curtin, *The Image of Africa,* 95–110; Brown, "From Slaves to Subjects"; Brown, *Moral Capital,* 253–330.

7. For planter comment on the Sierra Leone experiment, see the following: Simon Taylor to Chaloner Arcedeckne, 6 September 1789, Vanneck Manuscripts, Bundle 2/15; Simon Taylor to Chaloner Arcedeckne, 1 March 1790, Vanneck Manuscripts, Bundle 2/16; Simon Taylor to Chaloner Arcedeckne, 18 January 1794, Vanneck Manuscripts, Bundle 2/20; Simon Taylor to Stephen Fuller, 29 March 1793, Fuller Papers, Dickinson MSS, DD/DN 508, no. 2; and Simon Taylor to Stephen Fuller, 4 September 1793, Fuller Papers, Dickinson MSS, DD/DN 508, no.

33. When black settlers in the British Maritimes heard about the colony in Sierra Leone, they organized a mission to London to inquire whether they might join the fledgling settlement. The story of the Nova Scotia blacks who desired to immigrate to Sierra Leone after hearing about the adventure undertaken by the black poor is told in chapters 7–9. For details of how Caribbean slaves followed news of British abolition, see Scott, "The Common Wind," esp. chapter 3.

8. Among these, Gustavus Vassa the African is both the most famous and—since Vincent Carretta's very thoughtful work questioning the veracity of the African's African birth—the most controversial. Carretta, *Equiano, the African;* Equiano, *The Interesting Narrative and Other Writings,* rev. ed.; Carretta, "Questioning the Identity of Olaudah Equiano, or Gustavus Vassa, the African," 226–235; Carretta, "Olaudah Equiano or Gustavus Vassa?" 96–105.

9. Eltis, "Free and Coerced Migrations from the Old World to the New," 49–57. There remain additional and broader reasons for treating free and coerced migration together. Eltis is persuasive that there exist compelling similarities between free and coerced migration across the board and that such similarities should encourage and inform their being treated together. Both free and coerced migration, for example, unfolded in distinct waves, with distinctive, historical relationships developing between specific points of embarkation and disembarkation. Patterns of mortality, nutrition, reproduction, and socialization were also comparable in important ways. In terms of vital rates, writes Eltis, "the descendants of free and coerced migrants shared more with each other than with the populations that each of their forebears left behind in the Old World." In addition, New World societies, slave and free, tended to be more pluralistic than the Old World sources from which they hailed.

10. Sedgwick, "Slavery in New England," 421.

11. Thornton, *Africa and Africans in the Making of the Atlantic World,* 2nd ed., 320.

12. Bailyn, *The Peopling of British North America,* 113.

13. See, for example, Fischer, *Albion's Seed.* Contrast with Cressy, *Coming Over,* which focuses more on emigration and its consequences.

14. Some of the classic texts are Herskovits, *The Myth of the Negro Past;* Frazier, *The Negro Family in the United States;* Mintz and Price, *The Birth of African American Culture.* More recently, the debate over how African culture and society fared in the Americas has been carried on by such works as Berlin, *Many Thousands Gone;* Gomez, *Exchanging Our Country Marks;* Morgan, *Slave Counterpoint;* Thornton, *Africa and Africans in the Making of the Atlantic World,* 2nd ed.; Matory, "The English Professors of Brazil"; Sweet, *Recreating Africa;* Chambers, *Murder at Montpelier;* and Hall, *Slavery and African Ethnicities in the Americas.*

15. Uprootings and regroundings is one way that contemporary migration history and social science approaches the kinds of issues that lie behind longstanding debates in Afro-American history over the presence of African culture and society in the Americas (Ahmed et al., "Introduction: Uprootings/Regroundings: Questions of Home and Migration," 2).

16. Eltis, "Free and Coerced Migrations from the Old World to the New," 36. It is a problem worth pondering, writes Eltis, how it came to be that "transatlantic migration before 1800 was for so long associated in the minds of both specialist scholars and the general public with first, Europe, and second, freedom."

17. The modern literature on the transatlantic slave trade—a literature for a long time dominated by statistical and economic studies—long exemplified such an approach. Joseph Miller's *Way of Death* and Patrick Manning's *Slavery and African Life* early on pointed out

the necessity of grappling with the humanistic aspects of the terror, privation, and tragedy at the heart of the slave trade. Recently, some very important work in this vein has followed. See, for example, Smallwood, *Saltwater Slavery;* Brown, *The Reaper's Garden;* Rediker, *The Slave Ship;* Hartman, *Lose Your Mother.*

PART I. CAPTIVES

1. From the turn of the eighteenth century to about 1740, for instance, Biafran slave traders provided on average less than four thousand captives per year to Europe's premier slavers, the British. In the six succeeding decades, in contrast, Biafran traders packed British ships with, on average, more than fourteen thousand captives per year. For the expansion and perfection of the mechanics of slave trading in the Biafran interior, see Northrup, *Trade Without Rulers,* 54 and chapter 4; Nwokeji, "The Biafran Frontier," chapter 3. On the commercial explosion of slave trading at Bonny, Elem Kalbari, and Old Calabar, see Lovejoy and Richardson, "'This Horrid Hole,'" 367–370; Richardson, "The Eighteenth-Century British Slave Trade," Table 7 (statistics on British slave trading); Eltis and Richardson, "West Africa and the Transatlantic Slave Trade," 18–19, 29 (statistics on all European carriers).

2. For a description of the settlement, see Pereira, *Esmeraldo de situ Orbis,* 3rd ed., 156: "E assi trazem muitos escravos . . . e por oito e dez manilhas se pode aqui haver um bom escravo." G. I. Jones and E. J. Alagoa speculate that the town described by Pereira may have been Bonny (Jones, *The Trading States of the Oil Rivers,* 33–34; Alagoa, *A History of the Niger Delta,* 154–155).

3. Falconbridge, *An Account of the Slave Trade on the Coast of Africa,* 51, 7, 16, 52 (description of cityscape, number of ships calling at Bonny, announcements of Guineamen and canoe traders, and sailors' burial ground). On the cityscape, cf. Hutchinson, *Impressions of Western Africa,* 104–105. John Adams, who made ten voyages to African between 1786 and 1800, also commented on the announcements of Guineamen and canoe traders in his *Remarks on the Country Extending from Cape Palmas to the River Congo,* 135.

4. Hair et al., eds., *Barbot on Guinea,* 2:676, 681, 693, 695 (year of sailing and number of slaves, description of the *Albion,* quotation, and comparison of Bonny and Elem Kalabari).

5. British slavers' habit of calling by ship or boat at both Bonny and Old Calabar, if they called at either, is evident in the confusion apparent in the record of destination and arrival kept by some slavers wherein New Calabar and Bonny are both listed. See, for example, the records compiled by David Richardson for the *Phoenix, Elizabeth, Antelope, Thomas,* and *Eliza* in Richardson, *Bristol, Africa and the Eighteenth-Century Slave Trade to America,* 4:10, 44, 62, 107, 184. On the expansive Atlantic perspective of New Calabar, consult Northrup, *Trade Without Rulers,* 88–89.

6. On the founding and development of Old Calabar, see Ardener, "Documentary and Linguistic Evidence," 106, 109–113, 126; Latham, *Old Calabar,* chapters 1–2; Watts, *A True Relation,* 12.

7. Evidence of Alexander Falconbridge in House of Commons Sessional Papers (HCSP hereafter), 69:70–71; evidence of James Penny in HCSP 69:70–71. "At Bonny they have little Trade but Slaves, and some Ivory," Alexander Falconbridge told his inquisitors from the Board of Trade at an interview conducted in the late 1780s. James Penny cast a similar portrait of New Calabar, farther inland, saying that the town imported much of its food from the interior.

8. Evidence of Captain Hall in HCSP 69:71 (first quotation); Adams, *Sketches Taken*

during Ten Voyages to Africa, 43 (second quotation). Randy Sparks tells a fascinating story of Old Calabar, its elite, and the Atlantic world in a monograph and article recounting the enslavement of two of the towns "princes" and their eventual return to Old Calabar (Sparks, "Two Princes of Calabar"; Sparks, *The Two Princes of Calabar).*

9. As *Obong,* Edem Ekpo was invested with the rights-in-trade of Old Calabar society. By collecting and recording customs from arriving captains, he opened or "broke trade" with European ships entering the river. Then and only then could the visitors trade for slaves, and incidentally for elephant's teeth, palm oil, yams, and barwood. Consequently, there were Guinea captains who thought Edem Ekpo was the town's ruler. In truth, the *Obong* was but one of several Old Calabar oligarchs. On Edem Ekpo's career and functions as *Obong* and the organization of transatlantic trade at Old Calabar in general, see Latham, *Old Calabar,* 42–45; Lovejoy and Richardson, "Trust, Pawnship, and Atlantic History," 333–355.

10. For details on Old Calabar slave society, see Latham, *Old Calabar,* chapter 3; Jones, "The Political Organization of Old Calabar," 116–160, esp. 132–135 and 144–148. For an account of the executions conducted at the hall of the Ekpe Society, see Duke, "The Diary of Antera Duke," 46, 97, 100–101 (2, 3, 4, and 5 July 1786 and 2, 6, 8, and 9 November 1786).

11. Granted, there were slaves across Old Calabar who through deed and accumulation had all but erased their slave status and thus their vulnerability to the kind of assaults just described. For example, Eyo Nsa, known as Willy Honesty to his Old Calabar and European peers, had once been a slave but was no doubt among the gathering of Old Calabar gentlemen who punctuated the passing of Duke Ephraim by slaying fifty slaves. Still, most of the Old Calabar's slaves were strangers—they were not, that is, natives—and for them the violence executed at the hall of the Ekpe Society on November 6 was of a kind to which slaves, as the basest strangers, were particularly vulnerable (Latham, *Old Calabar,* 46–47).

ONE

THE SLAVE TRADE FROM THE BIAFRAN INTERIOR

1. Adams, *Remarks on the Country Extending from Cape Palmas to the River Congo,* 129; Equiano, *The Interesting Narrative and Other Writings,* rev. ed., 32, 241 n. 41; Simon Taylor to Chaloner Arcedeckne, 1 November 1789, Vanneck Manuscripts, Bundle 2/15.

2. Gomez, *Exchanging Our Country Marks;* Chambers, "'My Own Nation,'" 72–97; Chambers, "The Significance of Igbo in the Bight of Biafra Slave-Trade," 101–120; Chambers, *Murder at Montpelier.*

3. Thornton, *Africa and Africans in the Making of the Atlantic World, 1400–1800,* 2nd ed., 321. Both Chambers and Gomez, for instance, rightly hypothesize that becoming Igbo was a social process, but this insight is not fully explored in their subsequent work dealing with the nation as a concept for social and cultural analysis of black life in the African diaspora. Thus their work is more prone to describe being Eboe as possessing certain traits, performing certain actions, and practicing certain behaviors than it is to interrogate the process (or processes) of becoming Igbo (Chambers, "'My Own Nation,'" 84–91; Gomez, *Exchanging Our Country Marks,* 114–134. David Northrup's critique of Chambers's work flows mostly from just this kind of oversight. See Northrup, "Igbo and Myth Igbo," 1–20; Kolapo, "The Igbo and Their Neighbours during the Era of the Atlantic Slave Trade," 114–115.

4. Ofomata, *Nigeria in Maps,* esp. 8–9, 30–37. In the main, the Biafran interior is characterized by lowland plains, but these in turn are crisscrossed by a dizzying variety of microlandscapes. Marshy lowlands predominate along the western Niger Delta and astride

that river's main course. Low plains fan out behind the delta proper, rising slowly toward the north until transformed into a sloping hill country. More angular hills and valleys mark parts of the Cross River basin to the east, and two major and many minor escarpments slash across the northern end of the whole expanse. Topographically the territory's terrain is as diverse as its landforms. Here is freshwater swamp; there complexes of lowland rainforest; and where man has been most active for the longest period of time a mosaic of secondary forest and grassland prevails.

5. Onwuejeogwu, "The Igbo Culture Area," 1–10; Ottenberg, "Ibo Oracles and Intergroup Relations," 296; Jones, "Ecology and Social Structure Among the North Eastern Ibo," 117–134; Jones, "Ibo Land Tenure," 309–323.

6. Early British missionaries having already begun translating the Bible and other Christian tracts into Onitsha Igbo discovered the limits of the dialect rather belatedly. Green, "The Present Linguistic Situation in Ibo Country," 508–523. For the situation along the Cross River, examine Adams and Ward, "The Arochuku Dialect of Ibo," 57–70. For further insight on Igbo dialects, their social meanings, and how speakers overcome linguistic differences in practice, see the following: Afigbo, "The Impact of Colonialism on Igbo Language," 355–386; Emenanjo, "How Do the Igbo Understand Themselves?" 60–74; Manfredi, "Agbo and Ehughbo"; Ward, "A Linguistic Tour in Southern Nigeria," 90–97. The diversity and social manifestation of Igbo dialects show themselves in the story linguist R. F. G. Adams told concerning moving from the areas around the Onitsha and Awka village groups toward Afikpo and environs in the first decades of the last century. Adams had acquired a journeyman proficiency in speaking with farmers in his former situation that he realized was completely useless in his new position. He thus found himself relying on the translation skills of a native speaker he had brought with him from around Onitsha, a "small boy" who after listening to the language spoken at Afikpo replied: "It is no good trying to talk to these people: they do not speak our language." See Adams and Ward, "The Arochuku Dialect of Ibo," 60.

7. On politics and authority in the Biafran interior, see Cookey, "An Ethnohistorical Reconstruction of Traditional Igbo Society," 327–347. On the art history of the region, see Jones, *The Art of Eastern Nigeria;* Jones, *Ibo Art;* Cole and Aniakor, *Igbo Arts.* In 1988, *African Arts* published a special issue dedicated to Igbo arts introduced by Herbert M. Cole, "Igbo Arts and Ethnicity: Problems and Issues," 26–27. Two essays in the collection pay particular attention to regional and local variation: Picton, "Ekpeye Masks and Masking," 46–53; Bentor, "Life as an Artistic Process," 66–71. Also note, Willis, "*Uli* Painting and the Igbo World View," 62–67.

8. Ottenberg, "Ibo Oracles and Intergroup Relations," 297–299; Ottenberg, "Ibo Receptivity to Change," 130–143; Jones, "Dual Organization in Ibo Social Structure," 150–156; Jones, "Ecology and Social Structure Among the North Eastern Ibo," 120–122; Onwuejeogwu, *An Igbo Civilization.*

9. Onwuejeogwu, *An Igbo Civilization;* Dike and Ekejiuba, *The Aro of South-Eastern Nigeria, 1650–1980,* esp. chapters 6 and 7; Nwokeji, "The Biafran Frontier," chapter 3. As M. A. Onwuejeogwu has informed us, the widespread authority of the Nri village group was spread through large parts of the Biafran interior not by war or territorial expansion but through segmentary migration and the clarity and force of Nri ideology. Aback the Cross River, to cite another instance, the Aro facilitated a brisk trade in slaves and other articles throughout the whole Biafran interior during the eighteenth century. In the process, Aro traders and their allies depended at times on warfare, punitive raids, and the threat of the same in order to guarantee ascendancy over various hinterland trade routes and goods. But such as they were,

Aro depredations did not result in an Aro empire in any sense of the word. Rather, as has been persuasively argued by Kenneth Dike and Felicia Ekejiuba, and recently elaborated by G. Ugo Nwokeji, Aro expansion created a series of loosely linked Aro diasporas and/or frontiers.

10. See generally, Uchendu, *The Igbo of Southeast Nigeria*.

11. Shelton, *The Igbo-Igala Borderland*, 28. According to Shelton, to the peoples of the Biafran interior "the 'we' virtually always referring to a tightly related consanguineous group extending its membership hesitantly and with numerous serious reservations affinally, usually within a non-exogamous village-group called a 'town' in English, and the 'they' referring to all other peoples not of the consanguineous familial group, nor of the affinal and 'town' groups."

12. For Olu, Enugu, Aniocha, Ndiuzu, and Umudioka, see Dike and Ekejiuba, *The Aro of South-Eastern Nigeria, 1650–1980*, 6–7. For Ngwa-Ukwu, see Martin, *Palm Oil and Protest*, 17–35; Oriji, *Ngwa History*. For Onicha-Ukwu, see Okwechime, *Onicha-Ugbo through the Centuries*, 9–36.

13. See John Adams's remarks on p. 17 above. James Barbot, who sailed to Old Calabar in 1698, mentioned Igbo markets and returned to London from Africa with samples of Igbo-manufactured weaponry. He rendered Igbo as "Hackbous" (Hair et al., eds., *Barbot on Guinea*, 2:693, 694, 710–711 n. 65). Also see the eighteenth-century references to Igbo mentioned in Ogude, *No Roots Here*, 3–4.

14. Koelle, *Polyglotta Africana*, 7–8. By way of explaining the anomaly that he had uncovered, Koelle speculated that, through a process presently unknown, Igbos settled in Sierra Leone must have somehow "lost their general national name." In reflections on his own journey on the Niger in 1854, William Balfour Baikie made a point of disagreeing with the German philologist, writing as follows: "Here let me notice a conjecture of Koelle in his 'Polyglotta Africana,' namely, that I'bo is a name unknown to the natives, until they learn it from white men. This is quite erroneous, as the name I'bo or I'gbo is as familiarly employed among the natives as London is among ourselves" (Baikie, "Brief Summary of an Exploring Trip," 111). I agree with A. E. Afigbo that Baikie was subject to overreach in his application and interpretation of Igbo (see Afigbo, *Igbo Genesis*, 4–5). And it should also be pointed out that Baikie's gloss of Koelle was defective inasmuch as the author of *Polyglotta Africana* did not put such a fine point on the matter (Koelle did not argue that Igbo was a term learned from white men). Still Baikie was no doubt correct that the term Igbo was known and used in the Biafran interior. Jean Barbot and others, after all, encountered the term at the littoral in the late seventeenth century (Hair et al., eds., *Barbot on Guinea*, 2:673, 694, plate 53, plate 54, and 702 n. 5). More revealing, however, is the fact that when Baikie summarized his thoughts on Igbo as an ethnonym a year later—and after having benefitted from interviewing people from the Biafran interior then in Fernando Po and Sierra Leone—he was more circumspect concerning *how* Igbo was used in the Biafran interior. In his 1856 monograph, for instance, Baikie conceded Koelle's point concerning the primacy of local identifications among people in the interior. Consequently, if he meant in his 1855 article to suggest that Igbo was a term of self-identification, in his subsequent monograph Baikie's thoughts on the matter were more reserved, even opaque. "In I'gbo," wrote Baikie, "each person hails, as a sailor would say, from the particular district where he was born, but when away from home *all* are I'gbos" (Baikie, *Narrative of an exploring voyage*, 307 [emphasis is mine]). This is a tautology, but a useful one inasmuch as it acknowledges (not unlike Koelle in its conclusions) that Igbo consciousness was a process, not a given. Other nineteenth-century accounts of the people and places along the course of the Niger, taken as a whole, do not contradict this point, and, among these,

Samuel Crowther's 1854 journal displays a striking cognizance of the problems associated with assuming, as Baikie was sometimes inclined, that Igbo was an internally generated and accepted ethnonym of self-identification (Allen and Thomson, *A narrative of the expedition sent;* Crowther, *Journal of an expedition up,* see especially the entries for October 23, 24, 28, and 29, 1854; Laird and Oldfield, *Narrative of an expedition into the interior of Africa;* Schèon and Crowther, *Journals of the Rev. James Frederick Schèon and Mr. Samuel Crowther,* 2nd ed.). The earliest manuscript evidence from the Biafran interior, then, suggests that Igbo was a term unknown to some and known and used by others. But among those to whom the term was known, it was not ordinarily embraced as a term of self-identification.

15. W. D. W. Jeffreys, "Awka Division Intelligence Report," 18 January 1937 [?], NA-Nigeria, CSE 1.85.4596, File No. EP8766 (first quotation); C. W. Meek, "Comments by the Anthropological Officer on Mr. Jeffrey's Anthropological Report," 24 January 1932 [37?], NA-Nigeria, CSE.1.86.228 (second quotation).

16. Henderson, *The King in Every Man,* 40–41; Forde and Jones, *The Ibo and Ibibio-Speaking Peoples of South-Eastern Nigeria,* 9; Shelton, *The Igbo-Igala Borderland,* 6–7. In the 1930s, an enterprising if overreaching British anthropological officer put it this way: "An examination of the term Igbo shows that it belongs to the same category that the following words do in English. Viz. Kafir, Heathen; Barbarian, Welsh. All of these terms used in English are, with the exception of Heathen and Welsh, alien words used in alien languages to describe foreigners: i.e. persons not of the same race and language as the speaker. It would seem that Igbo is from a Sudanic root which means "bush" or people of the bush and its analogue in English would be Heathen i.e. people of the heath. It is thus clear that as there is no heathen race or nation per se, so actually there is no Igbo race [or] language and none of the peoples described today as [Igbo] by the European will admit the term as descriptive of his race or language nor will he use it of himself" (see W. D. W. Jeffreys, "Awka Division Intelligence Report," 18 January 1937 [?], NA-Nigeria, CSE 1.85.4596, File No. EP8766).

17. For Eboe, see Equiano, *The Interesting Narrative and Other Writings,* rev. ed., 32, 241 n. 41. Some of the most useful historical and critical evaluations of Equiano's memoir are Walvin, *An African's Life;* Green, "The Publishing History of Olaudah Equiano's *Interesting Narrative,*" 362–375; Afigbo, "Through a Glass Darkly," 145–186; Ogude, *No Roots Here;* Edwards, "Introduction to 'The Life of Olaudah Equiano,'" 302–338; Edwards, "Embrenché and Ndichie," 401–402; Edwards and Shaw, "The Invisible *CHI* in Equiano's 'Interesting Narrative,'" 146–156; Carretta, "'Property of Author,'" 130–150; Carretta, *Equiano the African.* Compare Ogude's "No Roots Here" to Acholonu's *The Igbo Roots of Olaudah Equiano.*

18. Equiano, *The Interesting Narrative of the Life of Olaudah Equiano, or Gustavus Vassa, the African,* 295–296.

19. Vassa claims to have been kidnapped at the age of eleven. Vincent Carretta's review of the documentary evidence related to Vassa's early life suggest that the author of the *Interesting Narrative* may have been as young as "between six and eight years old when initially kidnapped in Africa" (Carretta, "Olaudah Equiano or Gustavus Vassa?" 103).

20. Carretta, "Olaudah Equiano or Gustavus Vassa?"; Carretta, "Questioning the Identity of Olaudah Equiano, or Gustavus Vassa, the African." Also see Lovejoy, "Issues of Motivation"; Lovejoy, "Autobiography and Memory"; Carretta, "Response to Paul Lovejoy's 'Autobiography and Memory.'"

21. Byrd, "Eboe, Country, Nation and Gustavus Vassa's *Interesting Narrative,*" 123–148.

22. Joseph Miller and Joseph Inikori have addressed the disparity of attention to which I allude and have focused intensively on segments of the Atlantic trade preceding the actual

sea voyage. Stephanie Smallwood's and Marcus Rediker's very fine recent books both take similar tacks. Miller, *Way of Death;* Inikori, "The Sources of Supply," 31–32; Smallwood, *Saltwater Slavery;* Rediker, *The Slave Ship.* For average sailing times from the Bight of Biafra to Jamaica, see Klein, "The English Slave Trade to Jamaica," 35.

23. Equiano, *The Interesting Narrative and Other Writings,* rev. ed., 47. In what follows, I refer to the author of *The Interesting Narrative* by the name he used most in public: Gustavus Vassa. When describing incidents from *The Interesting Narrative* concerning Vassa's ostensive enslavement and that do not concern Vassa as an author, I write of the experiences of Equiano. It is a choice that allows a useful distinction, I think, between Vassa the author and the events described in the African chapters of his *Interesting Narrative.* This usage is not meant to betray a position on whether Vassa was born in Africa, nor on whether his birth name was indeed Olaudah Equiano. On these matters I am, at the moment, agnostic. In the notes and bibliography, *The Interesting Narrative* is cited under the name Olaudah Equiano because this is how the book is cataloged in most libraries in the United States.

24. Equiano, *The Interesting Narrative and Other Writings,* rev. ed., 47.

25. Ibid., 47.

26. Ibid., 47–48.

27. Ibid., 48–50.

28. Ibid., 50–51.

29. Ibid., 52–54.

30. Obichere, "Slavery and the Slave Trade in the Niger Delta Cross River Basin," 48. Such trials of the slave trade in the interior are less pronounced in Vassa's *Interesting Narrative.* For his part, Vassa indicated that the "sable destroyers of human rights" who forced Equiano from his home to the sea at no time offered any ill treatment to him or to the slaves who were his companions except for "tying them, when necessary, to keep them from running away." Given so much evidence to the contrary, however, it is likely that Vassa's point is largely rhetorical. A prime object of his account was to indict European slave traders, not their African counterparts (Equiano, *The Interesting Narrative and Other Writings,* rev. ed., 51).

31. Equiano, *The Interesting Narrative and Other Writings,* rev. ed., 48–50.

32. Ibid., 51. Concerning the acquisition of new dialects, Equiano writes: "From the time I left my own nation I always found somebody that understood me till I came to the sea coast. The languages of different nations did not totally differ, nor were they so copious as those of the Europeans, particularly the English. They were therefore easily learned; and, while I was journeying thus through Africa, I acquired two or three different tongues." G. I. Jones believes this was because before Equiano began in earnest toward the sea, he was all the while not very far from home (Jones, "Olaudah Equiano of the Niger Ibo," 67–68).

33. Kopytoff and Miers, "African 'Slavery' as an Institution of Marginality," 14–15, 3–81 passim; Uchendu, "Slaves and Slavery in Igboland," 121–132.

34. Evidence of Alexander Falconbridge in HCSP 69:48.

35. Evidence of James Penny in HCSP 69:47.

36. William Woodville to James Rogers, 20 April 1791, NA-Kew, C 107/13. ". . . some of the ships have been here from sixteen to nineteen weeks but as the provisions in the back country is now planted the times are much minded in respect to the briskness of the trade although the prices remain the same." Also see Evidence of James Fraser in HCSP 71:19. Fraser testified that "most of the Slaves we purchase at Bonny confess themselves to have been Slaves," a point of fact he took to mean that a "great many in the country are born Slaves," but the observation could just as well support the point I have made here.

37. Falconbridge, *An Account of the Slave Trade on the Coast of Africa,* 17. Vassa paid special attention to Equiano's crossing into this part of Africa—a place sustained by water transport and coursing with international commerce. The people there, Vassa wrote, "cooked in iron pots and had European cutlasses and crossbows." And they all but lived on the water. As Vassa portrayed these scenes decades later, as a man and a deep-sea sailor, he held that as a boy he was "beyond measure astonished" at what he saw (Equiano, *The Interesting Narrative and Other Writings,* rev. ed., 54).

38. Falconbridge, *An Account of the Slave Trade on the Coast of Africa,* 16.

39. William Woodville to James Rogers, 20 April 1791, NA-Kew, C 107/13. For more on the notion of trust, see Lovejoy and Richardson, "Trust, Pawnship, and Atlantic History," 333–355.

40. Falconbridge, *An Account of the Slave Trade on the Coast of Africa,* 17. "The speed with which the information of the arrival of ships upon the coast is conveyed to the fairs . . . is really surprising. In a very short time after any ships arrive upon the coast, especially if several make their appearance together, those who dispose of the negroes at the fairs are frequently known to increase the price of them."

41. Quotations in this sentence and the three previous ones were taken from Evidence of Alexander Falconbridge in HCSP 69; Falconbridge, *An Account of the Slave Trade on the Coast of Africa,* 19.

42. Evidence of William James in HCSP 69:49.

43. Falconbridge, *An Account of the Slave Trade on the Coast of Africa,* 17.

44. Evidence of William James in HCSP 69:49; Falconbridge, *An Account of the Slave Trade on the Coast of Africa,* 17. James, who made three voyages to Africa as a boy, recounted of the canoe trade: "When the bargain is made they are brought away. This is generally at the Close of the Evening." Falconbridge concurred.

45. Thus it is an act of rather confusing prolepsis to speak of the Igbo in eighteenth-century Africa as one would the Igbo of twentieth-century Nigeria. The Igbo of the era of the slave trade simply did not exist in the same way as did the Igbo of colonial and post-colonial Nigeria. Further, if Inikori's research on the slave trade from the Bight of Biafra pans out, it will have to be confessed that the majority of slaves exported from Biafra in the eighteenth and nineteenth centuries were not even the predecessors of the peoples now considered Igbo. That is, they were not from the present confines of Igboland, nor did they speak Igbo languages. Based on tenuous but intriguing demographic evidence, Inikori has argued that a majority of the slaves exported from Biafran ports must have been from north of the present confines of Igboland. Inikori, "The Sources of Supply," 29–30, 34–36; Kolapo, "The Igbo and Their Neighbours during the Era of the Atlantic Slave Trade," 114–133.

46. Hair et al., eds., *Barbot on Guinea,* 2:673, plate 53, and 702 n. 5.

47. Ibid., 2:693, 694, and plate 54.

48. Evidence of James Fraser in HCSP 71:19, 22, 46. See also, Evidence of Alexander Falconbridge in HCSP 72:299.

49. Alagoa, *A History of the Niger Delta,* 180–183.

50. Jones, *The Trading States of the Oil Rivers;* Horton, "From Fishing Village to City-State," 37–58.

51. Horton, "From Fishing Village to City-State," 54.

52. Jones, "The Political Organization of Old Calabar." Though in Old Calabar, under the auspices of Ekpe, this was a painfully slow and uneven process relative to the custom at Bonny and Elem Kalabari.

53. Dike, *Trade and Politics in the Niger Delta,* 30.

54. See especially Hodgkin, *Nationalism in Colonial Africa,* chapters 1–2; Cohen, *Custom and Politics in Urban Africa;* Mitchell, *The Kalela Dance;* Mitchell, *Cities, Society, and Social Perception,* chapter 6; Werbner, "The Manchester School in South-Central Africa," 157–185; Cohen, *Urban Ethnicity;* Nnoli, *Ethnicity and Development in Nigeria;* Nnoli, *Ethnic Politics in Nigeria;* Asiwaju, *The Birth of Yewaland.*

55. Evidence of James Fraser in HCSP 71:46.

TWO

THE SLAVE SHIP AND THE BEGINNINGS OF IGBO
SOCIETY IN THE AFRICAN DIASPORA

1. Chambers's and Michael Gomez's work on Igbo captives and culture in the Americas is illuminating in this sense (Chambers, *Murder at Montpelier,* chapters 1–4, and esp. page 22; Gomez, *Exchanging Our Country Marks,* chapter 6).

2. Evidence of John Ashley Hall in HCSP 72:230 (quotation and the manacling of male captives); Evidence of Alexander Falconbridge in HCSP 72:305; Evidence of William Littleton in HCSP 68:293 (securing men slaves to the ship's deck).

3. Evidence of James Penny in HCSP 69:117; Evidence of John Ashley Hall in HCSP 72:247.

4. Evidence of James Penny in HCSP 69:117 (quotation). Also see Evidence of Robert Heatley in HCSP 69:123.

5. Evidence of John Ashley Hall in HCSP 72:236; Evidence of Alexander Falconbridge in HCSP 72:306.

6. Evidence of James Penny in HCSP 69:117. ". . . the upper Decks are swept clean, where they have been fed. . . ."

7. Evidence of David Henderson in HCSP 69:139. See also, Evidence of James Penny in HCSP 69:117; Evidence of Alexander Falconbridge in HCSP 72:305; Evidence of John Matthews in HCSP 68:19; Evidence of John Ashley Hall in HCSP 72:231.

8. Evidence of James Penny in HCSP 69:117; Evidence of Robert Norris in HCSP 69:119; Evidence of Robert Norris in HCSP 68:5.

9. Evidence of Robert Norris in HCSP 69:119 (quotation); Evidence of James Penny in HCSP 69:117.

10. Evidence of Robert Norris in HCSP 68:4; Evidence of Archibald Dalziel in HCSP 68:32; Evidence of Robert Heatley in HCSP 69:123; Evidence of Alexander Falconbridge in HCSP 72:323.

11. Evidence of Robert Norris in HCSP 68:9, 10; Evidence of John Knox in HCSP 68:155; Evidence of James Penny in HCSP 68:40; Evidence of John Matthews in HCSP 68:43.

12. Henry Smeathman, "Extracts from Mr. Smeathman's Journal," 1771–1772, Smeathman's Journal, MS D 26, 17 December 1771. Here, Smeathman is describing a slaver on the Windward Coast, but ships working rivers in the Bight of Biafra attired themselves in a similar fashion. Two theories persuaded masters to array their anchored ships with temporary houses and barricades. The shelters were supposed to protect the ship's crew from the tropical sun and violent rains characteristic of the coast. The chambers about the main deck were meant to harbor slaves brought on board, separating women and children from the men while at the same time foiling attempts at overboard escape. In practice, all of the shipboard constructions described above answered each of their respective purposes "but very ineffectually." Water seeped and then poured through a ship's houses whenever the rains

were heavy (and they often were). And slaves desperate for the shore quite often slashed and tore their way through the lattice work and nets that were supposed to prevent escape. See Falconbridge, *An Account of the Slave Trade on the Coast of Africa*, 5–7.

13. Minchinton, "Characteristics of British Slaving Vessels, 1698–1775," 53–81 (variety of slaving ships); Falconbridge, *An Account of the Slave Trade on the Coast of Africa*, 7 (conditions shipboard).

14. Evidence of Robert Norris in HCSP 68:8; Evidence of John Knox in HCSP 68:157–158; Evidence of William James in HCSP 69:137; Evidence of David Henderson in HCSP 69:139.

15. Evidence of John Knox in HCSP 68:88–89; Evidence of William James in HCSP 69:137.

16. Evidence of Alexander Falconbridge in HCSP 72:301.

17. Evidence of George Young in HCSP 69:115.

18. Evidence of John Ashley Hall in HCSP 72:231; Evidence of Isaac Wilson in HCSP 72:275–276.

19. Evidence of David Henderson in HCSP 69:139.

20. Evidence of James Arnold in HCSP 69:127.

21. Evidence of Alexander Falconbridge in HCSP 72:303, 301.

22. Evidence of Isaac Wilson in HCSP 72:275–276.

23. Evidence of James Fraser in HCSP 71:45–46. Captain Fraser admitted the following about coaxing slaves to eat: "I have sometimes threatened them when they were sulky, and would not eat their provisions; namely, that they should have no yams if they did not eat their beans." For those slaves who were still not persuaded, he had another method of which he seemed particularly proud: "Being sick in my cabin, the chief mate and surgeon, at different times informed me, that there was a man upon the main deck, that would neither eat, drink, or speak—I desired them to use every means in their power to persuade him to speak, and assign reasons for his silence—I desired them to make some of the other Slaves endeavour to make him speak—when I was informed he still remained obstinate, and not knowing whether it was sulkiness or insanity, I ordered the chief mate, or surgeon, or both, to present him with a piece of fire in one hand and a piece of yam in the other, and to let me know what effect that had upon him—it was reported to me, that he took the yam and eat [*sic*] it, and threw the fire overboard."

24. Evidence of Captain Hall in HCSP 69:122. A case reported by the Guinea surgeon Isaac Wilson best relates how captives' inability and/or refusal to eat turned ship meals into moments of violent drama. A certain African "had not been very long on board" before the surgeon and others suspected that he intended to starve himself, as they could not recall a moment when he had actually eaten the provisions offered him. The crew attempted persuasion, informing the man that he could have anything he desired if he would simply eat. He refused, keeping his mouth shut and teeth clenched in rebuttal. The slave's obstinateness rather quickly convinced the surgeon that the cat might persuade the captive to end his strike, but cutting the slave with the whip "proved to have as little success" as previous methods. Calling for a speculum, the ship's doctor decided to pry the slave's mouth open and force-feed him. Remarkably, this too failed, and the African was finally left alone. Four or five days later, the man was brought from between decks, apparently unconscious, but when the crew attempted once again to convince him to eat, the captive refused with the same commitment as before. Two days later he was brought up again in the most pitiful state imaginable. This time, when the crew and a translator attended him, he asked for water. When it was brought to him, he drank with a vigor convincing those around him that they

had finally succeeded in dissuading him from his own destruction. After taking the water, however, the African "shut his teeth as fast as ever" and again appeared utterly "resolved to die." Two days afterward he succeeded (Evidence of Isaac Wilson in HCSP 72:280). Slave trade sympathizers thought such incidents indicated the lengths Guinea crew would go to to save slaves from themselves. Abolitionists interpreted the facts in the obvious way.

25. Evidence of David Henderson in HCSP 69:139.

26. Evidence of James Fraser in HCSP 71:28. According to Fraser, captives were "generally of a cheerful disposition, which we encourage, and they have frequent amusements peculiar to their own country, such as some little games with stones or shells, dancing, and jumping, and wrestling."

27. Evidence of John Ashley Hall in HCSP 72:231. See also, Evidence of Alexander Falconbridge in HCSP 72. "After every meal. . . [the slaves] are made to jump in their irons; but I cannot call it dancing."

28. Evidence of James Arnold in HCSP 69:126.

29. Evidence of David Henderson in HCSP 69:139.

30. For details on the frequency—from once a day to several times a week—and method of cleaning between decks, see the following: Evidence of William Littleton in HCSP 68:215; Evidence of Alexander Falconbridge in HCSP 72:322; Evidence of Robert Heatley in HCSP 69:123.

31. Evidence of William James in HCSP 69:137.

32. Cohn, "Maritime Mortality in the Eighteenth and Nineteenth Centuries," 173.

33. See the summary of the mortality literature in Cohn, "Deaths of Slaves in the Middle Passage," 685–692.

34. There has been some disagreement concerning the relationship between slave mortality and ship conditions—whether Guineaships more or less caused slave deaths, or whether ships were more the stage on which captives succumbed to sicknesses initially contracted in the interior. The latest synthesis suggests that this is an area in which general studies must give way to regional explanations and an approach that investigates how both factors—conditions shipboard and circumstances in the interior—interacted at particular places at particular times. Preliminary work in this vein suggests that once ill and exhausted captives were hoisted shipboard—whatever gauntlets the slaves had survived previously—they became at increased risk for the kinds of infection and disease encouraged by the close, unsanitary conditions of the Guineaship—namely various kinds of dysentery. For the debate over the incidence and timing of slave deaths, compare the following: Miller, "Mortality in the Atlantic Slave Trade," 385–423; Eltis, "Mortality and Voyage Length in the Middle Passage," 301–308; Cohn and Jensen, "Mortality in the Atlantic Slave Trade," 317–329; Cohn and Jensen, "The Determinants of Slave Mortality Rates on the Middle Passage," 2 69–282. For an emerging synthesis, see Steckel and Jensen, "New Evidence on the Causes of Slave and Crew Mortality in the Atlantic Slave Trade," 57–77, and Klein et al., "Transoceanic Mortality," 92–118. Comments on the particularly high mortality characteristic of the Bight of Biafra are scattered throughout the just mentioned studies, but see particularly Klein and Engerman, "Slave Mortality on British Ships, 1791–1797," 113–125, esp. 116–119; and Klein et al., "Transoceanic Mortality," 101–102. The reasons behind the high mortality rates for captives embarked along the Bight of Biafra are not well understood.

35. By the late eighteenth century, the spectacular mortality characteristic of Guineaships fifty years before—when Africans boarding slavers at the Bight of Biafra routinely perished at rates exceeding 40 percent of their number—gave way to less-breathtaking, simply grinding levels of mortality of around 15 percent. For slaves, however, the threat and actuality of

disease and death, even under the relatively healthier regime of late in the century, added an appreciating level of dread to their captivity. Under the best of circumstances, a healthy number of captives boarding ships at Biafran ports were constantly ill or recovering from illness, and hardly a week passed during loading when slaves did not perish. See Klein and Engerman, "Long-Term Trends in African Mortality in the Transatlantic Slave Trade," Table 2; Steckel and Jensen, "New Evidence on the Causes of Slave and Crew Mortality in the Atlantic Slave Trade," Table 1; Klein et al., "Transoceanic Mortality," Table VI (a).

36. Evidence of Alexander Falconbridge in HCSP 72:337. This former Guinea surgeon testified that he believed he had never cured a man who had a bad dysentery. When asked whether he thought his experience was general, Falconbridge replied: "I believe every man of candour will acknowledge it. I have often palliated the symptoms by large doses of opium, but never remember effecting a perfect cure. I mean to apply this observation to ship-board."

37. Evidence of Alexander Falconbridge in HCSP 72:302.

38. Evidence of James Arnold in HCSP 69:127.

39. Evidence of William James in HCSP 69:138. In eighteenth-century parlance, a puncheon referred to a large cask for storing liquids. A small puncheon might hold seventy-two gallons, a large one more than 100 gallons.

40. Evidence of John Ashley Hall in HCSP 72:259.

41. On some ships all of the time and on many ships some of the time—because of the season, the market, or the inclination of the master—scarcity of provisions was a major problem. Such disclosures surface only occasionally in Parliamentary testimony but are documented regularly in the business correspondence that passed between the masters of slave ships and their employers. See Richard Martin to James Rogers, 14 December 1790, NA-Kew, C 107/12; William Woodville to James Rogers, 10 August 1791, NA-Kew, C 107/13; Samuel Stribling to James Rogers, 17 March 1792, NA-Kew, C 107/13; H. Forsyth to James Rogers, 9 July 1792, NA-Kew, C 107/13; Evidence of John Knox in HCSP 68:150–151.

42. Evidence of John Matthews in HCSP 68:23; Evidence of William Littleton in HCSP 68:299. Also see, Evidence of John Knox in HCSP 68:155; Evidence of James Penny in HCSP 68:39. Matthews, trying to deflect his Parliamentary questioners, who were intent on drawing out details concerning the stifling heat that commonly prevailed between decks, replied as follows concerning captives' complaints upon going below: "When they first go down of an Evening, when the Sides and Deck are heated by the Sun, they complain of Heat; but three or four Hours afterwards, and during the Night, they more frequently complain of Cold."

43. For the general proposition of how many slaves might board per day, see Evidence of Alexander Falconbridge in HCSP 72:299. The *Rodney*'s numbers are drawn from the following: William Woodville to James Rogers, 20 April 1791, NA-Kew, C 107/13; William Woodville to James Rogers, 2 May 1791, NA-Kew, C 107/13; William Woodville to James Rogers, 16 May 1791, NA-Kew, C 107/13; William Woodville to James Rogers, 25 May 1791, NA-Kew, C 107/13; William Woodville to James Rogers, 10 August 1791, NA-Kew, C 107/13. For a description of the factors that determined how long a ship might slave at the coast, see Byrd, "Captives and Voyagers," Ph.D. diss., Appendix 1–2.

44. Evidence of John Ashley Hall in HCSP 72:242.

45. Evidence of Alexander Falconbridge in HCSP 72:300; Evidence of John Ashley Hall in HCSP 72:230. When asked whether Africans appeared "dejected when brought on board?" Falconbridge responded, "All that I have seen in my voyage did appear so." When asked a similar question, Hall replied, "Always. . . ."

46. Evidence of Isaac Wilson in HCSP 72:274. For a compelling description of white

society on slave ships along the west African coast, see Christopher, *Slave Ship Sailors and Their Captive Cargoes, 1730–1807.*

47. Evidence of Alexander Falconbridge in HCSP 72:300; Evidence of Isaac Wilson in HCSP 72:275. When the *Alexander*'s surgeon was asked whether the woman's sentiment was one slaves commonly expressed, he replied, "Many of them have done so." Similarly, when Isaac Wilson was asked on what he based his opinion that a pervasive melancholy overcame the generality of a slave ship's captives, his most direct piece of evidence was that, as he put it, "I have heard them say in their language, that they wished to die."

48. Evidence of Alexander Falconbridge in HCSP 72:304.

49. Evidence of Isaac Wilson in HCSP 72:279–280. Remarkably, this was not the first suicide among the ship's women. Previously, another woman had carried rope below. She was not berthed on a platform but managed to break her neck by fastening the loose end of her noose to the armorer's vice, which was stored in the room. She pulled violently against the rope until dead, again all of this apparently within view of her fellow captives.

50. William Woodville to James Rogers, 16 May 1791, NA-Kew, C 107/13. William Woodville outlined the rationale behind this practice in a letter to his employer, James Rogers: The slaves "are all at present healthy except one woman whom I have sent on shore to try if that would help her recovery & it has had the desired effect she is now mending fast when we have trusty persons with whom we can lodge a sick slave I think it is the best method—for our surgeons are so little acquainted with their modes of life & their habits which are extremely different from ours & the effect of their food which appears from what I can learn to be almost entirely vegetable—that either not withstanding how these circumstances operate upon the constitution or not considering them they scarcely ever treat them with propriety."

51. Evidence of Alexander Falconbridge in HCSP 72:305.

52. Evidence of Isaac Wilson in HCSP 72:281.

53. Evidence of James Arnold in HCSP 69:126.

54. Evidence of Alexander Falconbridge in HCSP 72:305. When it came time to expose the *Emilia*'s cargo for sale in Jamaica, the crew brought the woman out when they were certain she had entered into one of her more relaxed states.

55. The transformations in Equiano's state of mind can be followed in Equiano, *The Interesting Narrative and Other Writings*, rev. ed., 55–60 (quoted passage from pp. 56 and 58). Interestingly, the nature of life aboard a Guineaship appears to have resulted in similar kinds of reactions among the ship's crew. It is clear, for instance, that death and the specter of death foisted ship masters into a malaise consisting of alternating turns of denial and panic. William Woodville, who directed the slave ship *Rodney* to Bonny in May 1791 and slaved through the rainy season, illustrated something of this mania in the letters sent to his employer from Africa and the Caribbean. From the coast, Woodville's notes highlighted the terrible morbidity in which he found himself, and from which members of his crew perished as if on cue: "[S]ince my last we have become very sickly in our white men three of whome are dead . . . all my mates except the chief & third mate . . . are sick." Yet throughout, the master held out every hope for the slaves on board and those then loading. While his crew suffered, he offered only the slightest hint that the slaves did anything but prosper: "We have now one hundred & twenty three slaves & . . . they are all at present healthy except one woman. . . ." A week later, as his crew languished, Woodville intimated simultaneously that conditions had taken a turn for the worse for the 161 Africans then on board, but that they were nearly perfectly healthy all the same. "We are very sickly in our white men & since my last we have had a continual rain almost incessant which has affected a few of our slaves notwithstanding every

precaution—a number of fires & flannen shirts to those who were ailing Such there is only one boy who is very bad & him I think irrecoverable the rest mend there are three besides the boy who are sick." Only after the *Rodney*'s captives began to die in droves just after the ship left the coast did Woodville admit that the Africans occupied anything less than an enviable state of health. From the Caribbean, an anxious, panicky Woodville acknowledged the full scope of the matter: Though his letters from the coast contained only the vaguest hints of sickness among the slaves, on the passage itself he lost more than sixty of his 370 captives. The *Rodney*'s owner, sensing misconduct and perhaps suspecting the veracity of Woodville's Bonny correspondence, dismissed him. William Woodville to James Rogers, 16, 25 May 1791, NA-Kew, C 107/13; Joseph Caton to James Rogers, 12 January 1792, NA-Kew, C 107/10; and William Woodville to James Rogers, 10 January 1792, NA-Kew, C 107/10.

56. Evidence of Alexander Falconbridge in HCSP 72:307; Evidence of David Henderson in HCSP 69:139.

57. Evidence of James Arnold in HCSP 69:127. Arnold made a difference between the songs the ship's crew encouraged above deck and the songs the slaves sang on their own accord. He said the following concerning the ship master's response to the latter: "At other Times when the Women were sitting by themselves below, he had heard them singing; but always at these Times in Tears. Their Songs then contained the History of their Lives, and their Separation from their Friends and Country. These Songs were very disagreeable to the Captain, who has taken them up, and flogged them in so terrible a Manner for no other reason than this."

58. Evidence of Captain Hall in HCSP 69:122. See also Evidence of Alexander Falconbridge in HCSP 72:303. Falconbridge believed that fetters were a prime cause of mortality and morbidity among enslaved men. He thought the fact that women were not generally fettered a reason they exhibited better health during their captivity.

59. Evidence of John Newton in HCSP 69:118. See also Evidence of John Ashley Hall in HCSP 72:230. Concerning captives' melancholy, Hall testified that "it soon wears off with the young Slaves, and some of the women; but the men are dejected, and appear unhappy in the extreme, the whole of the voyage."

60. Evidence of John Barnes in HCSP 68:19; Evidence of John Fountain in HCSP 68:268. While witnesses were in agreement that captives from the coast reacted differently from those marched down from the hinterland, they were not in agreement as to the nature of this difference. Some argued that Africans enslaved at the coast, because they knew something about their captors and destinations, were less prone to the debilitating panics that ordinarily affected their fellows from farther inland. Some witnesses testified that knowledge of their captors and destinations and their previous involvement with the trade made such slaves more prone to even more severe depression.

61. Evidence of Archibald Dalzell in HCSP 69:122. Dalzell, who slaved west of the Bight of Biafra, offered that among the slaves he had observed, "The Old Men are sometimes sullen and dejected; the Young Men are soon reconciled to their Situation, and do not appear to regret their Country; Delinquents, who know their Lives are forfeited, of course do not wish to return."

62. Evidence of Isaac Wilson in HCSP 72:275; Evidence of Alexander Falconbridge in HCSP 72:303.

63. Evidence of Alexander Falconbridge in HCSP 72:303; Evidence of James Penny in HCSP 68:40.

64. Falconbridge, *An Account of the Slave Trade on the Coast of Africa*, 22.

65. Evidence of John Ashley Hall in HCSP 72:230; Evidence of Alexander Falconbridge in HCSP 72:305; Evidence of William Littleton in HCSP 68:293.

66. Evidence of James Arnold in HCSP 69:126. Arnold continued that "This was the Case on Board the Ruby; one of the Boys had been very active in tormenting one of the Men, the Man, however, having caught him unexpectedly, gave him a Pinch, the Boy immediately cried out; the Captain in consequence of this ordered the Man to be tied up whom he flogged on all Parts of his Body."

67. Falconbridge, *An Account of the Slave Trade on the Coast of Africa,* 22. Falconbridge gave the following example concerning the baubles sometimes passed out among the women: "The women are furnished with beads for the purpose of affording them some diversion. But this end is generally defeated by the squabbles which are occasioned, in consequence of their stealing them from each other."

68. Evidence of James Penny in HCSP 68:41. When asked to offer a Guinea sailor's definition of stowing, Penny answered, "I mean when it is necessary for an Officer to go down, to prevent Disputes among them, and to place them properly, and to see that each has no more Room than his Share."

69. Evidence of John Ashley Hall in HCSP 72:518.

70. Evidence of James Bowen in HCSP 69:125. Said Bowen of disputes between shackled captives: "they being linked together in Irons, as it sometimes happens they are Men of different Nations, they would quarrel and fight; One Man would drag the other after him when it was necessary for him to move."

71. Falconbridge, *An Account of the Slave Trade on the Coast of Africa,* 20 (first and second quotations); Evidence of Robert Norris in HCSP 68:18 (disputes among women).

72. Evidence of Isaac Wilson in HCSP 72:282. "Upon the news of" the death of her brother, "the sister wept bitterly, tore her hair, and showed other signs of distraction."

73. Evidence of William James in HCSP 69:137–138. The record reads, "Mr. James has seen Relations on Board the same Ship. In the King George, a young Woman had been complaining that her Father had been brought on Board at the same Time, but that she had never seen him since. This was occasioned by the large Bulk Head across the Ship, which made it difficult for the one to see the other. On coming, however, into St. Kitts, all the Slaves were on Deck. She looked about for her Father, and espied him first. Her Sensations on this Occasion were not easy to be described. She went towards him in Raptures; but considering her Situation, was checked by Fear, not knowing whether she would be permitted to got to him or not."

74. Evidence of James Fraser in HCSP 71:32. Fraser, who slaved at Angola and in the Bight of Biafra, made this comment while discussing Angola in particular. When discussing either, however, he was in the habit, as is the case here, of making general points pertaining to both.

75. Crow, *Memoirs of the Late Captain Hugh Crow,* 200.

76. Analyzing slave ship insurrections allows insights into the nature of black society aboard slave ships. Ships calling at ports in the Bight of Biafra, though, did not suffer an inordinate number of revolts (that distinction belongs to the Upper Guinea coast). See Taylor, *If We Must Die;* Behrendt et al., "The Costs of Coercion," 454–476; Richardson, "Shipboard Revolts, African Authority, and the Atlantic Slave Trade," 69–92.

77. The story of the insurrection aboard the *Ruby* comes from Evidence of James Arnold in HCSP 69:133–134.

78. For an excellent essay on the importance of both types of identification, see Brubaker and Cooper, "Beyond 'Identity,'" 1–47.

79. See, for example, Samuel Stribling to James Rogers, 17 January 1792, NA-Kew, C 107/13; Richard Martin to James Rogers, 9 September 1790, NA-Kew, C 107/12.

80. Crow, *Memoirs of the Late Captain Hugh Crow*, 38. See also the pioneering article by Smallwood, "African Guardians, European Slave Ships, and the Changing Dynamics of Power in the Early Modern Atlantic."

81. Ibid., 38.

82. Ibid., 232–233.

83. Cohn, "Maritime Mortality in the Eighteenth and Nineteenth Centuries," 173.

84. James Bailie to James Rogers, 14 December 1790, NA-Kew, C 107/12.

85. Henry LaRouche to James Rogers, 1 October 1791, NA-Kew, C 107/12.

86. W. Prent to James Rogers, 10 April 1789, NA-Kew, C 107/9; Munroe McFarlane and Co. to James Rogers, 4 September 1792, NA-Kew, C 107/5; Henry LaRouche to James Rogers, 1 October 1791, NA-Kew, C 107/12; John Cunningham to James Rogers, 21 January 1793, NA-Kew, C 107/13; William Jenkins to James Rogers, 4 September 1792, NA-Kew, C 107/5.

87. Lytcott and Maxwell to James Rogers, 3 March 1789, NA-Kew, C 107/9.

88. Samuel Chollet to James Rogers, 25 February 1789, NA-Kew, C 107/9.

89. W. Prent to James Rogers, 10 April 1789, NA-Kew, C 107/9. "I must confess," Prent later wrote, "it was rather an agreeable surprise to me to receive a consignment of Negroes unsolicited & unconditionally from a House which I had not the honour of being known or even recommended so far as I am informed."

90. Henry LaRouche to James Rogers, 1 October 1791, NA-Kew, C 107/12.

91. James Bailie to James Rogers, 31 October 1791, NA-Kew, C 107/7.

92. Francis Grant to James Rogers, 11 September 1791, NA-Kew, C 107/13.

93. Munroe McFarlane and Co. to James Rogers, 4 September 1792, NA-Kew, C 107/5; Francis Grant to James Rogers, 4 August 1789, NA-Kew, C 107/9.

94. Munroe McFarlane and Co. to James Rogers, 4 September 1792, NA-Kew, C 107/5.

95. Jamaica House of Assembly, "Second Report: Presented the 12th Day of November, 1788." "From the examination of Mr. Lindo it appears, that out of 7,873 negroes, consigned to him as factor in the years 1786, 1787, 1788, and reported at the custom-house, no less than 363 perished in the harbour of Kingston before the day of sale; and if the same proportion of deaths be allowed to the whole of the Africans imported since the conquest of the island to the present time (an allowance which on many accounts, we conceive to be moderate), the number that have thus perished are very considerable. We have thought it necessary to investigate this circumstance, with as much precision as the subject will admit; and having, from the books of the Receiver-general, and other sufficient authorities, procured the most exact account that can be formed, of the imports and exports of negroes into and from this island, from the year 1655 (the time of its conquest) to December 1787, we find the imports to amount to 676,276 negroes; of which, according to the proportion above stated, no less that 31,181 will appear to have died shipboard after entry, although they stand in the book of office as constituting part of the actual numbers supposed to have been distributed among the planters, and destroyed by neglect, excessive labour, or other mal-treatment."

96. William Jenkins to James Rogers, 4 September 1792, NA-Kew, C 107/5. "I arrived here on Sunday Last After a Passage of 7 weeks & 3 day[s] and on my Arrival I applied to the Gentlemen as pr. Instructions but Messrs. James Baillie & Co would not have any thing to do with the Cargo therefore I have Consine [*sic*] the Cargo to Messrs. Munro McFarlane & Co to Do the Best they can for your Interest I am Sorry to Say I Beleive there was Never a Worse Cargo of Slave Ship'd from Africa which I am greatly afraid it will be greatly to your

Disadvantage, I have Bury'd 65 and the others very thin, God knows I hope I Never Shall Experience the uneasiyness [*sic*] of Mine [Mind] as I have this Passage, the White People is all in health, the Cargo is Advertised for Sale on Thursday the 13 Inst. I am Indivering [*sic*] to get them up till the day of Sale as much as Meath & Drink will do. . . ."

97. Savannah Unit, *Drums and Shadows*, 150, 185; Littlefield, *Rice and Slaves*, 10, 13; Chambers, "'My Own Nation,'" 74; Gomez, *Exchanging Our Country Marks*, 116–120.

98. This particular point raises another. Evidence adduced from the Biafran interior and from slave ships that sailed from the Biafran littoral does not, in and of itself, support the broader argument that all expressions of African ethnicity in the Atlantic world can be explained as I have done here (though, no doubt, some can). It does not even mean that all Africans who identified themselves as Igbo across the Atlantic world necessarily came to acknowledge as much in the way outlined above (though undoubtedly many did). To understand what it meant to be Igbo in the eighteenth-century diaspora, however, it is vital to come to terms with certain social and historical factors that contributed to the eventual development of Igbo consciousness. Among these factors, the nature of internal African migration preceding the middle passage and the slave ship experience are particularly important. All the same, because the experiences of Africans enslaved in the Biafran interior were not necessarily identical, and because the nature of the trade from the region changed over time, how the Igboness outlined here compared to others is a matter that will require and reward further investigation. Such work promises to shed light on how factors such as gender, age, time in transit, distance in transit, and transatlantic carrier, among others, shaped the experiences of enslaved Africans and related processes of Igbo identification. No doubt, there were different and perhaps even competing ways of being Igbo in the Atlantic world, each informed by different experiences of enslavement and deserving of close study.

99. Elkins, *Slavery*, 3rd ed., 98–103; Johnson, *Folk Culture on St. Helena Island, South Carolina*; Frazier, *The Negro Family in the United States*.

100. Curtin, *The Atlantic Slave Trade*, xix. For the most recent formulation of the point, see Eltis and Richardson, "The 'Numbers Game' and Routes to Slavery," 3. Also see Miller's *Way of Death* and Manning's *Slavery and African Life* for cliometric approaches that focus very much on the human dimensions of their subject.

101. See especially Joyner, *Down by the Riverside*; Genovese, *Roll, Jordan, Roll*; Raboteau, *Slave Religion*; Hall, *Africans in Colonial Louisiana*; Blassingame, *The Slave Community*, 2nd ed.; Thompson, *Flash of the Spirit*; Stuckey, *Slave Culture*; Stuckey, *Going Through the Storm*; Thornton, "Central African Names and African American Naming Patterns," 727–742; Sobel, *The World They Made Together*; Creel, *A Peculiar People*; White and White, "Slave Hair and African American Culture in the Eighteenth and Nineteenth Centuries," 45–76; White and White, "Slave Clothing and African-American Culture in the Eighteenth and Nineteenth Centuries," 149–186; Mullin, *Africa in America*; Thornton, "African Dimensions of the Stono Rebellion," 1101–1114; Thornton, "African Soldiers in the Haitian Revolution," 58–80.

102. Berlin, "From Creole to African," 267 (see 274 as well); Thornton, *Africa and Africans in the Making of the Atlantic World, 1400–1800*, 2nd ed., 320.

103. By nationalistic, I mean histories that understand the cultural and social effect of migration as the establishment and re-creation of former norms in a new setting (in the view of Bernard Bailyn, works that view the Americas as a kind of frontier as opposed to a periphery) (Bailyn, *The Peopling of British North America*, 112–113).

104. James Sweet's deeply researched *Recreating Africa: Culture, Kinship, and Religion in the African-Portuguese World, 1441–1770* is a good example of this trend.

THREE

WHITE POWER AND THE CONTEXT OF SLAVE SEASONING IN EIGHTEENTH-CENTURY JAMAICA

1. Burnard, "A Failed Settler Society: Marriage and Demographic Failure in Early Jamaica," 63; Burnard and Morgan, "The Dynamics of the Slave Market and Slave Purchasing Patterns in Jamaica, 1655–1788," 205–206; Richardson, "The British Empire and the Atlantic Slave Trade, 1660–1807," Table 20.4; Sheridan, "The Wealth of Jamaica in the Eighteenth Century," 292–311; Burnard, "'Prodigious Riches,'" 506–524; Higman, *Plantation Jamaica*, 1–3.

2. Higman, *Plantation Jamaica*, 3. There are fundamental questions about black life and labor on Jamaica, Higman has pointed out, that are impossible to answer without a close examination of how "capital and control" functioned on the island. "Why were the enslaved people of Jamaica so productive compared to other enslaved people? What was different about slavery in Jamaica? Answers to these questions must be sought first in decisions made by slave owners and those who wished to be slave owners, the free people of Jamaica and Great Britain."

3. For basic geographies of the Lesser and Greater Antilles, and of the slave trade to Jamaica, see Donovan and Jackson, *Caribbean Geography;* Sheridan, "The Slave Trade to Jamaica, 1702–1808," 1–16; Klein, "The English Slave Trade to Jamaica, 1782–1808," 141–174.

4. This uptake in slave imports was a recently revived phenomena. During the American war of 1776–1783, slave ships all but disappeared from Jamaican ports. Only at the close of the conflict did the former belligerents agree that their subjects should, without interference, return to the coast of Africa "according to the usage which has hitherto prevailed." Jamaica, in consequence, once again became a slave hypermarket—depended on by resident planters and supporting as well an extensive regional slave trade to neighboring foreign colonies. The post-war surge in slaves sales was quite dramatic. Twice as many slaves landed at Jamaica in 1784 as had in 1782. Assessing this spike, the controller at the port of Kingston was all but certain that the trend would continue. Testifying to the recent doubling of slave imports about the island, he informed the governor that he expected still a further increase. "And there is not a Doubt," he wrote, "but as long as Peace Continues there will be Annually A larger Number brought in." The prediction was right on target. The 1784 increase was the beginning of an explosion in the overall trade as Jamaicans and the neighbors who depended on their slave marts forced more captives onto the island than had landed previously during any other comparable period of time. Between 1783 and 1795 more than 170,000 slaves touched at Jamaica—on average some 13,000 captives per year. In contrast, during the late war the yearly volume had hovered around 7,000. On the effects of the American war on slave importations and the agreement concerning the slave trade made at the end of that conflict, see Hertzog, "Naval Operation in West Africa and the Disruption of the Slave Trade during the American Revolution," 42–48; Chalmers, "The Definitive Treaty of Peace and Friendship," Article XII. For details on the subsequent expansions of slave importations at Jamaica, see "An Account of the Number of Negroes imported into, and exported from, the Island of Jamaica: Also, An Account of the Number Annually retained in the Island, as far back as the same can be made up," HCSP 67:239 (slave imports 1782 and 1784); Alured Clarke, "Circular," 29 January 1785, NA-Kew, CO 137/85; Eltis et al., eds., *The Trans-Atlantic Slave Trade* (data for 1783–1795 and 1776–1782).

5. Burnard and Morgan, "The Dynamics of the Slave Market and Slave Purchasing Pat-

terns in Jamaica, 1655–1788," 208–209. In the main, captives arrived at Jamaica at one of the island's two principal entrepôts—Kingston on the south side or Montego Bay on the north. Other ports attracted Guineamen—Black River, Martha Brae, Port Antonio, Annotto Bay, and Lucea, for instance—only in much lesser numbers. The diversity of landings meant that captives might approach the island from quite different vantages—dodging the keys and shoals for the bustling urban compact of Kingston, riding into one of two twin harbors to anchor before the sandy beaches fronting Port Antonio, or stopping short of the wide mouth and swampy shoulders of the Black River and its namesake hamlet. For brief geographies of Kingston, Port Antonio, and Black River, see Long, *The History of Jamaica,* 2:102–107, 170, plate 13, 183, and 185–186.

6. Falconbridge, *An Account of the Slave Trade on the Coast of Africa,* 33; Evidence of Reverend Ramsay in HCSP 69:141–142.

7. Thomas Barritt to Nathaniel Phillips, 18 June 1790, Slebech Papers and Documents, MSS 8358; John Taylor to Simon Taylor, 29 November 1791, Taylor Papers, XIV/A/84. Wrote Taylor: "Soon after the date of my last letter, a Ship of James Jones's arrived here with 280 Slaves from New Calabar, consigned to me. Messrs Andersons Ship the Duke of Buccleuch arrived at same time with 350 Slaves from [B]ance island. . . . Mr James Gairdener came over & picked out of the Eboe Cargo (before the sale) 16 Men & 16 women for Montrose Penn, & Mr. Walker at same time got 10 men for M. Bay Penn. John chose out 10 Women from the Duke of Buccleuchs cargo for your Penn, the whole of their lotts were very prime indeed. I could not allow a pick for Mt. Pleasant & G. Grove; being uncertain whether or not the overseer would wish to have Negroes at this time, untill I recd. their answers to my letter to them on that subject, which I did not untill the day before the sale, and durst not then allow any person to pick for fear of ruining the Sale. Mr. Graham got no negroes for Mt. Pleasant. There was 19 taken from the two sales for G. Grove & Batchelors Hall Penn."

8. Falconbridge, *An Account of the Slave Trade on the Coast of Africa,* 34; Edwards, *The History, Civil and Commercial, of the British Colonies in the West Indies,* 3rd ed., 2:150–151.

9. Falconbridge, *An Account of the Slave Trade on the Coast of Africa,* 34–35; Evidence of Alexander Falconbridge in HCSP 72:308 (slaves rushing overboard, captives maneuvering near others, and ship masters counseling purchasers). Of the efforts by Jamaican planters and ship masters to keep together captives claiming some relations, the mealymouthed quality that infected the language of slaveholders when they addressed this point speaks to the vitality with which they enforced this dictum: "that care shall be taken not to separate different branches of the same family. I am afraid it hath been found difficult, in all cases, to enforce this latter regulation; but it is usual with most planters, I believe, to enquire of the Negroes themselves, by means of an interpreter, whether they have relations on board, and to purchase families together; or, by exchanging with other buyers, to prevent, if possible, that cruel separation between parents and children, and brothers and sisters, which must sometimes, I doubt, unavoidably take place. I never knew an instance where such a purchase or accommodation was knowingly declined or refused" (Edwards, *The History, Civil and Commercial, of the British Colonies in the West Indies,* 3rd ed., 2:151).

10. John Taylor to Simon Taylor, 6 January 1790, Taylor Papers, XIV/A/51.

11. Higman, *Montpelier,* 2–3. "In most parts of plantation America the large-scale plantation was archetypical rather than dominant and most slaves did not actually live out their lives on such units. In Jamaica, however, the 'plantation legend' was a reality. . . . At the time of emancipation, Jamaica had 670 sugar plantations with an average population of 223 slaves, accounting for one-half of the island's 312,000 slaves."

12. Klein, *African Slavery in Latin America and the Caribbean,* 54–55.

13. Higman, *Jamaica Surveyed,* 80–81; Higman, *Montpelier,* 129–131, 136–145; Armstrong, *The Old Village and the Great House,* 97–98.

14. Higman, "The Spatial Economy of Jamaican Sugar Plantations," 25, 28, 30. Depending on less systematic data, other scholars have commented as well on the relative compactness of Jamaican sugar plantations. Philip Manderson Sherlock has argued the geography of sugar works, great house, and slave quarters "made up a compact unit which expressed in stone, timber and thatch the values and the structure of plantation society" (*West Indian Nations,* 139). Douglass Armstrong has followed a similar line: "Even when a plantation's holdings were large, its settlement tended to be compact and centrally located around the main house, or residence of the planter or plantation manager, which was the center of authority and supervision on the plantation" (*The Old Village and the Great House,* 89).

15. "Return of the number of White Inhabitants, Free People of Colour and Slaves in the Island of Jamaica," November 1788, NA-Kew, CO 137/87.

16. John Vanheelen to Joseph Foster Barham, 4 February 1786, Barham Papers, C.357, Bundle 1.

17. Thomas Barritt to Nathaniel Phillips, 10 October 1792, Slebech Papers and Documents, MSS 8404.

18. Simon Taylor to Chaloner Arcedeckne, 6 December 1787, Vanneck Manuscripts, Bundle 2/13.

19. Simon Taylor to Chaloner Arcedeckne, 6 September 1783, Vanneck Manuscripts, Bundle 2/11.

20. Nathaniel Phillips to Thomas Barritt and Robert Logan, 26 September 1784, Slebech Papers and Documents, MSS 11484. Planters also looked to the slave ships when they wanted to decrease the amount of plantation work they were obliged to outsource, or job, to enslaved laborers owned by others. On the property Simon Taylor managed for Chaloner Arcedeckne, an overarching goal informing many of his planned purchases was to arrive at a situation where, as he put it, "I do not see any occassion we shall have to Jobb any more on the Estate" (see Simon Taylor to Chaloner Arcedeckne, 4 September 1793, Vanneck Manuscripts, Bundle 2/19).

21. Simon Taylor to Chaloner Arcedeckne, 1 November 1789, Vanneck Manuscripts, Bundle 2/15. For examples of Taylor's tirades against anti-slavery advocates, see Simon Taylor to Robert Taylor, 6 September 1795, Taylor Papers, XIII/B/13; Simon Taylor to Chaloner Arcedeckne, 9 May 1798, Vanneck Manuscripts, Bundle 2/22; Simon Taylor to Chaloner Arcedeckne, 24 December 1789, Vanneck Manuscripts, Bundle 2/15.

22. Simon Taylor to Chaloner Arcedeckne, 1 November 1789, Vanneck Manuscripts, Bundle 2/15. James Wedderburn considered a similar scheme on Joseph Barham's Mesopotamia estate: "In the present Situation of Blast upon the Estate when small crops may be expected, we should consider a further purchase of Slaves might be improper—otherwise we would recommend, the Annual purchase of ten Ebo Girls from ten to Twelve years of Age for three years or the Same Number at the Shorter period of Eighteen Months, this would give a Sufficiency of females to keep up the number in future on your Estate" (James Wedderburn and John Graham to Joseph Foster Barham, 2 August 1793, Barham Papers, C.357, Bundle 2).

23. John Vanheelen to Joseph Foster Barham, 23 June 1788, Barham Papers, C.357, Bundle 1. See also James Wedderburn and John Graham to Joseph Foster Barham, 16 December 1790, Barham Papers, C.357, Bundle 2; James Wedderburn to Joseph Foster Barham, 19

February 1791, Barham Papers, C.357, Bundle 2. In the latter note, Wedderburn writes: "We particularly observe your object in the improvement of your Mesopotamia Estate and shall accordingly attend to the extension of the Penn and confining the Sugar Crop to the strength, which you may rely may not be improperly exerted" and "you say you Wish 3 Negroes to do the labour of 2, from your Strength and Crops I think your Slaves are full hard Worked."

24. John Taylor to Simon Taylor, 6 November 1791, Taylor Papers, XIV/A/83; Thomas Barritt to Nathaniel Phillips, 10 May 1790, Slebech Papers and Documents, MSS 8357. In examples of the kind of assessments planters and their factors made of arriving Guineamen, John wrote Simon, "There has been no cargo of slaves here for some Months, butt two small & *very bad* Eboe ships Messrs Rainfords Sold"; and Barritt informed Phillips, "I have not yet been able to make a choice of the New Negroes you desired to be purchased for Suffolk Park, as the late Cargos have been but indifferent, and what few good ones were among them they were soon pick'd up with great scrambling."

25. Thomas Barritt to Nathaniel Phillips, 4 August 1792, Slebech Papers and Documents, MSS 8401. See also Thomas Barritt to Nathaniel Phillips, 18 June 1790, Slebech Papers and Documents, MSS 8358; Thomas Barritt to Nathaniel Phillips, 7 March 1793, Slebech Papers and Documents, MSS 8412.

26. Simon Taylor to Chaloner Arcedeckne, 23 May 1793 and 5 June 1793, Vanneck Manuscripts, Bundle 2/19. "I shall go up to Windward tomorrow & see how provisions stand there & if I can venture to buy any more for you immediately, as I put on some time ago twenty on Batchelors Hall & fifteen upon Golden Grove. I would not willingly buy at this time of year as there is a risk of Hurricanes. but I know this that from the Failure of the Houses of Greigson & Dawson in Liverpool & of Rogers, Jacks & Fitzhenry of Bristol that there will be very few ships fitted out during the Warr for Africa & I think that there will by & by be a very great demand for Negroes, even if no abolition takes place & I would wish you to be supplied before that time arrives. tho except I should see the highest probability of our being able to feed them I will not run risks."

27. John Graham to Joseph Foster Barham, 12 June 1792, Barham Papers, C.357, Bundle 2 (emphasis in original). It is not altogether clear whether Graham meant to buy only ten additional slaves, for later in the letter he writes that the additional purchase will amount to twenty.

28. Simon Taylor to Chaloner Arcedeckne, 1 May 1787, Vanneck Manuscripts, Bundle 2/13.

29. Simon Taylor to Chaloner Arcedeckne, 21 September 1787, Vanneck Manuscripts, Bundle 2/13.

30. James Wedderburn to Joseph Foster Barham, 12 September 1791, Barham Papers, C.357, Bundle 2.

31. Simon Taylor to Chaloner Arcedeckne, 21 July 1788, Vanneck Manuscripts, Bundle 2/14.

32. Simon Taylor to Chaloner Arcedeckne, 10 October 1794, Vanneck Manuscripts, Bundle 2/20. See as well Simon Taylor to Chaloner Arcedeckne, 5 August 1789, Vanneck Manuscripts, Bundle 2/15. Wrote Taylor in the summer of 1789: "I did propose to you to lett the Produce of Batchelors hall Penn be laid out in New Negroes for it, and I think you are right in consenting to it, for lett it be much or little the putting on a few Negroes at a time, they can be better attended to, and there is less difficulty in finding them."

33. Simon Taylor to Chaloner Arcedeckne, 6 December 1787, Vanneck Manuscripts, Bundle 2/13.

34. Simon Taylor to Chaloner Arcedeckne, 27 August 1781, Vanneck Manuscripts, Bundle 2/9.

35. John Vanheelen to Joseph Foster Barham, 13 February 1787, Barham Papers, C.357, Bundle 1; Charles Rowe to Joseph Foster Barham, 20 April 1789, Barham Papers, C.357, Bundle 2.

36. Simon Taylor to Chaloner Arcedeckne, 23 April 1791, Vanneck Manuscripts, Bundle 2/17.

37. John Graham to Joseph Foster Barham, 9 May 1790, Barham Papers, C.357, Bundle 2; John Graham to Joseph Foster Barham, 16 June 1790, Barham Papers, C.357, Bundle 2; John Graham to Joseph Foster Barham, 18 July 1790, Barham Papers, C.357, Bundle 2; John Graham to Joseph Foster Barham, 6 September 1790, Barham Papers, C.357, Bundle 2. Before any of this could be effected, the island suffered a storm, which prompted Barham's agents simply to table all of their purchase plans until they received the owner's "further directions." In the midst this kind of uncertainty, Barham's decision would bear great weight for any Africans his people might purchase

38. William Miles to John Tharp, 10 January 1783, Tharp Family Papers, R55.7.128 (b)*.

39. Simon Taylor to Chaloner Arcedeckne, 16 October 1793, Vanneck Manuscripts, Bundle 2/19.

40. Simon Taylor to Chaloner Arcedeckne, 30 March 1783, Vanneck Manuscripts, Bundle 2/11. See also John Vanheelen to Joseph Foster Barham, 15 April 1783, Barham Papers, C.357, Bundle 1. Wrote Vanheelen: "Now Peace is Concluded on I hope you will soon please to think of putting Strength on your Estate. the Land of your Island Estate is certainly as good as any Land I see in this Country & with proper Cultivation must turn out to advantage, but this cannot be obtained without a proper number of negroes to Carry it into Execution, the property is now got into a proper Train & Cannot fail of making you good returns Was you to add for the present only Twenty able Working Negroes. If you will allow me to look out for those I know will answer, I am clear I shall be able to make such terms as will make the payment quite easy."

41. Charles Rowe to Joseph Foster Barham, 25 September 1792, Barham Papers, C.357, Bundle 2. Sometimes, however, the response of ship owners to news about abolition could have the opposite effect on slave prices by encouraging a large number of ships to fit out for western Africa, thus creating something of glut at various American ports. See, for instance, Simon Taylor to Chaloner Arcedeckne, 30 December 1792, Vanneck Manuscripts, Bundle 2/18. Taylor writes: "The Price of Negroes has increased here to a most alarming degree, but as there having been a vast Number of Ships fitting out this year for the Coast of Africa, and the Trinidad & Hispaniola cannot buy any, I am hopefull the Price will fall, for there are now one [no] less than 8 Ships from Africa in the Port of Kingston who have not yet opened . . . and there are a great many duly expected."

42. Simon Taylor to Chaloner Arcedeckne, 23 May 1793 and 5 June 1793, Vanneck Manuscripts, Bundle 2/19.

43. Simon Taylor to Robert Taylor, 6 September 1794, Taylor Papers, XIII/B/3.

44. Simon Taylor to Chaloner Arcedeckne, 30 August 1788, Vanneck Manuscripts, Bundle 2/14. Taylor used *embarrassed* in a now obsolete sense meaning "Perplexed (in thought)" or "Confused, constrained (in manner or behaviour)" (*Oxford English Dictionary,* 2nd ed., s.v., OED online, http://dictionary.oed.com/cgi/entry/00073586).

45. Simon Taylor to Chaloner Arcedeckne, 8 May 1782, Vanneck Manuscripts, Bundle 2/10.

46. Simon Taylor to Chaloner Arcedeckne, 11 June 1782, Vanneck Manuscripts, Bundle 2/10.

47. Simon Taylor to Chaloner Arcedeckne, 8 September 1792, Vanneck Manuscripts, Bundle 2/18.

48. Simon Taylor to Chaloner Arcedeckne, 9 April 1787, Vanneck Manuscripts, Bundle 2/13. "I bought for you a few days ago Seven New Negroes for Golden Grove and if we have plenty of Provisions as I expect, I will buy 13 more. But I am afraid to buy New Negroes for Batchelors Hall, for fear of the Yaws, and its being a Wett Place, if you approve of it I will look out for a Gang of Seasoned Negroes of 20 or thirty to buy for it." See as well, Simon Taylor to Chaloner Arcedeckne, 31 March 1790, Vanneck Manuscripts, Manuscripts Department, Cambridge University Library. "Wet" was a relative term for Taylor. In general, he thought the tropical nature of the whole island contributed greatly to slave mortality. "I would rather raise than buy Negroes if I could, but I aver it is impossible in a Wett Country to keep up the Stock of Negroes by birth, at least I have hitherto never found it, neither have we yett found out the possibility of Keeping up the Stock of White People here by Births, altho they do not work in the Field."

49. Simon Taylor to Chaloner Arcedeckne, 13 November 1790, Vanneck Manuscripts, Bundle 2/16.

50. Simon Taylor to Chaloner Arcedeckne, 5 December 1789, Vanneck Manuscripts, Bundle 2/16.

51. Simon Taylor to Chaloner Arcedeckne, 4 May 1794, Vanneck Manuscripts, Bundle 2/20.

52. John Kelly to Chaloner Arcedeckne, 23 April 1782, Vanneck Manuscripts, Bundle 2/10.

53. Simon Taylor to Chaloner Arcedeckne, 16 January 1783, Vanneck Manuscripts, Bundle 2/11; Simon Taylor to Chaloner Arcedeckne, 7 September 1790, Vanneck Manuscripts, Bundle 2/16. See in these letters Taylor's exasperation at dealing with a strong-willed black man named Philander, in whom Taylor perceives only passion and miscreancy, traits he believes common to blacks by birth.

54. Simon Taylor to Chaloner Arcedeckne, 11 June 1782, Vanneck Manuscripts, Bundle 2/10.

55. Simon Taylor to Chaloner Arcedeckne, 30 January 1782, Vanneck Manuscripts, Bundle 2/10.

56. Simon Taylor to Chaloner Arcedeckne, 5 July 1789, Vanneck Manuscripts, Bundle 2/15; Simon Taylor to Chaloner Arcedeckne, 5 August 1789, Vanneck Manuscripts, Bundle 2/15 (quotation); Simon Taylor to Chaloner Arcedeckne, 24 December 1789, Vanneck Manuscripts, Bundle 2/15; Simon Taylor to Chaloner Arcedeckne, 16 January 1783, Vanneck Manuscripts, Bundle 2/11; Simon Taylor to Chaloner Arcedeckne, 24 February 1783, Vanneck Manuscripts, Bundle 2/11.

57. Simon Taylor to Chaloner Arcedeckne, 24 February 1783, Vanneck Manuscripts, Bundle 2/11.

58. Simon Taylor to Chaloner Arcedeckne, 19 March 1782, Vanneck Manuscripts, Bundle 2/10. "Whatever you are told of Turneys Plantain Walk is a Fable there are no Plantains there & it is a design to hurt Turney that it is mentioned there were a few before the Storm the Overseer is not the Person to be blamed for not having ground Provisions. . . . He would do well was he left to follow his own way."

59. Simon Taylor to Chaloner Arcedeckne, 30 January 1782, Vanneck Manuscripts, Bundle 2/10. Of twenty barrels of flour sent to Golden Grove, charged Taylor, eight were appropriated outright to other ends. Of an unspecified quantity of herrings that were sent out, Kelly allegedly *borrowed* some seventy barrels. In another letter, Taylor described the problem as follows: "The matter was he had lived so long at Golden Grove that he began to

think it was his own, & in short made use of every thing there just as if it was" (Simon Taylor to Chaloner Arcedeckne, 11 June 1782, Vanneck Manuscripts, Bundle 2/10).

60. Simon Taylor to Chaloner Arcedeckne, 1 June 1783, Vanneck Manuscripts, Bundle 2/11.

61. "Extract of a Letter [from Simon Taylor to Chaloner Arcedeckne]," n.d. [29 October 1782], Vanneck Manuscripts, Bundle 2/10.

62. Simon Taylor to Chaloner Arcedeckne, 11 June 1782, Vanneck Manuscripts, Bundle 2/10.

63. John Kelly to Chaloner Arcedeckne, 19 September 1782, Vanneck Manuscripts, Bundle 2/10; John Kelly to Chaloner Arcedeckne, 21 March 1782, Vanneck Manuscripts, Bundle 2/10; John Kelly to Chaloner Arcedeckne, 18 May 1782, Vanneck Manuscripts, Bundle 2/10. For his part, Kelly thought Taylor's wrath originated partly in prejudice and partly in self-interest. According to Kelly, Taylor got it into his head that Kelly advised Arcedeckne to increase the rent on a section of Golden Grove leased to Taylor. The perceived move against his interest, thought Kelly, spurred Taylor's bile, and as Kelly put it, "I need not Mention to you the implacable resentment Mr. Taylor ever shews when he takes a Dislike whether Justly founded or not." But even without this cause, Kelly thought Taylor "could never like any man come from the Country I was born in." Kelly was Irish.

64. Simon Taylor to Chaloner Arcedeckne, 1 May 1788, Vanneck Manuscripts, Bundle 2/14.

65. John Graham to Joseph Foster Barham, 5 September 1794, Barham Papers, C.357, Bundle 2.

66. John Graham to Joseph Foster Barham, 5 September 1794, Barham Papers, C.357, Bundle 2. Even eight months later, conditions were not much improved (James Wedderburn to Joseph Foster Barham, 21 May 1795, Barham Papers, C.357, Bundle 2).

67. Simon Taylor to Chaloner Arcedeckne, 25 March 1789, Vanneck Manuscripts, Bundle 2/15.

68. Simon Taylor to Chaloner Arcedeckne, 19 July 1790, Vanneck Manuscripts, Bundle 2/16.

69. Simon Taylor to Chaloner Arcedeckne, 5 July 1789, Vanneck Manuscripts, Bundle 2/15.

70. Simon Taylor to Chaloner Arcedeckne, 8 April 1791, Vanneck Manuscripts, Bundle 2/17.

71. Simon Taylor to Chaloner Arcedeckne, 5 July 1789, Vanneck Manuscripts, Bundle 2/15.

72. Simon Taylor to Chaloner Arcedeckne, 26 July 1786, Vanneck Manuscripts, Bundle 2/12.

73. Nathaniel Phillips to Thomas Barritt and Robert Logan, 24 October 1784, Slebech Papers and Documents, MSS 11484.

74. John Vanheelen to Joseph Foster Barham, 9 May 1783, Barham Papers, C.357, Bundle 1. "We have been Fortunate last year the Number of Negroes have Increased four. the present Overseer is Very Attentive in taking Care of them & they seem happy & Contended & have Abundance of provisions."

75. Simon Taylor to Chaloner Arcedeckne, 26 July 1786, Vanneck Manuscripts, Bundle 2/12. "There is at present the greatest Scarcity of provisions among the Negroes that I ever Remember from the West End to the East End indeed it is little Short of a fammine, Flour it is true from some coming in now and then from America fluctuates between three pounds & five pounds per Barrell of 180 lbs, but the planters actually have not money to buy it for the Negroes." In 1786, there were quite a number of sugar plantations in financial distress across Jamaica. In another letter, Simon Taylor spoke as follows on the predicament of other slaveowners: "I must say that I do not believe that there are ten Estates in St. Thomas in the East but what are entailed one, that will not change Proprietors & go into the Hands of the Creditors, & sold for whatever they will bring in the course of & years & in the other Parishes of westmoreland & Hanover there are hardly one but is in that predicament, the people there being in the greatest distress, & from the continued Calamities that have befallen them the Estates actually do not make as much as will pay the Contengencies & Taxes & consequently

there is nothing left for the Maintenance of the Proprietor or to pay the Interest of the Money he owes" (Simon Taylor to Chaloner Arcedeckne, 1 June 1786, Vanneck Manuscripts, Bundle 2/12). For Taylor's description of the plantation of a cash-strapped slaveowner, see also Simon Taylor to Chaloner Arcedeckne, 24 December 1790, Vanneck Manuscripts, Bundle 2/16.

76. Simon Taylor to Chaloner Arcedeckne, 8 May 1782, Vanneck Manuscripts, Bundle 2/10. "I have also ordered the overseer to discharge the Gang that has always been both at the House & Hot house that your own People may have something for themselves."

77. Thomas Barritt to Nathaniel Phillips, 1 July 1795, Slebech Papers and Documents, MSS 9205 and 9204.

78. Morgan, *Slave Counterpoint;* Morgan, "Three Planters and Their Slaves."

79. The literature on slavery and paternalism is vast. Some key works touching the American South and Brazil are Genovese, *Roll, Jordan, Roll;* Rodney, "African Slavery and Other Forms of Social Oppression"; Faust, *James Henry Hammond and the Old South;* Freyre and Putnam, *The Masters and the Slaves (Casa-Grande and Senzala).* For slavery in Africa, researchers have employed the term "domestic slavery" to get at some of the same ideas that American historians explore with paternalism (see Rodney, "African Slavery and Other Forms of Social Oppression," 431–443).

80. Burnard, *Mastery, Tyranny, and Desire,* 84.

81. Simon Taylor to Chaloner Arcedeckne, 8 May 1782, Vanneck Manuscripts, Bundle 2/10.

82. John Graham to Joseph Foster Barham, 18 January 1790, Barham Papers, C.357, Bundle 2.

83. Nathaniel Phillips to Thomas Barritt and Robert Logan, 26 September 1784, Slebech Papers and Documents, MSS 11484 (emphasis in original).

84. Thomas Barritt to Nathaniel Phillips, 28 June 1792, Slebech Papers and Documents, MSS 8399.

85. Thomas Barritt to Nathaniel Phillips, 16 October 1793, Slebech Papers and Documents, MSS 8423.

86. Thomas Barritt to Nathaniel Phillips, 10 April 1793, Slebech Papers and Documents, MSS 8413. The blacks on Phillips's properties were speaking specifically to the quality of clothing, goods, and supplies.

87. Thomas Barritt to Nathaniel Phillips, 25 May 1791, Slebech Papers and Documents, MSS 8375.

88. Thomas Barritt to Nathaniel Phillips, 14 October 1789, Slebech Papers and Documents, MSS 8347.

89. Simon Taylor to Chaloner Arcedeckne, 24 December 1789, Vanneck Manuscripts, Bundle 2/15. J. R. Ward detects a similar trend throughout the British Caribbean in *British West Indian Slavery, 1750–1834,* 211–215.

90. Charles Rowe to Joseph Foster Barham, 17 March 1790, Barham Papers, C.357, Bundle 2.

91. John Vanheelen to Joseph Foster Barham, 30 November 1784, Barham Papers, C.357, Bundle 1.

92. Simon Taylor to Chaloner Arcedeckne, 24 November 1793, Vanneck Manuscripts, Bundle 2/20.

93. Simon Taylor to Chaloner Arcedeckne, 9 August 1794, Vanneck Manuscripts, Bundle 2/20.

94. Cooper, *Plantation Slavery on the East Coast of Africa,* 154. Cooper clarifies in this study, perhaps more clearly than any historian of slavery, the centrality of violence and subjugation to the practice of paternalism in slave societies.

95. James Wedderburn to Joseph Foster Barham, 25 September 1795, Barham Papers, C.357, Bundle 2.

96. Charles Rowe to Joseph Foster Barham, 4 February 1794, Barham Papers, C.357, Bundle 2.

97. Simon Taylor to Chaloner Arcedeckne, 4 February 1794, Vanneck Manuscripts, Bundle 2/20. For a similar example, see John Vanheelen to John Foster Barham, 1 December 1783, Barham Papers, C.357, Bundle 1.

98. Simon Taylor to Elizabeth Haughton Taylor, 13 August 1786, Taylor Papers, III/B/2; Simon Taylor to Elizabeth Haughton Taylor, 30 April 1787, Taylor Papers, III/B/9. In the first letter, Simon Taylor implies that Haughton Court blacks laid off their work upon Haughton Taylor's departure and the arrival of the new overseer. Apparently, the overseer complained to Simon Taylor that he acted as he had toward the property's blacks because they were shirking their duties. Taylor replied to the overseer that he must not exert too palpably his power over the slaves. Yes, "do the work of the Estate they must," agreed Taylor, but he must eschew "Cruelty" while ensuring that the slaves were at their duty. In the same letter, Taylor implies that one way to this end is for the overseer to display more often toward the slaves an interest in their basic physical needs. Thus Taylor wrote his sister-in-law, "as he [the new overseer] is indefatigable in putting in provisions for them, I am hopefull when I go down next to find they like him as much as they hated him." In the second letter, Taylor lays out in greater detail a point made briefly in the first as to the Haughton Court blacks' intentions to "thwart" the overseer as well as changes in the man's behavior that eventually returned the plantation to some kind of equilibrium: "it is always the disposition of Negroes to endeavour to take the advantage of a New Master or Overseer, and I am, very well persuaded in my own Mind, that they were putt on to behave amiss, that Stewart should punish them, and then to go to My Brother and you to endeavour to get the overseer turned away, but now they see he is fixed there, so far ar[e] they from being dissatisfied, . . . came and thanked me for putting him there, indeed he has been exceedingly Attentive to them when sick, and this has gained their Hearts." Taylor no doubt exaggerates here, perhaps because the Haughton Court blacks themselves exaggerated the shift. The larger point here, attended to in the following paragraph, is that the Haughton Court slaves in their owners absence moved rather quickly and successfully to check the power of their new overseer, spurred and informed all the while by their rather firm grasp of planters' ideology. Walter Johnson describes enslaved blacks using similar strategies concerning the slave markets of Louisiana (Johnson, *Soul by Soul*, 35–37).

99. Simon Taylor to Elizabeth Haughton Taylor, 13 August 1786, Taylor Papers, III/B/2.

100. Dusinberre, *Them Dark Days*, 201.

101. Morgan, *Slave Counterpoint*, 284; Morgan, "Three Planters and Their Slaves," 78.

102. Dusinberre, *Them Dark Days*, 201–202.

103. Burnard, *Mastery, Tyranny, and Desire*, 148, 149.

104. John Vanheelen to Joseph Foster Barham, 1 December 1783, Barham Papers, C.357, Bundle 1; Johnson, *Soul by Soul*, 107–111.

105. To confront paternalism as an ideology as opposed to paternalism as a practice is to define the term from the perspective of slaveholders like Simon Taylor and thus to accept unexamined the word's dubious gentle connotations. Approached from the perspective of enslaved Africans, the violent connotations of slaveowners's paternalism remains ever clear because the focus on practice and master-slave social relations ensures as much. Dusinberre believes "paternalism" should be avoided when describing and analyzing "the system of punishments, allowances, and privileges which planters imposed on their bondsmen and

women." I am of the mind that using the word in this sense as well as when describing planter ideology and motive is desirable because it highlights the dialectic at the heart of the term in a way that actually rescues paternalism from the sole preserve of planter rhetoric.

FOUR

ROUTINES OF DISASTER AND REVOLUTION

1. Sheridan, "The Crisis of Slave Subsistence," 625–626, 632.

2. Matthew Mulcahy has explored in depth the role of hurricanes in the development of British colonial society in the West Indies and environs. See Mulcahy, *Hurricanes and Society in the British Greater Caribbean.*

3. There is something to be said for starting with sugar, starting that is with the main work of Jamaican slaves, in order to make the same point. Sugar certainly shaped the bulk of slave life in Jamaica (its rhythm, its pace, and much of its possibilities). But enslaved blacks were certainly not interested in sugar in the way they were committed to their provisions and to their provision grounds. Enslaved blacks' provision grounds and their provisions were part of their internal lives in ways sugar was not. And so exploring enslaved Jamaicans' relationship to their grounds speaks more directly to the disaster (and the opportunity) that framed black life on the island in the late eighteenth century. For an excellent collection exploring the centrality of labor to slave life, see Berlin and Morgan, *Culture and Cultivation.* Roderick McDonald's excellent study speaks to the special importance of provisioning and provision grounds to slave culture and society in Jamaica (McDonald, *The Economy and Material Culture of Slaves*).

4. Simon Taylor to Chaloner Arcedeckne, 11 February 1786, Vanneck Manuscripts, Bundle 2/12. This kind of variety, however, was ideal. Achieving it meant neglecting, to an extent, the bottom line of a sugar property: making and shipping sugar and rum. Consequently, on many properties the least labor-intensive crop comprised the bulk of slave-grown provisions: plantains.

5. Dirks, *The Black Saturnalia*, 80.

6. Ibid., 78; Ward, *British West Indian Slavery*, 23.

7. John Kelly to Chaloner Arcedeckne, 4 December 1781, Vanneck Manuscripts, Bundle 2/10.

8. Alured [?] Clarke to Lord Sydney, 15 August 1784, NA-Kew, CO 137/84.

9. Charles Rowe to Joseph Foster Barham, 11 August 1784, Barham Papers, C.357, Bundle 1. Years later John Taylor admitted of another storm that "the first accounts of the dammage done on an Estate by such misfortunes is generally the worst" (John Taylor to Chaloner Arcedeckne, 5 November 1791, Vanneck Manuscripts, Bundle 2/18).

10. All quotations taken from "Copy of Minutes of Council and their resolutions relative to provisions and lands," 4 August 1784 through 7 August 1784, NA-Kew, CO 137/84.

11. John Vanheelen to Joseph Foster Barham, 7 September 1785, Barham Papers, C.357, Bundle 1 (quotations from Barham attorney); Alured Clarke to Lord Sydney, 10 September 1785, NA-Kew, CO 137/85 (quotations from governor).

12. Alured Clarke to Lord Sydney, 5 November 1786, NA-Kew, CO 137/86.

13. Simon Taylor to Chaloner Arcedeckne, 17 November 1786, Vanneck Manuscripts, Bundle 2/12.

14. Simon Taylor to Chaloner Arcedeckne, 7 April 1788, Vanneck Manuscripts, Bundle 2/14. Previously, the attorney at Golden Grove had put in a good deal of ground provisions, so the loss of the plantain walks did not signify a coming famine. On estates more dependent on plantains, the people were probably not so sanguine.

15. Simon Taylor to Chaloner Arcedeckne, 29 May 1788, Vanneck Manuscripts, Bundle 2/14.

16. Simon Taylor to Chaloner Arcedeckne, 30 August 1788, Vanneck Manuscripts, Bundle 2/14.

17. John Wedderburn to Joseph Foster Barham, 6 April 1789, Barham Papers, C.357, Bundle 2.

18. Simon Taylor to Chaloner Arcedeckne, 24 December 1789, Vanneck Manuscripts, Bundle 2/15.

19. John Graham to Joseph Foster Barham, 8 April 1790, Barham Papers, C.357, Bundle 2; John Graham to Joseph Foster Barham, 4 March 1790, Barham Papers, C.357, Bundle 2; Simon Taylor to Chaloner Arcedeckne, 1 March 1790, Vanneck Manuscripts, Bundle 2/16; Simon Taylor to Chaloner Arcedeckne, 20 April 1790, Vanneck Manuscripts, Bundle 2/16. From Westmoreland and environs there were complaints of excessively wet weather in April and May of 1790. At the same time, to the south and east the island was positively parched.

20. John Graham to Joseph Foster Barham, 6 September 1790, Barham Papers, C.357, Bundle 2.

21. James Wedderburn to Joseph Foster Barham, 2 September 1790, Barham Papers, C.357, Bundle 2.

22. Simon Taylor to Chaloner Arcedeckne, 7 September 1790, Vanneck Manuscripts, Bundle 2/16 (quote). On the relative strength of the storm in the different quarters of the island, see James Wedderburn to Joseph Foster Barham, 2 September 1790, Barham Papers, C.357, Bundle 2; Simon Taylor to Chaloner Arcedeckne, 6 October 1790, Vanneck Manuscripts, Bundle 2/16. Over the medium term, he came to think that the gale did more damage than was immediately apparent: "The Gale of the 1st of Sept. has done infinitely more damage than we supposed it had at the time, but I believe it was more owning to the excessive drought we had had the year and months preceding for vegetation had been stopt and consequently the Canes were coming to maturity too early and the Wind then breaking many they never vegetated again" (Simon Taylor to Chaloner Arcedeckne, 8 April 1791, Vanneck Manuscripts, Bundle 2/17).

23. John Taylor to Chaloner Arcedeckne, 5 November 1791, Vanneck Manuscripts, Bundle 2/18; John Taylor to Simon Taylor, 6 November 1791, Taylor Papers, XIV/A/83.

24. The course of the slave revolt-turned-revolution in St. Domingue can be followed in three remarkably literary and incisive accounts: James, *The Black Jacobins,* 2nd ed.; Dubois, *Avengers of the New World;* and Bell, *Toussaint Louverture.*

25. Simon Taylor to Chaloner Arcedeckne, 25 April 1793, Vanneck Manuscripts, Bundle 2/19.

26. Simon Taylor to Chaloner Arcedeckne, 18 June 1793, Vanneck Manuscripts, Bundle 2/19.

27. Simon Taylor to Stephen Fuller, 20 June 1793, Fuller Papers, Dickinson MSS, DD/DN 508, no. 1.

28. Simon Taylor to Chaloner Arcedeckne, 27 June 1793, Vanneck Manuscripts, Bundle 2/19.

29. Charles Rowe to Joseph Foster Barham, 12 June 1794, Barham Papers, C.357, Bundle 2.

30. "Resolution of the Council of Jamaica," 7 August 1793, NA-Kew, CO 137/91.

31. Charles Rowe to Joseph Foster Barham, 22 July 1793, Barham Papers, C.357, Bundle 2.

32. The war in the Caribbean is captured by Geggus, *Slavery, War, and Revolution;* Duffy, *Soldiers, Sugar, and Seapower.*

33. Adam Williamson to Henry Dundas, 28 April 1794, NA-Kew, CO 137/93.

34. Simon Taylor to Chaloner Arcedeckne, 4 May 1794, Vanneck Manuscripts, Bundle 2/20.

35. Simon Taylor to Chaloner Arcedeckne, 4 June 1794, Vanneck Manuscripts, Bundle 2/20; Simon Taylor to Chaloner Arcedeckne, 15 July 1794, Vanneck Manuscripts, Bundle 2/20.

36. Adam Wiliamson to Henry Dundas, 10 August 1793, NA-Kew, CO 137/91.

37. Simon Taylor to Chaloner Arcedeckne, 16 October 1793, Vanneck Manuscripts, Bundle 2/19.

38. Simon Taylor to Robert Taylor, 4 January 1796, Taylor Papers, XIII/B/17 (initial drought); Simon Taylor to Chaloner Arcedeckne, 17 April 1796, Vanneck Manuscripts, Bundle 2/21 (first quotation); Thomas Barritt to Nathaniel Phillips, 28 April 1796, Slebech Papers and Documents, MSS 11572 (second quotation); Thomas Barritt to Nathaniel Phillips, 20 May 1796, Slebech Papers and Documents, MSS 11573 (end of drought). See also Thomas Barritt to Nathaniel Phillips, 20 May 1796, Slebech Papers and Documents, MSS 11573; Thomas Barritt to Nathaniel Phillips, 4 June 1796, Slebech Papers and Documents, MSS 11575; Thomas Barritt to Nathaniel Phillips, 15 July 1796, Slebech Papers and Documents, MSS 11576; Thomas Barritt to Nathaniel Phillips, 18 August 1796, Slebech Papers and Documents, MSS 11576; Thomas Barritt to Nathaniel Phillips, 28 September 1796, Slebech Papers and Documents, MSS 11576; Thomas Barritt to Nathaniel Phillips, 14 October 1796, Slebech Papers and Documents, MSS 11577; Thomas Barritt to Nathaniel Phillips, 30 November 1796, Slebech Papers and Documents, MSS 11578; Simon Taylor to Chaloner Arcedeckne, 15 December 1795; 5, 10 January 1796; 1 May 1796, Vanneck Manuscripts, Bundle 2/21.

39. Burnard, *Mastery, Tyranny, and Desire,* 225. Enslaved Jamaicans, Burnard has written, "lived close to subsistence and near to disaster even at the best of times."

40. John Graham to Joseph Foster Barham, 30 June 1795, Barham Papers, C.357, Bundle 2. "The hot house is at present crowded with Negroes in fevers and small Complaints of the Bowels, which is always the result of clearing the provisions in the Mountains; whether it is caused from change of water, or lodging, or both, I cannot say, but I hear constantly this to be the case, And I do not know but it will be better allways to hire Negroes for this labour and only send a few of the Estates people to stimulate the workg. of the others"

41. John Graham to Joseph Foster Barham, 16 June 1790, 18 July 1790, Barham Papers, C.357, Bundle 2.

42. Thomas Barritt to Nathaniel Phillips, 4 August 1792, Slebech Papers and Documents, MSS 8401 (pox); Thomas Barritt to Nathaniel Phillips, 13 June 1792, Slebech Papers and Documents, MSS 8398 (dysentery and venereal disease); John Graham to Joseph Foster Barham, 8 August 1792, Barham Papers, C.357, Bundle 2 (quote).

43. Jamaica House of Assembly, "Second Report: Presented the 12th Day of November, 1788," 13–14.

44. Ibid., 15.

45. N.a., "Extract of two letters from Jamaica to a Gentleman now in London," n.d. [1787], NA-Kew, BT 6/76.

46. Charles Rowe to Joseph Foster Barham, 11 August 1784, 2 November 1784, 17 January 1785, Barham Papers, C.357, Bundle 1.

47. Thomas Barritt to Nathaniel Phillips, 16 December 1789, Slebech Papers and Documents, MSS 8349. Barritt wrote as follows concerning the flu: "This Complaint has been very general throughout the Island, and in many places mortal. It began first about Kingston the middle of Oct. last, and scarcely a white or black escaped it, soon after it made its appearance in the country, and many negroes have had it severely, but those who have only been afflicted with the Common influenza soon get well, but many others who were attacked with the bastard [?] or real pleurisy have very few escaped. Sorry am I to say that the latter has been so severe among the Farm gang that from the 17 ___ to the 4th inst. we lost 3 men and 2 women ____. Darby, Gardemin [?], Liander [?], Cle__sy, and Dole. These were not the most healthiest people of that gang, and of a full habit of body whom it seems /by the Doctors account/

that disorders generally attacks most severely, tho' there has been others severely dealt with, And at present Copia and Flora at the Farm can scarcely be said to be out of danger. Here we los Old Dick by this same complaint, and Old John and Kelly at Phillipsfield has been exceeding bad but now well there is no other at present with that complaint." See also Dr. Turney to Chaloner Arcedeckne, 29 March 1790, Vanneck Manuscripts, Bundle 2/16; John Graham to Joseph Foster Barham, 8 September 1789, Barham Papers, C.357, Bundle 2; Simon Taylor to Chaloner Arcedeckne, 1 November 1789, Vanneck Manuscripts, Bundle 2/15.

48. John Taylor to Simon Taylor, 7 August 1791, Taylor Papers, XIV/A/81; John Taylor to Simon Taylor, 6 November 1791, Taylor Papers, XIV/A/83.

49. John Graham to Joseph Foster Barham, 15 October 1793, 2 November 1793, Barham Papers, C.357, Bundle 2.

50. John Graham to Joseph Foster Barham, 15 October 1793, 2 November 1793, Barham Papers, C.357, Bundle 2 (influenza); Thomas Barritt to Nathaniel Phillips, 16 October 1793, Slebech Papers and Documents, MSS 8423 (scarlet fever).

51. Simon Taylor to Chaloner Arcedeckne, 16 October 1793, Vanneck Manuscripts, Bundle 2/19.

52. On the progress of the yellow fever and measles epidemics, see Simon Taylor to Chaloner Arcedeckne, 15 July 1794, Vanneck Manuscripts, Bundle 2/20; Alexander Balcarres to Duke of Portland, 24 May 1795, NA-Kew, CO 137/95; Thomas Barritt to Nathaniel Phillips, 25 February 1795, Slebech Papers and Documents, MSS 9201; Thomas Barritt to Nathaniel Phillips, 28 April 1795, Slebech Papers and Documents, MSS 9202; Thomas Barritt to Nathaniel Phillips, 13 May 1795, Slebech Papers and Documents, MSS 9202; Thomas Barritt to Nathaniel Phillips, 27 May 1795, Slebech Papers and Documents, MSS 9204; Thomas Barritt to Nathaniel Phillips, 1 July 1795, Slebech Papers and Documents, MSS 9205 and 9204; Thomas Barritt to Nathaniel Phillips, 17 July 1795, Slebech Papers and Documents, MSS 9206; Thomas Barritt to Nathaniel Phillips, 15 August 1795, Slebech Papers and Documents, MSS 9207; Simon Taylor to Chaloner Arcedeckne, 9 August 1794, Vanneck Manuscripts, Bundle 2/20; Thomas Barritt to Nathaniel Phillips, 16 January 1795, Slebech Papers and Documents, MSS 9201.

53. Dr. Turney to Chaloner Arcedeckne, 29 March 1790, Vanneck Manuscripts, Bundle 2/16; Dr. Turney to Chaloner Arcedeckne, 21 July 1790, Vanneck Manuscripts, Bundle 2/16. In the former letter, the doctor wrote, "I have to inform you the Lying in House has answered the highest expectation, & U have no doubt of its continuing to do so. Since the 1st Janry. we have had eight Childrn. born besides four or five belonging to Holland Estate, all of whom are alive and well. The only difficulty in carrying the plan into execution lay with the Mothers in the beginning, but the more sensible of them now begin to see the good effects of it, & in a little time I have no doubt of their giving up their old habits with alacrity, when they find the preservation of their Children will be their reward." In the latter missive, he confirms that things have unfolded as he suspected on this front.

54. John Graham to Joseph Foster Barham, 3 September 1793, Barham Papers, C.357, Bundle 2.

55. Charles Rowe to Joseph Foster Barham, 17 March 1790, Barham Papers, C.357, Bundle 2.

56. Thomas Barritt to Nathaniel Phillips, 4 July 1793, Slebech Papers and Documents, MSS 8419 (yaws is a tropical skin disease, now mostly eradicated). See also Charles Rowe to Joseph Foster Barham, 3 August 1791, Barham Papers, C.357, Bundle 2. Rowe writes, "I am very sorry to acquaint you since my last of having learnt the unfortunate death of one of

the finest Negro men out of the last purchased parcel, who I had previously pleased to learn to Occupation of a Cooper & was . . . persuaded away by another of his own Country who strolled across the Island over to Trelawney, where in attempting to rescue himself from the people that captured them, he was so desperately wounded in the affray as shortly after to expire in the workhouse for that parish before any indication of his Capture could be made known to me. I am really concerned for the fellows loss as he was in every particular well disposed, and bid fair had not this unforeseen event taken place to have made you a very able slave."

57. See, for example, Mullin, *Africa in America*, 62–74, 159–173; McDonald, *The Economy and Material Culture of Slaves*, 16–49; Craton, *Searching for the Invisible Man*, 161–167; Higman, "The Slave Family and Household in the British West Indies, 1800–1834," 261–287";Household Structure and Fertility on Jamaican Slave Plantations," 527–550; Craton, "Changing Patterns of Slave Families in the British West Indies," 1–35.

58. Stephen Fuller to Henry Dundas, n.d., NA-Kew, CO 137/93 (Miscellaneous Papers).

59. Simon Taylor to Chaloner Arcedeckne, 11 June 1782, Vanneck Manuscripts, Bundle 2/10.

60. Simon Taylor to Chaloner Arcedeckne, 1 November 1789, Vanneck Manuscripts, Bundle 2/15. Taylor continued, "but after they are 16 or 18, there is no danger of their Splitting in the boring."

61. Simon Taylor to Chaloner Arcedeckne, 4 February 1794, Vanneck Manuscripts, Bundle 2/20.

62. John Taylor to Simon Taylor, 12 September 1791, Taylor Papers, XIV/A/82; John Taylor to Chaloner Arcedeckne, 5 November 1791, Vanneck Manuscripts, Bundle 2/18; Simon Taylor to Chaloner Arcedeckne, 5 November 1791, Vanneck Manuscripts, Bundle 2/18. Initially, there was some confusion about who was Quashie's father. In his first letter on the subject, John Taylor makes him out to be the issue of John Kelly, the former attorney for the estate. In a later letter it is clarified that Quashie belonged to a Golden Grove blacksmith named Guy. Given that John Taylor was functioning as acting attorney for the estate during the time in question and was not at all nearly as familiar with the blacks on the plantation as was Simon Taylor, who was then in London, given the outcome of the inquiry into the incident, and given the fact that John Kelly had long been turned out as the estate's attorney and thus not longer lived at Golden Grove, I have taken Simon Taylor's later clarification of Quashie's father as more reliable than the initial identification in John Taylor's first letter on the subject.

63. John Taylor to Simon Taylor, 12 September 1791, Taylor Papers, XIV/A/82.

64. John Taylor to Simon Taylor, 6 November 1791, Taylor Papers, XIV/A/83.

65. John Taylor to Chaloner Arcedeckne, 8 April 1792, Vanneck Manuscripts, Bundle 2/18.

66. Mullin has argued that alcoholism might have been especially prevalent among American-born slaves (Mullin, *Africa in America,* 233).

67. Thomas Barritt to Nathaniel Phillips, 1 July 1795, Slebech Papers and Documents, MSS 9205 and 9204.

68. Thomas Barritt to Nathaniel Phillips, 16 October 1795, Slebech Papers and Documents, MSS 9209 (quotation); Thomas Barritt to Nathaniel Phillips, 1 January 1796, Slebech Papers and Documents, MSS 9211 (Pera and labor comparison). Barritt went on to say of Pera, "He has been broke for some time, and only lately reinstated, and I hope he is now sensible of his fault, and will behave as he should do!"

69. John Graham to Joseph Foster Barham, 27 June 1791, Barham Papers, C.357, Bundle 2.

70. Alured Clarke to Lord Sydney, 9 December 1788, NA-Kew, CO 137/87.

71. Charles Rowe to Joseph Foster Barham, 16 June 1790 (first quotation), 24 July 1790 (second quotation), Barham Papers, C.357, Bundle 2.

72. Simon Taylor to Chaloner Arcedeckne, 4 June 1794, Vanneck Manuscripts, Bundle 2/20 (first quotation); Simon Taylor to Chaloner Arcedeckne, 9 August 1794, Vanneck Manuscripts, Bundle 2/20 (second quotation); Simon Taylor to Chaloner Arcedeckne, 14 December 1786, Vanneck Manuscripts, Bundle 2/12 (third quotation); Simon Taylor to Chaloner Arcedeckne, 24 September 1786, Vanneck Manuscripts, Bundle 2/12 (fourth quotation).

73. Simon Taylor to Chaloner Arcedeckne, 14 December 1786, Vanneck Manuscripts, Bundle 2/12.

74. Jamaica House of Assembly, "Second Report: Presented the 12th Day of November, 1788," 15.

75. Simon Taylor to Chaloner Arcedeckne, 8 September 1792, Vanneck Manuscripts, Bundle 2/18.

76. N.a., "Extract of two letters from Jamaica to a Gentleman now in London," n.d. [1787], NA-Kew, BT 6/76. "The Famine we have had will occasion the deaths of Fifteen to twenty thousand negroes in this island, this year: many hundreds have been killed in robbing provision grounds; many have died of actual hunger; And thousands are now bloated and in Dropsies from the same cause." The abstract was probably compiled in 1787, the letter quoted above was dated September 1785.

77. Simon Taylor to Chaloner Arcedeckne, 11 October 1786, Vanneck Manuscripts, Bundle 2/12.

78. Simon Taylor to Chaloner Arcedeckne, 19 March 1786, Vanneck Manuscripts, Bundle 2/12.

79. The works of Orlando Patterson and Trevor G. Burnard best capture this aspect of black society on Jamaica (Patterson, *The Sociology of Slavery;* Burnard, *Mastery, Tyranny, and Desire*).

80. Craton, "Hobbesian or Panglossian," 324–356.

81. Scott, "The Common Wind."

82. Mintz and Hall, "The Origins of the Jamaican Internal Marketing System," 312–322, 329–330.

83. "Minutes of the proceedings of the Committee of Secrecy and Safety in the Parish of St. James,'" NA-Kew, CO 137/90.

84. John Taylor to Simon Taylor, 16 November 1790, Taylor Papers, XIV/A/71; John Taylor to Simon Taylor, 22 January 1790, Taylor Papers, XIV/A/54. The former letter contains the following, apparently about a slave messenger, "Your Boy went away yesterday before I saw him." On the outside of the latter missive is written "per. Sandy with a Horse to pass. J. Taylor."

85. Bolster, *Black Jacks,* 59–61, 131–132.

86. John Graham to Joseph Foster Barham, 25 June 1792, Barham Papers, C.357, Bundle 2: "It is with much concern I inform you that Cupid has been for some time past in a bad state of Health, he had got a complaint in his head, which puzzled the Medical gentlemen, and the disease has unfortunately settled on his Lungs. By the Doctors advice he was to have taken a trip to America as soon as a Vessel offered, and in the mean time has been sent up to St. Elizabeths, since he went there the Doctor informs [me] his disorder has taken a different turn, and it is much feared will get the better of him; in this event you will sustain the loss of one of the very best of Slaves. Jackie who used formerly to be a waiting man about the House is also troubled with a complain almost similar. Mr. Wedderburn and Self have concluded

upon sending him [Jackie] to America in the Commerce Captain Foot, which Vessel will sail in about three weeks. he will return again with the Ship that takes in a Cargo of Lumber for this port. The Doctors advise and think the Negroe will be much benefited by the Voyage." For news of Cupid's death and confirmation of Jackie's departure, see John Graham to Joseph Foster Barham, 8 August 1792, Barham Papers, C.357, Bundle 2.

87. Thomas Barritt to Nathaniel Phillips, 20 May 1796, Slebech Papers and Documents, MSS 11573 (quote). Also, John Graham to Joseph Foster Barham, 10 January 1792, 23 February 1795, Barham Papers, C.357, Bundle 2. In the former, Graham complains of certain habitual runaway blacks. In the latter, he reports their reclamation.

88. Simon Taylor to Chaloner Arcedeckne, 17 January 1791, Vanneck Manuscripts, Bundle 2/17. A plantation doctor described these gatherings as occasions where blacks "dance immoderately drink to excess, sleep in the cold ground or commit many acts of sensuality and intemperance." See William Wright, "Answers to Queries, concerning Negroe Slaves in the Island of Jamaica," 1 March 1788, Vanneck Manuscripts, Bundle 2/63.

89. Frey, *Water from the Rock*, 182.

90. Simon Taylor to Elizabeth Haughton Taylor, 16 February 1787, Taylor Papers, III/B/6; and Simon Taylor to Haughton Taylor, 7 September 1787, Taylor Papers, III/B/13.

91. Scott, "The Common Wind," 89–103.

92. Simon Taylor to Chaloner Arcedeckne, 19 March 1782, Vanneck Manuscripts, Bundle 2/10. So many slaves were drafted from Chaloner Arcedeckne's Golden Grove plantation during the taking off of the crop in 1782 that there came times when if not for hired labor the attorneys would have had to stop the mills. Taking off the crop was among the hardest periods for sugar slaves. Whatever work to which the slaves drafted off Golden Grove were put on the fortifications of the island, it is unlikely that it was more demanding.

93. John Kelly to Chaloner Arcedeckne, 19 March 1782, Vanneck Manuscripts, Bundle 2/10.

94. John Vanheelen to Joseph Foster Barham, 9 April 1782, Barham Papers, C.357, Bundle 1.

95. John Vanheelen to Joseph Foster Barham, 9 April 1782, Barham Papers, C.357, Bundle 1.

96. John Vanheelen to Joseph Foster Barham, 27 April 1782, Barham Papers, C.357, Bundle 1.

97. For the initial secret letter from officials at Whitehall to the lieutenant governor of Jamaica concerning impending war, see Baron Grenville to Lord Effingham, 6 May 1790, NA-Kew, CO 137/88.

98. Baron Grenville to Lord Effingham, 22 May 1790, NA-Kew, CO 137/88.

99. Simon Taylor to Chaloner Arcedeckne, 17 June 1790, Vanneck Manuscripts, Bundle 2/16.

100. Simon Taylor to Chaloner Arcedeckne, 19 July 1790, Vanneck Manuscripts, Bundle 2/16.

101. Simon Taylor to Chaloner Arcedeckne, 7 August 1790, Vanneck Manuscripts, Bundle 2/16.

102. In order, see Simon Taylor to Chaloner Arcedeckne, 7 August 1790, Vanneck Manuscripts, Bundle 2/16; Charles Rowe to Joseph Foster Barham, 8 September 1790, Barham Papers, C.357, Bundle 2; John Taylor to Simon Taylor, 25 September 1790, Taylor Papers, XIV/A/64; Charles Rowe to Joseph Foster Barham, 9 November 1790, Barham Papers, C.357, Bundle 2; Simon Taylor to Chaloner Arcedeckne, 13 November 1790, Vanneck Manuscripts, Bundle 2/16; Adam Williamson to Baron Grenville, 27 December 1790, NA-Kew, CO 137/89; Lord Effingham to Baron Grenville, 31 May 1791, NA-Kew, CO 137/89.

103. "The memorial and humble petition of the Council and Assembly of Jamaica," 15

December 1789, NA-Kew, CO 137/88. In the Americas, this was a common problem for British colonials whose borders abutted Spanish settlements. See, for instance, Landers, *Black Society in Spanish Florida*.

104. "Proceedings . . . ," 24 January 1791 (original 31 October 1789?), NA-Kew, CO 137/89.

105. Ibid.; and John W. McGregor, "Narration of Facts, representing the protection the Spainairds of Cuba, give all Negroes belonging to the West Indies Islands," 1 September 1790, NA-Kew, CO 137/88 (Miscellaneous Papers).

106. "Proceedings . . . ," 24 January 1791 (original 31 October 1789?), NA-Kew, CO 137/89.

107. Henry Dundas to Lord Effingham, 8 August 1791, NA-Kew, CO 137/89.

108. "Minutes of the proceedings of the Committee of Secrecy and Safety in the Parish of St. James,'" NA-Kew, CO 137/90.

109. Adam Williamson to Henry Dundas, 10 September 1791, NA-Kew, CO 137/89. "Many of the Slaves here are very inquisitive & inteligent, & are immediately informed of every kind of news that arrives. I do not hear of their having shown any signs of revolt, tho' they have composed songs of the Negroes having made a rebellion at Hispaniola with their usual chorus to it; & I have not a doubt but there are numbers who are ripe for any mischief & whenever any insurrection begins, it will be in the parishes on the North side of the Island."

110. Stephen Fuller to Henry Dundas, 30 October 1791, NA-Kew, CO 137/89 (Miscellaneous Papers). "I have this morning receiv'd letters from Jamaica by the Carteset Packet . . . adding that several canoes had arrived at the E. end of Jamaica with Negroes from Hispaniola."

111. Adam Williamson to Henry Dundas, 20 January 1794, NA-Kew, CO 137/92. "The French Inhabitants, Emigrants, & Refugees that are continually coming to the Kings House, and who I must in some degree entertain are without numbers. I am very often obliged to furnish them with Carriages &c; for having been just stript by the Commissaries, and afterwards plundered by our privateers, they literally have not a Louis D'or left to help them."

112. Simon Taylor to Chaloner Arcedeckne, 9 August 1794, Vanneck Manuscripts, Bundle 2/20. "There has as yet been no French Negroes brought down here & I hope to God none will."

113. Henry Dundas to Adam Williamson, 28 November 1793, NA-Kew, CO 137/91; Adam Williamson to Henry Dundas, 4 February 1794, NA-Kew, CO 137/92.

114. Earl of Balcarres to Duke of Portland, 30 May 1795, NA-Kew, CO 137/95. In this letter Balcarres notes that there were 229 French families on the island. The government of Jamaica provided relief for 107 of these families, which consisted of 309 people (thus the estimate of the official total noted above).

115. Simon Taylor to Chaloner Arcedeckne, 10 October 1794, Vanneck Manuscripts, Bundle 2/20.

116. Adam Williamson to Henry Dundas, 12 February 1792, NA-Kew, CO 137/90.

117. Simon Taylor to Chaloner Arcedeckne, 4 May 1794, Vanneck Manuscripts, Bundle 2/20. "We have been much afraid of an Intercourse of their negroes and ours, and there is a very severe law passed, respecting the bringing any of them down here, and any that are taken, are not permitted to be sold, but for transportation. . . . I cannot tell what will be the Ultimate Fate of the Matter, but it is impossible to prevent the Smuggling of Negroes into the Islands, if we have the [French] ones added to Ours."

118. "Proclamation No. 1," 10 December 1791, NA-Kew, CO 137/90; and "Proclamation No. 2," 10 December 1791, NA-Kew, CO 137/90. The first reads: "Whereas we have been requested by our House of Assembly now sitting to prohibit all free people of colour and free Negroes from Saint Domingo from landing in this Island until they have found two substantial House Keepers white persons resident here and approved of by the Curator or Chief magistrate of the Parish where they arrive as sureties for their good behaviour during their residence in this Island; and commanding all Foreigners of the above description forthwith to quit the Island unless they can find such securities for their good behaviour; —We do therefore Issue this our Royal Proclamation prohibiting all free people of Colour and free Negroes from the Island of Saint Domingo from landing in this our said Island without having first obtained such securities for their good behaviour." The second declaration continues: "Whereas from the representations of our House of Assembly it appears to us of the greatest consequence at this juncture to prohibit all Foreigners trading to this our Island of Jamaica from landing either themselves or Slaves without our Special licence, we do therefore hereby signify it to be our will and pleasure that no Foreigners trading to this Island be permitted on any pretence whatsoever, to land either themselves or any of their Slaves on any part of this Island without a special licence first obtained from our commander in chief, or from some other person or persons hereinafter mentioned to whom we have thought proper to give our authority for that purpose, of which all officers civil and Military and all other our subjects are enjoined to take notice at their peril; And we do hereby Authorize and empower the Custos and commanding officers of the Militia, in their several parishes and districts to examine all foreign vessels which shall arrive in any Harbour creek or Bay within the same, and to give such licence as aforesaid; but it is our will and pleasure that no licence be granted to free persons of Colour or free negroes from the Island of Saint Domingo unless the Conditions expressed in our Royal Proclamation of this date respecting them are observed and fulfilled and we do hereby order that all Foreigners /trading or aforesaid/ who shall be found on shore six days after the date hereof without such licence be apprehended and carried before the Commanding Officer for examination who shall report the same to Head Quarters and await our pleasure, And we do direct the Custos or Senior Magistrates of the Several Parishes of this Island forthwith to make enquiry and return of all Foreigners resident in their several districts."

119. Alured Clarke to Lord Sydney, 22 April 1788, NA-Kew, CO 137/87. "The Petitions which have been presented to the House of Commons relative to the Slave-Trade have already occasioned great alarm in all ranks of people here. . . . Your Lordship may rely on my particular attention to prevent any disturbance in Consequence of the rumours which must necessarily be spread among the Negroes upon the occasion, avoiding as much as possible to create unnecessary Suspicion or alarm and that I shall in no case resort to any measure of Rigoor or Severity, but such as the exigency of circumstances may render indispensable."

120. Committee of Correspondence, Jamaica to Stephen Fuller, 5 November 1791, NA-Kew, CO 137/90 (Miscellaneous Papers). The sixteen signatories complained that the British abolitionist movement taught slaves to believe "that they are held in a condition of servitude, which is reprobated in the mother country, and that the ultimate end of these Gentlemen whom they call their Friends in England, is to place them on a footing with the civilized part of the Community; an opinion which in the present ideas of right & wrong can lead only to involve them in one common destruction with ourselves. Perhaps nothing has contributed so much to the dissemination of these notions among our Negroes, as the publication of several examinations, which were taken before the Committee of the House of Commons, and most

insidiously sent out by persons in England, and explained to our Slaves by free people of their own complexion. We hope this will be prevented in future."

121. "Enclosures in The Humble Memorial of Stephen Fuller Esq. Agent for Jamaica," 29 September 1792, NA-Kew, CO 137/90 (Miscellaneous Papers).

122. The following account is taken from "Minutes of the proceedings of the Committee of Secrecy and Safety in the Parish of St. James,'" NA-Kew, CO 137/90 (section XXIV B).

123. "Examination of Sundry Slaves in the Parish of St. Ann Jamaica respecting an intention to revolt," 31 December 1791–11 January 1792, NA-Kew, CO 137/90.

PART II. VOYAGERS

1. Thomas B. Thompson, "Captain's Log Nautilus," 23, 24 February 1787, NA-Kew, ADM 51/627.

2. Ibid., 27 February 1787.

3. Thomas B. Thompson to Navy Board, 21 March 1787, NA-Kew, T1/643; George Marsh et al. to Captain Thompson, 24 March 1787, NA-Kew, ADM 106/2347.

4. Thomas B. Thompson, "Captain's Log Nautilus," 10 May 1787, NA-Kew, ADM 51/627.

5. Clarkson, "Mission to America," 30 November 1791. The first two passages quoted in the succeeding paragraphs are from ff 190, and the third is from ff 193.

6. Clarkson, "Mission to America," 30 November 1791.

7. Ibid.

8. Walker, *A History Blacks in Canada*, 35; Sierra Leone Company, *Substance of the report delivered by the Court of Directors*, 5–6 (emigration offer).

9. Walker, *The Black Loyalists;* Wilson, *The Loyal Blacks;* Winks, *The Blacks in Canada*. Historians of blacks in Canada and of the migration to Sierra Leone have generally framed the 1791–1792 emigration movement as an exodus. The term holds significant literary utility, and given the religious bent of many of the migrants themselves, the phrase resonates, no doubt, something of their own interpretation of events. I argue, in the pages that follow, that the term is also of great analytical benefit.

FIVE

SOCIAL MOVEMENT AND IMAGINING FREEDOM
IN THE BRITISH CAPITAL

1. *Public Advertiser,* 16 January 1786, 4; *Public Advertiser,* 17 February 1786, 1. The custom during the eighteenth century was to number the city's Asian-born inhabitants among its black residents. Some of these lascars, as they were called, were servants from eastern Africa, India, Malaysia, and beyond who arrived in London bonded to wealthy British merchants. More were sailors forced to make their way in the city after being discharged from either the King's ships or the service of the East India Company. All told, servants and seamen from in and around the Indian subcontinent may have accounted for little more that 2 percent of the capital's eighteenth-century black population. See Visram, *Ayahs, Lascars and Princes,* esp. 34–54; Hecht, *Continental and Colonial Servants in Eighteenth-Century England;* Myers, *Reconstructing the Black Past,* 108. Lascar is a corruption of the Persian *lashkar,* meaning army or camp. The Portuguese in India used the word to mean solider, but when taken up by the Dutch and English afterward it was more often used to refer to "an inferior class of

artilleryman," to camp laborers, and more commonly to sailors (Yule and Burnell, *Hobson-Jobson,* 2nd ed., s.v. "Lascar").

2. Gerzina, *Black England,* 40–42; Myers, *Reconstructing the Black Past,* 18–37, 118–124; Braidwood, *Black Poor and White Philanthropists,* 26–27; Schwarz, *London in the Age of Industrialisation,* 125–128. London's total population during the period was less than 1 million.

3. Braidwood, *Black Poor and White Philanthropists,* 63–64; *Morning Post,* 15 March 1786, 1b, quoted in Braidwood, *Black Poor and White Philanthropists,* 69.

4. *Morning Post,* 15 March 1786, 1b, quoted in Braidwood, *Black Poor and White Philanthropists,* 71.

5. A motivating factor behind the expansion of the committee's original focus on East Indian sailors and one rationale for the early success of the committee's public subscription was the fact that many of London's impoverished blacks were loyalists from the American war. In the aftermath of that conflict, it was generally understood that the nation owed a debt to colonists who aligned themselves with the king and were made refugees because of their allegiance. Of course, white Britons and their public officials drew sharp distinctions between their obligations to loyalists in general and to black loyalists in particular, almost always to the detriment of the latter. But while prevailing prejudices circumscribed the responsibility white Britons felt for the black sailors, soldiers, and pioneers among them, such biases did not extinguish their sense of obligation. In consequence, as voluntary subscriptions to the committee trailed off, the Lords of the Treasury were persuaded to take an interest in the present support and subsequent emigration of London's blacks. The government endorsed a plan to do with the black poor what was done with a great many Afro-American loyalists during the British evacuation of New York at the end of the late war: to settle them in Nova Scotia (Braidwood, *Black Poor and White Philanthropists,* 77–78 [plans for Sierra Leone]). On British loyalists, black and white, during and after the war, see Norton, *The British-Americans;* Moore, *The Loyalists;* Norton, "The Fate of Some Black Loyalists of the American Revolution," 404–405. The commission established to pay restitution and offer assistance to loyalists denied more than half of the claims brought by blacks, while almost always offering assistance to white claimants.

6. In the Treasury Office papers, the first set of surviving meeting minutes dates from early May: "Proceedings of the Committee for the Relief of Black Poor," 10 May 1786, NA-Kew, T1/631.

7. For background on Smeathman and references to his February introduction, his March presentation, and his detailed plan for transporting the black poor, see respectively, Fyfe, *A History of Sierra Leone,* 15; Coleman, *Romantic Colonization and British Anti-Slavery;* "Proceedings of the Committee for the Relief of Black Poor," 10 May 1786, NA-Kew, T1/631; Henry Smeathman, "The Memorial of Henry Smeathman[:] Proposals for taking Black Poor to Grain Coast of Africa," 17 May 1786, NA-Kew, T1/631.

8. "Proceedings of the Committee for the Relief of Black Poor," 17 May 1786, NA-Kew, T1/631; "Instrument of Agreement," n.d. [1786], NA-Kew, T1/632.

9. Braidwood, *Black Poor and White Philanthropists,* 69 (average number of blacks assisted); "Proceedings of the Committee for the Relief of Black Poor," 17 May 1786, NA-Kew, T1/631 (blacks received at the Yorkshire Stingo). During the first month of relief operations, almost 150 blacks gathered for assistance at the two public houses. Between February and mid-March, on average, more than 200 gathered there for relief. These numbers are in addition to the forty or fifty blacks, on average, who were lodged in the Warren Street hospital. By May, almost 350 blacks gathered weekly at the Yorkshire Stingo alone.

10. Sharp, *Memoirs of Granville Sharp,* 260; "Proceedings of the Committee for the Relief

of Black Poor," 10, 17 May 1786, NA-Kew, T1/631; Smeathman, *Plan of a Settlement*. In a letter Granville Sharp wrote in 1788 recapitulating the circumstances around the founding of the colony at Sierra Leone, Sharp suggested that Smeathman recruited blacks directly. According to Sharp, Smeathman proposed emigration to black Londoners soon after the committee initiated its subscription drive. "In the meantime, a proposal was made to them by the late Mr. Smeathman, to form a free settlement at Sierra Leone." In consequence, wrote Sharp, "Many of them came to consult me about the proposal: sometimes they came in large bodies together." It is also clear from the committee's minutes that Smeathman was in close conversation with potential migrants weeks before the committee itself decided to advertise the Sierra Leone proposal. For example, the same week the committee decided to draft a contract between themselves and potential migrants—May 10, 1786—Smeathman submitted to the committee a question some of London's blacks had previously inquired of him: If we agree to go to Sierra Leone, will we be provided guns and ammunition for our protection? Also, prior to the committee's decision to print and distribute a handbill with an outline of the Sierra Leone proposal, as many as 130 people had already committed themselves to Smeathman's plan.

11. Smeathman, *Plan of a Settlement*, 6–9. "Such are the mildness and fertility of the climate and country, that a man possessed of a change of cloathing, a wood axe, a hoe, and a pocket knife, may soon place himself in an easy and comfortable situation. All the cloathing wanted is what decency requires; and it is not necessary to turn up the earth more, than from the depth of two or three inches, with a slight hoe, in order to cultivate any type of grain."

12. Sharp, *Memoirs of Granville Sharp*, 259–260 (quotation); "Proceedings of the Committee for the Relief of Black Poor," 7 June 1786, NA-Kew, T1/632 (blacks treated as vagrants); "Expences of the Sickhouse in Warren Street," n.d. [26 May 1786?], NA-Kew, T1/632 (pawning clothes); "Proceedings of the Committee for the Relief of the [*sic*] Black Poor," 10 July 1786, NA-Kew, T1/633 (morbidity). The writer of Granville Sharp's obituary described the predicament of the capital's free blacks in the wake of the Somerset decision as follows: "being locked up, as it were, in London, and having now no masters to support them, . . . and having besides no parish which they could call their own, [black Londoners] fell by degrees into great distress, so that they were alarmingly conspicuous throughout the streets as common beggars."

13. N.a., *The Gentleman's Magazine* 24 (October 1764), quoted in Gerzina, *Black England*, 41; and Simon Taylor to Elizabeth Haughton Taylor, 16 February 1787, Taylor Papers, III/B/6.

14. On James Somerset and the Somerset case, see Davis, *The Problem of Slavery in the Age of Revolution*, 480–482; Sharp, *Memoirs of Granville Sharp*, 70, 83–84; Hochschild, *Bury the Chains*, 48–52; Wise, *Though the Heavens May Fall*. Details about Somerset's life contained in the court proceedings and in the preparatory materials of his counsel suggest that before his dash for freedom, Somerset may have moved even more widely in the Atlantic world than indicated above. His abolitionist counselors, in their correspondence and at trial, repeatedly referred to their client as hailing from Virginia. In addition, there is evidence that he may have been born in Africa, as was suggested during a moment of the trial when one of Somerset's counsel assumed the voice of the aggrieved slave: "It is true, I was a slave; kept as a slave, in Africa. I was first put in chains on board a British ship, and carried from Africa to America." Whether Somerset's lawyer at this juncture in the trial was drawing directly on his client's life history, or whether he was providing a generalized description of the experiences and actions of runaway slaves throughout the capital, we cannot know. The speech was probably conceived as a mixture of both.

15. Equiano, *The Interesting Narrative and Other Writings,* rev. ed., 179–181.

16. Norton, "The Fate of Some Black Loyalists of the American Revolution," 402–426; Granville Sharp to Archbishop of Canterbury, 1 August 1786, in Sharp, *Memoirs of Granville Sharp* (hereafter MGS), 261–264, 263. "The present set of unfortunate Negroes that are starving in our streets were brought here on very different occasions. Some, indeed, have been brought as servants, but chiefly by officers; others were Royalists from America; but most are seamen, who have navigated the King's ships from the East and West Indies, or have served in the war."

17. Coke, "Memorial of Benjn. Whitcuff," 132.

18. Coke, "Memorial of John Twine—a Black," 197; Coke, "Memorial of Samuel Burke—Black," 197–198.

19. Smeathman, *Plan of a Settlement;* Smeathman, "Henry Smeathman to Dr. [Thomas?] Knowles (21 July 1783)," 281–287.

20. Sharp, *Memoirs of Granville Sharp,* 260–261.

21. Smeathman, "Henry Smeathman to Dr. [Thomas?] Knowles (21 July 1783)," 279–280. In this introductory letter to a longer piece more directly concerned with Smeathman's Sierra Leone proposal, the doctor writes as follows concerning his relationship with slave traders: "Mr. Wilding is my particular friend, and though engaged in the Slave Trade, in other respects a man of great sense, honor and candor. I should be glad however to have no sort of connection with any concerned in the Slave Trade."

22. Smeathman, *Plan of a Settlement,* 1 (first quotation), 6 (second quotation), 13–14 (third quotation), and 18 (fourth quotation).

23. Ibid., 9, 10.

24. Ibid., 10–12. "The adventurers on this new establishment will be under the care of a Physician, who has had four years practice on the coast of Africa, and as many in the West Indies. He is qualified, from his knowledge of the country, and of the disorders that generally prevail there, to afford them much valuable information; and being well provided, and accompanied by skillful assistants, in Surgery, Midwifery, Chemistry, and other medical arts; and by several prudent and experienced women, they will enjoy every necessary assistance."

25. Smeathman, *Plan of a Settlement,* 5–6 (raising the town), 12 (the school), and 15–16 (the judiciary).

26. "Proceedings of the Committee for the Relief of Black Poor," 10 May 1786, NA-Kew, T1/631 (firearms); "Proceedings of the Committee for the Relief of Black Poor," 17 May 1786, NA-Kew, T1/631; "State of the Black Poor Accounts," 16 May 1786, NA-Kew, T1/631 (potential migrants). From May 10–15, 1786, the committee paid six pence to some 327 people.

27. "Proceedings of the Committee for the Relief of Black Poor," 7 June 1786, NA-Kew, T1/632.

28. "Proceedings of the Committee for the Relief of Black Poor," 7 June 1786, NA-Kew, T1/632; "Instrument of Agreement," n.d. [1786], NA-Kew, T1/632.

29. "Proceedings of the Committee for the Relief of Black Poor," 17 May 1786, NA-Kew, T1/631; "Proceedings of the Committee for the Relief of Black Poor," 7 June 1786, NA-Kew, T1/632.

30. "Proceedings of the Committee for the Relief of Black Poor," 14 June 1786, NA-Kew, T1/632. A main issue in the committee meeting of this date was "bringing the Design to the more speedy and happy Issue." To keep from offending some parties, the committee also resolved as follows: "That in order to prevent the countenancing of any Person to emigrate

against the Rights of Parents or Masters, it be advertised in the Gazette and in two Evening Papers that all Persons, Blacks and People of Colour, intended for an African Settlement may be seen at the White Raven behind the London Hospital at the next Payment of their Allowance, and if the Lords of the treasury think any other Precaution necessary they will please to give directions to their Solicitor in order that the same be not omitted."

31. "Proceedings of the Committee for the Relief of Black Poor," 24 May 1786, NA-Kew, T1/631; "Proceedings of the Committee for the Relief of Black Poor," 7 June 1786, NA-Kew, T1/632 (the delegates); "Proceedings of the Committee for the Relief of the [sic] Black Poor," 3 July 1786, NA-Kew, T1/633 (Smeathman's death). At the May 24, 1786, meeting the committee expressed a desire that those receiving assistance be organized into companies under the direction of a corporal. The selection of representatives, however, may have already been a fate accompli, for at Hanway's meeting with potential migrants on June 3, though there is little evidence that they had arranged themselves into companies, there is an indication that there already existed a group of informal delegates, for nine men were ready to meet with Hanway to express the concerns of the larger group.

32. Sharp, *Memoirs of Granville Sharp*, 268; "Proceedings of the Committee for Relief of Black Poor," 5 July 1786, NA-Kew, T1/633. On the same day the government agreed to back Smeathman's emigration plan, the doctor was too tired to share the news in person with his supporter Granville Sharp. In a letter dated April 12, 1786, Smeathman apologized for missing an appointment, writing that "Extreme fatigue prevents him from having the honour of waiting on Mr. S[harp]." On July 4, Jonas Hanway met with a representative from the Treasury to ask whether the government was firm on the destination to which the black poor were to be shipped. The official replied that the government had no opinion on the matter, except that it held the Committee for the Black Poor responsible for determining and organizing whatever was to be done with the capital's black beggars.

33. Before endorsing a settlement in the Bahamas, the committee briefly considered Canada and Gambia. "Proceedings of the Committee for Relief of Black Poor," 5 July 1786, NA-Kew, T1/633 (Bahamas); "Proceedings of the Committee for the Relief of the [sic] Black Poor," 12 July 1786, NA-Kew, T1/633 (Nova Scotia); "Proceedings of the Committee for Relief of Black Poor," 28 July 1786, NA-Kew, T1/636 (Gambia); "Proceedings of the Committee for the Relief of the [sic] Black Poor," 10 July 1786, NA-Kew, T1/633 (settling on the Bahamas).

34. "Proceedings of the Committee for Relief of Black Poor," 15 July 1786, NA-Kew, T1/633.

35. "Proceedings of the Committee for Relief of Black Poor," 15 July 1786, NA-Kew, T1/633. The penultimate resolution of the meeting read: "Resolved That Messrs. Bryan be desired to wait on the Lords of the Treasury with the following Note signed by the Chairman, Viz. 'My Lords, Messrs. Bryan the Persons named in the Minutes appearing to the Committee to be well qualified to take the Charge of conveying the Black Poor abroad and superintending them till they can be properly settled; the committee think it their duty to give them this Introduction to Your Lordships, that you may hear their Proposals and take such Measures as may be judged necessary.'"

36. "Proceedings of the Committee for Relief of Black Poor," 26 July 1786, NA-Kew, T1/634 (quotations). To the committee, the authors of the Bahamas proposal appeared "very intelligent and well acquainted with the West Indies" ("Proceedings of the Committee for the Relief of the [sic] Black Poor," 10 July 1786, NA-Kew, T1/633). If so, their proposal for a settlement at Great Inagua was simply callous. Great Inagua is the driest island in the Bahamas archipelago (the settlement proposal claimed it was among the wettest). Geopolitically, the place was terribly vulnerable: the island lay in the shadow of Spanish Cuba and French

St. Domingue. Agriculturally, it was only of nominal value, a fact granted by the authors of the proposal when they admitted that it was not possible to settle the black poor on any other island in the Bahamas since "the Old Inhabitants of Providence and the Loyalist[s] have taken up all the places worth having And they would not approve of those People to mix with them." Indeed, as late as 1810, less than fifty people called Great Inagua home. Wm. Bryan and Brister Bryan, "Messrs. Bryans Proposals," n.d. [c.a. 8 July 1786], Enclosed with to George Marsh et. al. to Thomas Steele. 2 August 1786, NA-Kew, T1/634; Craton and Saunders, *Islanders in the Stream,* vol. 1: map 2, table 5.

37. "Proceedings of the Committee for Relief of Black Poor," 28 July 1786, NA-Kew, T1/636.

38. "Proceedings of the Committee for Relief of Black Poor," 28 July 1786, NA-Kew, T1/636; Jonas Hanway to The Rt. Honble. the Lords Commsrs. of his Majesty's Treasury, 28 July 1786, NA-Kew, T1/634. The July 28 meeting sounded a death knell for the Bahamas plan. Following that meeting, Jonas Hanway wrote the Treasury, "As to the Bahama Islands the Blacks are totally disinclined to go, and consequently that Proposal cannot be carried into execution."

39. Jonas Hanway to The Rt. Honble. the Lords Commsrs. of his Majesty's Treasury, 28 July 1786, NA-Kew, T1/634.

40. Macaulay, Turnbull, and Gregory, to The Right Honourable the Lords Commissioners of His Majesty's Treasury, 28 July 1786, NA-Kew, T1/634 (Canada proposal); "Proceedings of the Committee for Relief of Black Poor," 31 July 1786, NA-Kew, T1/634; George Peters to Thomas Steele, 31 July 1786, NA-Kew, T1/634 (black response).

41. "Proceedings of the Committee for the Relief of Black Poor," 4 August 1786, NA-Kew, T1/634 (all quotations). Apparently, Smeathman shared with the committee his ideas on slavery and the slave trade (ideas that were conspicuously absent from his 1786 *Plan* but pronounced in the 1783 version), because the committee later responded as follows concerning the strength of Smeathman's antislavery sentiment: "With respect to the deceased Mr. Smeathman, he had the art of telling his Story very well and represented things in the most favourable light, but in the latter days of his life he avowed his Intention of *trafficking in Men,* so far that he would buy though he would not sell. The Committee thought that his Judgment misled him if not his heart; and if he had not changed his mind or said that he would acquiesce in the Sentiments of the Committee, the Committee would have certainly dropped any further connection with him. . . . Mr. Smeathman held only that he would upon no consideration sell the Man that he should buy, but unluckily nobody believed or had faith in such a Doctrine. To buy and forgo all the advantages of selling was not credible."

42. "Proceedings of the Committee for the Relief of Black Poor," 4 August 1786, NA-Kew, T1/634.

SIX

MIGRATION AND THE IMPOSSIBLE DEMANDS OF LEAVING LONDON

1. "Proceedings of the Committee for Relief of Black Poor," 25 August 1786, NA-Kew, T1/635; George Marsh et al. to Committee for the Relief of the Black Poor, 30 August 1786, NA-Kew, ADM 106/2347; "Agreement Between Mr. Jos. Irwin and The Black Poor [Copy]," 6 October 1786, NA-Kew, T1/638; George Marsh et ai. to Secretaries Treasury, 19 October 1786, NA-Kew, T1/636; George Marsh et al. to Committee for the Relief of the Black Poor, 19 October 1786, NA-Kew, ADM 106/2347; George Peters to George Rose, 24 October 1786,

NA-Kew, T1/638; "Proceedings of the Committee for Relief of Black Poor," 24 October 1786, NA-Kew, T1/638.

2. "Proceedings of the Committee for Relief of Black Poor," 1 December 1786, NA-Kew, T1/638; George Marsh et al. to Mr. Irving, 4 December 1786, NA-Kew, ADM 106/2347. Vassa's appointment was made official in early December. But it is clear from the minutes of the Committee that he was at work aboard the transports as early as November.

3. "Proceedings of the Committee for Relief of Black Poor," 6 October 1786, NA-Kew, T1/636; "Proceedings of the Committee for Relief of the [sic] Black Poor," 13 October 1786, NA-Kew, T1/638; "Most Humbly submitted to the Consideration of the Committee as a Form of Certificate for each person when shipp'd going to Sierra Leona," n.d., Enclosed with Proceedings of the Committee for the Relief of Black Poor, 6 October 1786, NA-Kew, T1/636; George Peters to George Rose, 24 October 1786, NA-Kew, T1/638.

4. "Proceedings of the Committee for Relief of Black Poor," 6 October 1786, NA-Kew, T1/636; "Agreement Between Mr. Jos. Irwin and The Black Poor [Copy]," 6 October 1786, NA-Kew, T1/638.

5. "List of Names of Black Persons embarked on board the Atlantic Captn. Muirhead," 22 November 1786, NA-Kew, T1/638; "A List of Names of Black persons embarked on board the Bellisarius Captn Sill," 22 November 1786, NA-Kew, T1/638.

6. Samuel Hoare to George Rose, 6 December 1786, NA-Kew, T1/638. "The Committee submit to their Lordships whether it may not be proper to issue a Proclamation stating the Provision which is made for establishing a free Settlement on the Coast of Africa, and enjoining all those who have been relieved by the humanity of the British Government to go on board the Ships which are now ready for their reception, and that Ten Days after the Date thereof all Persons of that description who are found begging or lurking about the Street will be taken up on the Vagrants Act." Two days earlier, the Treasury suggested to the Committee that they might have to resort to strict enforcement of the Vagrancy Act in order to compel blacks to board the ships. Steven J. Braidwood thinks the plan never came to fruition (Braidwood, *Black Poor and White Philanthropists,* 139–142).

7. "Proceedings of the Committee for Relief of Black Poor," 16 January 1787, NA-Kew, T1/641; Gustavus Vassa, "A List of all the People who are embarked on board the Atlantic now lying at the Motherbank," 16 February 1787, Enclosed with George Marsh to Secretaries Treasury, 27 February 1787, NA-Kew, T1/643; Gustavus Vassa, "A List of all the Names of those People who are now on board the Vernon laying [sic] at Motherbank," 18 February 1787, Enclosed with George Marsh to Secretaries Treasury, 27 February 1787, NA-Kew, T1/643; Gustavus Vassa, "The Names of Men, Women & Children who are now on board the Belisarius Captn. Sill lying at the Motherbank," 16 February 1787, Enclosed with George Marsh to Secretaries Treasury, 27 February 1787, NA-Kew, T1/643; "Proceedings of the Committee for Relief of Black Poor," 1 December 1786, NA-Kew, T1/638; "Agreement Between Mr. Jos. Irwin and The Black Poor [Copy]," 6 October 1786, NA-Kew, T1/638.

8. Landers, *Death and the Metropolis,* 203–241; "Proceedings of the Committee for Relief of Black Poor," 1 December 1786, NA-Kew, T1/638; "Proceedings of the Committee for Relief of Black Poor," 16 January 1787, NA-Kew, T1/641; Equiano, *The Interesting Narrative and Other Writings,* rev. ed., 228.

9. Wadstrom, *An essay on colonization,* paragraphs 335 and 679; Equiano, *The Interesting Narrative and Other Writings,* rev. ed., 228. An advocate for African colonization and an apologist for the organizing acumen of the Committee, Wadstrom blamed the emigrants themselves for their illnesses, but in so doing confirmed the transports' unhealthy environ-

ment. "From the disorders they brought on board with them, aggravated by debauchery and confinement, these people became very sickly during their long detention in the British Channel. . . . From these causes 50 died before they left Plymouth" [the transports' last English port of call].

10. "Proceedings of the Committee for Relief of Black Poor," 24 October 1786, NA-Kew, T1/638 (quotation); George Marsh et al. to Committee for the Relief of the Black Poor, 29 November 1786, NA-Kew, ADM 106/2347; Robert Fanshawe to Philip Stephens, 29 March 1787, NA-Kew, T1/644; Equiano, *The Interesting Narrative and Other Writings*, rev. ed., 229; Wadstrom, *An essay on colonization*, paragraph 335.

11. George Rogers et al. to Secretaries Treasury, 1 January 1787, NA-Kew, T1/641; "Proceedings of the Committee for Relief of Black Poor," 19 January 1787, NA-Kew, T1/641; George Marsh et al. to Mr. Vasa [*sic*], 22 January 1787, NA-Kew, ADM 106/2347.

12. *Morning Herald*, 13 January 1787, 4; Equiano, *The Interesting Narrative and Other Writings*, rev. ed., 228; *Public Advertiser*, 4 April 1787, 3.

13. *Public Advertiser*, 6, 18, 22 December 1786 and 4, 12, 29 January 1787, quoted in Wilson, *The Loyal Blacks*, 145–146; Cugoano, *Thoughts and Sentiments on the Evil and Wicked Traffic of the Slavery and Commerce of the Human Species*, 142. "For can it be readily conceived that government would establish a free colony for them nearly on the spot, while it supports its forts and garrisons, to ensnare, merchandize, and to carry others into captivity and slavery."

14. Cross index, "An Alphabetical List of the Black People who have received the Bounty from Government," n.d. [6 December 1786?], NA-Kew, T1/638; Gustavus Vassa, "A List of all the People who are embarked on board the Atlantic now lying at the Motherbank," 16 February 1787, Enclosed with George Marsh to Secretaries Treasury, 27 February 1787, NA-Kew, T1/643; Gustavus Vassa, "A List of all the Names of those People who are now on board the Vernon laying [*sic*] at Motherbank," 18 February 1787, Enclosed with George Marsh to Secretaries Treasury, 27 February 1787, NA-Kew, T1/643; Gustavus Vassa, "The Names of Men, Women & Children who are now on board the Belisarius Captn. Sill lying at the Motherbank," 16 February 1787, Enclosed with George Marsh to Secretaries Treasury, 27 February 1787, NA-Kew, T1/643.

15. Eight lists form the basis of the following analysis: "A List of Names of Black persons embarked on board the Bellisarius Captn Sill," 22 November 1786, NA-Kew, T1/638; "List of Names of Black Persons embarked on board the Atlantic Captn. Muirhead," 22 November 1786, NA-Kew, T1/638; "An Alphabetical List of the Black People who have received the Bounty from Government," n.d. [6 December 1786?], NA-Kew, T1/638; "Agreement Between Mr. Jos. Irwin and The Black Poor [Copy]," 6 October 1786, NA-Kew, T1/638; Gustavus Vassa, "The Names of Men, Women & Children who are now on board the Belisarius Captn. Sill lying at the Motherbank," 16 February 1787, Enclosed with George Marsh to Secretaries Treasury, 27 February 1787, NA-Kew, T1/643; Gustavus Vassa, "List of Black Poor who have embarked on board the Atlantic, Vernon, & Belisarius Transports," 27 February 1787, NA-Kew, T1/643; Gustavus Vassa, "A List of all the People who are embarked on board the Atlantic now lying at the Motherbank," 16 February 1787, Enclosed with George Marsh to Secretaries Treasury, 27 February 1787, NA-Kew, T1/643; Gustavus Vassa, "A List of all the Names of those People who are now on board the Vernon laying [*sic*] at Motherbank," 18 February 1787, Enclosed with George Marsh to Secretaries Treasury, 27 February 1787, NA-Kew, T1/643.

16. "Proceedings of the Committee for the Relief of Black Poor," 17 May 1786, NA-Kew, T1/631 (quotation). Single black women's avoidance is in line with the kinds of choices black women made throughout the eighteenth-century Atlantic regarding flight or migration. In

the Americas, male slaves were much more likely to run away than were female slaves, whose domestic concerns, often children or family, tied them more firmly to a specific place. A similar dynamic may have been at work in London.

17. Gerzina, *Black England*, 68–89.

18. The following are the new recruits probably introduced to the agreement by their spouses (whose names are given in parenthesis): Mary Adams (George Adams); Hariot Allamaza (Joseph Allamaza); Elizabeth Benn (Isaac Benn); Fanny Castor (Charles Castor); Daniel Coventry (Rachael Coventry); Margaret Denham (Richard Denham); William Green (Elizabeth Green); Charlotte Harris (Thomas Harris); Mary Harvey (John Harvey); Ann Holder (Thomas Holder); Mary Johnson (James Johnson); Margaret London (John London); Elizabeth Minor (George Minor); Sarah Parker (James Parker); Sarah Parker (Thomas Parker); Elizabeth Ramsey (John William Ramsey); Jane Read (James Read); Elizabeth Robertson (Robert Robertson); Ann Sterling (Lewis Sterling); Catherine Thomas (John Thomas); Ann Thompson (Alexander Thompson); and Mary Thompson (Charles Thompson).

19. Mary Bradley (Richard Bradley); Darcus [Darius] Brooks (Aaron Brooks); Elizabeth Clarke (George Clark[e]); Elizabeth Damerain (Thomas Damerain [Demain]); Betsey Dover (William Dover); Elizabeth Dyer (John Dyer); Maria Green (William Green); Peggy [Margaret] Higgins (William Higgins); Rebecca Innis (Joseph Innis); Elizabeth Lemmen [Lemmon] (John Lemmon); Betsey Lynch (John Lynch); Mary Morris (John Morris [Morres]); Ann Pardo (Emanuel Pardo); Elizabeth Raper (William Raper); Jane Richardson (Thomas Richardson); Hannah Richardson (William Richardson); Susan Rose (Lewis Rose); Peggy Smyth [Smith] (William Smith); Barbara [Barbary] Thomas (John Thomas); and Mary Wood (Samuel Wood).

20. Norton, "The Fate of Some Black Loyalists of the American Revolution," 417–418.

21. The coming and going of married and related prospective migrants is only suggestive of what might have occurred among the majority of the eighty-three emigrants who left the ships during the forty days between the making of the November muster and when the *Atlantic* and *Belisarius* sailed toward Portsmouth. But because there is no firm evidence of great mortality as the transports waited first at Deptford and then at Gravesend and conversely because there is evidence that there was significant sickness on the transports during this same period of time, it is likely that the majority of those leaving the ships did so after calculating that it was in their best interests to do so.

22. "Proceedings of the Committee for Relief of Black Poor," 1 December 1786, NA-Kew, T1/638; Gustavus Vassa, "A List of all the People who are embarked on board the Atlantic now lying at the Motherbank," 16 February 1787, Enclosed with George Marsh to Secretaries Treasury, 27 February 1787, NA-Kew, T1/643; Gustavus Vassa, "A List of all the Names of those People who are now on board the Vernon laying [*sic*] at Motherbank," 18 February 1787, Enclosed with George Marsh to Secretaries Treasury, 27 February 1787, NA-Kew, T1/643.

23. For the population of black London, see note 5.2 above.

SEVEN

FROM SLAVES TO FREE SUBJECTS IN BRITISH NORTH AMERICA

1. Gipson, *The Triumphant Empire*, 127–155 (esp. 143–145); Conrad, *They Planted Well;* Conrad, *Intimate Relations;* Reid, "Change and Continuity in Nova Scotia, 1758–1775," 49; Hartlen, "Bound for Nova Scotia," 123–128; Winks, *The Blacks in Canada*, 1–28.

2. Several repositories preserve manuscript copies of the register, including the NA-Kew

(PRO 30/55/100); the National Archives (Papers of the Continental Congress: Miscellaneous Papers: Relating to Specific States); the Public Archives of Nova Scotia (PANS, vol. 423); and the Public Archives of Canada (PAC, Royal Institution, American Manuscripts, vol. 55). The "Book of Negroes" is available on microfilm in the "British Headquarter (Sir Guy Carleton) papers," and in parts among *The Papers of the Continental Congress, 1774–1789*, as "Inspection roll of Negro emigrants" (on M332, R7, f5, 21, 25, 26, 29, 30, 44, 47, and 53; and on M247, R66, i53, p276). A published version of the inspection rolls is in Hodges, *The Black Loyalist Directory*.

3. Walker, *The Black Loyalists*, 3; Wilson, *The Loyal Blacks*, 69; Sir Guy Carleton Branch United Empire Loyalists' Association of Canada, *Carleton's Loyalist Index*.

4. The onetime chattel of famous men—"Deborah . . . pock marked. . . . Formerly slave to General Washington"—headed to Nova Scotia with the remarkable former slaves of unremarkable men—"Prince Augustus . . . feeble old fellow. . . . Formerly slave to John Simon of Boston New England; left him upon the Evacuation of the Town." There were those whose accounts suggest that they had been born in Africa, worked as slaves in the Americas, regained their freedom in Europe, returned free to the colonies, and now wished to try their life in Nova Scotia. And emblematic of all of these—how little of black life during the war the "Book of Negroes" actually captures, yet how suggestive it is of the consequences attending the tangled routes blacks followed to Nova Scotia—there were voyagers who could not, to the satisfaction of the auditors, articulate anything about their previous course but by their actions made their intentions quite clear: Aboard the ship *Blacket*, officials found "Charles. . . . Came from Jamaica, can't understand him" (Hodges, *The Black Loyalist Directory*, 16 [Deborah], 69 [Prince Augustus], 15 [African], 31 [Charles]. Hodges, ed., *The Black Loyalist Directory*, 8 (soldiers), 105 (families, for instance Joseph and Silvie Tramell), 17 (former rebels, for instance Gad Saunders), 66 (women and children, for instance Sarah and Hannah Jackson, Mary Ann, Elizabeth, and Nancy), and 75 (children alone).

5. Mullin, *Africa in America*, Appendix II; Franklin and Schweninger, *Runaway Slaves*, Tables 3 and 4; Sir Guy Carleton Branch United Empire Loyalists' Association of Canada, *Carleton's Loyalist Index*.

6. White, *Ar'n't I a Woman?* 70–74; Franklin and Schweninger, *Runaway Slaves*, 210–213; Camp, *Closer to Freedom*, 36–39.

7. Quarles, *The Negro in the American Revolution*, chapters 2, 7, and 8. Since the first days of the Anglo-American conflict, British commanders sought to undermine American resistance by offering liberty to slaves and other unfree peoples who would desert their rebel masters. Among the king's forces in Virginia such expediencies were practiced as early as the winter of 1775. By the British invasion of Georgia and South Carolina in 1778, what began as expediency was all but official policy. Most likely, it was word of this policy that drew the Silver Bluff slaves toward Savannah.

8. Byrd, "Captives and Voyagers," Ph.D. diss., Appendix 3-1.

9. George, "An Account of the Life of Mr. David George," 477.

10. Ibid.

11. King, "Memoirs of the Life of Boston King, a Black Preacher," 110.

12. Ibid.

13. Ibid., 107.

14. Ibid.

15. George, "An Account of the Life of Mr. David George," 477. At his eventual arrival in Nova Scotia, George mentions that he gained leave to disembark the ship while others, his family included, remained on board. When introduced to the general then commanding

the Maritimes and upon showing him his papers, the commandant ordered a sergeant to fetch George's family from the just-arrived ship. Given George's habit of falling in with very helpful British officers wherever he landed, it is likely that he carried letters of introduction since leaving Savannah.

16. King, "Memoirs of the Life of Boston King, a Black Preacher," 108.

17. Ibid., 109.

18. Raboteau, *Slave Religion,* esp. 126, 149; Morgan, *Slave Counterpoint,* 420. In terms of sheer mass, black congregants were nearly inconsequential. Even if there were 2,000 black Christians in Virginia in 1770—and there is no evidence that there were—the state's enslaved population at that date exceeded 180,000 (more than ninety-five times the size of the exaggerated, hypothetical black Christian community just proposed). Similarly, in South Carolina during the 1760s contemporaries estimated that only about 1 percent of the enslaved population was baptized (see Morgan, *Slave Counterpoint,* Table 10 and 422; and Raboteau, *Slave Religion,* 131). For the scattered exceptions, see Pilcher, "Samuel Davies and the Instruction of Negroes in Virginia," 293–300; Sensbach, *A Separate Canaan;* Sensbach, *Rebecca's Revival;* Sobel, *Trabelin' On;* Sobel, *The World They Made Together.*

19. Windley, *Runaway Slave Advertisements,* 1:50–51, 339; Frey and Wood, *Come Shouting to Zion,* 114. The authors argue convincingly that "Wartime disturbances slowed down the momentum of the evangelical movement among whites but accelerated it among blacks."

20. George, "An Account of the Life of Mr. David George," 475.

21. Ibid., 475.

22. Ibid., 476. That the Silver Bluff church tripled in size during the period in which white, outside ministers were not allowed to attend testifies that Silver Bluff's black Baptists were hardly detoured by their quarantine. Indeed, it appears that the church—now cut off from outside support but also independent from outside censure—flourished *because of* and not in spite of its new isolation. Further, recall that when Silver Bluff's enslaved blacks left the estate for the promise of freedom held out by the British at Savannah, the troops receiving them jailed David George for fear that he was both inclined and capable of leading the just-arrived refugees back to Silver Bluff and, in due time, into their former servitude. Whether these were David George's intentions or whether it was the intention of the people themselves, the fact that the British believed jailing George was an antidote is, in itself, evidence of George's authority and how it developed in Silver Bluff during the time when the church was isolated from outside influence.

23. Rippon, "Sketch of the Black Baptist Church at Savannah," 344 (emphasis in original). At the time of his writing, George Liele was in Jamaica, where he was pastor to a black church in Kingston

24. Brooks, "The Priority of the Silver Bluff Church and Its Promoters," 127–196 (esp. 184–189); Little, "George Liele and the Rise of Independent Black Baptist Churches in the Lower South and Jamaica," 188–204; Rippon, "Sketch of the Black Baptist Church at Savannah," 339–343; George, "An Account of the Life of Mr. David George," 475; Rippon, "An Account of Several Baptist Churches," 336; Rippon, "Account of the Negro Church at Savannah, and of Two Negro Ministers," 541; Rippon, "From the Rev. Abraham Marshall, Who Formed the Negro Church at Savannah, to Mr. Rippon," 545.

25. King, "Memoirs of the Life of Boston King, a Black Preacher," 157.

26. Ibid.

27. Ibid.; Jones, "Sir Guy Carleton and the Close of the American War of Independence, 1782–83," 239–242.

28. King, "Memoirs of the Life of Boston King, a Black Preacher," 157–158.

29. Berlin, *Slaves Without Masters;* Hodges, *The Black Loyalist Directory,* passim (first quotation); Carretta, *Unchained Voices,* 348 n. 29 (second quotation). See also *Oxford English Dictionary,* 2nd ed., s.v. "bottom," OED Online, 7 Aug. 2005, http://dictionary.oed.com/. "[T]o stand on one's own bottom: to act for oneself, be independent."

EIGHT

BLACK SOCIETY AND THE LIMITS OF BRITISH FREEDOM

1. MacKinnon, *This Unfriendly Soil,* 1–26 passim and 30; Walker, *The Black Loyalists,* 28. In the main, the evacuees settled in three areas: in and around Halifax, the capital city; on the northwest side of the Nova Scotian peninsula at such towns as Annapolis Royal and Digby; and at a new settlement to the southwest developed solely in anticipation of the loyalist deluge, Port Roseway. Black loyalists followed these general patterns of settlement (a full 10 percent of the people at Halifax and environs, for instance, may have been black). But in addition to establishing themselves within larger loyalist settlements, blacks founded and were forced into segregated communities of color: At Port Roseway, black evacuees were among the vanguard who laid out and built the settlement's main town; yet these laborers, and other blacks who followed, settled en masse to the northwest, at a place they named Birchtown. Along the Bay of Fundy, there were hundreds of blacks at Digby and Annapolis Royal, but there was also the all-black hamlet of Brindley Town just outside of Digby proper. Bordering St. Georges and Chedabucto Bays along Nova Scotia's desolate eastern edge, blacks made their way to Manchester and Guysborough with most of that area's loyalists but established as well the region's all-black village of Little Tracadie. Such all-black communities varied in size. Birchtown had more than fifteen hundred inhabitants. Sixty-five black families lived at Brindley Town. Less than two hundred blacks settled at Little Tracadie (Walker, *The Black Loyalists,* 39 n. 59).

2. Ells, "Clearing the Decks for the Loyalists," 43–58; Ells, "Settling the Loyalists in Nova Scotia," 105–109.

3. Walker, *The Black Loyalists,* 23–30.

4. Rawlyk, "The Guysborough Negroes," 26; Dennis, *Down in Nova Scotia,* 358.

5. Raymond, "The Founding of Shelburne," 265 (first quotation); George, "An Account of the Life of Mr. David George," 480 (second quotation).

6. Clarkson, "Some Account of the New Colony at Sierra Leona," 160–162, 229–231. So palpable was the fear of this kind of re-enslavement, stories of such disasters resounded for generations. Even in the twentieth century, Birchtowners recalled how unscrupulous white captains used to sail into the harbor, entice black laborers aboard ship, and sail off again" (Dennis, *Down in Nova Scotia,* 359).

7. Dennis, *Down in Nova Scotia,* 359. Contemporary accounts of Birchtown, even when they do not specifically mention the nature of black loyalist accommodation, relay a similar sense of deprivation. When William Dyott, a young adjutant stationed in Nova Scotia, visited the black settlement in the winter of 1788, he found the "huts miserable to guard against the inclemency of a Nova Scotia winter" and the whole place "beyond description wretched" (see Dyott, *Dyott's Diary,* 1:57).

8. Powell and Niven, *Archaeological Surveys in Two Black Communities, 1998.*

9. George, "An Account of the Life of Mr. David George," 481–482; Hart, *History of the County of Guysborough,* 63. There is a Thomas Thompson in the "Book of Negroes" described

as a "stout fellow" around twenty years old. He was formerly held in bondage by a Andrew Middleton of South Carolina, from whom Thompson escaped around 1779. See Hodges, *The Black Loyalist Directory*, 205.

10. J. Chamberlain to Lawrence Hartshorne, 26 December 1791, Clarkson Papers.

11. Ibid.

12. Wilson, *The Loyal Blacks*, 107 (Richardson et al.); Walker, *The Black Loyalists*, 27–28 (Brownsprigg); Thomas Peters, n.d. [received 18 December 1790], "The Humble Memorial and Petition of Thomas Peters. . . ." NA-Kew, CO 217/63.

13. George, "An Account of the Life of Mr. David George," 478.

14. Ibid., 478–480.

15. Ibid., 480–481.

16. Walker, *The Black Loyalists*, 67–68 (Church of England), 72–73 (Methodists), and 71–72 (Huntingdonians).

17. King, "Memoirs of the Life of Boston King, a Black Preacher," 158. As evidenced in the earlier account of David George's surrender to Christ, Christian conversion was a protracted and public ordeal whereby supplicants both searched for and proved to others their salvation through a series of trials and transformations. Challenged and troubled by the word of God, the ignorant and the evil embarked on a search to ease their hearts. After long suffering the physical and mental persecutions of sin and disobedience, they accepted that the only way to peace was to surrender all to Christ, to become His instrument, to be born again. In eighteenth-century evangelical churches, converts relayed their experiences to fellow believers who, after recognizing the affinity of the supplicant's experience to their own, accepted them into the body of Christ. Thus, criteria for conversion—however they might vary from denomination to denomination—admitted a certain equality among believers by virtue of establishing a baseline of Christian experience. This admission of equality was in theory only tacit, and in practice constantly contested and denied. What matters more, however, is that any admission of rough equality before Christ existed at all and that it could be taken as a channel of communication and negotiation between parties whose social standing might ordinarily preclude both.

18. King, "Memoirs of the Life of Boston King, a Black Preacher," 158.

19. Ibid.

20. Ibid.

21. George, "An Account of the Life of Mr. David George," 480–481.

22. Garrettson, *American Methodist Pioneer*, 246, 128.

23. Spray, *The Blacks in New Brunswick*, Appendix IV. Spelling and punctuation have been modernized to clarify Fisher's meaning.

24. Thomas Peters, n.d. [received 18 December 1790], "The Humble Memorial and Petition of Thomas Peters. . . ." NA-Kew, CO 217/63.

NINE

THE EFFECTS OF EXODUS

1. Clarkson, "Some Account of the New Colony at Sierra Leona," 230.

2. The best essays on Peters are Nash, "Thomas Peters"; Fyfe, "Thomas Peters," 4–13. Also see Byrd, "Captives and Voyagers," Ph.D. diss., Appendix 3-2.

3. Wilson, *The Loyal Blacks*, 179. The secretary of state for the home department at this time, William Wyndham Grenville, was in charge of colonial affairs.

4. Thomas Peters, n.d. [received 18 December 1790], "The Humble Memorial and Petition of Thomas Peters. . . ." NA-Kew, CO 217/63.

5. Sharp, *Memoirs of Granville Sharp*, 270–274, 324; Sierra Leone Company, *Substance of the Report of the Court of Directors*, 6–7; Falconbridge, *Narrative of two voyages to the River Sierra Leone, during the years 1791–3*, 2nd ed., 9–10.

6. Anstey, *The Atlantic Slave Trade and British Abolition*, 255–273.

7. Braidwood, *Black Poor and White Philanthropists*, chapter 5; Falconbridge, *Narrative of two voyages to the River Sierra Leone, during the years 1791–3*, 2nd ed., 59–64, 90.

8. Sierra Leone Company, *Substance of the Report of the Court of Directors*, 46–47; Sierra Leone Company, *Postscript to the report of the court of directors*, 71–72.

9. Henry Dundas to John Parr, 6 August 1791, NA-Kew, CO 217/63. The apparent certainty of Dundas's orders were undercut by other instructions that arrived from an undersecretary in the Home Department, Evan Nepan. So, although there was an inquiry into Peters's charges, his accusations were ultimately found wanting in several particulars. Further, Robin Winks has suggested that Nepan's communications with Parr may have suggested to the governor that Dundas's letter of August 6 was not "to be taken literally" (Winks, *The Blacks in Canada*, 68–69). Eventually, the colonial office was successful in establishing black regiments manned from its American territories (see Buckley, *Slaves in Red Coats*).

10. Clarkson, "Mission to America," 6 August 1791 (first quotation); Clarkson, "Some Account of the New Colony at Sierra Leona," 230 (second quotation). More generally, see Wilson, *John Clarkson and the African Adventure*, 54–56.

11. Clarkson, "Mission to America," 6 October 1791; Thomas Peters to Lawrence Hartshorne, 10 October 1791, in Clarkson, "Mission to America." In practice, once Clarkson, Taylor, and Peters landed in the Maritimes, two modes of recruitment obtained. One involved black settlers meeting directly with agents of the company or the colonial government or encountering official advertisements in the local press about the settlement at Sierra Leone. In turn, these kinds of encounters informed a more electric mode of recruitment traveling along the communication networks of black Nova Scotians.

12. Details of the agents' visits to Preston and Port L'Hebert are taken from the following: Clarkson, "Mission to America," 12, 13, 20, 23 October 1791, 1 November 1791.

13. Stephen Bluck to Lawrence Hartshorne, 10 October 1791, in Clarkson, "Mission to America," 14 October 1791; Thomas Peters to Lawrence Hartshorne, in Clarkson, "Mission to America," 10 October 1791. Before the arrival of Clarkson and Taylor, Thomas Peters began to cut a swath toward the Bay of Fundy in order to alert those who sent him to London in the first place about the coming option for emigration. His trip, no doubt, must have helped spread the word about the company's proposals throughout central and western Nova Scotia.

14. Clarkson, "Mission to America," 25 October 1791.

15. Ibid., 26 October 1791.

16. Henry Dundas to John Parr, 6 August 1791, NA-Kew, CO 217/63; Clarkson, "Mission to America," 25 October 1791.

17. Sierra Leone Company, "[Proceedings of the Sierra Leone Company]," 2 August 1791, NA-Kew, CO 217/63; Sierra Leone Company, *Substance of the report delivered by the Court of Directors*, 5–6; Clarkson, "Mission to America," 25 October 1791.

18. Clarkson, "Mission to America," 25 October 1791.

19. Ibid.

20. Ibid.

21. Ibid., 26 October 1791.

22. Ibid., 12 November 1791. Clarkson and Taylor departed Shelburne for Halifax on 6 November 1791.

23. Wrigley et al., *English Population History from Family Reconstitution,* Tables 8.1 and 8.7; Bailyn, *Voyagers to the West,* 90–94, esp. Table 4.1.

24. Clarkson, "Mission to America," 21, 25 October 1791.

25. Ibid., 8 October 1791 (Philanthropos); 10 November 1791; 12 November 1791 (the former colony).

26. Ibid., 25 October 1791; 4 November 1791.

27. Ibid., 1 December 1791; 30 October 1791.

28. Mr. Williams to John Clarkson, 12 August 1791, Clarkson Papers; John Clarkson to Henry Thornton, 19 October 1791, in Clarkson, "Mission to America."

29. For brief backgrounds on Godfrey and Allen, see Hodges, *The Black Loyalist Directory,* 24–25. For Stephen Bluck's assessment of their character, see Stephen Bluck to Mr. Taylor, 24 November 1791, in Clarkson, "Mission to America."

30. Clarkson, "Mission to America," 13 November 1791; Stephen Bluck to Mr. Taylor, 24 November 1791, in Clarkson, "Mission to America."

31. Clarkson, "Mission to America," 24 November 1791.

32. Ibid., 2 November 1791; 30 October 1791. Clarkson, no student of Afro-Atlantic creole, recorded his conversation with the African as follows: "Took down the names of a man conditionally as before, he came originally from the coast of Africa, and spoke English indifferently: the following dialogue passed between us[:] 'Well my friend, I suppose you are thoroughly acquainted with the nature of the proposals offered to you by His Majesty' 'No Massa me no hear, nor no mind, me work like a slave cannot do worse Massa in any part of the world, therefore am determined to go with you Massa, if you please.' 'You must consider that this [is] a new Settlement, and should you keep your health must expect to meet with many difficulties if you engage in it' 'Me well know that Massa, me can work much, and care not for climate; if me die, me die, had rather die in me own Country than this cold place.'"

33. King, "Memoirs of the Life of Boston King, a Black Preacher," 261.

34. Clarkson, "Mission to America," 28, 29 October 1791; 18 November 1791. In his instructions to agents, Clarkson wrote: "I think you should object to take any people of the following description, those that are lame and cannot work for their living, as they will certainly starve in an unsettled Country; elderly single women, and in short any one who cannot maintain him or herself, unless the lame Man or Woman &c. has a Father, Brother, Sister, or some relation to take care of them. This I call common justice." In a letter to his superior in London, Clarkson admitted that of single women in particular he had "taken care that not one single woman has given in her name unless she could find a man to be answerable to maintain her; so that I have put them down in the different families accordingly" (John Clarkson to Henry Thornton, 1 December 1791, in Clarkson, "Mission to America").

35. For planning estimates, see Clarkson, "Mission to America," 12 November 1791. For informal censuses of the growing number of blacks émigrés in Halifax, see Clarkson, "Mission to America," 12, 18, 28 December 1791.

36. Clarkson, "Mission to America," 9 December 1791.

37. Ibid.

38. Ibid., 29 November 1791; 9, 10, 14 December 1791.

39. The Black People of Preston, "The Memorial of the Black People of Preston," n.d. [26 December 1791], in Clarkson, "Mission to America"; Clarkson, "Mission to America," 18 November 1791.

40. Clarkson, "Mission to America," 1, 18 November 1791; 12 December 1791.

41. Ibid., 9, 12, 13December 1791. In another place, Clarkson estimated that "upon a rough calculation there appears nearly 300 people almost naked" (Clarkson, "Mission to America," 10 December 1791).

42. Clarkson, "Mission to America," 15, 26 December 1791. For remarks on the Snowballs' flight from Virginia, and then from New York, see Hodges, *The Black Loyalist Directory*, 85, 115.

43. Clarkson, "Mission to America," 10 December 1791.

44. Ibid., 2 December 1791 (blacks working); 11 December 1791 (religious life); 13 December 1791 (religious life); 17 November 1791 (settlers' independence).

45. Ibid., 6, 26 December 1791.

46. Ibid., 10 December 1791 (relieving debt). A petition drafted by the inhabitants of Birchtown about the same time speaks as well to how circumstances of emigration may have contributed to a certain hyper-normalcy: "Whereas a number of us formerly were inhabitants of Birch Town near Shelburne Nova Scotia but now intending under inspection to embark for Sierra Leone would therefore humbly solicit; that on our arrival you will be pleased to Settle us as near as possible to the inhabitants of Preston, as they and us are intimately aquatinted, so in order to render us unanimous would be glad to be as nearly connected as possible, when the tract or tracts of land shall be laid out; humbly relying upon your interest in this matter, and in compliance with this request will be bound to pray" (John Stobo et al., "Petition," n.d. [26 December 1791], in Clarkson, "Mission to America").

47. Clarkson, "Mission to America," 6, 14 November 1791.

48. Ibid., 1, 11, 27, 28, 31 December 1791.

49. Ibid., 11 December 1791.

50. Ibid., 12 December 1791 (delegates' failure); John Clarkson to Henry Thornton, 19 October 1791, in Clarkson, "Mission to America," 19 October 1791 (first quotation); Clarkson, "Mission to America," 16 November 1791 (second quotation).

51. Clarkson, "Mission to America," 30 October 1791 (redeeming slaves); 10 December 1791 (debts). On provisions, see Clarkson, "Mission to America," 6 December 1791; 13 November 1791; John Clarkson and Lawrence Hartshorne to Richard Buckley, n.d. [13 December 1791], in Clarkson, "Mission to America"; Clarkson, "Mission to America," 15 December 1791. On ship conditions, see Clarkson, "Mission to America," 16, 17 November 1791; 1, 12, 14, 15, 27, 29, 30, 31 December 1791. The following is representative of Clarkson's efforts on behalf of enslaved would-be migrants: "In the afternoon, one of the free Blacks called upon me to say that he had stolen his son from his master, when he was going to carry him with him to America, and that he had secured him in the woods, till the vessel sail'd which was to take his master away. This boy was the occasion of my waiting upon two justices of the Peace on the 26th inst. the circumstance is as follows: The Master was a butcher of the most vile & abandoned character who had resided at Shelburne for some time, the boy had been bound as an apprentice to him till he arrived at the age of 21 years[.] his [*sic*] master was going to quit the Province and become a subject of the States of America, meaning to reside at Boston, and he had according to the laws of the Province notified his intentions in a public manner previous to his departure; he claimed the right to take his servant with him and the two justices partly acquiesced with him, but finding there was no time to lose as the vessel was upon the point of sailing, I told his parents to steal the child if they could and I would bring it to a trial for them afterwards as I was convinced the master meant upon his arrival at Boston to sell the boy for a slave. Having obtained the best legal opinion on the business, I secured the boy and came forward openly to justify the measure; but no one appearing

against he continued with his family and was enrolled for embarkation" (Clarkson, "Mission to America," 30 October 1791).

52. Clarkson, "Mission to America," 1 January 1792 (salute); John Clarkson to Henry Thornton, 19 October 1791, in Clarkson, "Mission to America" 19 October 1791 (Clarkson's commitment). As word circulated in Halifax about what had become of the former black colony at Sierra Leone, Clarkson wrote his superior in London concerning the safety of the people he was then conducting. "But I will now tell you what will certainly happen; should I meet with any determined resistance while the people are under my protection. . . . I will sacrifice my life in the defence of the meanest of them on board sooner than they should entertain a doubt of the sincerity of my intentions."

53. John Clarkson to Henry Thornton, 1 December 1791, in Clarkson, "Mission to America."

54. John Clarkson to Henry Thornton, 1 December 1791, in Clarkson, "Mission to America" (first quotation); Clarkson, "Mission to America," 11 December 1791 (second quotation); 14 November 1791 (third quotation); 3 December 1791 (my emphasis).

55. Clarkson, "Mission to America," 22 December 1791.

56. Fyfe, *"Our Children Free and Happy,"* 23.

TEN

ARRIVING IN SIERRA LEONE

1. Thomas B. Thompson, "Captain's Log Nautilus," 24 February 1787, NA-Kew, ADM 51/627.

2. Ibid., 27, 28 February 1787; 1 March 1787.

3. Ibid., 2, 13, 17, 18 March 1787.

4. *Public Advertiser,* 4 April 1787; Wadstrom, *An essay on colonization,* paragraphs 334 and 679. In the former passage Wadstrom implies that the majority of the mortality occurred while the ships were at Plymouth and in the channel. In the latter he suggests that a better part occurred before Plymouth. Griffith's letter lends support to the first interpretation. See also Sharp, *Memoirs of Granville Sharp,* 270.

5. *Public Advertiser,* 4 April 1787, 3.

6. George Marsh et al. to Secretaries Treasury, 23 March 1787, NA-Kew, T1/643 (quotation); Granville Sharp to Dr. Lettsom, 13 October 1788, M GS, 315–320.

7. Thomas B. Thompson to Navy Board, 21 March 1787, NA-Kew, T1/643; George Marsh et al. to Captain Thompson, 24 March 1787, NA-Kew, ADM 106/2347. Thompson did not let Irwin off without censure, writing that he did not find "Mr. Irwin the least calculated to conduct this business," and adding that he "never observed any wish of his to facilitate the sailing of the Ships, or any steps taken by him which might indicate that he had the welfare of the people the least at heart." All the same, Thompson eventually came down for Vassa's dismissal and the expulsion from the transports of some of the most discontented migrants, prompting the Navy Board to reply: "We have received your letter of [no dated given] and acquaint you we are sorry to hear of the conduct of the Commissary & Mr. Irwin, the former having always conducted himself properly whilst in the river; We wrote to the Lords of the Treasury & Admiralty thereon, and by the directions of the former have by this Post recall'd Mr. Vasa for his appointment, and you will receive orders from the Rt. Honble. the Lords Commissrs. of the Admiralty for your Pursers attending to the matters that were committed to Mr. Vasa's care."

8. Thomas B. Thompson, "Captain's Log Nautilus," 5 May 1787, NA-Kew, ADM 51/627.

Before arriving in Sierra Leone, Thompson discarded from the *Nautilus* "135 lbs of rotten cheese and 128 lbs of rancid butter." Provisions aboard the transports carrying the black poor would not have been better, and the commissary was probably not more motivated than Thompson to dump poor provisions. On crowding aboard the transports, see Granville Sharp to Dr. Lettsom, 13 October 1788, MGS, 315–320, 316.

9. Granville Sharp to Dr. J. Sharp, 23 June 1787, MGS, 312–313.

10. Thomas B. Thompson to Thomas Steele, 22 April 1787, NA-Kew, T1/647.

11. Thomas B. Thompson, "Captain's Log Nautilus," 23 April 1787, NA-Kew, ADM 51/627.

12. Ibid., 15, 17, 20 April 1787. See also Thomas B. Thompson, "Captain's Log Nautilus," 13, 14 April 1787, NA-Kew, ADM 51/627.

13. Thomas B. Thompson, "Captain's Log Nautilus," 8 May 1787, NA-Kew, ADM 51/627.

14. Thomas B. Thompson to Thomas Steele, 22 April 1787, NA-Kew, T1/647; Granville Sharp to Dr. J. Sharp, 23 June 1787, MGS, 312–313. Sharp similarly interpreted Thompson's early missives on the voyage, writing that "all the jealousies and animosities between the Whites and Blacks had subsided, and that they had been very orderly ever since Mr. Vassa and two or three other discontented persons had been left on shore at Plymouth."

15. Thomas B. Thompson, "Captain's Log Nautilus," 10 May 1787, NA-Kew, ADM 51/627.

16. Ibid., 11 May 1787.

17. Ibid., 25 May 1787; 12 June 1787; King Tom et al., "Cession of a Territory on the Banks of the River Sierra Leona, for the Accommodation of the Black Poor," 11 June 1787, HCSP 67:260.

18. Richard Weaver to Granville Sharp, 23 April 1788, MGS, 321–322.

19. Ibid.

20. King Tom et al., "Cession of a Territory on the Banks of the River Sierra Leona, for the Accommodation of the Black Poor," 11 June 1787, HCSP 67:260; Thomas B. Thompson, "Captain's Log Nautilus," 12 June 1787, NA-Kew, ADM 51/627.

21. Rain totals are from Thomas B. Thompson, "Captain's Log Nautilus," NA-Kew, ADM 51/627.

22. James Reid to Granville Sharp, September 1788, MGS, 322–323.

23. Richard Weaver to Granville Sharp, 23 April 1788, MGS, 321–322.

24. Abraham Elliot Griffith to Granville Sharp, 20 July 1787, MGS, 320–321.

25. James Reid to Granville Sharp, September 1788, MGS, 322–323.

26. Thomas B. Thompson, "Captain's Log Nautilus," 12 July 1787, 7 September 1787, NA-Kew, ADM 51/627.

27. James Reid to Granville Sharp, September 1788, MGS, 322–323. Wrote Reid: "We did not find our arrival at our new settlement according to our wishes; for we arrived in the rainy season and very sickly."

28. Abraham Elliot Griffith to Granville Sharp, 20 July 1787, MGS, 320–321.

29. Granville Sharp to Dr. Lettsom, 13 October 1788, MGS, 315–320.

30. Ibid.

31. Ibid.; Granville Sharp to John Jay, 7 March 1789, MGS, 334–336; Granville Sharp to Samuel Hopkins, 25 July 1789, MGS, 342–343; Sharp, *Memoirs of Granville Sharp.*

32. Abraham Elliot Griffith to Granville Sharp, 20 July 1787, MGS, 320–321.

33. Thomas B. Thompson to Philip Stephens, 23 July 1787, HCSP 67:254.

34. Thomas B. Thompson to Philip Stephens, 26 May 1787, HCSP 67:253.

35. Thomas B. Thompson, "Captain's Log Nautilus," 7 July 1787, NA-Kew, ADM 51/627. Probably stripes because this was Thompson's ordinary punishment. See, for example, Thomas B. Thompson, "Captain's Log Nautilus," 18 May 1787, 18, 21 June 1787, 5 September 1787, NA-Kew, ADM 51/627.

36. Thomas B. Thompson, "Captain's Log Nautilus," 16 July 1787, NA-Kew, ADM 51/627. "Dominick" was perhaps Edward Dominic, who sailed to Sierra Leone on the *Atlantic* (see Vassa, "A List of all the People who are embarked on board the Atlantic now lying at the Motherbank," 27 February 1787, NA-Kew, T1/643).

37. Thomas B. Thompson to Philip Stephens, 23 January 1788, HCSP 67:255.

38. Ibid.

39. Thomas B. Thompson to Philip Stephens, 23 July 1787, HCSP 67:254.

40. Granville Sharp to Dr. J. Sharp, 23 June 1787, MGS, 312–313.

41. James Reid to Granville Sharp, September 1788, MGS, 322–323.

42. Thomas B. Thompson to Philip Stephens, 23 July 1787, HCSP 67:254.

43. Abraham Elliot Griffith to Granville Sharp, 20 July 1787, MGS, 320–321.

44. Granville Sharp to Inhabitants of Granville Town, 11 November 1789, MGS, 344–347.

45. Granville Sharp to Dr. Lettsom, 13 October 1788, MGS, 315–320.

46. Thomas B. Thompson to Philip Stephens, 23 January 1788, HCSP 67:255; Thomas B. Thompson to Philip Stephens, 23 July 1787, HCSP 67:254; Granville Sharp to Anon. [female correspondent in New York], MGS, 313–314.

47. Thomas B. Thompson, "Captain's Log Nautilus," 2 August 1787, 13 September 1787, NA-Kew, ADM 51/627.

48. Evidence of Alexander Anderson in HCSP 68:358.

49. James Reid to Granville Sharp, September 1788, MGS, 322–323; Evidence of Alexander Anderson in HCSP 68:341–346, 354–367.

50. James Reid to Granville Sharp, September 1788, MGS, 322–323.

51. Thomas B. Thompson to Philip Stephens, 23 January 1788, HCSP 67:255.

52. James Reid to Granville Sharp, September 1788, MGS, 322–323.

53. Evidence of Alexander Anderson in HCSP 68:354.

54. Granville Sharp to Thomas Steele, n.d. [1789?], MGS, 338–339.

55. Granville Sharp to Inhabitants of Granville Town, 11 November 1789, MGS, 344–347.

56. Evidence of Alexander Anderson in HCSP 68:362.

57. Granville Sharp to Thomas Steele, 23 July 1789, MGS, 339–340.

58. Thomas B. Thompson, "Captain's Log Nautilus," 28 May 1787, NA-Kew, ADM 51/627.

59. Richard Weaver to Granville Sharp, 23 April 1788, MGS, 321–322.

60. Granville Sharp to Inhabitants of Granville Town, 11 November 1789, MGS, 344–347.

61. The Old Settlers at Sierra Leone to Granville Sharp, 3 September 1788, MGS, 331–333.

62. Evidence of Alexander Anderson in HCSP 68:356.

63. Ibid., 68:359–360.

64. Ibid., 68:361.

65. Ibid.

66. Ibid., 68:355.

67. Granville Sharp to Thomas Steele, n.d. [1789?], MGS, 338–339.

68. Granville Sharp to Thomas Steele, 23 July 1789, MGS, 339–340.

69. Evidence of Alexander Anderson in HCSP 68:354.

70. Granville Sharp to Inhabitants of Granville Town, 11 November 1789, MGS, 344–347.

71. Granville Sharp to Thomas Steele, n.d. [1789?], MGS, 338–339.

72. The Old Settlers at Sierra Leone to Granville Sharp, 3 September 1788, MGS, 331–333.

73. James Reid to Granville Sharp, September 1788, MGS, 322–323.

74. Granville Sharp to Inhabitants of Granville Town, 11 November 1789, MGS, 344–347.

75. Granville Sharp to Inhabitants of Granville Town, 11 November 1789, MGS, 344–347.

76. Thomas B. Thompson, "Captain's Log Nautilus," 10 May 1787, NA-Kew, ADM 51/627.

77. Ibid., 4 June 1787 (Dutch); 31 July 1787 (Antigua); 26 June 1787 (Gambia); 21 July 1787 (Banana Islands).

78. James Reid to Granville Sharp, September 1788, MGS, 322–323; Richard Weaver to Granville Sharp, 23 April 1788, MGS, 321–322.

79. Abraham Elliot Griffith to Granville Sharp, 20 July 1787, MGS, 320–321.

80. Evidence of Alexander Anderson in HCSP 68:359–360.

81. Hancock, *Citizens of the World;* Evidence of Alexander Anderson in HCSP 68:344, 345.

82. Minchinton, "Characteristics of British Slaving Vessels, 1698–1775," 69–71.

83. Evidence of Alexander Anderson in HCSP 68:363–364.

84. At this question, the chamber erupted with objections and Anderson and his counsel were wheeled out while the Parliamentary panel decided whether the last query was a proper one. The motion "passed in the negative" (Evidence of Alexander Anderson in HCSP 68:363–364).

85. Evidence of Alexander Anderson in HCSP 68:356.

86. Thomas B. Thompson, "Captain's Log Nautilus," 25 May 1787, NA-Kew, ADM 51/627.

87. Ibid., 26 May 1787.

88. Ibid., 12 June 1787.

89. Ibid.

90. Ibid., 29 May 1787.

91. Ibid., 13 July 1787.

92. Ibid., 16, 22 May 1787; 2 June 1787; 17 September 1787.

93. Ibid., 29 May 1787; 25, 27 June 1787. But also see the following: Thomas B. Thompson, "Captain's Log Nautilus," 11, 12 July 1787.

94. Thomas B. Thompson, "Captain's Log Nautilus," 25 May 1787, NA-Kew, ADM 51/627.

95. Ibid., 18 May 1787.

96. Ibid., 20 July 1787. These men were later put on board the *Vernon.* Thomas B. Thompson, "Captain's Log Nautilus," 24 July 1787, NA-Kew, ADM 51/627.

97. Thomas B. Thompson, "Captain's Log Nautilus," 9 July 1787, NA-Kew, ADM 51/627.

98. Ibid., 10 July 1787.

99. Ibid., 17 July 1787.

100. Ibid., 22 July 1787.

101. Ibid., 22 July 1787; 23 June 1787.

102. Ibid., 23 June 1787.

103. Ibid., 4 August 1787.

104. Ibid., 23 June 1787.

105. Ibid.

106. Abraham Elliot Griffith to Granville Sharp, 20 July 1787, MGS, 320–321.

107. Ibid.

108. The Old Settlers at Sierra Leone to Granville Sharp, 3 September 1788, MGS, 331–333.

109. Ibid.

110. Granville Sharp to Anon. [female correspondent in New York], MGS, 313–314; Granville Sharp to Inhabitants of the Province of Freedom, 16 May 1788, MGS, 324–327; Granville Sharp to John Jay, 7 March 1789, MGS, 334–336.

111. Richard Weaver to Granville Sharp, 23 April 1788, MGS, 321–322.

112. Granville Sharp to Dr. Lettsom, 13 October 1788, MGS, 315–320.

113. Granville Sharp to Samuel Hopkins, 25 July 1789, MGS, 342–343.

114. Granville Sharp to Thomas Steele, 4 May 1789, MGS, 337–338.

115. Granville Sharp to Samuel Hopkins, 25 July 1789, MGS, 342–343.

116. The Old Settlers at Sierra Leone to Granville Sharp, 3 September 1788, MGS, 331–333.

117. Ibid.

118. Sierra Leone Company, *Postscript to the report of the court of directors,* 6–7; Granville Sharp to William Pitt, 10 June 1790, MGS, 353–354; William Savage to Stephen Phillips, 27 May 1790, NA-Kew, ADM 1/2488; James Bowie, "Extract of a Letter addressed to John & Alexander Anderson . . . ," 22 December 1789, NA-Kew, Chatham Papers, PRO 30/8/363; John Tilly, "Extract of a Letter addressed to John & Alexander Anderson Esq. . . . ," 20 December 1789, NA-Kew, Chatham Papers, PRO 30/8/363.

119. Granville Sharp to William Pitt, 26 April 1790, MGS, 351–352; Granville Sharp to William Pitt, 10 June 1790, MGS, 353–354.

120. Granville Sharp to The Settlers at Sierra Leone, 27 September 1790, MGS, 357–359.

121. Ibid.

122. Ibid.

123. King Tom et al., "Cession of a Territory on the Banks of the River Sierra Leona, for the Accommodation of the Black Poor," 11 June 1787, HCSP 67:260.

124. Granville Sharp to Inhabitants of the Province of Freedom, 16 May 1788, MGS, 324–327.

125. Ibid.

126. Granville Sharp to William Pitt, 26 April 1790, MGS, 351–352.

127. Granville Sharp to William Pitt, 10 June 1790, MGS, 353–354.

128. Granville Sharp to The Settlers at Sierra Leone, 27 September 1790, MGS, 357–359.

129. Granville Sharp to The worthy British Settlers, late Inhabitants of the territory purchased by the King of Great Britain, in Sierra Leone, called the Province of Freedom, 22 January 1791, MGS, 359–361.

130. Granville Sharp to Anon., 5 October 1791, MGS, 362–363.

131. Braidwood, *Black Poor and White Philanthropists,* 208. High mortality, of course, did

not only affect the black settlers. Throughout the eighteenth and nineteenth centuries white workers and settlers in west Africa also suffered high rates of mortality and morbidity (see, for example, Curtin, *Migration and Mortality in Africa and in the Atlantic World*).

132. Ibid., 207.

133. Ibid., 208.

134. Walker, *The Black Loyalists*, 100.

135. Pybus, *Epic Journeys of Freedom*, 139.

136. Schama, *Rough Crossings*, 209. Writes Schama: "This succession of disasters seemed to bear out only too well the returned Captain Thompson's report that there was nothing good to be expected from the settlers since they were, for the most part, a drunken, vicious, scoundrelly lot, who either lived in anarchy or had sold out to the slavers. But of course Thompson would hardly take kindly to the conspicuous and, as he saw it, unseemly lack of deference on the part of the blacks. Sharp, the incurable optimist, was not going to give up on Granville Town."

137. Granville Sharp to Dr. J. Sharp, 31 October 1787, MGS, 313.

138. Fyfe, *A History of Sierra Leone*, 38; Schama, *Rough Crossings*, 305–310, 314–315.

139. Fyfe, *A History of Sierra Leone*, 38.

140. Ibid., 45.

141. Ibid., 46.

142. Ibid., 53–54, 83.

143. Ibid., 59–61; Schama, *Rough Crossings*, 367–371.

144. Schama, *Rough Crossings*, 341–342, 357–358, 371, 382; Pybus, *Epic Journeys of Freedom*, 154–155, 171–174, 184–185.

145. Pybus, *Epic Journeys of Freedom*, 171, 184–185, 191–194, 197.

146. Ibid., 194–195, 197.

147. "Beverhout Company to John Clarkson," 26 June 1792, in Fyfe, *"Our Children Free and Happy,"* 25–27.

148. Pybus, *Epic Journeys of Freedom*, 202; Schama, *Rough Crossings*, 377–383.

CONCLUSION

1. This is why Joseph Miller and Bernard's Bailyn's respective works on the slave trade from Angola to Brazil and European migration to the Americas repay being read in tandem (Miller, *Way of Death*; Bailyn, *Voyagers to the West*).

2. For work stressing continuity, see, for instance, Chambers, *Murder at Montpelier*; Gomez, *Exchanging Our Country Marks*; Thornton, *Africa and Africans in the Making of the Atlantic World, 1400–1680*, 2nd ed.; Fischer, *Albion's Seed*. For work stressing the transformative aspects of migration, see Mintz and Price, *The Birth of African American Culture*; Games, *Migration and the Origins of the English Atlantic World*; Morgan, *Slave Counterpoint*.

3. Mintz and Price, *The Birth of African American Culture*, 1.

4. See, for instance, Thornton, "'I am the Subject of the King of Congo,'" 181–214.

5. Cahill, "The Black Loyalist Myth in Atlantic Canada," 76–87; Walker, "Myth, History and Revisionism," 88–105.

6. John Thornton, though (with an awareness of the claim's tenuousness), has called attention to the ways that the American manifestation of Akan political ideology may have been "more open to achievement and democratic" than its African counterpart (Thornton, "War, the State, and Religious Norms in 'Coromantee' Thought," 199–200).

7. Miller, *Way of Death.*

8. Fenn, *Pox Americana,* 127–133.

9. Klein et al., "Transoceanic Mortality," Tables V and VI(a); Wadstrom, *An essay on colonization,* paragraphs 334 and 679. The loss ratio that obtained on British slave ships in the second half of the eighteenth century was a little less than 10 percent. Guineamen, of all flags that called at ports in the notoriously deadly Bight of Biafra in the late eighteenth century, lost on average almost 16 percent of their human cargo. In the spring of 1787, when the *Vernon, Nautilus, Atlantic,* and *Belisarius* waited at Plymouth, it was estimated at the time that one in ten passengers died.

10. Berlin, "From Creole to African," 267, 274. Writing of the first African slaves in French Louisiana, Berlin holds, "Despite the long transatlantic journey, once in the New World, they recovered much of what they had lost in the Old." This benign perspective on the consequences of migration is a shift apparent in other realms of history, too. In the history of nineteenth-century European migration to the United States, the subjects of Oscar Handlin's *The Uprooted* are certainly more affected by their voyages than the migrants whose stories John Bodnar relates in *The Transplanted.*

11. Thornton, *Africa and Africans in the Making of the Atlantic World,* 2nd ed., 320.

12. Ahmed et al., "Introduction: Uprootings/Regroundings: Questions of Home and Migration," 2.

13. Ibid.

14. Thornton, *Africa and Africans in the Making of the Atlantic World,* 2nd ed., 320.

15. Lovejoy, "Trans-Atlantic Transformations," 128.

16. Equiano, *The Interesting Narrative and Other Writings,* rev. ed., 51.

17. Thornton, *Africa and Africans in the Making of the Atlantic World,* 2nd ed., 322 (emphasis is mine).

18. My thinking in this paragraph has been influence by Irvine, "'Style' as Distinctiveness"; Irvine and Gal, "Language Ideology and Linguistic Differentiation."

19. The following are excellent examples of recent work that take seriously and subject to close analysis the violence and catastrophe that formed the backdrop of much of slave life: Brown, "Spiritual Terror and Sacred Authority in Jamaican Slave Society," 24–53; Painter, "Soul Murder and Slavery," 15–39; Hartman, *Scenes of Subjection;* Dusinberre, *Them Dark Days.*

20. There is a growing anthropological and historical literature dedicated to theorizing and more fully describing such complexities. See, for instance, Connell, "Efik in Abakuá," 223–238; Manfredi, "Philological Perspectives on the Southeastern Nigerian Diaspora," 239–287; Palmié, "Ecué's Atlantic"; Yelvington, *Afro-Atlantic Dialogues.*

21. Greene, "Beyond Power," 319–342.

22. Much of the apparent present confusion about the conceptual boundaries of the Atlantic world, it seems to me, result from neglecting the importance of this particular point. See, for example, Games, "Beyond the Atlantic," 675–692; Stern, "British Asia and British Atlantic," 693–712; Mapp, "Atlantic History from Imperial, Continental, and Pacific Perspectives," 713–724; Coclanis, "Atlantic World or Atlantic/World?" 725–742. Compare, though, with the following essays, more certain of the location of their Atlantic subject, Armitage and Braddick, eds., *The British Atlantic World, 1500–1800.*

23. Berlin, *Many Thousands Gone,* 217–365.

BIBLIOGRAPHY

ARCHIVAL SOURCES

Federal Republic of Nigeria
NA-Nigeria   Intelligence Reports, National Archives of Nigeria,
                              Enugu

Sweden
Smeathman's Journal   Extracts from Mr. [Henry] Smeathman's Journal,
                              Uppsala University Library, Uppsala

United Kingdom
Barham Papers   The Barham Papers, Bodleian Library, Oxford
                              University, Clarendon Deposit

Clarkson Papers   The Clarkson Papers, British Library, Manuscript
                              Students' Room, Additional Manuscripts 41,262A

Fuller Papers   Stephen Fuller Papers, Somerset Archive and
                              Record Service, Taunton

NA-Kew   The National Archives, Kew
                                    Admiralty: Navy Board In-Letters (ADM
                                    106); Captain's Log, *Nautilus* (ADM
                                    51/627); Letters from Captains, Surnames
                                    S (ADM 1/2488)
                              Board of Trade: Documents Concerning Trade,
                                    Jamaica (BT 6/76)
                              Chancery: Master's Senior Exhibits, RE Rogers
                                    Bankrupt (C 107/1–15). Copies consulted
                                    at Duke Univ. Rare Book, Special Collec-
                                    tions, and Manuscript Library as the
                                    James Rogers Papers
                              Chatham Papers, 2nd Series, Papers Relating to
                                    Africa (PRO 30/8/363)

Colonial Office: Jamaica, Original Correspondence
(CO 137); Jamaica, Entry Books (CO 138);
Jamaica, Sessional Papers (CO 140);
Nova Scotia and Cape Breton, Original
Correspondence (CO 217); Sierra Leone,
Original Correspondence (CO 268);
Sierra Leone, Sessional Papers (CO 270)
Treasury: Treasury Board Papers and In-Letters (T1)

Slebech Papers and
Documents

Slebech Papers and Documents, the National
Library of Wales, Aberystwyth

Taylor Papers

Simon Taylor Papers, Institute of Commonwealth
Studies, Archives and Special Collections

Tharp Family Papers

Tharp Family Papers, Cambridgeshire Record
Office

Vanneck Manuscripts

Vanneck Manuscripts, Cambridge University
Library, Manuscripts Department

United States
Clarkson, "Mission to
America"

John Clarkson, "Mission to America," New York
Historical Society

Rogers Papers

The Rogers Papers (Copies of C 107/1–15 from
the National Archives, Kew), Rare Book, Manuscript, and Special Collections Library, Duke University, Durham, North Carolina

NEWSPAPERS

Morning Chronicle and London Advertiser, 1786
Morning Herald (London), 1786–1787
Morning Post (London), 1786
Morning Post and Daily Advertiser (London), 1786
Public Advertiser (London), 1786–1787

GOVERNMENT RECORDS

Great Britain. Parliament. House of Commons. *House of Commons Sessional Papers.*

Edited by Shelia Lambert. Vols. 67–72. Wilmington, Del.: Scholarly Resources, 1975.

House of Assembly, Jamaica. *Two Reports from the Committee of the Honourable House of Assembly of Jamaica, on the Subject of the Slave-Trade.* London: Stephen Fuller, Esq. Agent for Jamaica, 1789.

———. "Second Report: Presented the 12th Day of November, 1788." In *Two Reports from the Committee of the Honourable House of Assembly of Jamaica, on the Subject of the Slave-Trade,* 4–19 (ff 283LH through 290RH). London: Stephen Fuller, Esq. Agent for Jamaica, 1789.

———. *Report, Resolutions, and Remonstrance of the Honourable the Council and Assembly of Jamaica at a Joint Committee, on the Subject of the Slave Trade, In a Session which began the 20th of October 1789.* London: Stephen Fuller, Esq. Agent for Jamaica, 1790.

———. *Proceedings of the Hon. House of Assembly of Jamaica on the Sugar and Slave Trade.* St. Jago de la Vega: Alexander Aikman, 1792.

PUBLISHED SOURCES

Acholonu, Catherine Obianuju. *The Igbo Roots of Olaudah Equiano.* Owerri [Nigeria]: AFA Publications, 1989.

Adams, John. *Remarks on the Country Extending from Cape Palmas to the River Congo.* London: Frank Cass, 1966.

———. *Sketches Taken during Ten Voyages to Africa.* London: James Smith, 1970.

Adams, R. F. G., and Ida C. Ward. "The Arochuku Dialect of Ibo." *Africa* 2, no. 1 (1929): 57–70.

Adderley, Rosanne Marion. *"New Negroes from Africa": Slave Trade Abolition and Free African Settlement in the Nineteenth-Century Caribbean.* Blacks in the Diaspora. Bloomington: Indiana Univ. Press, 2006.

Afigbo, A. E. "The Impact of Colonialism on Igbo Language: The Origins of a Dilemma." In *Ropes of Sand: Studies in Igbo Culture and History,* 355–386. Oxford: Oxford Univ. Press, 1981.

———. "Through a Glass Darkly: Eighteenth Century Igbo Society Through Equiano's Narrative." In *Ropes of Sand: Studies in Igbo Culture and History,* 145–186. Oxford: Oxford Univ. Press, 1981.

———. *Igbo Genesis.* Uturu [Nigeria]: Abia State Univ. Press for Centre for Igbo Studies, Abia State University Uturu, 2000.

Ahmed, Sara, Claudia Castañeda, Anne-Marie Fortier, and Mimi Sheller. "Introduction: Uprootings/Regroundings: Questions of Home and Migration." In *Uprootings/Regroundings: Questions of Home and Migration,* edited by Sara Ahmed, Claudia Castañeda, Anne-Marie Fortier, and Mimi Sheller, 1–19. Oxford: Berg, 2003.

Alagoa, Ebiegberi J. *A History of the Niger Delta: An Historical Interpretation of Ijo Oral Tradition.* Ibadan: Ibadan Univ. Press, 1972.

Allen, William, and Thomas Richard Heywood Thomson. *A narrative of the expedition sent by Her Majesty's Government to the River Niger in 1841 under the command of Captain H. D. Trotter,* 1st ed. 2 vols. 1848. Reprint, New York: Johnson Reprint Corporation, 1967.

Anstey, Roger. *The Atlantic Slave Trade and British Abolition, 1760–1810.* London: Macmillian, 1975.

Ardener, Edwin. "Documentary and Linguistic Evidence for the Rise of the Trading Polities between Rio del Rey and Cameroons, 1500–1650." In *History and Social Anthropology,* edited by I. M. Lewis, 81–126. London: Tavistock, 1968.

Armitage, David, and M. J. Braddick, eds. *The British Atlantic World, 1500–1800.* New York: Palgrave Macmillan, 2002.

Armstrong, Douglas V. *The Old Village and the Great House.* Urbana: Univ. of Illinois Press, 1990.

Asiwaju, A. I. *The Birth of Yewaland: Studies and Documents Relating to the Change of a Yoruba Sub-Ethnic Name from Egbado to Yewa in Ogun State of Nigeria.* Ibadan: STATCO, 1995.

Atkins, T. B. *History of Halifax City.* Vol. 8, Collections of the Nova Scotia Historical Society, 1895.

Baikie, William Balfour. "Brief Summary of an Exploring Trip up the Rivers Kwora and Chadda (Or Benue) in 1854." *Journal of the Royal Geographical Society of London* 25 (1855): 108–121.

———. *Narrative of an exploring voyage up the rivers Kwóra and Bínue, commonly known as the Niger and Tsádda in 1854.* London: Cass, 1966.

Bailyn, Bernard. *Voyagers to the West: A Passage in the Peopling of America on the Eve of the Revolution.* New York: Knopf, 1986.

———. *The Peopling of British North America: An Introduction.* New York: Vintage-Random House, 1988.

Baptist, Edward E., and Stephanie M. H. Camp, eds. *New Studies in the History of American Slavery.* Athens: Univ. of Georgia Press, 2006.

Behrendt, Stephen D., David Eltis, and David Richardson. "The Costs of Coercion: African Agency in the Pre-Modern Atlantic World." *Economic History Review* 54, no. 3 (2001): 454–476.

Bell, Madison Smartt. *Toussaint Louverture : A Biography.* New York: Pantheon Books, 2007.

Bentor, Eli. "Life as an Artistic Process: Igbo Ikenga and Ofo." *African Arts* 21, no. 2 (1988): 66–71.

Berlin, Ira. *Slaves Without Masters: The Free Negro in the Antebellum South.* New York: New Press, 1974.

———. "From Creole to African: Atlantic Creoles and the Origins of African-American Society in Mainland North America." *William and Mary Quarterly* 53, no. 2 (1996): 251–288.

———. *Many Thousands Gone: The First Two Centuries of Slavery in North America.* Cambridge, Mass.: Harvard Univ. Press, 1998.

Berlin, Ira, and Philip D. Morgan. *Culture and Cultivation*. Charlottesville: Univ. Press of Virginia, 1993.

Blassingame, John W. *The Slave Community*, 2nd ed. New York: Oxford Univ. Press, 1979.

Bodnar, John E. *The Transplanted: A History of Immigrants in Urban America*, Interdisciplinary Studies in History. Bloomington: Indiana Univ. Press, 1985.

Braidwood, Stephen J. *Black Poor and White Philanthropists: London's Blacks and the Foundation of the Sierra Leone Settlement, 1786–1791*. Liverpool: Liverpool Univ. Press, 1994.

Brathwaite, Edward. *The Development of Creole Society in Jamaica, 1770–1820*. London: Clarendon Press, 1971.

Brooks, George E. *Landlords and Strangers: Ecology, Society, and Trade in Western Africa, 1000–1630*. Boulder: Westview Press, 1993.

Brooks, Walter H. "The Priority of the Silver Bluff Church and Its Promoters." *Journal of Negro History* 7, no. 2 (1922): 127–196.

Brown, Christopher Leslie. "From Slaves to Subjects: Envisioning an Empire without Slavery, 1772–1834." In *Black Experience and the Empire*, edited by Philip D. Morgan and Sean Hawkins, 111–140. Oxford: Oxford Univ. Press, 2004.

———. *Moral Capital: Foundations of British Abolitionism*. Chapel Hill: Published for the Omohundro Institute of Early American History and Culture, Williamsburg, Virginia, by the Univ. of North Carolina Press, 2006.

Brown, Vincent. "Spiritual Terror and Sacred Authority in Jamaican Slave Society." *Slavery and Abolition* 24, no. 1 (2003): 24–53.

Brubaker, Rogers, and Frederick Cooper. "Beyond 'Identity.'" *Theory and Society* 29 (2000): 1–47.

Buckley, Roger Norman. *Slaves in Red Coats: The British West India Regiments, 1795–1815*. New Haven, Conn.: Yale Univ. Press, 1979.

Burnard, Trevor. "A Failed Settler Society: Marriage and Demographic Failure in Early Jamaica." *Journal of Social History* 28, no. 1 (1994): 63–82.

Burnard, Trevor, and Kenneth Morgan. "The Dynamics of the Slave Market and Slave Purchasing Patterns in Jamaica, 1655–1788." *William and Mary Quarterly* 58, no. 1 (2001): 205–228.

Burnard, T. G. "'Prodigious Riches': The Wealth of Jamaica before the American Revolution." *Economic History Review* 54, no. 3 (2001): 506–524.

Burnard, Trevor G. *Mastery, Tyranny, and Desire: Thomas Thistlewood and His Slaves in the Anglo-Jamaican World*. Chapel Hill: Univ. of North Carolina Press, 2004.

Byrd, Alexander X. "Eboe, Country, Nation and Gustavus Vassa's *Interesting Narrative*." *William and Mary Quarterly* 63, no. 1 (2006): 123–148.

———. "Violence, Migration, and Becoming Igbo in Gustavus Vassa's *Interesting Narrative*." In *Constructing Borders/Crossing Boundaries: Race, Ethnicity, and Immigration*, edited by Caroline B. Brettell, 31–58. Lanham, Md.: Lexington Books, 2007.

Cahill, Barry. "The Black Loyalist Myth in Atlantic Canada." *Acadiensis* 29, no. 1 (1999): 76–87.

Campbell, James T. *Middle Passages: African American Journeys to Africa, 1787–2005.* The Penguin History of American Life. New York: Penguin Press, 2006.

Carretta, Vincent. *Unchained Voices: An Anthology of Black Authors in the English-Speaking World of the 18th Century.* Lexington: Univ. Press of Kentucky, 1996.

———. "Olaudah Equiano or Gustavus Vassa? New Light on an Eighteenth-Century Question of Identity." *Slavery and Abolition* 20, no. 3 (1999): 96–105.

———. "'Property of Author': Olaudah Equiano's Place in the History of the Book." In *Genius in Bondage: Literature of the Early Black Atlantic,* edited by Vincent Carretta and Philip Gould, 130–150. Lexington: Univ. Press of Kentucky, 2001.

———. "Questioning the Identity of Olaudah Equiano, or Gustavus Vassa, the African." In *The Global Eighteenth Century,* edited by Felicity Nussbaum, 226–235. Baltimore: Johns Hopkins Univ. Press, 2003.

———. *Equiano, the African: Biography of a Self-Made Man.* Athens: Univ. of Georgia Press, 2005.

———. "Response to Paul Lovejoy's 'Autobiography and Memory: Gustavus Vassa, alias Olaudah Equiano, the African.'" *Slavery and Abolition* 28, no. 1 (2007): 115–119.

———. *Equiano the African: Biography of a Self-Made Man.* Athens: Univ. of Georgia Press, 2005.

Chalmers, George, ed. *The Definitive Treaty of Peace and Friendship, between his Britannic Majesty and the most Christian King signed at Versailles, the 3d of September 1783.* Vol. 1, Collection of Treaties between Great Britain and Other Powers. London, 1790.

Chambers, Douglas B. "'My Own Nation': Igbo Exiles in the Diaspora." *Slavery and Abolition* 18, no. 1 (1997): 72–97.

———. "The Significance of Igbo in the Bight of Biafra Slave-Trade: A Rejoinder to Northrup's 'Myth Igbo.'" *Slavery and Abolition* 23, no. 1 (2002): 101–120.

———. *Murder at Montpelier: Igbo Africans in Virginia.* Jackson: Univ. Press of Mississippi, 2005.

Christopher, Emma. *Slave Ship Sailors and Their Captive Cargoes, 1730–1807.* Cambridge: Cambridge Univ. Press, 2006.

Clarkson, John. "Mission to America." See entry in Archival Sources above.

Clarkson, Thomas. "Some Account of the New Colony at Sierra Leona, on the Coast of Africa." *The American Museum or Universal Magazine* 11 (1792): 160–162, 229–231.

Coclanis, Peter A. "Atlantic World or Atlantic/World?" *William and Mary Quarterly* 63, no. 4 (2006): 725–742.

Cohen, Abner. *Custom and Politics in Urban Africa: A Study of Hausa Migrants in Yoruba Towns.* London: Routledge, 1969.

———. *Urban Ethnicity.* London: Tavistock Publications, 1974.

Cohn, Raymond L. "Deaths of Slaves in the Middle Passage." *Journal of Economic History* 45, no. 3 (1985): 685–692.

———. "Maritime Mortality in the Eighteenth and Nineteenth Centuries: A Survey." *International Journal of Maritime History* 1, no. 1 (1989): 159–191.

Cohn, Raymond L., and Richard A. Jensen. "The Determinants of Slave Mortality Rates on the Middle Passage." *Explorations in Economic History* 19, no. 3 (1982): 269–282.

———. "Mortality in the Atlantic Slave Trade." *Journal of Interdisciplinary History* 13, no. 2 (1982): 317–329.

Coke, Daniel Parker. "Memorial of Benjn. Whitcuff." In *The Royal Commission on the Losses and Services of American Loyalists,* edited by Hugh Edward Egerton, 132. New York: Burt Franklin, 1971.

———. "Memorial of John Twine—a Black." In *The Royal Commission on the Losses and Services of American Loyalists,* edited by Hugh Edward Egerton, 197. New York: Burt Franklin, 1971.

———. "Memorial of Samuel Burke—Black." In *The Royal Commission on the Losses and Services of American Loyalists,* edited by Hugh Edward Egerton, 197–198. New York: Burt Franklin, 1971.

Cole, Herbert M. "Igbo Arts and Ethnicity: Problems and Issues." *African Arts* 21, no. 2 (1988): 26–27.

Cole, Herbert M., and Chike C. Aniakor. *Igbo Arts: Community and Cosmos.* Los Angeles: University of California, 1984.

Coleman, Deirdre. *Romantic Colonization and British Anti-Slavery.* Cambridge: Cambridge Univ. Press, 2005.

Company, Sierra Leone. *Substance of the Report of the Court of Directors of the Sierra Leone Company held at London the 19th of October 1791.* London: James Phillips, 1791.

———. *Postscript to the report of the court of directors of the Sierra Leone Company to the general court at London on Wednesday the 19th of October, 1791.* London: James Phillips, 1792.

———. *Substance of the report delivered by the Court of Directors of the Sierra Leone Company, to the General Court of Proprietors, on Thursday the 27th of March, 1794.* London: J. Phillips, 1794.

Connell, Bruce. "Efik in Abakuá: Linguistic Evidence for the Formation of a Diaspora Identity." *Contours* 2, no. 2 (2004): 223–238.

Conrad, Margaret. *They Planted Well: New England Planters in Maritime Canada.* New Brunswick: Acadiensis Press, 1988.

———. *Intimate Relations: Family and Community in Planter Nova Scotia, 1759–1800.* Fredericton [Canada]: Acadiensis Press, 1995.

Cookey, S. J. S. "An Ethnohistorical Reconstruction of Traditional Igbo Society." In *West African Cultural Dynamics: Archaeological and Historical Perspectives,* edited by B. K. Swartz Jr. and Raymond E. Dumett, 327–347. New York: Mouton, 1980.

Cooper, Frederick. *Plantation Slavery on the East Coast of Africa.* New Haven, Conn.: Yale Univ. Press, 1977.

Craton, Michael. "Hobbesian or Panglossian: The Two Extremes of Slave Conditions in the British Caribbean." *William and Mary Quarterly* 35 (1978): 324–356.

———. *Searching for the Invisible Man: Slaves and Plantation Life in Jamaica.* Cambridge, Mass.: Harvard Univ. Press, 1978.

————. "Changing Patterns of Slave Families in the British West Indies." *Journal of Interdisciplinary History* 10, no. 1 (1979): 1–35.

Craton, Michael, and Gail Saunders. *Islanders in the Stream: A History of the Bahamian People,* vol. 1. Athens: Univ. of Georgia Press, 1992.

Creel, Margaret Washington. *A Peculiar People: Slave Religion and Community-Culture Among the Gullahs.* New York: New York Univ. Press, 1988.

Cressy, David. *Coming Over: Migration and Communication between England and New England in the Seventeenth Century.* Cambridge: Cambridge Univ. Press, 1987.

Crow, Hugh. *Memoirs of the Late Captain Hugh Crow. . . .* London: Longman, Rees, Orme, Brown, and Green, 1830.

Crowther, Samuel. *Journal of an expedition up the Niger and Tshadda rivers, undertaken by Maegregor Laird in connection with the British Government in 1854.* 1855. Reprint, London: Cass, 1970.

Cugoano, Ottobah. *Thoughts and Sentiments on the Evil and Wicked Traffic of the Slavery and Commerce of the Human Species.* London, 1787.

Curtin, Philip D. *The Image of Africa: British Ideas and Action, 1780–1850.* Madison: Univ. of Wisconsin Press, 1964.

————. *The Atlantic Slave Trade: A Census.* Madison: Univ. of Wisconsin Press, 1969.

Curtin, Philip D. *Migration and Mortality in Africa and the Atlantic World, 1700–1900.* Aldershot, Hampshire, Great Britain; Burlington, Vt.: Ashgate/Variorum, 2001.

Davis, David Brion. *The Problem of Slavery in the Age of Revolution, 1770–1823.* Ithaca, N.Y.: Cornell Univ. Press, 1975.

Dennis, Clara. *Down in Nova Scotia: My Own, My Native Land.* Toronto: Ryerson Press, 1933.

Dike, K. Onwuka. *Trade and Politics in the Niger Delta.* Oxford: Clarendon, 1959.

Dike, Kenneth Onwuka, and Felicia Ekejiuba. *The Aro of South-Eastern Nigeria, 1650–1980: A Study of Socio-Economic Formation and Transformation in Nigeria.* Ibadan [Nigeria]: Univ. Press Limited, 1990.

Dirks, Robert. *The Black Saturnalia.* Gainesville: Univ. of Florida Press, 1987.

Donovan, Stephen K., and Trevor A. Jackson. *Caribbean Geography: An Introduction.* Kingston: University of the West Indies Publisher's Association (UWIPA), 1994.

Dubois, Laurent. *Avengers of the New World : The Story of the Haitian Revolution.* Cambridge, Mass.: Belknap Press of Harvard Univ. Press, 2004.

Duffy, Michael. *Soldiers, Sugar, and Seapower: The British Expeditions to the West Indies and the War against Revolutionary France.* Oxford: Clarendon Press, 1987.

Duke, Antera. "The Diary of Antera Duke, being three years in the life of an Efik chief, 18th January 1785 to 31st January 1788." In *Efik Traders of Old Calabar,* edited by Daryll Forde. London: Oxford Univ. Press, 1956.

Dusinberre, William. *Them Dark Days: Slavery in the American Rice Swamps.* New York: Oxford Univ. Press, 1996.

Dyott, William. *Dyott's Diary,* vol. 1. London: Archibald Constable and Company, 1907.

Edwards, Bryan. *The History, Civil and Commercial, of the British Colonies in the West Indies,* vol. 2, 3rd ed. London, 1801.

Edwards, Paul. "Embrenché and Ndichie." *Journal of the Historical Society of Nigeria* 2, no. 3 (1962): 401–402.

———. "Introduction to 'The Life of Olaudah Equiano.'" In *The Interesting Narrative of the Life of Olaudah Equiano,* edited by Werner Sollors, 302–338. New York: Norton, 2001.

Edwards, Paul, and Rosalind Shaw. "The Invisible *CHI* in Equiano's 'Interesting Narrative.'" *Journal of Religion in Africa* 19, no. 2 (1989): 146–156.

Elkins, Stanley. *Slavery: A Problem in American Institutional and Intellectual Life,* 3rd ed. Chicago: Univ. of Chicago Press, 1976.

Ells, Margaret. "Clearing the Decks for the Loyalists." *Report of the Annual Meeting—Canadian Historical Association* (1933): 43–58.

———. "Settling the Loyalists in Nova Scotia." *Report of the Annual Meeting—Canadian Historical Association* (1934): 105–109.

Eltis, David. "Mortality and Voyage Length in the Middle Passage: New Evidence from the Nineteenth Century." *Journal of Economic History* 44, no. 2 (1984): 301–308.

———. *The Rise of African Slavery in the Americas.* New York: Cambridge Univ. Press, 2000.

———. "Free and Coerced Migrations from the Old World to the New." In *Coerced and Free Migration: Global Perspectives,* edited by David Eltis, 33–74. Stanford, Calif.: Stanford Univ. Press, 2002.

Eltis, David, Stephen D. Behrendt, David Richardson, and Herbert S. Klein, eds. *The Trans-Atlantic Slave Trade: A Database on CD-ROM.* New York: Cambridge Univ. Press, 1999.

Eltis, David, and David Richardson. "The 'Numbers Game' and Routes to Slavery." *Slavery and Abolition* 18, no. 1 (1997): 1–15.

———. "West Africa and the Transatlantic Slave Trade: New Evidence of Long-Run Trends." *Slavery and Abolition* 18, no. 1 (1997): 16–35.

Emenanjo, E. Nolue. "How Do the Igbo Understand Themselves? A Preliminary Study of Mutual Intelligibility in the Igbo Culture Area." *Ikenga* 4, no. 1 (1979): 60–74.

Equiano, Olaudah. *The Interesting Narrative of the Life of Olaudah Equiano, or Gustavus Vassa, the African, Written by Himself: Authoritative Text, Contexts, Criticism.* Edited by Werner Sollors. New York: Norton, 2001.

———. *The Interesting Narrative and Other Writings,* revised ed. Edited by Vincent Carretta. New York: Penguin Books, 2003.

Falconbridge, Alexander. *An Account of the Slave Trade on the Coast of Africa.* London: J. Phillips, 1788.

Falconbridge, Anna Maria. *Narrative of Two Voyages to the River Sierra Leone, during the Years 1791–3,* 2nd ed. 1802. Reprint, London: Frank Cass, 1967.

Faust, Drew Gilpin. *James Henry Hammond and the Old South: A Design for Mastery.* Southern Biography Series. Baton Rouge: Louisiana State Univ. Press, 1982.

Fenn, Elizabeth A. *Pox Americana: The Great Smallpox Epidemic of 1775–82.* New York: Hill and Wang, 2001.

Fischer, David Hackett. *Albion's Seed: Four British Folkways in America.* New York: Oxford Univ. Press, 1989.

Forde, Daryll, and G. I. Jones. *The Ibo and Ibibio-Speaking Peoples of South-Eastern Nigeria.* 1950. Reprint, London: International African Institute, 1962.

Franklin, John Hope, and Loren Schweninger. *Runaway Slaves: Rebels on the Plantation.* New York: Oxford, 1999.

Frazier, E. Franklin. *The Negro Family in the United States.* Chicago: Univ. of Chicago Press, 1939.

Free English Territory in Africa. London, n.d. [1790?].

Frey, Sylvia R., and Betty Wood. *Come Shouting to Zion: African American Protestantism in the American South and British Caribbean to 1830.* Chapel Hill: Univ. of North Carolina Press, 1998.

Freyre, Gilberto, and Samuel Putnam. *The Masters and the Slaves (Casa-Grande and Senzala): A Study in the Development of Brazilian Civilization.* New York: Knopf, 1946.

Fyfe, Christopher. *A History of Sierra Leone.* London: Oxford Univ. Press, 1962.

———. *"Our Children Free and Happy": Letters from Black Settlers in Africa in the 1790s.* Edinburgh: Edinburgh Univ. Press, 1991.

Fyfe, C. F. [Christopher F.]. "Thomas Peters: History and Legend." *Sierra Leone Studies* New Series no. 1 (1953): 4–13.

Games, Alison. *Migration and the Origins of the English Atlantic World.* Cambridge, Mass.: Harvard Univ. Press, 1999.

———. "Beyond the Atlantic: English Globetrotters and Transoceanic Connections." *William and Mary Quarterly* 63, no. 4 (2006): 675–692.

Garrettson, Freeborn. *American Methodist Pioneer: The Life and Journals of the Rev. Freeborn Garrettson.* Rutland, Vt.: Academy Books, 1984.

Geggus, David Patrick. *Slavery, War, and Revolution: The British Occupation of Saint Domingue, 1793–1798.* Oxford: Clarendon Press; New York: Oxford Univ. Press, 1982.

Genovese, Eugene D. *Roll, Jordan, Roll: The World the Slaves Made.* New York: Vintage Books-Random House, 1974.

George, David. "An Account of the Life of Mr. David George, from Sierra Leone in Africa; given by himself in a Conversation with Brother Rippon of London, and Brother Pearce of Birmingham." *Baptist Annual Register* (1790): 473–484.

Gerzina, Gretchen. *Black England: Life before Emancipation.* London: John Murray, 1995.

Gipson, Larence Henry. *The Triumphant Empire: New Responsibilities within the Enlarged Empire, 1763–1766.* New York: Knopf, 1956.

Gomez, Michael A. *Exchanging Our Country Marks: The Transformation of African Identities in the Colonial and Antebellum South.* Chapel Hill: Univ. of North Carolina Press, 1998.

Green, James. "The Publishing History of Olaudah Equiano's *Interesting Narrative.*" *Slavery and Abolition* 16, no. 3 (1995): 362–375.

Green, Margaret M. "The Present Linguistic Situation in Ibo Country." *Africa* 9, no. 4 (1936): 508–523.

Greene, Jack P. "Beyond Power: Paradigm Subversion and the Reformulation and the Re-Creation of the Early Modern Atlantic World." In *Crossing Boundaries: Comparative History of Black People in Diaspora*, edited by Darlene Clark Hine and Jacqueline McLeod, 319–342. Bloomington: Indiana Univ. Press, 1999.

Hair, P. E. H., Adam Jones, and Robin Law, eds. *Barbot on Guinea: The Writings of Jean Barbot on West Africa, 1678–1712*, vol. 2. London: Hakluyt Society, 1992.

Hall, Gwendolyn Midlo. *Africans in Colonial Louisiana.* Baton Rouge: Louisiana State Univ. Press, 1992.

———. *Slavery and African Ethnicities in the Americas: Restoring the Links.* Chapel Hill: Univ. of North Carolina Press, 2005.

Hancock, David. *Citizens of the World: London Merchants and the Integration of the British Atlantic Community, 1735–1785.* New York: Cambridge Univ. Press, 1995.

Handlin, Oscar. *The Uprooted: The Epic Story of the Great Migrations That Made the American People*, 2nd ed. Philadelphia: Univ. of Pennsylvania Press, 2001.

Hart, Harriet Cunningham. *History of the County of Guysborough.* Belleville [Canada]: Mika Publishing Company, 1975.

Hartlen, Gary. "Bound for Nova Scotia: Slaves in the Planter Migration, 1759–1800." In *Making Adjustments: Change and Continuity in Planter Nova Scotia, 1759–1800*, edited by Margaret Conrad, 123–128. Fredericton [Canada]: Acadiensis Press, 1991.

Hartman, Saidiya V. *Scenes of Subjection: Terror, Slavery, and Self-Making in Nineteenth-Century America.* New York: Oxford Univ. Press, 1997.

———. *Lose Your Mother: A Journey along the Atlantic Slave Route.* New York: Farrar, Straus, and Giroux, 2007.

Hecht, J. J. *Continental and Colonial Servants in Eighteenth-Century England.* Northampton, Mass.: Smith College, 1954.

Henderson, Richard N. *The King in Every Man: Evolutionary Trends in Onitsha Ibo Society and Culture.* New Haven, Conn.: Yale Univ. Press, 1972.

Herskovits, Melville. *The Myth of the Negro Past.* Boston: Beacon Press, 1990.

Hertzog, Keith P. "Naval Operation in West Africa and the Disruption of the Slave Trade during the American Revolution." *American Neptune* 55, no. 1 (1995): 42–48.

Higman, B. W. "Household Structure and Fertility on Jamaican Slave Plantations: A Nineteenth-Century Example." *Population Studies* 27, no. 3 (1973): 527–550.

———. "The Slave Family and Household in the British West Indies, 1800–1834." *Journal of Interdisciplinary History* 6, no. 2 (1975): 261–287.

———. "The Spatial Economy of Jamaican Sugar Plantations: Cartographic Evidence from the Eighteenth and Nineteenth Centuries." *Journal of Historical Geography* 13, no. 1 (1987): 17–39.

————. *Jamaica Surveyed: Plantation Maps and Plans of the Eighteenth and Nineteenth Centuries.* Kingston: Institute of Jamaica, 1988.

————. *Montpelier: A Plantation Community in Slavery and Freedom, 1739–1912.* Kingston: The Press, University of the West Indies, 1998.

————. *Plantation Jamaica, 1750–1850: Captial and Control in a Colonial Economy.* Kingston: Univ. of the West Indies Press, 2005.

Hodges, Graham Russell, ed. *The Black Loyalist Directory: African Americans in Exile After the American Revolution.* New York: Garland Publishing, 1996.

Hodgkin, Thomas. *Nationalism in Colonial Africa.* New York: New York Univ. Press, 1956.

Horton, Robin. "From Fishing Village to City-State." In *Man in Africa,* edited by Mary Douglass and Phyllis Kaberry, 37–58. London: Tavistock Publications, 1969.

Hutchinson, Thomas J. *Impressions of Western Africa.* London: Frank Cass, 1970.

Inikori, Joseph E. "The Sources of Supply for the Atlantic Slave Trade Exports from the Bight of Benin and the Bight of Bonny (Biafra)." In *De La Traite À L'Esclavage,* edited by Serge Daget, 25–43. Nantes: Centre de Recherche Sur L'Histoire du Monde Atlantique, 1988.

Irvine, Judith T. "'Style' as Distinctiveness: The Culture and Ideology of Linguistic Differentiation." In *Style and Sociolinguistic Variation,* edited by Penelope Eckert and John R. Rickford, 21–43. Cambridge: Cambridge Univ. Press, 2002.

Irvine, Judith T., and Susan Gal. "Language Ideology and Linguistic Differentiation." In *Regimes of Language: Ideologies, Polities, and Identities,* edited by Paul V. Kroskrity, 35–83. Santa Fe, N.Mex.: School of American Research Press, 2000.

James, C.L.R. *The Black Jacobins: Toussaint L'Ouverture and the San Domingo Revolution,* 2nd ed. New York: Vintage–Random House, 1989.

Johnson, Guy B. *Folk Culture on St. Helena Island, South Carolina.* Chapel Hill: Univ. of North Carolina Press, 1930.

Johnson, Walter. *Soul by Soul: Life Inside the Antebellum Slave Market.* Cambridge, Mass.: Harvard Univ. Press, 1999.

Jones, G. I. "Dual Organization in Ibo Social Structure." *Africa* 19, no. 2 (1949): 150–156.

————. "Ibo Land Tenure." *Africa* 19, no. 4 (1949): 309–323.

————. "The Political Organization of Old Calabar." In *Efik Traders of Old Calabar,* edited by Daryll Forde, 116–160. London: Oxford Univ. Press, 1956.

————. "Ecology and Social Structure Among the North Eastern Ibo." *Africa* 31, no. 2 (1961): 117–134.

————. *The Trading States of the Oil Rivers: A Study of Political Development in Eastern Nigeria.* London: Oxford Univ. Press, 1963.

————. "Olaudah Equiano of the Niger Ibo." In *Africa Remembered,* edited by Philip D. Curtin, 60–69. Madison: Univ. of Wisconsin Press, 1967.

————. *The Art of Eastern Nigeria.* Cambridge: Cambridge Univ. Press, 1984.

————. *Ibo Art.* Aylesbury [Great Britain]: Shire Publications, 1989.

Joyner, Charles. *Down by the Riverside.* Urbana: Univ. of Illinois Press, 1984.

King, Boston. "Memoirs of the Life of Boston King, a Black Preacher." *Methodist Magazine* 21 (1798): 105–110, 157–161, 262–265.

Klein, Herbert. "The English Slave Trade to Jamaica, 1782–1808." In *The Middle Passage: Comparative Studies in the Atlantic Slave Trade.* Princeton, N.J.: Princeton Univ. Press, 1978.

Klein, Herbert S. "The English Slave Trade to Jamaica, 1782–1808." *Economic History Review* 31, no. 1 (1978): 25–45.

———. *African Slavery in Latin America and the Caribbean.* New York: Oxford Univ. Press, 1986.

Klein, Herbert S., and Stanley L. Engerman. "Slave Mortality on British Ships, 1791–1797." In *Liverpool, the African Slave Trade, and Abolition,* edited by Roger Anstey and P. E. H. Hair, 113–125. [Liverpool]: Historical Society of Lancashire and Cheshire, 1976.

———. "Long-Term Trends in African Mortality in the Transatlantic Slave Trade." *Slavery and Abolition* 18, no. 1 (1997): 36–48.

Klein, Herbert S., Stanley L. Engerman, Robin Haines, and Ralph Shlomowitz. "Transoceanic Mortality: The Slave Trade in Comparative Perspective." *William and Mary Quarterly* 58, no. 1 (2001): 93–118.

Koelle, Sigismund W. *Polyglotta Africana.* Edited by P. E. H. Hair and David Dalby. 1854. Reprint; Graz [Austria]: Akademische Druck, 1963.

Kolapo, Femi J. "The Igbo and Their Neighbours during the Era of the Atlantic Slave Trade." *Slavery and Abolition* 25, no. 1 (2004): 114–133.

Kopytoff, Igor, and Suzanne Miers. "African 'Slavery' as an Institution of Marginality." In *Slavery in Africa: Historical and Anthropological Perspectives,* edited by Suzanne Miers and Igor Kopytoff, 3–81. Madison: Univ. of Wisconsin Press, 1977.

Laird, MacGregor, and R. A. K. Oldfield. *Narrative of an expedition into the interior of Africa by the River Niger in the steam-vessels Quorra and Alburkah in 1832, 1833 and 1834.* 2 vols. 1837. Reprint, London: Frank Cass, 1971.

Landers, John. *Death and the Metropolis: Studies in the Demographic History of London, 1670–1830.* Cambridge: Cambridge Univ. Press, 1993.

Landers, Jane. *Black society in Spanish Florida,* Blacks in the New World. Urbana: Univ. of Illinois Press, 1999.

Latham, A. J. H. *Old Calabar, 1600–1891.* Oxford: Clarendon Press, 1973.

Little, Thomas J. "George Liele and the Rise of Independent Black Baptist Churches in the Lower South and Jamaica." *Slavery and Abolition* 16, no. 2 (1995): 188–204.

Littlefield, Daniel. *Rice and Slaves.* Urbana: Univ. of Illinois Press, 1981.

Long, Edward. *The History of Jamaica,* vol. 2. London: Frank Cass, 1970.

Lovejoy, Paul E. "Trans-Atlantic Transformations: The Origins and Identity of Africans in the Americas." In *The Atlantic World: Essays on Slavery, Migration, and Imagination,* edited by Wim Klooster and Alfred Padula, 126–146. Upper Saddle River, N.J.: Pearson-Prentice Hall, 2005.

Lovejoy, Paul E. "Autobiography and Memory: Gustavus Vassa, alias Olaudah Equiano, the African." *Slavery and Abolition* 27, no. 3 (2006): 317–347.

————. "Issues of Motivation—Vassa/Equiano and Carretta's Critique of the Evidence." *Slavery and Abolition* 28, no. 1 (2007): 121–125.

Lovejoy, Paul E., and David Richardson. "Trust, Pawnship, and Atlantic History: The Institutional Foundations of the Old Calabar Slave Trade." *American Historical Review* 104, no. 2 (1999): 333–355.

Lovejoy, Paul E., and David Richardson. "'This Horrid Hole': Royal Authority, Commerce and Credit at Bonny, 1690–1840." *Journal of African History* 45 (2004): 363–392.

MacKinnon, Neil. *This Unfriendly Soil: The Loyalist Experience in Nova Scotia, 1783–1791.* Montreal: McGill-Queen's Univ. Press, 1986.

Manfredi, Victor. "Philological Perspectives on the Southeastern Nigerian Diaspora." *Contours* 2, no. 2 (2004): 239–287.

Manning, Patrick. *Slavery and African Life: Occidental, Oriental, and African Slave Trades.* Cambridge: Cambridge Univ. Press, 1990.

Mapp, Paul W. "Atlantic History from Imperial, Continental, and Pacific Perspectives." *William and Mary Quarterly* 63, no. 4 (2006): 713–724.

Martin, Susan M. *Palm Oil and Protest: An Economic History of the Ngwa Region, South-Eastern Nigeria, 1800–1980.* Cambridge: Cambridge Univ. Press, 1988.

Matory, J. Lorand. "The English Professors of Brazil: On the Diasporic Roots of the Yorùbá Nation." *Comparative Studies in Society and History* 41, no. 1 (1999): 72–103.

McDonald, Roderick A. *The Economy and Material Culture of Slaves.* Baton Rouge: Louisiana State Univ. Press, 1993.

Miller, Joseph C. "Mortality in the Atlantic Slave Trade: Statistical Evidence on Causality." *Journal of Interdisciplinary History* 11, no. 3 (1981): 385–423.

————. *Way of Death: Merchant Capitalism and the Angolan Slave Trade, 1730–1830.* Madison: Univ. of Wisconsin Press, 1988.

Minchinton, Walter E. "Characteristics of British Slaving Vessels, 1698–1775." *Journal of Interdisciplinary History* 20, no. 1 (1989): 53–81.

Mintz, Sidney, and Richard Price. *The Birth of African American Culture.* Boston: Beacon Press, 1990.

Mitchell, J. Clyde. *The Kalela Dance,* The Rhodes-Livingstone Papers. Manchester: Manchester Univ. Press, 1956.

————. *Cities, Society, and Social Perception: A Central African Perspective.* Oxford: Clarendon Press, 1987.

Moore, Christopher. *The Loyalists: Revolution, Exile, Settlement.* Toronto: McClelland and Stewart, 1994.

Morgan, Philip D. "Three Planters and Their Slaves: Perspectives on Slavery in Virginia, South Carolina, and Jamaica." In *Race and Family in the Colonial South,* edited by Winthrop D. Jordan and Sheila L. Skemp, 37–79. Jackson: Univ. Press of Mississippi, 1987.

————. "British Encounters with Africans and African-Americans, circa 1600–1780." In *Strangers within the Realm: Cultural Margins of the First British Empire,* edited by Bernard Bailyn and Philip D. Morgan, 157–219. Chapel Hill: Published for the Institute of Early American History and Culture, Williamsburg, Virginia, by the Univ. of North Carolina Press, 1991.

———. *Slave Counterpoint: Black Culture in the Eighteenth-Century Chesapeake and Lowcountry.* Published for the Omohundro Institute of Early American History and Culture, Williamsburg, Virginia, by the Univ. of North Carolina Press, 1998.

Mulcahy, Matthew. *Hurricanes and Society in the British Greater Caribbean, 1624–1783,* Early America. Baltimore: Johns Hopkins Univ. Press, 2006.

Mullin, Michael. *Africa in America: Slave Acculturation and Resistance in the American South and the British Caribbean, 1736–1831.* Urbana: Univ. of Illinois Press, 1992.

Myers, Norma. *Reconstructing the Black Past: Blacks in Britain, 1780–1830.* London: Frank Cass, 1996.

Nash, Gary B. "Thomas Peters: Millwright and Deliverer," 15 December 2004. http://revolution.h-net.msu.edu/essays/nash.html (accessed 19 January 2008).

———. *The Forgotten Fifth: African Americans in the Age of Revolution,* Nathan I. Huggins lectures. Cambridge, Mass.: Harvard Univ. Press, 2006.

Nnoli, Okwudiba. *Ethnic Politics in Nigeria.* Enugu: Fourth Dimension Publishers, 1978.

———. *Ethnicity and Development in Nigeria.* Aldershot: Avebury, 1995.

Northrup, David. *Trade Without Rulers: Pre-Colonial Economic Development in South-Eastern Nigeria.* Oxford: Clarendon Press, 1978.

———. "Igbo and Myth Igbo: Culture and Ethnicity in the Atlantic World, 1600–1850." *Slavery and Abolition* 21, no. 3 (2000): 1–20.

Norton, Mary Beth. *The British-Americans: The Loyalist Exiles in England, 1774–1789.* Boston: Little, Brown, 1972.

———. "The Fate of Some Black Loyalists of the American Revolution." *Journal of Negro History* 58 (1973): 402–426.

Obichere, Boniface. "Slavery and the Slave Trade in the Niger Delta Cross River Basin." In *De La Traite À L'Esclavage,* edited by Serge Daget, 45–56. Nantes: Centre de Recherche Sur L'Histoire du Monde Atlantique, 1988.

Ofomata, G. E. K. *Nigeria in Maps: Eastern States.* Benin City: Ethiope Publishing House, 1975.

Ogude, S. E. *No Roots Here: On the Igbo Roots of Olaudah Equiano.* Edited by S. O. Asein. Vol. 5, Review of English and Literary Studies Monographs. Ibadan [Nigeria]: Bookman Educational and Communications Services, 1989.

Okwechime, Chudi. *Onicha-Ugbo through the Centuries.* Lagos [Nigeria]: Max-Henrie and Associates, 1994.

Onwuejeogwu, M. A. "The Igbo Culture Area." In *Igbo Language and Culture,* edited by F. C. Ogbalu and E. N. Emenanjo, 1–10. Oxford: Oxford Univ. Press, 1975.

———. *An Igbo Civilization: Nri Kingdom and Hegemony.* London: Ethnographica, 1981.

Oriji, John Nwachimereze. *Ngwa History: A Study of Social and Economic Changes in Igbo Mini-States in Time Perspective.* New York: Peter Lang, 1991.

Ottenberg, Simon. "Ibo Oracles and Intergroup Relations." *Southwestern Journal of Anthropology* 14, no. 3 (1958): 295–317.

———. "Ibo Receptivity to Change." In *Continuity and Change in African Cultures,* edited by William Bascom and Melville J. Herskovits, 130–143. Chicago: Univ. of Chicago Press, 1959.

Painter, Nell Irvin. "Soul Murder and Slavery: Toward a Fully Loaded Cost Accounting." In *Southern History Across the Color Line,* 15–39. Chapel Hill: Univ. of North Carolina Press, 2002.

Palmié, Stephan. "Ecué's Atlantic: An Essay in Methodology." *Journal of Religion in Africa* 37, no. 2 (2007): 275–315.

Patterson, Orlando. *The Sociology of Slavery: An Analysis of the Origins, Development and Structure of Negro Slave Society in Jamaica.* London: MacGibbon and Kee, 1967.

Pereira, Duarte Pacheco. *Esmeraldo de situ Orbis,* 3rd ed. Lisbon: Academia Portuguesa da Historia, 1954.

Picton, John. "Ekpeye Masks and Masking." *African Arts* 21, no. 2 (1988): 46–53.

Pilcher, George William. "Samuel Davies and the Instruction of Negroes in Virginia." *The Virginia Magazine of History and Biography* 74, no. 3 (1966): 293–300.

Powell, Stephen, and Laird Niven. *Archaeological Surveys in Two Black Communities, 1998: Surveying the Tracadie Area and Testing Two Sites in Birchtown.* Halifax: Nova Scotia Museum, 2000.

Pybus, Cassandra. *Epic Journeys of Freedom: Runaway Slaves of the American Revolution and Their Global Quest for Liberty.* Boston: Beacon Press, 2006.

Quarles, Benjamin. *The Negro in the American Revolution.* Published for the Institute of Early American History and Culture, Williamsburg, Virginia, by the Univ. of North Carolina Press, 1996.

Raboteau, Albert J. *Slave Religion: The "Invisible Institution" in the Antebellum South.* New York: Oxford Univ. Press, 1980.

Rawlyk, G. A. "The Guysborough Negroes: A Study in Isolation." *Dalhousie Review* (1968): 24–36.

Raymond, W. O. "The Founding of Shelburne: Benjamin Marston at Halifax, Shelburne and Miramichi." *Collections of the New Brunswick Historical Society,* no. 8 (1909): 204–297.

Rediker, Marcus Buford. *The Slave Ship: A Human History.* New York: Viking, 2007.

Reid, John G. "Change and Continuity in Nova Scotia, 1758–1775." In *Making Adjustments: Change and Continuity in Planter Nova Scotia, 1759–1800,* edited by Margaret Conrad, 45–59. Fredericton [Canada]: Acadiensis Press, 1991.

Richardson, David. "The Eighteenth-Century British Slave Trade: Estimates of Its Volume and Coastal Distribution in Africa." In *Research in Economic History,* 151–195. Greenwich, Conn.: JAI Press, 1989.

———. *Bristol, Africa and the Eighteenth-Century Slave Trade to America: The Final Years, 1770–1807,* vol. 4. Bristol: Bristol Record Society, 1996.

———. "The British Empire and the Atlantic Slave Trade, 1660–1807." In *The Oxford History of the British Empire—Volume 2, The Eighteenth Century,* edited by P. J.

Marshall, 440–464. New York: Oxford Univ. Press, 1998.

———. "Shipboard Revolts, African Authority, and the Atlantic Slave Trade." *William and Mary Quarterly* 58, no. 1 (2001): 69–92.

Rippon, John. "An Account of Several Baptist Churches, consisting Chiefly of Negro Slaves." *Baptist Annual Register* (1790): 336.

———. "Account of the Negro Church at Savannah, and of Two Negro Ministers." *Baptist Annual Register* (1790): 541.

———. "From the Rev. Abraham Marshall, Who Formed the Negro Church at Savannah, to Mr. Rippon." *Baptist Annual Register* (1790): 545.

———. "Sketch of the Black Baptist Church at Savannah, in Georgia; and of their Minister Andrew Bryan, extracted from Several Letters." *Baptist Annual Register* (1790): 339–343.

Rodney, Walter. "African Slavery and Other Forms of Social Oppression on the Upper Guinea Coast in the Context of the Atlantic Slave-Trade." *Journal of African History* 7, no. 3 (1966): 431–443.

———. *A History of the Upper Guinea Coast, 1545–1800.* New York: Monthly Review Press, 1982.

Savannah Unit, Georgia Writers' Project (Work Projects Administration). *Drums and Shadows.* Athens: Univ. of Georgia Press, 1986.

Schama, Simon. *Rough Crossings: Britain, the Slaves and the American Revolution.* London: BBC Books, 2005.

Schèon, James Frederick, and Samuel Crowther. *Journals of the Rev. James Frederick Schèon and Mr. Samuel Crowther: who, with the sanction of Her Majesty's Government, accompanied the expedition up the Niger in 1841 on behalf of the Church Missionary Society,* 2nd ed. 1842. Reprint, London: Cass, 1970.

Schwarz, L. D. *London in the Age of Industrialisation: Entrepreneurs, Labour Force and Living Conditions, 1700–1850.* New York: Cambridge Univ. Press, 1992.

Sedgwick, Catharine Maria [Miss Sedgwick]. "Slavery in New England." *Bentley's Miscellany* 1853, 417–424.

Sensbach, Jon F. *A Separate Canaan: The Making of an Afro-Moravian World in North Carolina, 1763–1840.* Chapel Hill: Univ. of North Carolina Press for the Omohundro Institute of Early American History and Culture, 1998.

———. *Rebecca's Revival: Creating Black Christianity in the Atlantic World.* Cambridge, Mass.: Harvard Univ. Press, 2005.

Sharp, Granville. *Memoirs of Granville Sharp,* edited and compiled by Prince Hoare. London: H. Colburn, 1820.

Shelton, Austin J. *The Igbo-Igala Borderland: Religion and Social Control in Indigenous African Colonialism.* Albany: State Univ. of New York Press, 1971.

Sheridan, R. B. "The Wealth of Jamaica in the Eighteenth Century." *Economic History Review* 18, no. 2 (1965): 292–311.

Sheridan, Richard B. "The Crisis of Slave Subsistence in the British West Indies During and After the American Revolution." *William and Mary Quarterly* 33, no. 3 (1976): 615–641.

————. "The Slave Trade to Jamaica, 1702–1808." In *Trade, Government, and Society in Caribbean History,* edited by Barry W. Higman, 1–16. Kingston: Heinemann, 1983.

Sherlock, Philip Manderson. *West Indian Nations: A New History.* New York: St. Martin's Press, 1973.

Sidbury, James. *Becoming African in America: Race and Nation in the Early Black Atlantic.* New York: Oxford Univ. Press, 2007.

Sir Guy Carleton Branch United Empire Loyalists' Association of Canada. Carleton's Loyalist Index: A Select Index to the Names of Loyalists and their Associates Contained in the British Headquarters Papers, New York City, 1774–1783 (the Carleton Papers) Also The Book of Negroes. Ottawa, 1996. CD-ROM.

Smallwood, Stephanie. *Saltwater Slavery: A Middle Passage from Africa to American Diaspora.* Cambridge, Mass.: Harvard Univ. Press, 2007.

————. "African Guardians, European Slave Ships, and the Changing Dynamics of Power in the Early Modern Atlantic." *William and Mary Quarterly* 64, no. 4 (2007): 679–716.

Smeathman, Henry. *Plan of a Settlement to be made near Sierra Leona, on the Grain Coast of Africa.* London, 1786.

————. "Henry Smeathman to Dr. [Thomas?] Knowles (21 July 1783)." *New Jerusalem Magazine* (1790–1791): 281–287.

Sobel, Mechal. *Trabelin' On: The Slave Journey to an Afro-Baptist Faith.* Westport, Conn.: Greenwood Press, 1979.

————. *The World They Made Together: Black and White Values in Eighteenth-Century Virginia.* Princeton, N.J.: Princeton Univ. Press, 1987.

Sparks, Randy J. "Two Princes of Calabar: An Atlantic Odyssey from Slavery to Freedom." *William and Mary Quarterly* 59, no. 3 (2002): http://www.historycooperative.org/journals/wm/59.3/sparks.html (accessed 22 July 2005).

————. *The Two Princes of Calabar: An Eighteenth-Century Atlantic Odyssey.* Cambridge, Mass.: Harvard Univ. Press, 2004.

Spray, W. A. *The Blacks in New Brunswick.* Fredericton [Canada]: Brunswick Press, 1972.

Steckel, Richard H., and Richard A. Jensen. "New Evidence on the Causes of Slave and Crew Mortality in the Atlantic Slave Trade." *Journal of Economic History* 46, no. 1 (1986): 57–77.

Stern, Philip J. "British Asia and British Atlantic: Comparisons and Connections." *William and Mary Quarterly* 63, no. 4 (2006): 693–712.

Stuckey, Sterling. *Slave Culture: Nationalist Theory and the Foundations of Black America.* New York: Oxford Univ. Press, 1987.

————. *Going Through the Storm.* New York: Oxford Univ. Press, 1994.

Sweet, James H. *Recreating Africa: Culture, Kinship, and Religion in the African-Portuguese World, 1441–1770.* Chapel Hill: Univ. of North Carolina Press, 2003.

Taylor, Eric Robert. *If We Must Die: Shipboard Insurrections in the Era of the Atlantic Slave Trade.* Baton Rouge: Louisiana State Univ. Press, 2006.

Thompson, Robert F. *Flash of the Spirit.* New York: Vintage Books-Random House, 1983.

Thornton, John K. "African Dimensions of the Stono Rebellion." *American Historical Review* 96, no. 4 (1991): 1101–1114.

———. "African Soldiers in the Haitian Revolution." *Journal of Caribbean History* 25, no. 1–2 (1991): 58–80.

———. "Central African Names and African American Naming Patterns." *William and Mary Quarterly* 50, no. 4 (1993): 727–742.

———. "'I am the Subject of the King of Congo': African Political Ideology and the Haitian Revolution." *Journal of World History* 4, no. 2 (1993): 181–214.

———. *Africa and Africans in the Making of the Atlantic World, 1400–1800,* 2nd ed. New York: Cambridge Univ. Press, 1998.

———. "War, the State, and Religious Norms in 'Coromantee' Thought: The Ideology of an African American Nation." In *Possible Pasts: Becoming Colonial in Early America,* edited by Robert Blair St. George, 181–200. Ithaca, N.Y.: Cornell Univ. Press, 2000.

Uchendu, Victor. "Slaves and Slavery in Igboland." In *Slavery in Africa: Historical and Anthropological Perspectives,* edited by Suzanne Miers and Igor Kopytoff, 121–132. Madison: Univ. of Wisconsin Press, 1977.

Uchendu, Victor Chikezie. *The Igbo of Southeast Nigeria.* Case Studies in Cultural Anthropology. New York: Holt, 1965.

Visram, Rozina. *Ayahs, Lascars and Princes: Indians in Britain, 1700–1947.* London: Pluto Press, 1986.

Wadstrom, Carl Bernhard. *An essay on colonization, particularly applied to the western coast of Africa, with some free thoughts on cultivation and commerce; also brief descriptions of the colonies already formed, or attempted in Africa, including those of Sierra Leona and Bulama.* Reprints of Economic Classics. New York: Augustus M. Kelley, 1968.

Walker, James St. G. *The Black Loyalists.* New York: Africana Publishing Company, 1976.

———. *A History Blacks in Canada: A Study Guide for Teachers and Students.* Hull: Canada, 1980.

———. "Myth, History and Revisionism: The Black Loyalists Revisited." *Acadiensis* 29, no. 1 (1999): 88–105.

Walvin, James. *An African's Life: The Life and Times of Olaudah Equiano, 1745–1797.* London: Cassell, 1998.

Ward, Ida C. "A Linguistic Tour in Southern Nigeria." *Africa* 8, no. 1 (1935): 90–97.

Ward, J. R. *British West Indian Slavery, 1750–1834.* Oxford: Clarendon Press, 1988.

Watts, John. *A True Relation of the Inhumane and Unparalled'd Actions, and Barbarous Murders of Negroes or Moors Committed on three English-men in Old Calabar in Guinny.* London: Thomas Passinger, 1672.

Werbner, Richard P. "The Manchester School in South-Central Africa." *Annual Review of Anthropology* 13 (1984): 157–185.

White, Deborah Gray. *Ar'n't I a Woman? Female Slaves in the Plantation South,* revised ed. New York: Norton, 1999.

White, Shane, and Graham White. "Slave Clothing and African-American Culture in the Eighteenth and Nineteenth Centuries." *Past and Present* no. 148 (1995): 149–186.

———. "Slave Hair and African American Culture in the Eighteenth and Nineteenth Centuries." *Journal of Southern History* 61, no. 1 (1995): 45–76.

Willis, Liz. "*Uli* Painting and the Igbo World View." *African Arts* 23, no. 1 (1989): 62–67.

Wilson, Ellen Gibson. *The Loyal Blacks.* New York: G. P. Putnam's Sons, 1976.

———. *John Clarkson and the African Adventure.* London: Macmillan, 1980.

Windley, Lathan A. *Runaway Slave Advertisements: A Documentary History from the 1730s to 1790,* vol. 1: Westport, Conn.: Greenwood Press, 1983.

Winks, Robin. *The Blacks in Canada: A History.* New Haven, Conn.: Yale Univ. Press, 1971.

Wise, Steven M. *Though the Heavens May Fall: The Landmark Trial That Led to the End of Human Slavery.* Cambridge, Mass.: Da Cappo Press, 2005.

Wrigley, E. A., R. S. Davies, J. E. Oeppen, and R. S. Schofield. *English Population History from Family Reconstitution, 1580–1837.* Cambridge: Cambridge Univ. Press, 1997.

Yelvington, Kevin A. *Afro-Atlantic Dialogues: Anthropology in the Diaspora.* School of American Research Advanced Seminar Series. Santa Fe, N.Mex.: School of American Research Press, 2006.

Yule, Henry, and A. C. Burnell. *Hobson-Jobson: A Glossary of Colloquial Anglo-Indian Words and Phrases, and of Kindred Terms, Etmological, Historical, Geographical, and Discursive,* 2nd ed. Delhi: Munshiram Manoharlal, 1968.

UNPUBLISHED SECONDARY SOURCES

Byrd, Alexander X. "Captives and Voyagers: Black Migrants Across the Eighteenth-Century World of Olaudah Equiano." Ph.D. diss., Duke University, 2001.

Jones, Eldon Lewis. "Sir Guy Carleton and the Close of the American War of Independence, 1782–83." Ph.D. diss., Duke University, 1968.

Manfredi, Victor. "Agbo and Ehughbo: Igbo Linguistic Consciousness, Its Origins and Limits." Ph.D. diss., Harvard University, 1991.

Nwokeji, G. Ugo. "The Biafran Frontier: Trade, Slaves, and Aro Society, c. 1750–1905." Ph.D. diss., University of Toronto, 1999.

Scott, Julius, III. "The Common Wind: Currents of Afro-American Communication in the Era of the Haitian Revolution." Ph.D. diss., Duke University, 1986.

INDEX

groundings in, 248; story of Sierra Leone as, 240–241; transformation of societies by, 7, 198–199, 270n103; urban dimension of, 163–164; uprootings in, 248, 254n15; violence and privation in, 246; wartime, 155, 163, 177; women and, 296n16

Miles, William, 68

Mintz, Sidney, 105, 245

Montego Bay, Jamaica, 59, 91, 106, 272n5

Moore, Robert and Amelia, in Bance Island affair, 218–219, 220, 225

Morgan, Philip D., 78, 84

music: drums and singing on slave ships, 34, 37, 43; hymn singing, 161, 171; revolutionary songs, 113, 287n109

Myro, rescue mission of, 231–234, 235

Nanny (enslaved Jamaican in London), 128

Nassau, Peter, 235

HMS *Nautilus:* captain and crew of, 201–205, 207, 208, 211, 229, 239; as projection of British power, 204–205, 227–229; provisions on, 204, 306n8; Sierra Leone expedition of, 1, 121, 148, 201, 202, 204, 205, 207, 213–217, 253n1

New Brunswick, 137, 154, 174, 187; blacks in, 175–176, 178, 191; landholders in, 191; Nova Scotia and, 175–176; Sierra Leone immigrants from, 185–186. *See also* Maritimes; Nova Scotia

New Calabar (Elem Kalabari), 13, 29, 41, 49, 50, 51, 52, 54, 55, 164, 245, 261n52: elite of, 30; Igbos in, 30, 31; polyglot nature of, 29–30; as slave port, 1, 14, 57; slaves at, 17, 27, 29, 31, 39; slaves from, 272n7; slave ships at, 29, 32, 33, 39, 255n5; traders of, 11, 31, 39, 40

New Calabar River, 29

New England, 2, 6, 56, 154

New York, 129, 134, 156, 164, 244, 246; evacuation of, 57, 155, 164–165, 175, 191

Ngwa-Ukwu village group, 20, 31

Niger Delta, 13, 18, 21, 26, 54; description of, 256n4; eastern, 11, 13, 42; languages of, 20; map of, *12;* western, 256n4

Nigeria, southeastern, 1, 8, 18, 20

Niger River, 51, 257n4; "Igbo" and, 20–21, 258n14

North America, 105; Afro-Baptists in, 164;

European immigrants in, 5–6; free blacks in, 4; naval actions off coast of, 109–110; trade of, with Jamaica, 76, 91, 277n75

North Atlantic, 1, *3,* 59, 170

North Carolina, 149, 164, 173

Nova Scotia: black Christianity in, 163, 171–175; black exodus from, 124, 153, 177–199, 289n9; blacks in, 122–123, 154, 155, 156, 166, 245, 300n1; black society in, 170–176; former slaves in, 166, 175, 298n3; governor of, 183, 184, 187, 302n9; indentured servants in, 122, 168, 187, 304n51; land grants in, 167, 171, 188, 189; loyalist emigrants in, 167; map of, *168;* as possible settlement for black Londoners, 126, 290n5; racial violence in, 168–169. *See also* black Nova Scotians; Sierra Leone, Nova Scotians in

Nri village group, 19, 257n9; use of "Igbo" in, 21

Nsuka, 51

Obichere, Boniface, 24

Old Calabar, 41, 44, 47, 49, 51, 52, 54, 55, 57, 164, 245; agriculture in, 14, 256n9; as Atlantic entrepôt, 13; description of, 14; Ekpe Society in, 14, 30, 261n52; elite of, 256n9; Igbos in, 30, 31, 258n13; polyglot nature of, 29–30; reputation of, for slaves of, 52, 53, 54; slaves at, 14–15, 17, 27, 29, 31, 256n11; slave ships at, 32, 33, 51, 255n5; traders of, 11, 14, 31, 40

Old Town, 13. *See also* Old Calabar

Onicha-Ukwu village group, 20

Onitsha, 18, 20; Igbo, 21, 257n6

Orchard estate (Hanover, Jamaica), 113

overseers, 72, 74, 76, 80, 81, 88, 90, 100, 101, 277n74, 278n76; Irish, 75, 277n63; mismanagement of, 71–73; new, 83, 279n98; slaves and, 107–108, 118

palm oil, 14, 33, 256n9

Panter, escape of, to Cuba, 111–112

Parliament: abolitionists and, 114–115, 179, 288n119; acts of incorporation in, 179, 237; panels of, 308n84

Parr, John, 180, 183, 184, 302n9

paternalism: of Clarkson, 196; distinct meanings of, 83; as experienced by slaves,

DATE DUE